Edwin Newman On Language

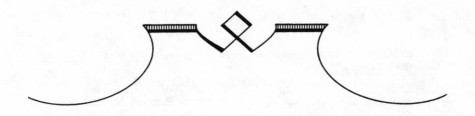

Edwin Newman On Language

STRICTLY SPEAKING

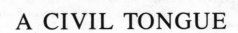

A CIVIL TONGUE

Galahad Books
•
New York

Published in 1992 by
Galahad Books
A division of LDAP, Inc.
386 Park Avenue South
Suite 1913
New York, NY 10016

Galahad Books is a registered trademark of LDAP, Inc.
Published by arrangement with Macmillan Publishing Co.

Library of Congress Catalog Card Number: 92-72504
ISBN: 0-88365-795-3

Printed in the United States of America.

For
my wife
and
daughter

Contents

Strictly Speaking

Acknowledgments

This book is dedicated to my wife and daughter. My wife's contributions have been so many and varied that it is not possible to list them. There would be no book without her. My daughter supplied many suggestions, much encouragement, and, through the years, tolerance of my kind of humor above and beyond the call of duty.

Jeannette Hopkins provided the impetus for the book and edited it. Carol Bok did the typing and the research. To both of them, my deep thanks. Mary Heathcote was the invaluable copy editor.

I want also to thank NBC News, on whose time and in whose employ I had many of the experiences and gathered much of the material on which the book is based. The NBC library gave generous help.

Finally, for permission to use, mostly in changed form, material that originally appeared in their pages, I thank the *Atlantic Monthly, TV Guide,* Overseas Press Club *Bulletin,* and *Punch.*

Contents

INTRODUCTION

A Protective Interest in the English Language

Will America be the death of English? I'm glad I asked me that. My well-thought-out mature judgment is that it will. The outlook is dire; it is a later point in time than you think. The evidence is all around us:

In March, 1974, the White House press secretary, Ron Ziegler, explained a request for a four-day extension of a subpoena from the Watergate prosecutor for certain files. The extension was needed, Ziegler said, so that James St. Clair, President Nixon's attorney, could "evaluate and make a judgment in terms of a response."

We are all of us ready to man the barricades for the right to evaluate and make a judgment in terms of a response, but Ziegler could have said that St. Clair wanted more time to think about it. That he didn't is a commentary on the state of language in the United States, and the state of the language is a commentary on the state of our society. It must be obvious that our society, like our language, is in serious trouble when a man who represents the President speaks of evaluating and making a judgment in terms of a response; when the President himself feels no embarrassment (on any score, apparently) in saying, "There must be no whitewash at the White House," describes a possible course of action as taking the hang-out road, and, on asking his legal counsel for a detailed statement, is told, "Let me give you my overall first"; when a vice-president of the United States achieves fame of a sort through alliterative device: "pampered prodigies," "vicars of vacillation," "nattering nabobs of negativism"; when his successor denounces "prophets of negativity" and endorses the administration "policy-wise"; when Mayor John Lindsay of New York, about to step down, says that his youngest child will go to a boys' school because "he needs peer stuff"; when a publisher will put out what purports to be a book of poetry, *Pages,* by Aram Saroyan, in which, occupying an entire page, this constitutes a poem: "Something moving in the garden a cat"; and this: "incomprehensible birds"; and this: "Alice"; and this: "lobstee"; and when nobody takes medicine but rather medication. Indian tribes soon will have medication men. Ours is a time when Secretary of the Treasury William Simon advises Congress, "One cannot ad hoc tax reform." He might have added that there are no bargains at ad hoc shops.

It is a time when, in the interest of fuel conservation, the federal government adopted the comic strip character Snoopy as a symbol and showed us Snoopy on top of his dog house, flat on his back, with a balloon coming out of his mouth containing the words, "I believe in conserving energy!" while below there was this exhortation: savEnergy.

savEnergy. An entire letter e at the end of save was savd. In addition, an entire space was savd. Perhaps the government should say onlYou can prevent forest fires.

Ours is also a time when Harry Ashmore, a former newspaper editor apparently overborne by being president of the Center for the Study of Democratic Institutions, describes an idea he considers unfounded as "a spurious construct," and speaks of television in a presidential election year as facing "the quadrennial challenge of giving focus and perspective to the polemics of contending partisans"; and when one of Ashmore's associates, a writer, gives his occupation as social critic. ("What do you want to be when you grow up, son?" "Gee, Dad, I thought I'd be a social critic.") And when the president of the Organization of American Historians, John Hope Franklin, identifies 1974 as "this antepenultimate year of our bicentennial."

There are those who think it better to say impacted on than hit. A young actress said she hoped she would not be made an escapegoat if the show she was in failed. An author told me there was too much largis available in Washington. Derbis, the stuff that lies around after a wreck, is part of history at NBC News. So is a letter from a viewer who thought she saw—I don't remember in what connection—the hammer and cycle on one of our programs, possibly a program on which another viewer accused us of providing grist for the fires. Hubert Humphrey has said more than once that he believes in going at politics hook and tong. Others of strong ambition believe, perhaps, in going at it hook and ladder.

I have seen scripts by television news writers who proposed to tell the American people that "Old Man Winter wound up today and threw a roundhouse punch." Ron Ziegler (Again? Yes. After all, spokesmen are made to be quoted) believes that a photograph of someone taken with the President might be sent to that person as a momento. A guest on the "Today" show assured me that blacks running rampart through the streets were not representative of most blacks in this country. Kevin White, mayor of Boston, has spoken of "young juveniles." Dr. Oscar Sussman of the New Jersey State Health Department wondered aloud during a television interview: "Can we stop something, preventive medicinewise, from happening?" There are people who speak of seven A.M. in the morning and four P.M. in the afternoon; I heard that on the NBC television station in Los Angeles. On the ABC station in Washington, a newscaster spoke of three families that had suffered kidnapings as having the same thing in common.

Most conversation these days is as pleasing to the ear as a

Flash-Frozen Wonder Dinner is to the palate, consisting largely of "You've got to be kidding," "It's a bad scene," "How does that grab you?" "Just for openers," "It's a fun idea," "Fantastic," "It's the in place," "Is he for real?" "Back to square one," "I just heard this great Polish [Hungarian, Italian, etc.] joke," "That's the name of the game," "Who's counting?" "That's the bottom line," "Wild," "What's the plot?" "Would you believe?" "Out of sight," "Lots of luck," "What can I tell you?" "What have you done for me lately?" and "How do you structure your day?"*

There is a recording of Sammy Davis, Jr., singing "And then they nursed it, rehearsed it, And gave out the news—You better believe it—That the Southland gave birth to the blues." Inserting "You better believe it" must have seemed a fun idea at the time. In the same way, wearing a button with somebody else's commercially produced clever remark on it or the apron bearing the words "For this I spent four years in college?" seems to many great for openers, even to many who spent four years in college. The conversation thus opened, "Everything you ever wanted to know about . . . but were afraid to ask," and ". . . is alive and well and living in . . ." soon make it a new ball game.

Language is in decline. Not only has eloquence departed but simple, direct speech as well, though pomposity and banality have not. Some who share my views on this believe that one of the nation's most pressing needs is an Anti-Thrust Act. ("What is the thrust of your report?") Others believe that if there is one word that expresses the spirit of the age, it is parameter, a mathematical term now widely misused so that nobody finds himself in the hateful position of having to say boundary or limit. I would choose viable. Thus Senator Howard Baker, Republican of Tennessee, commenting on Judge John Sirica's decision to give the

---

* Also "I feel so vulnerable," "I feel threatened," "Will the real _____ please stand up?" "Back to the drawing board," "I've got news for you," "I couldn't care less," "Meanwhile, back at the ranch," "What is your philosophy on that?" "Let me give you my thinking on that," "Can do," "No can do," "The _____ bit," "Track record," "For the birds," "He's inner-directed but she's outer-directed."

Watergate grand jury's report on President Nixon to the House Judiciary Committee, was not content to say that the judge had no alternative. He said that Sirica had no viable alternative.

I don't know what Baker thought it added, but automatic recall should be visited on anyone on the public payroll who says viable. Something drastic is needed, for while language— the poor state of language in the United States—may not be at the heart of our problems, it isn't divorced from them either. It is at least conceivable that our politics would be improved if our English were, and so would other parts of our national life. If we were more careful about what we say, and how, we might be more critical and less gullible. Those for whom words have lost their value are likely to find that ideas have also lost their value. Maybe some people discipline themselves in one and not in the other, but they must be rare.

Jack Gould, when he was television critic of the *New York Times,* thought a sticky wicket was something you squeezed through. Howard Cosell noted that the result of a particular athletic event left the French people "numbstruck." I regret that I do not remember how this, to use one of Cosell's favorite words, eventuated. An official of the Office of Economic Opportunity was quoted as saying, "That's the loggerhead no one has yet gotten past." There is an apartment building in Miami Beach known as the Maison Grandé. There was a massage parlor in New York called the Club Monmarté. I have eaten Béaucoup Mints. In Wilkes-Barre, Pennsylvania, you may purchase a Monseur hairpiece. At the Ramada Inn in Washington, D.C., you will find the Haypenny Bar.

Is it important? Obviously much of it isn't. The drinks at the Haypenny Bar probably would be no better or worse if the spelling were more nearly authentic, and the Béaucoup Mints would not have had a mintier taste without the uncalled-for acute accent, which, by the way, was the accent that appeared over the last letter in the name of W. C. Fields's alter ego, Egbert Sousé. Fields, probably because he liked the sound in French, always referred to it as an accent grave.

A world without mistakes would unquestionably be less fun. I cherish the memory of the Long Island Railroad union leader who felt he was chasing Willie the Wisp during contract negotiations, and I thank the *New York Post* for describing Ho Chi Minh as a small wisp of a man, for it thereby left no stone unturned and no stone not turned over as well. Nor will I ever forget the estate agent in Norwich, England, who told us that we should not expect that city to be like the metrolopis. A friend of my early youth thought that the English actor Clive Brook was Civil Brook, and my life has been richer for it. What could be more civil than a brook? And I have only the kindest memories of a colleague in the navy in World War II who wanted to know what a lert was, inasmuch as we were about to go on one.

There is a story, which I am assured is true, about the caretaker of a cemetery in Barbados that had a particularly interesting tomb. One day a number of women came to see it without making arrangements beforehand. The caretaker felt they were presuming and wanted to be certain that his gesture was not misunderstood. "I'll show it to you ladies," he said, "but don't get the idea that I am going to be here to show it to Bobtail and his crew." How can language be better served than that?

How can it be served better than it was by the taxi driver who told me how much he admired the actress Mildred Natwick? "Ah," he said, nodding, "she can portray."

Harry Truman used to say irrevelant and stress the third syllable in incomparable. But Mr. Truman never had any trouble getting his points across.

As a veteran I was in an army hospital in 1947, and a fellow patient asked me what another patient did for a living. I said he was a teacher. "Oh," was the reply, "them is my chief dread." A lifetime was summed up in those six syllables. There is no way to improve on that.

In 1950 two members of the British Foreign Office, Guy Burgess and Donald Maclean, defected to the Russians and became notorious as "The Missing Diplomats." On the trail too late, like dozens of other reporters, I went to Maclean's house in

Buckinghamshire and found only the gardener on the premises. I asked what his reaction had been on hearing the news. He was a country man. "Oi were thunderstruck," he said.

There is no way to improve on that, either.

The argument for preciseness of language has limits, of course. I don't know whether grammarians were less taken in by, for example, the Gulf of Tonkin affair than other groups in the population. I assume that professors of logic often arrive at the wrong conclusion. Nine justices of the United States Supreme Court may consult the same laws, check the same precedents, and come out with contradictory conclusions, elegantly expressed. Certainly, too, those involved in Watergate had had far more education that the national average. Yet one of the things the Watergate hearings revealed was a poverty of expression, an inability to say anything in a striking way, an addiction to a language that was almost denatured, and in which what little humor did occur was usually unintentional.

It has often been said that the Watergate people hid what they were doing from themselves behind a cloud of fuzzy notions they never rigorously examined. I am more inclined to believe that they knew what they were doing and did it, for the most part, out of plain self-interest. But the fuzzy notions provided an easy escape. The haven was there, for those who wanted it, in phrases like "higher national interest," "excess of zeal" (looked at this way, the Nixon administration's major problem was zeal production's outrunning the demand for it), "good team player," and the like.

Watergate, in the course of revealing so much else about American life, also revealed the sad state of language; apparently form and substance are related. In Washington, as we learned from the White House transcripts, a president may speak of kicking butts, call a problem a can of worms, decide not to be in the position of basically hunkering down, anticipate something hitting the fan, propose to tough it through, sight minefields down the road, see somebody playing hard ball, claim political savvy, and wonder what stroke some of his associates have with others.

He may be told by members of his staff what is the bottom line, that a situation has cycled somewhat while another situation is a bullet biter, that a lawyer has done some dove-tailing for him, that a lot of people have to pull oars, and that another man was a ballplayer who carried tremendous water for the President's cause. That was private talk; in public, Watergate language lost the men's club flavor and became distended. In addition to the notorious "at that point in time," first cousin to "in point of fact," John Ehrlichman spoke of "that time era," and John Mitchell of "that time frame," though Ehrlichman did say "labor the point" rather than "belabor the point," a heroic act in the circumstances.

In Watergate, nobody ever discussed a subject. It was always subject matter. The discussion never took place before a particular date. It was always prior to. Nor was anything said, it was indicated; just as nothing was done, it was undertaken. If it was undertaken, it was never after the indications about the subject matter; it was subsequent to them. A danger in using subsequent is that some people think it means before rather than after, which made the Watergate hearings, to which subsequent was almost a password, even harder to follow. Those hearings popped up, ghostlike, at the trial in New York of John Mitchell and Maurice Stans, during the cross-examination of John Dean:

PROSECUTOR: Am I correct that you approached various prosecutors and asked for immunity from prosecution in return for your testimony?

DEAN: No, sir.

PROSECUTOR: Did your lawyer do it?

DEAN: Yes, sir.

PROSECUTOR: You haven't taken the Fifth Amendment before another grand jury?

DEAN: Subsequent to my appearance here, yes.

Ah, Watergate! John Mitchell, former attorney general of the United States, spoke of "grievious" damage and "dilatorious" action. Sam Ervin, senator from North Carolina and chairman of the Watergate Committee, thought claims should be "substantuated" and discerned "gradiations" of difference. A White House lawyer, Richard Moore, spoke, as he put it, "in the context of hindsight." Herbert Kalmbach, President Nixon's personal attorney or not President Nixon's personal attorney, as the case may be, while telling the Senate committee of his changing "level of concern," referred to "the meeting I recall with particularity."

Language used to obfuscate or conceal or dress with false dignity is not confined to politics and did not burst upon us for the first time with Watergate. In our time, however, it has achieved a greater acceptance than ever before, so that stiffness and bloat are almost everywhere. Any number of people might render the line in the television commercial, "I ate the whole thing," as "I ate the thing in its totality." In Britain, this sign was chalked on the blackboard at London Airport: "All BEA flights subject to delays, reactionary to fog at Heathrow Airport earlier this morning." My daughter spotted a sign that urged restaurant employes in an English city to use "any hygienic hand washing media." But while this has been going on in part of our society, a different process has been under way in another part, where respect for rules has been breaking down and correct expression is considered almost a badge of dishonor.

I believe that the decline in language stems in part from large causes. One of those causes is the great and rapid change this country went through in the 1960s. Take the environment issue. It raised questions that challenged the fundamental assumptions of American life. Is it sensible to consume as much as we do? How do you calculate a standard of living—do you include quality of air and water, for example, and the amount of time you spend in traffic jams? Is economic growth necessarily a good thing? What social obligations does a corporation take on when it builds a plant to earn profits?

Another aspect of that change was that people who felt oppressed by society organized to enforce their demands either for the first time or with greater success than ever before—blacks, Indians, Chicanos, women, homosexuals, lesbians, prison inmates, welfare recipients. Perhaps the most remarkable manifestation of this was the strike by black garbage collectors in

Memphis, Tennessee, during which Martin Luther King, Jr., was killed. A few years earlier such a strike would have been unimaginable.

It came as a shock that all these groups could bargain with society over what they wanted, and that made older and more settled people uncomfortable. But the greatest capacity for creating such discomfort lay with those things that reminded people of their age, reminded them that the future did not belong to them and that maybe not even the present did. Thus the generation gap.

Here I must pause to say that the generation gap is not something I fully accept. Still less is it something I unreservedly deplore. The notion that the trouble between generations is caused by a failure in communication may have some merit, but it makes a large and not necessarily justified assumption: that there should be communication and that if there is, things will be better. I am not so sure. It may be that we have entered a time when some groups would do better to ignore each other than to communicate with each other. Not communicating saves energy; it keeps people from worrying about things they cannot do anything about; and it eliminates an enormous amount of useless talk.

I take myself as an example. I have no wish to dress as many younger people do nowadays. I cannot accept the discomfort that many of them do, or the lack of privacy. I have no wish to impair my hearing by listening to their music, and a communication gap between an electronic rock group and me is something I devotedly cherish and would hate to see disappear.

Or take the job of drama critic, which I happened to have at NBC in New York for six seasons, 1965–66 through 1970–71. It was often troublesome and annoying, not because most of the plays were bad, although they were. It was because a number of the plays I saw did not seem to be directed at me, but at younger people.

I watched these plays and, it sometimes happened, I got little out of them. Inevitably I asked myself whether there was something wrong with me. For example, in the 1968–69 season there was a play called *Beclch,* which, if you examine it, is "Belch" with an extra c in it.

The character of that name was a white queen somewhere in Africa, where she ruled in an amorous, bloodthirsty, and extremely verbose way. The action of the play included shouting, scratching, fighting, lovemaking, biting, dancing, massage, murder, fits, ritual slaughter, nudity, and self-strangulation. The climax of the play came when one of the male characters, who was naked apart from elephantiasis makeup on one leg, choked himself to death. It took him quite a long time, and all I learned from the scene was that he had red hair, and I wondered whether the lack was in me.

This was not a matter of great importance in itself. Nonetheless, *Beclch* did symbolize the difficulties that come with age, when change is taking place and you are not among those changing. For *Beclch* was a product of the cult of youth and the cult of change, cults in whose creation the war in Vietnam played an enormous part. Because people of age and experience and position led us into Vietnam, they made age and experience and position look ridiculous. This conferred a kind of blessing on youth and inexperience and not being in the establishment. To many it made change and experiment intrinsically desirable. The effect was almost beyond measuring, and we still do not know its full extent, but we do know that when age, experience, and position were discredited, there was a wholesale breakdown in the enforcement of rules, and in the rules of language more than most. One reason is that, in language, changes can be registered quickly and passed along literally by word of mouth. Another reason is that the language people use is a ready guide to the side they are on, and correct and relatively conventional language was widely abandoned by those in revolt. Finally, language lies to hand not only as a symbol of change but as its instrument.

Television played its part, too. It exalted the picture and depreciated the word. The "talking head"—which may someday take its place as a name for English pubs alongside the King's Heads and Boar's Heads and Saracen's Heads and the rest—was considered dull television and to be avoided whenever possible in favor of something, anything, moving, though a head that talks well is a pearl beyond price.

The decline in language comes in part, as I said, from such large causes. It also stems from the naïve but stuffy conviction that certain occasions call ineluctably for an idiom that is, somehow, worthy. In June, 1972, I recall, the unwelcome news came that the government of the state of Connecticut, which had been looking for a state song for six months, had found one. As could easily have been predicted, the song is terrible. Maybe the music isn't; I have not heard it. But the words are. What is worse, the new song means that the Yale University fight song, "Boola Boola," which had sneaked in in the absence of an official song, will no longer be played on official occasions in Connecticut.

It was Governor Thomas Meskill who recommended that the state legislature adopt "The Hills of Connecticut" as the official song. This is how it goes:

> There's a place that's nearest to heaven,
> Where the hills roll up to the sky,
> And the land is peaceful and lovely,
> It's where I want to live and die.
> I love the hills of Connecticut,
> I love its valleys and its streams,
> I've got my loved ones in Connecticut,
> And they're always in my dreams.
> My heart is home among those friendly hills,
> And no matter where I roam,
> I love the hills of my Connecticut,
> Connecticut, my home.

Those are unexceptionable sentiments, but we have thousands of songs about valleys and streams, and people in our dreams, and no matter where we roam, and this and that, my home. Compare those sentiments with what they replaced:

"Boola boola, boola boola, boola boola, boola boola, boola boola, boola boola, boola boola, boola boo."

I checked with Yale University and found that there are additional words—the usual stuff about what the Yales intend to do to the Harvards and the Princetons on the fields of friendly strife. I also learned that boola boola is an adaptation of the Hawaiian hoola boola, which is a term of exultation and ecstasy used to accent the rhythm of dances. But those are irrelevancies. For the last seven decades, when the Yales have sung Boola boola, boola boola, boola boola, boola boola, boola boola, boola boola, boola boola, boola boo, that simple affirmative statement is all they had in mind.

In 1972, the same year that gave the world "The Hills of Connecticut," Gough Whitlam became prime minister of Australia on a platform that included the promise of a new national anthem to replace "God Save the Queen." The winner, established by public opinion poll, was "Advance Australia Fair," a song that already existed. The Australian government takes the position that only the music matters; the words that go with the tune are not regarded as part of the official anthem. One would like to think that its view has something to do with what the words, written by P. D. McCormick in 1885, are, but that is unlikely.

In any case, the lyrics *are* sung, and have drawn a complaint from the Women's Electoral Lobby, though on feminist rather than literary grounds. There are four stanzas; here are one and three:

> Australia's sons, let us rejoice,
> For we are young and free;
> We've golden soil and wealth for toil,
> Our home is girt by sea;
> Our land abounds in nature's gifts
> Of beauty rich and rare;
> In history's page, let every stage
> Advance Australia fair.
> In joyful strains then let us sing
> Advance Australia fair.

While other nations of the globe
Behold us from afar,
We'll rise to high renown
And shine like our glorious southern star.
From England, Scotia, Erin's Isle,
Who come our lot to share
Let all combine with heart and hand to
Advance Australia fair.

Connecticut also abounds in gifts of beauty rich and rare, though "The Hills of Connecticut" is conspicuously not among them. Governor Meskill, on hearing of my objections to the song, remarked that I had a nose for news but no ear for music. A good line for a governor, better than we expect. But when the Governor announced that he would not run for reelection in 1974, I was not sad. He has done enough. Can a state song be repealed?

Can a *phrase* be repealed? I have in mind Y'know. The prevalence of Y'know is one of the most far-reaching and depressing developments of our time, disfiguring conversation wherever you go. I attend meetings at NBC and elsewhere in which people of high rank and station, with salaries to match, say almost nothing else.

For a while I thought it clever to ask people who were spattering me with Y'knows why, if I knew, they were telling me? After having lunch alone with some regularity, I dropped the question. In Britain, a National Society for the Suppression of Y'know, Y'know, Y'know in the Diction of Broadcasters was organized in 1969. It put out a list of the broadcasters who were the worst offenders. Reporters then interviewed the offenders and quoted all the Y'knows in their answers when they were asked whether they really said Y'know that often. Nothing changed.

Once it takes its grip, Y'know is hard to throw off. Some people collapse into Y'know after giving up trying to say what they mean. Others scatter it broadside, these, I suspect, being for some reason embarrassed by a silence of any duration during which they might be suspected of thinking about what they were going to say next. It is not uncommon to hear Y'know used a dozen times in a minute.

We know less about the origin of Y'know than about the origin of Boola boola, but there is some reason to believe that in this country it began among poor blacks who, because of the various disabilities imposed on them, often did not speak well and for whom Y'know was a request for assurance that they had been understood. From that sad beginning it spread, among people who wanted to show themselves sympathetic to blacks, and among those who saw it as the latest thing and either could not resist or did not want to be left out.

Those who wanted to show that they were down to earth, and so not above using Y'know, or—much the same thing— telling you that somebody is like six feet tall, have been particularly influential. They include makers of television commercials who begin the sales pitch with Y'know, and so gain the confidence of the viewer, who realizes at once that the person doing the commercial is down to earth, regular, not stuck-up, and therefore to be trusted.

It also included, on May 1, 1970, the day after he announced the American and South Vietnamese invasion of Cambodia, President Nixon. To a gathering of employes at the Pentagon, he made these remarks about antiwar students at universities:

"You see these bums, you know, blowing up the campuses. Listen, the boys that are on the college campuses today are the luckiest people in the world, going to the greatest universities, and here they are burning up the books, storming around about this issue. You name it. Get rid of the war and there will be another one." The White House Watergate transcripts show Mr. Nixon to be fairly devoted to Y'know, even without one use deleted by the White House but shown in the House Judiciary Committee's version: "One of these blacks, y'know, goes in there and holds up a store with a Goddamn gun, and they give him two years and then probation afterward."

The technique might be extended to other fields, perhaps to make Shakespeare more popular in the schools.

HAMLET: To be or not to be, that is the question. Y'know? Or: I pledge, y'know, allegiance to the flag, and to the y'know, republic for which it stands. One nation indivisible, like I mean with liberty and justice for all. Y'know?

The White House transcript did not show it, but the President also dropped the g at the end of some ing words, apparently to ensure that his down-to-earthness would be recognized.* The g at the end of ing words must be thought by politicians to have class connotations that may offend the masses of voters. For that reason it is often dropped in party songs. In 1960, for example, the Democrats' song was "Walkin' Down to Washington," and the Republicans had one about "The Good Time Train," which was "a-waitin' at the station" in the first stanza and "a-waitin' for the nation" in the second.

To choose a lower order of speech is, I suppose, antiestablishment in motive and carries a certain scorn for organized, grammatical, and precise expression. Object to it and you are likely to be told that you are a pedant, a crank, an elitist, and behind the times. "Right on," "uptight," and "chicken out," to take only a few examples, are looked upon as vivid phrases that enrich and renew the language.

They do enrich it, but they are exhausted very rapidly by overuse. When that happens they wrinkle into clichés before our eyes. Nor does it matter where they come from. "Right on" was a black expression. "It's a new ball game" came from sports. "In orbit" came from the space program. Space was also indirectly responsible for "A nation that can put a man on the moon ought to be able to . . ." Since July 20, 1969, this has been popular with those urging the government to improve mass transit, take care of

---

* Mr. Nixon supplied another and even less graceful demonstration of how down to earth and regular he was when he was visited by a former prisoner of war who gave him an American flag he had made while he was in North Vietnam. The President asked about the man's wife and was told that she had divorced him during his stay in prison camp. Mr. Nixon assured the former prisoner that he would be popular at Washington dinner parties, and added, "Watch out for some of those dogs they have you sit by." Mr. Nixon quickly thought better of this and said, "No, there are some very nice girls in Washington."

old people, take care of children, take care of the sick, win the Winter Olympics, win the Summer Olympics, build a nonpolluting automobile engine, see to it that meat in supermarkets is wrapped in packages transparent on both sides, and so on and so on. Those who say these things believe that they have put forward compelling ideas, and such pronouncements do often pass for thought. In reality they camouflage its absence.

Much written and spoken expression these days is equivalent to the background music that incessantly encroaches on us, in banks, restaurants, department stores, trains, shops, airports, airplanes, dentists' offices, hospitals, elevators, waiting rooms, hotel lobbies, pools, apartment building lobbies, bars, and, to my personal knowledge, at least one museum. It thumps and tinkles away, mechanical, without color, inflection, vigor, charm, or distinction. People who work in the presence of background music often tell you, and sometimes with pride, that they don't hear it anymore. The parallel with language is alarming.

Language, then, sets the tone of our society. Since we must speak and read, and spend much of our lives doing so, it seems sensible to get some pleasure and inspiration from these activities. The wisecrack is a wonderful thing, and the colorful phrase, and the flight of fancy. So is the accurate description of a place or an event, and so is the precise formulation of an idea. They brighten the world.

It need not be elaborate. In January, 1974, during the struggle over wages between the British miners' union and the government, there was speculation that Prime Minister Edward Heath would call an election. A BBC man went out to interview miners:

BBC MAN: Do you want an election?

MINER: Yes.

BBC MAN: Why?

MINER: To get the buggers out.

In March, 1958, I was in Tunis to cover a speech by President Bourguiba about Tunisian independence. I started to leave the building where the speech was being made, and a policeman told me that if I did, I could not get back in.

NEWMAN: Mais je suis journaliste.

POLICEMAN: Oui, monsieur, et moi, je suis policier.

I stayed.

In the summer of 1966 I attended a concert in the Alhambra in Granada as the guest of Andrés Segovia. A pianist played a Beethoven concerto with the Madrid Symphony and received polite applause. At once he sat down and played an encore. Segovia leaned over to me. "Too queeck," he said.

Maestro!

Most of us will never speak that succinctly or concretely. We may, however, aspire to. For direct and precise language, if people could be persuaded to try it, would make conversations more interesting, which is no small thing; it would help to substitute facts for bluster, also no small thing; and it would promote the practice of organized thought and even of occasional silence, which would be an immeasurable blessing.

I do not want to overstate the case. The rules of language cannot be frozen and immutable; they will reflect what is happening in society whether we want them to or not. Moreover, just as libraries, which are storehouses of wisdom, are also storehouses of unwisdom, so will good English, being available to all, be enlisted in evil causes. Still, it remains true that since nothing is more important to a society than the language it uses—there would be no society without it—we would be better off if we spoke and wrote with exactness and grace, and if we preserved, rather than destroyed, the value of our language.

It is not as complicated as it is sometimes made out to be. At an English girls' school one of the mistresses was asked whether the children were allowed to have comic books. She cited no studies, surveys, or research projects. "Oh, no," she said. "Such inferior language."

I speak, then, for a world from which the stilted and pompous phrase, the slogan and the cliché, have not been banished— that would be too much to hope for—but which they do not dominate. This book is intended to help bring about, good-naturedly, I hope (please, not hopefully), that outcome.

1
Hopefully, Fit to Print

In American journalism we have created no legend to compare with Lunchtime O'Booze, star reporter for the British satirical magazine *Private Eye*. It may be because we also have no journalistic practices as old-fashioned and outrageous as those still engaged in by some British papers—"I Fly to the Flashpoint Island," "Fare Shock!" "Airline Chaos Faces Holiday Thousands" (a clear favorite among British headline writers, perhaps because of envy), and "Lisbon, Thursday: The heady wine of revolution flows freely in the streets of Lisbon tonight as citizens uncork the bottles and hand them to the rebel troops who toppled Prime Minister Marcello Caetano in a one-day coup." With these real-life models, Lunchtime coaxes many a rousing story from his battered but sturdy portable:

I SEE SINAI HELL-HOLE HORROR
Make no mistake, this is war! Today with my own eyes I saw the holocaust that is turning the Middle East into a blood-

bath that puts the Red Sea to shame. Just what is going on, it was hard to make out. But one thing is certain. This is war. Even the normally tight-lipped Israeli generals are openly admitting it.

FEAR STALKS PARADISE ISLE

Today I saw with my own eyes the stark terror which overnight has turned this paradise on earth into a living nightmare. They are calling it The Island of Death—this international playground for millionaires and sun-seekers alike. The question everyone here is asking is: Why did it have to happen here on this exotic sun-drenched haven hideaway?

I CALL IT LONDON'S DAY OF SHAME!

Hell on four wheels! That was the picture yesterday as London ground to a halt in what a [Royal Automobile Club] spokesman described as "the worst snarl-up in the entire history of the world."

All over central London, the scene of chaos was the same, as tens of thousands of motorists battled their way to and from work in a sea of frustration and fury. Tempers boiled over and fists were raised as normally sober citizens were reduced by London's Day of Shame to what a High Court judge described as nothing more than a pack of wild animals.

American journalism is, however, not without its resources, and the hack phrase, the labored point, and the stereotyped treatment are by no means unknown, and Lunchtime O'Booze would not scorn the columnist Joseph Alsop.

In May, 1974, Alsop wrote a column headed, "The Undiluted Horror That Lies Ahead." The undiluted horror lay ahead four times in the column, once for an interminable period, and horror unundiluted lay ahead once. The United States government was described as paralyzed by Watergate four times (this *was* the undiluted horror) and also as being in the vulnerable state of a beached whale and afflicted by Watergate mania (twice) with the result that what the government was doing about anything was "zero," which "profoundly imperiled" all America's interests overseas and all America's friends overseas.

"Altogether," Alsop concluded, "if the undiluted horror does not lead to far greater disasters, it will be proof that this country is in God's own care."

Lunchtime, look to your laurels.

Here is a story from the *New York Times*:

"Moscow, Nov. 5—Marshal Boris P. Bugayev, the Soviet Minister of Civil Aviation, personally directed the successful foiling of an attempt to hijack a Soviet domestic airliner to Sweden last Friday, unofficial sources said today."

The story went on from there, but it never did tell us how close Bugayev came to unsuccessfully foiling the attempt to hijack the airliner.

I do not recall seeing a report of a successful foiling before that one in the *Times* in 1973. The phrase had, however, a certain inevitability about it, the way having been paved by totally destroyed, completely destroyed, surrounded on three sides, partially surrounded, completely surrounded, partially damaged, completely abandoned, completely eliminated, most unique, rather unique, very unique, and totally unique.

Think back to Victorian melodrama. The villain has tied the heroine to the railroad track as the express approaches. This is part of his revenge on the hero. The hero, however, arrives in the nick of time, frees the girl, and rolls with her to safety as the train thunders by. The villain gnashes his teeth over this safe escape. "Successfully foiled again," he mutters as the curtain falls.

The Associated Press from San Francisco, February 14, 1971:

"Marathon talks continued today in an effort to end an eight-day strike of city employes that has paralyzed public transit."

Marathon talks are a relatively new development in labor negotiations. As the representatives of employer and union pound along, gasping out proposals about wage differentials and grievance procedures, and accusing each other of not engaging in genuine collective bargaining, the virtue of marathon talks becomes clear. It is that the parties quickly tire of the pace and, rather than go on running, come to an agreement. Even if they keep going, an artfully placed last ditch is provided for them to fall into, and these last-ditch talks avert, as last-ditch talks will, a costly walkout. It is a more effective and healthier method than the one so often recommended by irate citizens, locking them in a room until they come up with a contract.

Marathon talks may, however, lead to less than equitable results. If the employer representative finds the going hard, and is clearly winded, he may have to yield a whopping wage increase to get some rest. Whenever this happens, it raises one of the most intriguing questions in American journalism: When does an increase begin to whop? There is a school of thought among economists that this takes place unfailingly between ninety and one hundred twenty days of inflation beginning to soar. Historically, however, the determination has been left to the discretion of individual reporters and has never been firmly established.

Foreign journalists are not without sin, and it was on the BBC that I heard a reference to Bach's taxing Goldberg Variations, though in a government of laws, not men, the ways of taxing Goldberg are no more numerous than the ways of taxing anyone else. When I was stationed in Rome in the late 1950s, archeologists dug up the mummy of a female thought to be about twenty centuries old. The story at once went out that it was the mummy of a beautiful young woman, and there was speculation about how she came to be there—died for love, buried alive by an ardent tyrant to whom she refused to yield (the proper journalistic phrase for this is Slain for Love), all the usual sort of thing. Experts were called in to analyze the remains and concluded that it was the skeleton of a nine-year-old girl with rickets.

The following story was carried by the AP on October 5, 1973:

"Buenos Aires, Argentina—AP: A high-ranking police officer was shot to death in front of his home Thursday night in the fourth political murder since Juan D. Peron was elected President less than two weeks ago."

Juan D. Peron. The D. is there to keep you from confusing Juan D. Peron with the Juan Q. Peron also elected president of Argentina two weeks earlier. It is there as well because wire services love middle initials. So do newspapers and news magazines. So do television networks. Middle initials are thought to add authenticity and the ring of history. That is why they are so often heard in nominating speeches at party conventions. That is why, when newspapers call on President Nixon to resign, they always specify that it is President Richard M. Nixon they have in mind.

The desire for weightiness even creeps into the language of television weather forecasters. In Denver one night, after the local newscaster had said that something had been done "as best as possible," he referred to an "alleged shoot-out," which not merely was alleged but had taken place, with three people killed. The alleged probably was intended to cover the fact that there was a dispute over who should be prosecuted for it. With that, however, our newscaster reached familiar ground, turned brightly to the weatherman, and asked, "Will we have more major thunderstorm activity?"

The weatherman spotted the cue and, with equal spontaneity and an unerring instinct for the lively phrase, replied, "You better believe it, Ron. That is the prospect," he continued, "as of right now."

I long ago stopped wondering why major thunderstorm activity is preferred to major thunderstorms. It is because of the national affection for unnecessary word activity. Once upon a time, weathermen spoke of showers. (I heard one of them say, "We may have a scattered shower.") Showers were succeeded by shower activity. More recently, the shower area has taken over. All this has happened because we love to pump air into the language and make it soft and gaseous. Newsmen borrow the style from those they consider authoritative, such as the air-force general who talked one day about the nuclear deterrent and how well it deterred. It deterred so well, the general said, that the Russians were not in a position to attack us with any confidence factor. The general did not say the Russians lacked confidence. They lacked a confidence factor.

In the same way, head winds no longer delay commercial airliners. Head wind components do. They don't blow at any more miles an hour than head winds do, but a wind is only a wind, while a component is knowledgeable and has know-how. Psychologists no longer speak of children playing but of children in a play situation. My daughter, when she was doing social work, heard it said of a child that he had "not mastered the reading situation." People burying their dead are now said to be in an acute grief situation, and funeral pre-planning is recommended as a way of helping them to deal with it.

Television sportcasters do it, too. They do not say that a team is forced to punt but that it is in a punting situation. A phrase like "punting situation" need be used only once and hordes of journalists descend on it and make it their own. Somebody once described a legal brief as lengthy. Now there is no other kind. There is no record of anybody's ever submitting a short brief, or brief brief. Lengthy is automatic, like powerful before Ways and Means Committee, and all-important before Rules Committee, and uneasy before truce.

When President Nixon announced the agreement for the separation of Egyptian and Israeli forces along the Suez Canal after the fighting in October, 1973, he remarked that the recent history of the Middle East had been one of outbreaks of fighting, each of them succeeded by an uneasy truce.* True enough. But who ever heard of an easy truce, or a comfortable one? If one did turn

---

* Mr. Nixon missed a bet here by not speaking of the oil-rich Middle East, but we all slip up occasionally. He had begun sounding like a commentator much earlier, when he was out of office in the 1960s. My impression was that he did this to emphasize his already long experience and

up, it would escape notice, because reporters would not be sent
to cover it. They go to the Middle East because it is a tinderbox
filled with fertile soil (in spite of its being oil-rich) in which an
uneasy truce may grow.

Later, if an uneasy truce has held up, the same reporters will
probably be present when the parties to it sit down to negotiate.
This process could be interrupted by setbacks, during which the
negotiations grind to a halt and each side spells out its minimum
demands (m-i-n-i-m-u-m d-e-m-a-n-d-s) and insists that all it
wants is a settlement that will be viable and that the ball is in the
other side's court. At this point the scenario (30 LASHES 30 would
be an appropriate punishment for anybody using *that* word) calls
for globe-trotting diplomat Henry Kissinger (H-e-n-r-y K-i-s-s-
i-n-g-e-r) to arrive. Kissinger, who habitually carries heavy objects on his person while trotting, even when wearing more than
one hat, gives a hammer to each side. Both take the cue, whereupon an agreement is hammered out.

As automatic as uneasy before truce was Marxist before the
title of the late President Allende of Chile. You would have

---

the positions he had held, so as to set himself above his rivals. In May,
1967, he held a news conference in Chicago and said that the Republicans
would have more candidates for the presidential nomination than either
party had had in the century. He listed a number of "potential candidates"
in addition to those generally known. He noted that some people regarded
him as a candidate. Then he said that the Republicans would win and,
commentating harder than ever, forecast a photo finish.

A week earlier Mr. Nixon had returned from a tour of Latin America.
The picture there, he said, offering what I suppose must be called com-
mentation, was of "a desperate race between production and population."
With that, he began sounding like a television newsman on one of the
year-end programs, when he reports on his area and makes a prediction.
"Castro is waging unrelenting verbal warfare against the unstable regimes
of Latin America," Mr. Nixon said. "There will be some rocky roads and
some explosion points. The next few years will tell the tale." Becoming
president did not change Mr. Nixon. On October 26, 1973, after a cease
fire had been established between Egypt and Syria on the one side and
Israel on the other, he held a news conference which included "A very
significant and potentially explosive crisis," and "My up-to-the-minute
report on that—and I just talked to Dr. Kissinger five minutes before
coming down—is this." He did everything but promise to be back after
this message.

thought that Marxist President was the position Allende had run for and been elected to.

An earlier specimen of Marxist President was Walther Ulbricht of East Germany. His full name, actually, was Spade-bearded Walther Ulbricht, but an odd thing happened as he grew older. His first name changed from Spade-bearded to Aging, possibly—since he was a well-known puppet of Moscow—out of deference to the aging Soviet Politburo. Ulbricht would sometimes meet other prominent politicians whose first names were Balding and Left-leaning.

In addition to Marxist President, a political office that sometimes has to be filled is that of Ailing Premier. Openings in this position often occur in Japan, probably because the incumbents, given the condition they are required to be in to get the job—i.e., ailing—rarely finish their terms. If they are in particularly frail health, a meeting with somebody who holds the position of Right-wing Strongman in another country may finish them; so may trouble at home with the holder of the post of Balky Defense Minister; and of course, for anybody who is Aging and Ailing at the same time, the end cannot be far off. For example, in Vientiane, in 1962, I met Right-wing Laotian Strongman Phoumi Nosavan, who shortly thereafter turned out to be Right-wing Laotian Weakman Phoumi Nosavan instead.

When politicians called Aging, Ailing, and even Left-leaning* go abroad, they stay in swank hotels which they prefer to Hiltons and others. In New York, they may leave their swank hotels for a visit to the United Nations' posh headquarters. Posh headquarters reveal themselves not only by their poshness but by having been built with public money. Headquarters built with private money, even for prestigious law firms, do not qualify.

Foreign leaders may also, if their tastes run that way, visit a sprawling installation or two. The sprawling Marshall Space Flight Center in Huntsville, Alabama, is among those available, and there are countless others, equally ungraceful, including the

---

* Senator Robert Dole once called former Attorney General Ramsey Clark a left-leaning marshmallow. Clark's reply, if any, is not recorded.

sprawling ethyl plant in Baton Rouge, Louisiana. Wives of foreign leaders may visit sprawling shopping centers.

Having visited the world organization at its posh headquarters, the foreign leader may go to Washington to call on the chief executive, or the embattled chief executive, if *he* happens to be in office. If the visitor is unpopular, there may be demonstrations against him, with the television reporters explaining that "The demonstrators were protesting alleged repressive measures in his homeland." If the police are called in, there may soon thereafter be reports of demonstrators protesting alleged police brutality. In some countries, where customs are different, demonstrators, frequently university students, may instead rampage through appropriate neighborhoods and buildings while protesting alleged government corruption. This, as the UPI told us, was the case in Patna, India, in March, 1974. Anybody who rampages is inviting alleged repression with concomitant alleged police brutality.

Back, however, to the meeting between the foreign leader and the chief executive. When they meet, the mysterious corps of diplomatic observers, its whereabouts known only to correspondents who cover foreign policy matters, goes into action. Two kinds of diplomatic observers are available, ordinary and seasoned. The situation being dealt with here—foreign leader in wide-ranging parley with chief executive—is fairly straightforward and does not warrant disturbing the seasoned diplomatic observers. Ordinary diplomatic observers suffice, and they cease observing ordinarily long enough to tell reporters covering the story that the top-level meeting is necessary to prevent a situation already difficult from escalating into an eyeball-to-eyeball confrontation.

In the early days of American involvement in Vietnam, after Lyndon Johnson had faced Aging Mao Tse-tung eyeball-to-eyeball in the Gulf of Tonkin and had shown him to be a paper tiger by making the Chinese leader blink—blinking in such confrontations being the infallible sign of paper-tigerness—I remarked on the air that an eyeball-to-eyeball confrontation between Johnson and Mao must have been difficult to arrange, given the considerable difference in height and eye shapes. A professor in California at once wrote to accuse me of a racist attempt to whip up anti-Chinese feeling. I blinked.

I took part in a television program in which Senator Henry Jackson, describing the somewhat faltering progress of the détente between the Soviet Union and the United States, described the situation as half-an-eyeball-to-half-an-eyeball. Presumably, if things improved, the half-an-eyeball confrontation would give way to confrontation by peripheral vision, and finally, on the bright sunlit uplands of peace, the two parties would not be looking at each other at all.

Eyeball-to-eyeball, though it came close to burlesque even at the beginning (for example, when hard-nosed private eyes are private-eyeball-to-private-eyeball, does eye or nose prevail?), was once a fairly graphic phrase. Because of overuse, it has been devalued. American journalism has a way of seeing to that, of fastening on words and sucking them dry. Controversial is such a word, because it is applied to almost every issue that arises in politics, and because reporters feel obliged to tell us that issues that are resolved in the Senate by votes of fifty-one to forty-nine are controversial. Again, as anyone can discern from book jackets, scarcely a book appears that is not controversial, even when it is also witty, warm, and wise.

The television critic of the *New York Times*, John O'Connor, recently shed some light on *The Merchant of Venice* by describing Shylock as controversial. Macbeth was, too, of course: some say it was his fault, some say it was his wife's.

Nelson Rockefeller explained why his Commission on Critical Choices would not ask the federal government for money: "Like anything in these days of controversy, this commission, privately organized, got into a controversial situation. We decided not to pursue a request for funding from either the Executive or Congress. It was bound to be controversial."

I in turn regarded Rockefeller's decision as controversial, but it is his commission, and he can do what he likes with it.

Meanwhile has gone the same way that controversial has; it now serves about as much purpose as a clearing of the throat.

Massive has also, and here the matter is more serious. Massive was robbed of its original meaning, which is to say forming a large mass, heavy, bulky, solid, so that it could be used to mean large, a word considered no longer able to stand on its own but requiring size after it. Massive doesn't even mean large anymore. It goes by without registering. It means nothing.

Still worse is the destruction of rhetoric. Rhetoric does not mean fustian, exaggeration, or grand and empty phrases. It means—it meant—the effective use of language, and the study of that use. Suddenly beloved of politicians and journalists, rhetoric is now used to mean something doubtful and not quite honest, instead of something desirable. Its misapplication could hardly tell more than it does. The director of the Center for Russian and East European Studies at the University of Michigan, William Zimmerman, has written of someone's "rhetorical thrust." This is a veritable synthesis.

Not only words become hackneyed. People do too. As long ago as October, 1951, while working in London, I invented the Winkfield Award, given for journalistic achievement above and beyond the call of duty. I wrote about it in *Punch*:

I never thought the day would come when I'd interview my old friend Dymchurch. He and I had made our modest starts in journalism together, and for a while he was no more prominent than I, which is to say not prominent at all. Even recently he hadn't seemed to me to be doing anything out of the ordinary, and then, to my surprise, came his winning of the Winkfield Journalism Award for outstanding public service.

"It's an old story," he told me, "a cliché. I started low and worked up. Of course I didn't realize it at the time, but looking back now I can see exactly how it began. It was my not interviewing somebody who won seventy-five thousand pounds in a football pool. That gave me my start.

"You can't plan these things," he went on. "It was pure accident, and so was the next step—not interviewing a woman who, in response to a newspaper advertisement, was about to travel five thousand miles to marry a man she'd never seen.

"Up to then, it was fairly routine stuff," he continued, "but it was the sort of experience that helps later on. You may recall that I became a war correspondent. I got to Chungking, and it was there that I never interviewed Chou En-lai. Later the opportunity arose of not interviewing Mao Tse-tung in a cave in Yenan."

"Which you took?" I asked.

"Oh, yes," he said, smiling with satisfaction. "By that time I was firmly on the road. Soon after, I did not submit a list of written questions to Stalin. War corresponding was a highly competitive business, you know. You have no idea what that did for my prestige."

"After hitting the high spots that way," I said, "it must have been difficult for you when the war ended."

"It was," he said. "I had to keep my hand in by not asking American tourists how they liked it here, and not asking G. I. brides who came back to see their families how they liked it there. It wasn't much but it kept me from getting rusty. Then things took a turn for the better, and I was able not to interview Communists who changed their minds."

"So you were ready when the big chance came?" I asked.

"Absolutely," he said emphatically. "That's how I won the award. I told myself it was now or never, and then I went out and did not interview Tito. I don't like to boast, but I ask you, in all honesty, how many journalists, or non-journalists, for that matter, can make that claim?"

I admitted it was very few.

"Of course," he went on expansively, "there are some people who believe that the non-interview of Tito was not the best thing I've done. They think that came later, with my not interviewing Mossadegh at his bedside. They may be right. I confess I don't know which I prefer myself. But the Winkfield people seem more impressed by the Tito thing. It was a bit of a coup."

"I suppose," I said, "that you feel there are no more worlds for you to conquer."

"There is that problem," he said. "But something always turns up. The big thing is to be ready for it." He lowered his voice. "You're an old friend," he said. "I can trust you. I've got something up my sleeve. I've noticed a few interviews with General Franco lately. That sounds like the beginning. I think an opportunity is building up there. It's a question of timing. I'll let a few months go by and then I'll do my stuff."

His eyes lit up, and he rubbed his hands gleefully. "It could be my greatest triumph," he said.

In that piece for *Punch* I was wrong. Franco never allowed himself to become an easy interview subject. The days of Tito, Mossadegh (prime minister of Iran, 1951–53, nationalizer of the Iranian oil industry, usually interviewed propped up in bed and wearing pajamas), and, later, Gamal Abdel Nasser in Egypt, were heady days for seekers of the Winkfield Award and were never equaled. In our own time, some have made a stab at comparable glory. They have never asked for comment from men in the street, strasse, rue, calle, piazza, or prospekt. They did not interview Princess Anne at the time of her wedding; they did not interview Captain Mark Phillips; and they did not interview Princess Anne and Captain Mark Phillips together. One journalist, a woman of original mind, refrained from interviewing Abba Eban and then, understandably keyed up, in quick succession did not question the reigning Federal Energy Czar and made no attempt to draw out Senator Edward Kennedy on his plans for 1976.

Nobody can deny that she deserves well of her countrymen, but hers is still not a winning performance. There are too many people not to interview now. Television has done that, and jet aircraft, and the large number of new countries. The possibilities are endless. Wherefore the Winkfield Award is no more.

It is too bad. I can almost hear the exchange between the award committee chairman and the winner when the trophy is handed over.

"We are all eager to know how you came to refrain from interviewing the Federal Energy Czar. Will you tell us?"

The winner looks weary, as befits one who has been under the strain of not interviewing so many of the world's great figures. "It was," he replies, "because he is there."

"The *New York Times*," I hear you saying. "Surely the *New York Times* is free of these things. There was that successful foiling of the hijacking, but that must have been an aberration. No?"

No. While the motto of the *Times*, "All the News That's Fit to Print," is not exactly shy and retiring, it is not the news in the *Times* I mean to have at. It is the English. The English is not always fit to print. Far from it.

For long years now, one of the worst things the *Times* has done is to use the construction "convince to." You may convince that. You may convince of. You may not convince to. Unfortunately, this use has caught on and is now virtually accepted. There is no more chance of heading it off than there is of preserving media as a plural. Someone should convince the *Times* that it will bear a large part of the blame.

Here is an editorial in which the *Times* remarks that the Soviet Union "evidently is not able to convince Cairo to accept a rapid cease-fire." Here is a story about the tenor Richard Tucker, who wanted to sing *La Juive* but "was unable to convince Rudolf Bing to stage the work"; and one about Lockheed hoping "to convince airlines to accept modifications of its basic model—the L-1011-1—that would give it transatlantic range"; and one about a new cigarette filter that Columbia University became interested in, in which the *Times* speaks of convincing heavy smokers to cut down their smoking.

The *Times* was not exclusively to blame for the last one, because Columbia University itself, in its press release about the filter, said, "It may be impossible to convince many people to stop smoking." Maybe Columbia should filter its press releases through its English Department.

If the *Times* can do it, why not others?

United Press International from Ankara:

"Two U. S. Congressmen tried to convince Turkey today to

reconsider its decision to resume cultivation of the opium poppy, source of heroin."

Associated Press, from Philadelphia:

"A group of University of Pennsylvania students has called for a 'streak for impeachment' April 1 around the White House.

"They say they are hoping to convince President Nixon to 'lay bare the facts' about Watergate."

Time magazine, March 25, 1974:

"Ervin was aided by Paul Verkuil, a professor at the University of North Carolina, in gathering the evidence that convinced Congress to adopt the provision."

In any case, why do people say—and, more particularly, journalists write—"He was convinced to withdraw his candidacy"? Only a few years ago they would have correctly said, "He was persuaded to." Why, further, do so many people say comprised of instead of composed of? Composed of filled the bill for a very long time. Why, after centuries, has more importantly, misused, begun to replace more important? The *Times* does nothing to resist it: "There has been a gradual shift, over the past 25 years, in the balance of economic power, and even more importantly, in the attitudes governing the relationships between the United States and her neighbors in the Western Hemisphere." "More importantly, in getting kids to read, the impulse to 'read the book, see the movie' works both ways." The ultimate: "Most importantly, he would like to help in prisons." It has, naturally, made its way into commercials, so that it is said of a Guerlain spray, "More importantly, it travels." More importantly, more unfortunately, does too.

What makes the incorrect more attractive than the correct? Gresham's Law tells us that the less valuable currency will force the more valuable out of circulation. That, however, does not explain the case; it merely states it. There is at work here the desire to be up with the latest in thing. But that leaves the question of how the latest in thing came to be. People say, "Hopefully, something will happen." They could, as they did for so long, use the simple and straightforward, "I hope." They don't say, "Hopelessly, nothing will happen." Why should James Reston write in the *Times,* ". . . we are left to our instincts and emotions, and hopefully to our common sense"? Why does the *Times* write, "Hopefully, the Americans believe that this would increase the chances for a peaceful resolution of the Arab-Israeli conflict"? Is it a hope or belief the Americans have? Or is it that the *Times* hopes the Americans believe it? Maybe in the scramble of daily journalism there isn't time to catch these things. But why should Robert Alan Aurthur write ". . . if the city fell apart from a simple power failure, soon hopefully to be repaired, what would happen in the event of a real disaster?" and why should *Esquire,* a monthly, accept it?

Why do American politicians invariably say "I would hope"? ("Right now we are experiencing rather critical shortages in various parts of states, most of it centered on the east coast. I would hope our allocation program would take care of that."— William Simon.) They never specify the conditions under which their hoping would come to pass.

Vice-President Ford said, "I would hope that the White House would cooperate," about the tapes the House Judiciary Committee wanted from President Nixon. (Otherwise, he said, there might be a head-to-head confrontation, this being one in which the eyeballs face the ground while the tops of the skulls are in contact.)

British politicians go a step further. They say "I would have hoped," which implies a wistful detachment. Wistful detachment has not been a recommended attitude for American politicians since the days of Adlai Stevenson, so we may be spared this.

When—and more to the point, why—did a troop become the same thing as a soldier? A troop is a body of men. This, from the *Times* in February, 1974, on the fighting in the Moslem insurgency in the Philippines, is the sort of thing that has become common: "The government admits to more than 300 dead, giving a 'body count' of 225 rebels, about 50 civilians and only 29 of its own troops."

Suppose the casualties were one, one, and one. Would the report then speak of a body count of one rebel, one civilian, and one troop? If *Times* foreign affairs columnist C. L. Sulzberger were writing it, perhaps not. "There are still," he wrote in March, 1974, "about 313,000 U. S. forces in Europe's defense, of whom 190,000 are ground troops in Germany." Sulzberger might make it one rebel, one civilian, and one force.

Here are other tidbits from recent issues of the *Times*: "Equally as costly." Equally as is redundant. "As for example." Redundant. "Different than," rather than different from, is wrong. So is "augur for." Augur does not take for after it. It cannot take for after it. Also, ". . . anyone who feels that either Sills or Lorengar are milking the piece for more than it is worth . . ." Most critics felt that neither soprano were, though in other music, each perhaps do. "Both men had worked together at the Columbia Broadcasting System." On the well-known man-bites-dog principle, the *Times* should have reported this only if one man had worked together at CBS. In the 1973 American League playoff, the *Times* had Jim Palmer of Baltimore and Vida Blue of Oakland engaging in a "flaunted pitching classic." It could have been worse. It could have been flouted.

Not long ago the *Times* put an advertisement in the *Times* for its own help-wanted columns. The advertisement said: "Are you a housewife and have the time to earn extra money while enjoying a change of pace? A temporary job may be the answer." A suitable reply would have been: "No, I aren't have the time to earn extra money while enjoying a change of pace. Are you?"

A headline: "Clean Air Likely to Cost Taxpayer." One in arrears, I trust. From James Reston, a reference to a serious economic crisis facing Egypt. For the Egyptians' sake, I hope so. A serious crisis is the only kind to have. Crises that are not serious are not worth the trouble. It's like the true facts politicians so often demand or, conversely, insist that they are giving us. True facts are the only facts worth having. False facts are no use at all, a point that escaped a State Department spokesman who said of an article in *Foreign Policy:* "Some of the facts are true, some are distorted, and some are untrue." True facts, in (true) fact, are like the factual numbers to which William Simon was devoted as Federal Energy Czar. Nonfactual numbers don't count.

When Alexander Solzhenitsyn arranged for the publication of his account of Soviet prison camps, *The Gulag Archipelago,* in Paris in December, 1973, the *Times* reported that the Soviet government was in a dilemma. Doing nothing would show it to be ineffective, while "The other horn of the dilemma," the *Times* pointed out, seeing to the heart of the matter, "is equally unattractive." A dilemma has to get up pretty early in the morning to fool the *New York Times.*

In March, 1974, the *Times* reported an attack by *Pravda,* the Soviet Communist party newspaper, on Secretary of State Kissinger. The *Times* began by describing *Pravda* as authoritative, which it certainly is. Then it quoted *Pravda* as saying that in Kissinger's Middle East negotiations, "the mountain produced a mouse." The *Times,* thinking this cryptic, added, "an allusion to the Aesopian fable about monumental efforts producing pitifully small results." Always helpful, the *Times.*

When Ibsen's *A Doll's House* was about to open in New York, the *Times* had an article about a rehearsal. It began, "The cast was a half hour late for rehearsal and Patricia Elliott, one of the few to arrive early, was waxing ecstatically about the new set." The *Times* thereby created a picture of Miss Elliott happily shining the furniture on the theater stage, presumably after an agreement between Actors Equity and the Stagehands Union.

So it goes. The *Times* has described Cuban peasants as "prone to pressure from the government, the army, and the plantation owners." With those pressures, no wonder the peasants are prone. It has told us of a soprano with a big-sized voice and a dance company that gave "the most number of performances in years," and of a parcel of land that was square-shaped, thereby saving countless people from believing that it was square-colored.

Some mistakes in the *Times* are hard to classify. When Kwame Nkrumah was deposed in Ghana, the *Times* spoke of his "oustering." Maybe it meant his removaling. It banished a blameless baritone to limbo in its review of a Metropolitan Opera performance of *Otello:* "Except for David Holloway, as the Herald, the other members of the cast were William Lewis (Cassio), Jean Kraft (Emilia) and Paul Plishka (Lodovico)."

Look at this sentence: "With frequent disdain for grammar, logic and, often, accuracy, Hedda Hopper produced a Hollywood gossip column for 28 years." The *Times* evidently believed there was a difference between doing something frequently and doing it often. Which leads to an item from Jack Gould's television column: "But particularly intriguing is the possible consequences of the subway strike on Mr. Lindsay's video fortunes." Gould was right. Consequences often is intriguing. Not frequently, perhaps, but often. That's how consequences on video fortunes is.

Sentences like that one came frequently, as well as often, from Gould. There was this about Mia Farrow:

"Miss Farrow is an interesting personality to know more about, and her attempts to articulate her own set of faith and convictions is probably pertinent to comprehending the 'Now Generation.' "

Gould also gave us this:

"In the judgment of some entertainment executives, the relationship between TV and the motion-picture industry has come full circle. The Hollywood tycoons, in the all-time classic misjudgment of show business, at first ignored TV. Then they sold off their libraries. Now they and TV are becoming partners."

That's full circle.

What follows is not Gould, but try it anyway:

"Dr. Nigrelli, and his wife, Margaret, who live at 11 West 183rd Street, the Bronx, is a native of Pittston, Pa."

Past participles trouble the *Times:*

"Mr. Ives portrays the richest man in the world, a widower, who seeked social status for himself and his children."

"J. W. Fulbright, chairman of the committee, plainly indicated he thought Mr. McNamara had treaded close to deception."

". . . an individual who has bestrode American life for a quarter of a century—Eisenhower of Abilene, Normandy and Washington."

From the sports pages of the *Times*, in an article about Bill Russell at the time he was appointed coach and general manager of the Seattle Supersonics of the National Basketball Association: "This is the second time around for Russell as a coach. As the playing coach of the Celtics for three seasons, Boston won two titles."

That is a non sequitur, as well as a misplaced, dangling modifier, but I suppose that it can be understood as easily as the confused notice now so often seen: "Having left my bed and board, I am no longer responsible for debts incurred by my wife." Or this, from a UPI story about motherly weather in Utah: "After stuffing the apparel in the Cessna 210's windows to keep out the blistering winds, a snowstorm completely covered the craft."

Like many people, the *Times* has trouble with former. A story on the society page said that Leslie J. Leathers, son of the Viscount Leathers "who was a former British Minister of Transport," had announced the engagement of his daughter. This suggests that when Lord Leathers joined the government, the Prime Minister called him in and said, "Leathers, I hereby appoint you former Minister of Transport." That came later, after he'd had the job for a while.

This line appeared in the *Times's* news summary one recent March twenty-second: "Despite weather, spring arrives on schedule." This seemed odd, since the arrival of spring is what might be called a predictable event, and there is no case on record of spring's not arriving at the appointed time. The *Times*, however, did not look at it that way. "Spring arrives, despite clouds," it said in a headline on page 27. Any newspaper likes to have an exclusive angle, and the *Times* had one, that if the clouds had been more lowering, or spring less determined, spring would not have made it.

Such developments come thick and fast at the *Times*. The

arrival of spring was a key and/or major development in the calendar. In a recent period of three weeks the *Times* conferred keyness on local news; labor and management negotiators (who were also top-level bargainers); Democrats in Congress; an election in West Germany; a cabinet post in Israel; the position of Herbert Kalmbach as a Watergate witness; a British insurance broker and parts of letters he was accused of forging; a piece of evidence in the Watergate affair, against which some witnesses were only potentially key; five initiatives that some Arizona citizens who had joined in a loose coalition wanted to put on the ballot in November; and a problem in the development of solar power.

It ascribed the state of being major to newspapers and print publications; a beneficiary of political maneuvering in Israel who might have been expected to work himself into that position since he had, the *Times* pointed out, a reputation for capability; candidates in the French presidential election; television as a source of news; questions facing President Nixon; crimes; a news story; a military defeat in Cambodia; the reason a referendum on divorce was expected to be a political watershed in Italy; the economy as a political issue; the importance of matters on which Yitzhak Rabin, as Israeli ambassador to Washington, consulted Golda Meir; a stumbling block in a labor negotiation; guerrilla groups in the Middle East; criticism in the Lebanese parliament; a speech in Moscow on Lenin's birthday; a confrontation between the White House and the Watergate prosecutor; Saudi Arabia; banks; a piece of consumer legislation in Albany; cities; car rental dealers; strategic weapons systems; a study of the Arms Control and Disarmament Agency; the winter oil shortage and price explosion; the collapse in automobile sales and production; the impact of an indictment; issues in Albany; Governor Wilson's presence in Albany; Henry Kissinger's influence on President Sadat of Egypt; an element in the survival of Japanese soldiers recently found alive in the Philippines; a singer from Brittany, in France; recruiting programs for the armed services; the part of the cost of emergency service borne by hospitals; a post office construction program; the role Henry Kissinger allegedly played in investigations of Daniel Ellsberg; a Portuguese resort; industrial countries; a stroke suffered by the son of Emperor Haile Selassie; steel producers; car manufacturers; an American effort to help poor countries; a smallpox area; the revamping of a television news program; the appointment of William Simon as secretary of the treasury; building projects in urban areas; and a function of the educational staff of the Metropolitan Museum of Art.

Then there is spelling. In the *Times* it is sometimes exotic. Maybe I am only knitpicking, as the *Times* had one of Mayor Abe Beame's men saying when his ethics were questioned. Still, the *Times* has had a black-and-white-striped robe flowing majesterially to the floor. It has told us, in a headline, about "India and the Kashmiri shiek," and otherwise has found the teeming subcontinent teeming with orthographic difficulties, so that it used the spelling Ghandi four times in five sentences, hardly a feather in its hatma Gandhi. Dearth has been spelled dirth in the *Times*. Maybe a dirth is an unclean scarcity. Germane has been spelled germain by one of the learned book reviewers. Germane, she cries in vain.

Of course, it isn't only the *Times*. I received a letter a while ago that ended by thanking me in advance for past courtesies, a bit of politesse not unlike something that happened just before one of the Apollo space flights. A box arrived at NBC News in New York with a map in it from the Topographic Command of the United States Army Corps of Engineers in Washington. It was addressed to us at 30 Rockerfellow Plaza.

There are many people who think that Rockefeller is uncouth, a form of dese and dose English. They therefore address us at Rockafellow or Rockerfellow Plaza. As in Nelson Rockafellow, or John D. Rockerfellow III. This package went them one better, however. It carried the warning: "Handel with care." That is good advice. Handel with care. Going Chopin? Liszt with care. Bizet? Take care. Ravel with care. On the other hand, if you are about to unravel, it doesn't matter so much. But Handel with care. Otherwise you might spill the water music.

2

Ongoing Dialogue
vs.
Adversary Relationship

There are few reputations for eloquence in Washington. Henry Kissinger has one, more or less deserved. His speech is organized, which is to say that it comes out in phrases, sentences, and paragraphs, all apparently premeditated, and that the argument proceeds in an orderly and logical way. Occasionally he is even humorous. Moreover, Kissinger often has an idea that he seeks to communicate; ponderous he may be, but he is genuinely engaged in persuasion.

Such is the astonishment brought on by a man for whom there is a connection between thought and speech that the reaction is out of proportion. We are told that Kissinger is "majestic," that he has offered "an intellectual tour de force," that he was "at his magisterial best," and so on. In fact—and this is not to belittle Kissinger, who, after all, is not responsible for others—in fact, Kissinger stands out also because of a lack of competition, because the level of most of those around him is so low. It does not take much to be thought eloquent in Washington.

Another beneficiary of this condition is William F. Buckley, Jr. Buckley does not so much speak as exhale, but he exhales polysyllabically, and the results are remarkable. "Epiphenomenon," says Buckley, "epistemology, maieutic," and, so we are led to believe, people swoon all over the nation.

I have sometimes thought that Buckley is considered intellectually imposing because some people, unable otherwise to account for his manner of speech, take him to be English. Many Americans feel themselves inferior in the presence of anyone with an English accent, which is why an English accent has become fashionable in television commercials: it is thought to sound authoritative. Buckley reminds me of a character created by the British comedian Spike Milligan and known as the "pronouner." Looting a bombed-out house during the Second World War, he came upon a dictionary, fell in love with words of many syllables, and devoted the rest of his life to pronouning them. His wife kept the dictionary binding polished, and his work mates waited daily for his latest pronunations. When Buckley pulled out the word anfractuosity to describe the American tax system, I thought of the pronouner. He would have been proud.

Washington—appropriately, since it is the capital of the United States—is the place where language is most thoroughly debased—more than Hollywood, which is not what it used to be; more than the world of advertising, which is; more even than the academic world, a realm of unlimited horizons, in which somebody talking to somebody else is considered to be engaged in information transfer.

A respect for language requires some standards of judgment. In Washington they are lacking. There the chief characteristic of language is self-importance, and it casts its spell quickly. I remember receiving a press release from a first-term congressman headed "Major Policy Statement." He was being as helpful as the producer who tells you that he has made a Major Motion Picture; it saves everybody else the trouble of making up his mind.

Self-importance in Washington begins, naturally, at the White

House, and it was an accurate measure of the self-importance that permeated the Nixon White House that the tape-recording system that came to haunt the President should have been put in place. The Johnson administration also had a recording system and at least an equal amount of self-esteem. At the outset of the Kennedy administration, which was bowed down early under a sense of history in the making, an official White House photographer was on the scene incessantly, so that no expression or moment should be lost. Before that, evidently on somebody's sudden inspiration, on January 16, 1961, four days before the inauguration, a telegram went out in some numbers over the signature of President-elect and Mrs. Kennedy:

"During our forthcoming administration we hope to effect a productive relationship with our writers artists composers philosophers scientists and heads of cultural institutions," they said, and went on to say that the recipients of the telegram were invited to attend the inaugural ceremonies "as a beginning in recognition of their importance."

The press, taking its cue from the monarchic our and we, and possibly seeing itself in the role of courtier, soon invoked "Camelot" and "The New Versailles," and talked limitlessly about "style," which had earlier been given a tryout in the days of Adlai Stevenson. Style has since refused to go away, and banks yearning after your money now tell you that they have a thrift style to go with your life style, while sociologists speak of "the legitimacy of multiple body styles." This does not mean multiple body styles in a single, or nonmultiple, body. It means it is all right to be fat.

Sometimes reality entirely flees the White House. On October 3, 1966, Nicholas Katzenbach was sworn in as undersecretary of state. Katzenbach had been attorney general, and President Johnson spoke to the television cameras about that. "He has stood here for the cause of freedom," Mr. Johnson said. "He has pursued justice for all Americans. Every man is in his heart."

Then the President spoke about Katzenbach's new post. "Now the scope of his work is the world, and the qualities of mind and spirit which have made him the champion of social change and human progress at home will make him their advocate throughout the world."

There cannot have been many hearts beating faster because Katzenbach was undersecretary of state. But Mr. Johnson did not merely announce his appointments; he congratulated himself on them, and congratulated the nation as well. He made the nomination of an ambassador to Poland sound earth-shaking. Lawrence O'Brien, as the new postmaster general, received such a tribute that it might have seemed he would carry all the mail himself.

The pressure to measure up to such extravagant standards is intense in Washington. President Nixon described the Smithsonian monetary agreement of December, 1971, as the most important agreement of its kind in the history of the world; he described revenue sharing and a guaranteed family income as the second American revolution; and he called the first manned flight to the moon the most important event since the Creation. He must have thought that if he called it epochal nobody would notice. Vice-President Ford, possibly preparing for higher duties, assessed Kissinger's part in the Syrian-Israeli troop disengagement as "the great diplomatic triumph of this century or perhaps any other."

When Campobello Island in Nova Scotia was given to the Canadian and American governments as a "peace park" by the industrialist Armand Hammer and his brother Victor, papers had to be signed by Prime Minister Lester Pearson and President Johnson. A photograph of the ceremony on January 22, 1964, shows the nonsense that has been allowed to grow up around the presidency, for just as words lose their value, so do ceremonies and events. On the left side, Mr. Pearson is signing. He has one pen. On the right side, Mr. Johnson is signing. In front of him sits what looks like a giant punchboard, with pens stuck into it nibs up. As nearly as I could make out, it had spaces for one hundred forty-four pens, plus an inkpot. I don't know how many historic pens Mr. Johnson gave out that day, but at the time the photograph was taken, more than a hundred were in the board.

Pens do something to the American presidential psyche. When President Nixon went to Paris in April, 1974, for the memorial service after the death of President Georges Pompidou, he went out in the street and gave away ball point pens. The French have a word, protocolaire, to describe what is fitting and proper. Giving away pens in such circumstances wasn't.

President Johnson liked things big. The Lyndon B. Johnson Library at the University of Texas in Austin is eight stories high and measures 100,000 square feet. It contains 31,000,000 documents (There's a freighted word! When does a sheet of paper metamorphose into a document?), 500,000 photographs, 500,-000 feet of moving-picture film, and 30,000 gifts sent to the Johnsons. With the Lyndon B. Johnson School of Public Affairs at the university, it cost $18,600,000 to build. The cost to the taxpayers of maintaining the library was $540,000 a year at the beginning. It must be more now.

Mr. Johnson was president for more than five years. The Kennedy Library, a memorial to a man who was president for less than three years, threatens to undo an entire neighborhood in Cambridge, Massachusetts, it is to be so big.

Presidential libraries, like many things, came to a climax of sorts under President Nixon when it turned out that his brother Edward had been retained as a consultant by the Richard Nixon Foundation, a tax-exempt undertaking. Edward Nixon advised the foundation where the Nixon family would like the Nixon presidential library to be, a chore that involved him in consulting himself, and for which he was paid $1,500 a month for fourteen months. According to Leonard Firestone, head of the foundation, Edward visited six sites and recommended that the final selection be made from among three in Orange County, California, an area that might otherwise have escaped attention, since its only claim to consideration was that the President was born and began his legal and political careers there.

About Edward Nixon's compensation Firestone said, "If people think that is too much, let them try to hire a consultant these days and see what they come up with." The plain meaning of that comment was that consultants were becoming so scarce in the United States that low-grade ones had to be used, just as rising prices make low-grade ores economical when they were not economical before. The quality of life is deteriorating in unforeseen and surprising ways.

The Rockefeller brothers, perhaps in expectation, perhaps in aspiration—it's hard to know—have announced plans to build a $4,500,000 archive center holding perhaps 20,000,000 papers related to their family's activities and history. They are to build it on their own land at Pocantico Village, New York, and near their own houses, which will be convenient for popping historic documents into it on the way to and from work.

The outlook for presidential and other libraries is, I am happy to say, cloudy, because in 1969 a law was passed ending tax deductions for the contribution of personal papers to libraries, universities, and the like. Shakespeare said (*The Tempest,* Act II, Scene 1), "What's past is prologue"; we made it for a while, What's past is deductible, but after President Nixon's celebrated and later disallowed $576,000 deduction for his vice-presidential papers (the his is used loosely; it is hard to see how they were his, or how Hubert Humphrey's were Hubert Humphrey's, or those of anybody else in public office those of anybody else in public office), the law is not likely to be repealed.

The papers Mr. Nixon sent to the National Archives in exchange for the $576,000 deduction were 414,000 letters; 87,000 items relating to public appearances, including speech texts, 27,000 invitations, with acceptances and refusals; and 57,000 items relating to trips abroad. In this mass of materials were newspaper clippings and unclipped newspapers.

I don't know how the stuff Mr. Nixon had delivered to the National Archives, where Shakespeare's line cited above adorns the façade, compares with similar material contributed by others. I think that by rule of thumb—extended in the way the baseball umpire signals "out"—at least 90 percent of it could be thrown away with no loss to anyone. A sense of history and a debt to scholarship are all very well, but how can words and ideas have any value when there are millions of them? The word documents is robbed of meaning when it is claimed that there are 31,000,000 of them.

There is something spooky about the desire to pronounce oneself historic ahead of time. Only history decides on that; anticipation increases the discomforting exaltation we have seen in our recent presidents. It is, for example, expressed in the weighty announcement, "Ladies and gentlemen, the President of the United States," and the playing of "Hail to the Chief." No doubt, if an actress about to receive an award can be serenaded with "A Pretty Girl Is Like a Melody," a president can have "Hail to the Chief" proclaim his arrival. But it does lend an aura of destiny to the daily round when it is hard enough for a president to maintain a sense of proportion, and it might be worse still if presidents knew the words of the song, which come from Sir Walter Scott's "Lady of the Lake":

> Hail to the chief, who in triumph advances,
> Honor'd and blessed be the evergreen pine!
> Long may the tree in his banner that glances,
> Flourish, the shelter and grace of our line.
> Hail to the chief, who in triumph advances,
> Honor'd and bless'd be the evergreen pine!
> Long may the tree in his banner that glances,
> Flourish, the shelter and grace of our line.
> Heav'n send it happy dew,
> Earth lend it sap anew;
> Gaily to burgeon and broadly to grow;
> While ev'ry highland glen,
> Sends our shout back again,
> Roderigh Vich Alpine dhu, ho! i-e-roe!

Not much has been heard lately about former Senator John Williams, Republican of Delaware, who was responsible for the 1969 law ending deductions for personal papers. I would like to put up a memorial to him, but I am afraid somebody would want to put documents in it. I speak as one who for two years took deductions of $4,215 and $1,340 for papers contributed to the Wisconsin State Historical Society. This also was ridiculous.

The project for a Nixon presidential library is in abeyance and, because of Watergate, may never come to anything. However, Mr. Nixon has announced that he and his wife intend to give their house at San Clemente to the people of the United States. This is the structure that has a sign outside identifying it as the Western White House, which it isn't even though the bills charged to the American people could have confused them into thinking they had bought it, and even though most of the press, in an exercise of self-importance by association, is happy to go along. Nor is the Nixon house in Key Biscayne the Florida White House, any more than Lyndon Johnson's ranch was the Texas White House, though that is what he liked to call it; or John Kennedy's place at Hyannis Port the Cape Cod White House; or the Eisenhower farm the Gettysburg White House. The naval base at Key West, Florida, did not turn into a White House when Harry Truman was there. The White House is in Washington. Presidents do not take it with them when they travel.

Washington is the seat of government because it is where other people in the government sit. If it is objected that presidents are isolated in Washington, a jet flight to Florida or California, followed by a helicopter flight to a guarded compound, is unlikely to remedy that. I am not trying to make the White House a mystic shrine. I am trying to distinguish it from its tenants, who are transient.

It may be that there is something wrong with the White House. Perhaps, with tourists trooping through it, it offers those who live in it no real privacy. For we have seen a strange development in the past few decades. Men dedicate their lives to getting to the White House. What Richard Nixon went through to get there is almost unimaginable, including Barry Goldwater's saying of him in 1964, "Nixon is sounding more like Harold Stassen every day." Once there, they can hardly wait to leave it. A president is no longer important because he is in the White House but because he is out of it, and the more places at his disposal the better. Likewise the press. It is more glamorous to be not on your regular beat but somewhere else, and it is still more glamorous to be en route.

I know this kind of thing from my own experience. One night during the Suez Crisis of 1956 I made a broadcast from London in a dinner jacket. It was the crown of my career until I made a broadcast in swimming trunks from the Eisenhower-Macmillan conference in Bermuda in 1957. That in turn held up until I was summoned from a tennis court when the East Germans began putting up the Berlin Wall in August, 1961. These are the things that tell you that you are important.

A similar inflation expresses itself in the attitudes of the press toward words like sources, documents, and intelligence. Say sources and the eyes sparkle. Say documents and a hush falls. Say intelligence and people gasp in awe, as when Mephistopheles in *Faust* strikes a tavern sign and brings forth wine. Yet intelligence is only information, or misinformation. Documents are only papers, sometimes classified, or overclassified. A source is only somebody who told you something, possibly for his own purposes, and possibly incorrect.

No practice in Washington is more beloved than that of attributing statements to sources who cannot be named. It has the same appeal as secret societies with mystic rites and passwords and carries some of the same prestige a columnist acquires by referring to Gerald Ford as Gerry, Melvin Laird as Mel, Alexander Haig as Al, or the late Charles E. Bohlen as Chip. Highly placed, or well placed, the sources may be; reliable they may be; informed, well informed, in a position to know, acquainted with the case, close to the investigation, familiar with the documents, but unnamed.

There is nothing like the Richter scale that measures earthquakes on which to rate sources; but well placed is a step below highly placed, reliable means the source has been used before, and usually reliable is a hedge. Compared to informed, well informed is slightly defensive. Acquainted with, in a position to know, close to, familiar with are only variations on informed, but may sound better in stories about trials and investigations. Authoritative is the best, since unimpeachable has been removed to another context.

There are those who prefer sources to be unnamed even though it means that those sources cannot be held responsible for what they say. It gives people in government the feeling that they are on the inside, with everybody else on the outside, and that they are among the makers and shakers in a city where competition in making and shaking is intense. Reporters enjoy the feeling that they are on the inside, too, for nothing is as valuable as an unnamed source that others cannot reach. In 1946 a member of the Anglo-American commission on Palestine told me that President Truman had privately denounced the British blockade of Palestine against ships carrying Jews. Nobody was able to match it, and nobody could knock it down because the White House would not comment. Note that even now I do not tell who the source ("a guest who sat at the President's right at the White House dinner at which he made the denunciation") was.

Using unnamed sources is often, of course, the only way information can be put out. The dogged reporting of Watergate by a small number of people demonstrated that. But it can be abused, and is too often indulged in for its own sake; and again, language is destroyed when words like reliable and sources are shrugged off and laughed at.

I have had occasion to laugh at them myself. In October, 1966, during the second of my six seasons as a play reviewer, the Broadway producer David Merrick withdrew my first-night tickets because, he said, I was unqualified and I didn't like anything. (This is a generous way of putting it. He said I had been a washroom attendant before becoming a "Hey you, critic"; that is, the head of NBC News walked into the washroom and said, "Hey you, there's a play opening tonight. Go and review it.") All this was reported at the time on radio and television, in the newspapers and in the news magazines. Later, things were patched up and my tickets were restored and NBC no longer had to pay my way into Merrick's plays.

A few years later a book called *Reviewing for the Mass Media,* whose author had asked for and received copies of some of my reviews, stated that Merrick had withdrawn my first-night tickets because I had insisted on reviewing preview performances of his productions, something I had never done with any producer. I wrote the author, who had never questioned me about the incident, telling him that he was wrong and pointing out that the facts of the incident were public knowledge at the time and getting far more attention than they were worth, which was Merrick's intention all along. The author replied that he was sorry about the mistake but he had relied on his sources.

I had visions of a clandestine phone call to the author of *Reviewing for the Mass Media,* with the source, a man of furtive movements, darting into a pay phone booth in the outer recesses of Brooklyn, identifying himself by a prearranged code, and tersely telling the phony preview story. As for why he would tell it, I supposed it must have been for the glory of being a source.

One reason that language is debased in Washington is that it rests so often on assumptions that are unexamined. As soon as a presidential election ends, it becomes the fashion to write stories and put together television programs describing the winner as close to a political genius, and finding a latent significance in every act of his childhood and early youth.

In the early and middle 1950s any British magazine editor could tell you with only a small margin of error how many copies it was worth to him to have the Queen on the cover, or the Duke of Edinburgh, or any other member of the royal family. Sensibly employed, and before satiety set in, the royal family was one of the greatest selling points the British press had. It has never entirely lost its commercial usefulness; people want to read enough about the royal family to be able to have opinions about them—that the Queen seems happy, that the Duke has made lots of changes in the palace, that poor Princess Margaret is not happy and got more than she bargained for, that Princess Anne has spirit, that Prince Charles is a quiet one but he'll come out all right. In April, 1974, a British women's magazine reminded its readers that the Queen was also a wife, a mother, and a woman with a mind of her own in an article called "The Queen the Public Doesn't Know." The subheadings were: Moved perilously close to tears; Her feet were aching so she took off her shoes; At home, she is an easy, lively conversationalist; Hurt and indignant, she asked for her coat; and It is Philip who sits at the head of the table.

Not that it is likely ever to go back to where it was at coronation time in 1953. I was riding in a bus one day along the coronation route, and men were jumping up and down on the spectators' stands that had just been erected. A little girl behind me asked her mother why the men were doing that, and the mother explained that they wanted to be sure the stands wouldn't collapse when there were people in them on Coronation Day because "That wouldn't be very nice for the Queen, would it?"

We in the American press do somewhat the same thing with our presidents and their families, especially just before and just after they take office. We are proud of them; we find qualities in them that they do not have; we want them to personify the nation, which is impossible; we write about their responsibility and opportunity to give the country moral leadership, which would be presumptuous for anybody to offer, especially somebody engaged in the day-to-day business of politics; we give the nation a fixation on them. Any journalist worth his salt writes at least a couple of articles about the new political era and new political style, and even journalists not worth their salt, though oppressed by their shortcomings, manage nonetheless. We dig up teachers who always knew that he would do great things someday. "I remember him coming to get milk and sugar for his mother," a storekeeper tells us. "He was always very careful to get the correct change. I always figured he'd make something of himself. Even then, he was all business." Quick switch to lawyer from his home town. "There was something about the way he spoke. I thought he'd become a judge for sure. Never thought he'd go into politics, though." (Chuckles.) "He seemed too serious."

A year or so after the new president has come in, two years

at the most, the press discovers that he has had some failures. This makes possible another series of articles saying that the new political era may be short-lived, and that it is off to a patchy start. The press, in short, is disappointed, which it has every right to be, after taking seriously such notions as President Kennedy's Grand Design for partnership between the United States and Western Europe, the Multilateral Nuclear Force, affectionately known as the MLF, and the Alliance for Progress, also called the Alianza para el Progreso so that our neighbors to the South, who were to be transformed by it, would not feel left out. When you have an Alliance for Progress, you can count on writing articles headed The Alliance Falters quite soon.

This is not a court I enter with clean hands. I unloaded a number of stories about the Multilateral Nuclear Force and I am sure that I made loose use of Great Society and War on Poverty. It may be said that they were convenient shorthand, but there are times when that is not sufficient justification. I referred a few times to the San Antonio Formula, a proposal President Johnson put forward in San Antonio, Texas, for ending the war in Vietnam and which had not the slightest chance of doing so. I believe, however, that I never mentioned the New Frontier.

The press did it with President Johnson. He was presented as a dominating politician of near-genius, creating the Great Society in spite of other distractions. He wound up virtually a prisoner in the White House. Hubert Humphrey, as Mr. Johnson's vice-president, proclaimed that we would build the Great Society not only here but in Southeast Asia. This could have led to disappointment on a monumental scale, but it went too far. Nobody believed it.

It was done with Robert McNamara, not a president, of course, but presented as the secretary of defense with the computer brain. Computers must have data fed into them. The data are called software, a kind of mush McNamara used to ingest before he emitted the solution to whatever defense problem was bothering the country. Clicking and whirring sounds would be heard; he would look uncomfortable; and out would come a readout advocating an electronic fence along the border between the two Vietnams.

The Washington press corps, as it likes to call itself, measures happiness by the amount of its contact with the president. A failure by a president to meet the corps—a possible alternative title to "Meet the Press"—more or less regularly is seen as demeaning to the corps and, still worse, a dereliction of his duty to the American people.

I have my doubts about this, and I don't care whether the president calls me by my first name, or invites me to dinner, or telephones to congratulate me on a story, which is just as well, since all these things a succession of presidents has so far resisted the temptation to do. Information does not have to come from presidents. Can I find out what I want to find out? Is the government suppressing what should be known? These are the things that matter.

The presidential news conference is vastly overrated, anyway. This may be heresy—and I hope it is, for few things are more enjoyable than being heretical without penalty—but it would hardly matter if it weren't held at all. I am not *against* presidential news conferences if people are happy having them, and circumstances do alter cases, as they did in the Watergate summer of 1973, when we reached the stage where it was taken as an act of courage for the president of the United States to answer questions from reporters.

But no president answers anything he does not want to. It is a simple matter to say, "No comment," even though, beginning with President Kennedy's time, it seems to have been thought not sporting and shameful to do so. It is also simple to sidestep, or to drown the question rather than answer it, a technique brought to perfection by politicans on the Sunday television programs. You cannot pin down a president who does not want to be pinned down, and that is as it should be. I was bawled out by President Truman because he did not like a follow-up question I asked. He was quite right. I should not have asked it, though maybe he shouldn't have been there at a press conference to be asked it, either.

It may be argued that since those who hold news conferences choose to hold them, anything goes. We all have our fantasies:

"So, Mr. President, you thought you could get out from under with that half-baked answer. Well, you reckoned without Lank Lancelot, investigative reporter for the Honesty-Is-the-Best-Policy Syndicate."

The President tries to bluff his way out. "Listen, Lancelot, I know your kind. If you want an adversary relationship—and this goes for anybody else in this room—I can be more adversarial than you ever dreamed."

Lancelot's eyes narrow to a steely glare. "An adversary relationship is exactly what I want, Mr. President. It goes with the press card."

The President, seeing himself overmatched, tells all.

There is a cozy notion that presidential news conferences are free-swinging, no-holds-barred methods of enlightening the American people, and that they take the place of parliamentary question periods in other countries. They are not free-swinging and no-holds-barred because they cannot be, since one person at the conference is president of the United States and everybody else is not.

Nor are news conferences in any way equivalent to question periods in parliamentary countries. Those are conducted by the government and the opposition, which is an alternative government. The press is neither. Not that it might not be fun to try the parliamentary style at our news conferences. Questions are submitted in advance, "supplementaries" are allowed the questioner after the answer is given, and the Speaker may call other members who wish to ask questions:

PRESIDENT: Since I cannot accept the false premises on which the question is based, I am afraid that I am therefore unable to answer. However, I will be glad to supply detailed and factual information to show how the act cited is being carried out. (Cries of "Hear, hear" from aides gathered behind President, and from reporters sympathetic to his point of view.)

REPORTER: Bearing in mind what the Right Honorable Gentleman has said, will he acknowledge that his administration has failed miserably in carrying out the terms of the act and that the result has been the atrociously unfair treatment of those in need? (Cries of "Hear, hear" from reporters sympathetic to Questioner's point of view.)

PRESIDENT: No, sir.

SECOND REPORTER: Will my Right Honorable friend bear in mind that absurd and tendentious questions such as the one he has just been asked serve only to bring opposition parts of the press into the disrepute they so well deserve? (Cheers from President's aides and sympathetic reporters.)

PRESIDENT: I will bear that in mind, and I thank my honorable friend.

We are told that a president must communicate with the people, that those who govern must take the people into their confidence, that there must—this is the clincher—there must be an ongoing dialogue. (It is impossible to calculate how many academic and government careers have been preserved and furthered by the devising of ongoing, or the amount of foundation money shaken loose, but that is by the way.) News conferences take care of this. So we are told.

On February 2, 1967, President Johnson held a fairly typical news conference. Would he assess the prospects for peace in Vietnam? He had said many times that we wanted a peaceful settlement and were ready for discussions, but he was not aware of any serious effort by the other side to stop the fighting. Would he be willing to take part in negotiations himself? He had no sign that the other side was willing to settle on decent terms. Would the United States compromise on its objectives? Both sides would have to make concessions, but he knew of no serious indication that the other side was ready to stop fighting. Did he note any signs of fluidity in the other side's position? He had seen no serious effort to go to the conference table or bring the war to an end.

Four questions, and essentially one answer.

Later, the President was asked what we would like from North Vietnam in exchange for stopping the bombing. He replied that he had seen no indication of reciprocal action. Still later, this question was pretty much repeated and the President pretty much repeated his answer.

Six questions, and essentially one answer.

The President was also asked about China, the new Congress, politics, Eastern Europe, and—some Washington reporters cannot resist this one—his opinion of Washington reporters (the corps!) and how he liked his job.

Presidential news conferences make news when presidents want them to, and they do not instruct presidents about what the people consider important and pressing ("the ongoing dialogue") unless presidents want them to, in which case the president probably has a shrewd idea about it all without questions from the press. Presidents don't usually think of reporters as tribunes of the people, anyway, and an ongoing dialogue would take a different form. The president begins by saying "Good evening," with 210,000,000 voices replying "Good evening" in unison, no small trick. The president announces he has good news, provoking shouts of "We'll be the judge of that" and "Let him speak." The announcement itself gets a divided reception, 42 percent in favor, 36 against, 14 don't know, and 8 don't give a damn. The president tries to reason with those who dislike his proposal; this inflames tempers further; fighting breaks out; there are occasional cries of "Thank you, Mr. President" from those who have watched too many television news conferences; the president leaves, and the ongoing dialogue ceases on to go.

Some critics of President Johnson said that in his administration a dialogue never onwent, that he never sufficiently explained his aims and intentions in Vietnam, was not candid with the people. That was not entirely so. President Johnson communicated and communicated and communicated. He exhorted, he entreated, he adjured. He pleaded. He appealed to pride and he appealed to patriotism—March 2, 1967: "I think the American people should know that this is a question between their President, their country, their troops, and Mr. Ho Chi Minh and the troops that he is sending from the North. Everyone can take whatever side of the matter he wants to." He explained, repeatedly and at length. It is true, however, that in his administration a dialogue never onwent. A monologue onwent.

President Nixon fell into the same problem over Watergate. Every time he said something about it, his position grew worse.

There is a moral here. Communicate, by all means. But *what* is communicated may still matter. No amount of Q. and A. can change that.

I also think it childish and time-wasting for presidents and other officials to go through "briefings" and rehearsals for news conferences in which their assistants play the parts of reporters and ask the "toughest" questions they can. It would not surprise me if reservations like those made for a popular book at a circulating library were put in early for the right to play Dan Rather, Clark Mollenhoff, and Sarah McClendon.

Here again we run into that familiar blight on public life and language, excessive calculation. Do I, then, recommend off-the-cuff answers to reporters? No. They can be too dangerous. During the Korean war, President Truman made an offhand, ambiguous answer to a question about whether consideration was being given to the use of atomic weapons. In a matter of hours the British Prime Minister, Clement Attlee, was in the air and on the way to Washington to find out what the President had meant. What he'd meant turned out to be quite different from what he'd said.

Another of Mr. Truman's offhand news conference remarks created complications of a different kind. It came during his first term, when an attorney was trying to organize a union of major league baseball players. A wartime law empowered the President to seize and operate any industry vital to national defense if its production was being interfered with, and the possibility had arisen of a strike by the Pittsburgh Pirates, the team the attorney was concentrating on. Somebody jokingly asked Mr. Truman whether he might seize them.

"I'll tell you one thing," Mr. Truman replied. "If I do, the Cardinals will have a damn good team."

When the conference ended, I was dictating a little feature about the President's remark to the United Press, for which I was then working, when one of the presidential news secretaries knocked on the door of the UP booth in the White House press room.

"Are you using the story about the Pittsburgh Pirates?" he asked.

I said I was.

"Don't have the President saying damn," he said. "It only leads to trouble."

The secretary meant that there would be letters, telegrams, and telephone calls to the White House about it, and maybe some petitions, and perhaps an anti-damn resolution passed here and there. So I left damn out. So did everyone else. Those were innocent days, but we shouldn't have. Also, it spoiled the story. A quarter of a century later we might have had Mr. Truman saying, "I'll tell you one thing. If I do, the Cardinals will have a (expletive deleted) good team," a device that puts the burden of supplying the profanity on the reader but does nothing to reduce the no-nonsense impression the curser (or precurser, really) seeks to give.

Displays of virtuosity in answering questions may be amusing, but, though I treasure the wisecrack, I do not look to the White House for amusement. A president must be able to persuade, but if he does it better, and with less risk, in ways other than the news conference, that is his business.

In any case, it is less useful to the country to have reporters questioning a president than it is for reporters to preserve their independence. Secretary of State Dean Rusk lost his temper with some reporters about Vietnam and asked, "Which side are you on?" They were where they should have been, on the side of accurate reporting.

Secretary Rusk may well have thought theirs an "adversary relationship." It sounds persuasive, exhilarating, like a shoot-out at the O.K. Corral, and many people in government believe in it. That is no reason for the press to accept the idea. The press may be shoved into an adversary position from time to time, as it was over the Pentagon papers, but newspapers exist to print news, not to suppress it, and once they got the Pentagon papers, they had no choice, in spite of the government's attempt to enjoin publication.

It was much the same in the summer of 1973 when President Nixon, holding a news conference after going five months without one, was asked whether his authority had been eroded. He said that it had been, inevitably, because he had been attacked nightly for twelve or fifteen minutes on the news programs. The President had not been attacked; he had been reported on. These were some of the things reported:

The Watergate break-in and cover-up; the insistence by the judge in the Watergate trial on going beyond where the prosecution wanted to go; the Watergate hearings; the resistance to the idea of a special prosecutor; the unwillingness to hand over White House tapes; the break-in at the office of Daniel Ellsberg's psychiatrist; the offer of the job of FBI director to the judge in the Ellsberg case; the "enemies lists"; questionable campaign contributions; creation of the "plumbers' unit"; approval of the Huston plan, including breaking and entering, wire tapping, and mail covers; wire tapping, without court order, of a dozen journalists and White House employes; wire tapping of the President's brother Donald; the indictment of some of the President's associates, the guilty pleas entered by others, and the resignations of still others; the disgrace and resignation of the man he twice chose for vice-president; the money spent on his houses; his tax returns; the questions raised by the ITT affair, the dairy industry affair, and the Soviet wheat deal; the pressure on corporations to contribute to his reelection campaign; the secret bombing of Cambodia and the falsification of records about it.

Walter Cronkite himself would have found his authority eroded by these things, let alone a mere president of the United States. All of this, moreover, was in addition to the firing of the special prosecutor, Archibald Cox, and the resignations of Attorney General Elliot Richardson and Deputy Attorney General William Ruckelshaus; the now-you-see-them, now-you-don't White House tapes; and the suspicions aroused by the military alert during the Middle East fighting in October, 1973.

Sometimes the President complained not that he had been attacked but that he had been subjected to a "daily pounding by the press." One of his assistants, Bruce Herschensohn, said that the President had taken a "battering" over his decision to bomb Hanoi and Haiphong in December, 1972. Vice-President Agnew had a more technical and fashionable way of putting it when he resigned. "Media interest" in his case would distract public attention from other and more important matters, Agnew said, and that was one reason he had decided to step aside. In short, it wasn't what he did but what we did, and news organizations could have chosen to cover or not to cover the case of a vice-president under grand jury investigation, as they pleased. If there had been no media interest, who knows? He might have stayed on.

Media interest appears to mean that news organizations are covering stories you don't want them to cover. This was President Kennedy's reaction—though he did not make it publicly known—when news stories began to come out of Vietnam that showed the war ongoing not as he expected it to and, probably, not as he was being told it was. The most prominent reporter sending back not supportive but nonsupportive stories was David Halberstam of the *New York Times,* and Mr. Kennedy asked that he be replaced. The *Times* said, adversarily, no.

In an earlier intervention, Mr. Kennedy asked the *New York Times* not to print a story about the preparations being made for the Bay of Pigs invasion. The *Times* unadversarily said yes, and later Mr. Kennedy became something of a hero to parts of the press by saying that he wished the *Times* had turned him down and printed the story, because it would have saved the United States from a disaster. It was a peculiarly silly comment, since if the *Times* had printed the story, Mr. Kennedy would not have known the outcome of the invasion, and the *Times* would have been denounced for blocking an attempt to eliminate a Communist government from Cuba.

The fact is that Mr. Kennedy had quite a different view of media interest in the days after the Bay of Pigs. I covered a speech he made at the Waldorf-Astoria in New York to a meeting of newspaper publishers. He asked them to institute a system of voluntary censorship about military matters based on the operations of the Office of War Information in the Second World War. The speech was delivered in embarrassed silence and the idea was heard of no more.

On April 1, 1968, the day after he announced that he would not run for another term, President Johnson flew to Chicago and spoke to the National Association of Broadcasters. He never quite specified his complaint, but he circled it and stalked it:

"You, the broadcasting industry, have enormous power in your hands. You have the power to clarify. And you have the power to confuse. Men in public life cannot remotely rival your opportunities because day after day, night after night, hour after hour . . . you shape the nation's dialogue.

"The commentary that you provide can give the real meaning to the issues of the day or it can distort them beyond all meaning."

When Mr. Johnson told the broadcasters, "You shape the nation's dialogue," it was what a psychologist would call projection. "The nation's dialogue" was shaped by what was done in Vietnam, principally by him. Unless, of course, the news organizations had decided that a war in which 500,000 Americans were involved, which took 50,000 American lives and crippled thousands more, and cost $30,000,000,000 a year—not to mention what it did to the countries where it was fought—did not warrant media interest.

We in the news business—"media folks," Mayor Richard Daley of Chicago called us in July, 1968, when he rejoiced over the prospect that a strike by electrical workers might hold up installation of communications facilities and lead to "a good old-fashioned, old-time Democratic convention, with the delegates in charge and maybe without you media folks all over the place" —we folks in the media interest business must be careful about what we accept. The reason is that what we accept we pass along to the nonmedia folks at home.

The war in Indochina produced a host of terms that media folks accepted at their peril: protective reaction strike, surgical bombing, free-fire zone, interdiction, contingency capability, New Life Hamlet—which in sterner days was a refugee camp— and many more. Money paid to the family of a South Vietnamese civilian killed by mistake was a condolence award.

In February, 1971, South Vietnamese ground forces, with American air support, moved into Laos. Rarely had the importance the government attached to language been made so clear. An incursion, Washington called it, and there were official objections to our calling it an invasion, evidently in the belief that incursion implied something softer than invasion did, and that an incursion was permissible where perhaps an invasion was not.

At this point, media interest led to the dictionary, where an incursionist was defined as an invader, incursionary as invading, and incursion as entering into territory with hostile intent; a sudden invasion; a predatory or harassing inroad; a raid. The first definition of invasion mentioned conquest and plunder, and the United States was not bent on those, but the operation in Laos met other meanings of invasion precisely: an inroad of any kind, as an entry into or establishment in an area not previously occupied; the introduction or spread of something hurtful or pernicious; and a penetration or occupation by outside force or agency.

All this may be simply expressed: invasion = incursion. This being the case, why not say incursion and give the government its heart's desire? Because calling it an incursion was a public relations exercise, an attempt to make it appear less grim than it was and acceptable to the American people.

The distinction between incursion and invasion was a distinction without a difference, in grammar and in fact. The incursion into, or invasion of, Cambodia in 1970 enormously increased death and destruction there, and the incursion into, or invasion of, Laos increased death and destruction there. It is not the business of news people to exaggerate any of this, but it is not their business to water it down either.

Administrations seem to feel that he who is not in a supportive relationship with me is in an adversary relationship with me. People in the news business should turn a cold and appraising eye on all ideas, including that one. Especially that one.

A confession: I once used the word supportive while appearing on the "Dick Cavett Show." I heard it coming out and tried to pull it back. But too late. A judgment of ignominy should have been pronounced.

3

Mr. Chairman,
I Find It
Incumbent
Upon Me

Politics has a way of bringing on meaningless language.
Late in 1966, while discussing the war in Vietnam, Senator Everett Dirksen of Illinois, then the Republican leader
in the Senate, reported that he heard the American people asking, "Where are we going?" just as, Dirksen said, the people of
ancient Rome had asked "Quo vadis?" when Rome was nearing
the end. It was a little like suggesting that the ancient Romans
went around muttering "Nehercule, hoc quidem lapsus ea ruina"
("Gee whiz, this really is a decline and fall"). Dirksen probably
drew his comment from a card file of appropriate reactions, under the heading Crisis Situations, or Watersheds, though the
reaction was not appropriate, since it is not the Roman people
but St. Peter who is usually credited with asking "Quo vadis?"
and in circumstances notably different from those Dirksen set
out. Still, such files are standard equipment, and few politicians
are without one.

During the Republican convention in Chicago in 1960 I was walking along Michigan Boulevard when I became aware of a knot of people on the other side of the avenue. I crossed over and found Richard Nixon, then vice-president and about to be nominated for president, crouching near a shoeshine boy who was black. Crouching with him were the three Nixon women and a few cameramen.

As I arrived I heard Mr. Nixon say, "What do you want to be when you grow up?" The boy, Leon Thompson, ten years old, considered this for a while, then replied, "Well, I don't want to be no police." Mr. Nixon had a ready answer. "You don't have to be a policeman if you don't want to," he said. "In this country, you can be anything you like."

The vistas thus thrown wide, the boy considered his glowing future once more. After a while it was agreed, in the absence of other suggestions, that he would go into the army. Mr. Nixon then went on his way, and the next day NBC's "Today" show displayed its delicacy of feeling by having Leon Thompson on the program and giving him (before the cameras) a check for $200.

The politician who tries to get away from the formula reply risks creating impatience and boredom. But consider what may happen to the one who uses it. I remember Mr. Nixon representing the United States as vice-president at the independence ceremonies in Accra, Ghana, in 1957. He went to a school to announce the establishment of an Eisenhower fellowship and in the course of his speech said, "I agree with your great educator, Aggrey.* If you want to make beautiful music, you must play the black and the white notes together." As he said this, Mr. Nixon was looking out on some hundreds of black notes who were celebrating the expulsion of white notes from their country, after eighty-three years in which the black notes might almost not have been on the piano at all. The speech, probably drawn

---

* James Emman Kwegyir Aggrey (1875–1927), who studied at Livingston College in Salisbury, N.C., and at Columbia University in New York.

from the card file under "Negro Audiences," was not a rousing success.

There may be, nonetheless, a certain safety in language by formula, even in conversation, now that private matters have become increasingly public.

L. Patrick Gray has testified that when he called President Nixon on July 6, 1972, to tell him that some members of his staff were trying to wound him mortally, the President replied, "Pat, you just continue to conduct your thorough and aggressive investigation." This is not conclusive evidence that Mr. Nixon was speaking for the record, or for the recording, since he could have said, "Pat, you carry on with your thorough, aggressive, free-swinging, fearless, unremitting and let-the-chips-fall-where-they-may investigation." In any case, the President said this in San Clemente, where, so far as we know, there were no recording facilities.

However, Gray has testified that during another telephone conversation, on March 23, 1973, Mr. Nixon reminded him that he had told him to conduct a thorough investigation. Gray said this gave him "an eerie feeling," as though the President were speaking not to him but to another audience.

The White House has said that the practice of recording the President's conversations has been ended. In a way it is too bad, for conversations in which both parties, rather than only one, know they are being recorded might be models of carefully guarded talk, well worth preserving:

NIXON: Good evening, Pat.

GRAY: Good evening, Mr. President.

NIXON: What can I do for you?

GRAY: I hope this won't seem a trivial matter I've called you about.

NIXON: No need to worry. The affairs of state often weigh heavily on me—indeed, they do tonight—but I believe I must make myself available to all members of my administration for advice and counsel, if the people's interests are to be served.

GRAY: That is very good of you, Mr. President.

NIXON: Not at all. It is only what the taxpayers deserve. Now then, Pat, what is it?

GRAY: Well, Mr. President, I happened to be working late tonight—I often do—and as luck would have it a file that for months had seemed an inpenetrable mystery, and had defied my best efforts and most intense study, has at last, I have reason to believe, yielded its secret.

NIXON: I congratulate you, Pat. But are you sure that it is information that I, even as president, should have? Is it perhaps personal in nature and therefore best kept secret, even if the interests of the nation might, at a glance and superficially considered, indicate otherwise?

GRAY: Mr. President, I put forward my own view with some hesitation, but that view is that public service often demands sacrifice, and it may compel us to engage in activities we would ordinarily find distasteful, even repellent, and which we would prefer to keep clear of. This, I believe, is such a case.

NIXON: Go on then, Pat, and you may be reassured to know that I had the FBI run a check on me after my visit to Peking. I was worried about my motives and whether I had bargained hard enough, and I thought I should be checked out. Unfortunately, with those doubts in my mind, I did not feel free to look at all the information on me that the FBI had gathered, but, on the whole, I was satisfied with my own patriotism and reliability, so I think you can go ahead.

GRAY: Mr. President, I have to inform you that a dispute has broken out in certain circles of your administration over the interpretation of your inspiring admonition, "When the going gets tough, the tough get going."

NIXON: Surely the meaning of that is beyond dispute for any real American, though I would not for one moment question the motives of anyone who did not accept that meaning, whatever the cost to the country or the additional burdens placed on me as I make the difficult decisions that peace for our children and our children's children requires.

GRAY: I quite agree, Mr. President. I had thought it not only beyond dispute but beyond cavil, as well.* Nonetheless, they have been overheard—strike that—they have been heard to say that the meaning to be drawn from the phrase depends on the interpretation of the second going. Not—if I may be allowed a small joke, Mr. President—not to be confused with the Second Coming.

NIXON: Very good, Pat.

GRAY: Thank you, sir. They say that the second going can be interpreted as meaning going in a literal sense, i.e., leaving the field of battle.

NIXON: Never! Though I respect their right to an interpretation that can only help those who do not wish America well.

GRAY: Do you want a written report on this, Mr. President?

NIXON: No. I would regard that as an unjustifiable invasion of privacy. I think this calls for a directive, but naming no names. Perhaps I can write it this weekend. No rest for the weary, eh, Pat?

GRAY: Exactly, Mr. President. Thank you, Mr. President.

Still, there is no need to invent language for those in Washington. The real thing serves very well:

"I am considering offering my capacity for state-wide leadership." Representative Hugh Carey of New York, on being asked whether he would run for the Democratic nomination for governor in 1974.

"No serious thoughts [of the nomination] will be permitted in my mind while I am undertaking the most painful duty of my political career." Senator Howard Baker of Tennessee, on being asked whether he would try for the Republican presidential nomination in 1976.

"I believe the present situation clearly indicates that in the second quarter we're going to be in a posture where gas ration-

---

* Beyond good and cavil.—Author's note.

ing may well be a reality." Senator Henry Jackson, Democrat of Washington, speaking about the gasoline situation after three days of hearings in January, 1974.

"At once original, bold, comprehensive, measured and timely." James Lynn, Secretary of Housing and Urban Development, commenting on President Nixon's housing message of 1973.

The above is a fair sampling of Washington language, spoken by those who seek to show themselves worthy of larger responsibilities, who solemnly demonstrate that they put the nation's interest before their own, and who sternly, uncompromisingly, and ambiguously face facts.

Lynn's dutiful hyperbole sounded as though it came from his department's public relations machine. Very likely it did. Much of the language in Washington is produced by speech writers, and while some of them are clever, speech writers are bad for language.

There undoubtedly are politicians who, nine months old and about to move from breast to bottle, thanked their mothers for making the determination that they should be weaned and for nourishment that had been comprehensive, measured, and timely. They can make stilted speeches without help. I have been told, too, that an actor may come to feel that the words the playwright gave him are his own. Politicians probably do the same with the words cranked out for them, and once they speak the words, the responsibility is theirs. But when speech writers are used, what is personal to the speaker is minimized, whereas when a politician uses his own words, they tell us something about the speaker. William Simon, when he was head of the Federal Energy Office, replied, "That would be judgmental," when asked when gasoline rationing might begin if it were ordered. In an earlier era the equivalent answer would have been, "That's an iffy question." Iffy is coy but people who used it merely thought they were clever. People who say judgmental think they are important.

In any case, we in the news business are being unfair to

writers, and inaccurate as well. For years we should have been reporting, "President Kennedy, in a speech largely written by Theodore Sorenson and Arthur Schlesinger, Jr., said today . . ." and "President Nixon, using words and ideas principally supplied by Patrick Buchanan, said today . . ." On January 16, 1974, we should have reported, "Vice-President Ford today attacked George Meany, president of the AFL-CIO, Americans for Democratic Action, and other 'pressure organizations' calling for the impeachment of President Nixon. The original draft of Ford's speech was prepared by writers in the White House."

Ford explained later that he had had to use White House speech writers because his own staff was still in process of formation and he could not call on writers of his own. He also said that the original draft had been prepared from ideas he supplied. That may have been Ford's pride speaking, but suppose Ford had not supplied the ideas? Suppose the White House led him to make the first bellicose speech of his vice-presidency, thereby antagonizing some of those who wanted him to replace President Nixon as soon as possible, and so strengthening Mr. Nixon's grip on the White House? Ford made the speech. The responsibility for it would still have been his.

I do not, however, withdraw my statement that we in the news business are being unfair and inaccurate when we do not say who the writers of a particular speech are. Writers are identified at the end of television programs. Maybe they should be identified at the end of political speeches. The term used for the list of names given at the end of television programs is credits. That takes a lot for granted, but the practice is sound.

If the speech writer is an enemy of language because he conceals, or in some cases distorts, the politician's personality and talent, so is the public opinion poll, for it also depersonalizes, and anything that depersonalizes is an enemy of language. The poll has a deadening effect on politics, and its effect on language is an extension of that. It encourages predictability, and it encourages the tailoring of positions, and so of language, to whatever the poll indicates is desirable.

I am reminded of something that happened in January, 1972, when, God help us, ten months before the election, campaigning in the New Hampshire primary was about to begin. There were many new voters in New Hampshire that year—either young people newly enfranchised or people who had moved in from other states—and so somebody associated with Senator Edmund Muskie was quoted as saying, "The big problem is that we know virtually nothing about these voters," while associates of Senator George McGovern were devising a questionnaire to find out who the new voters were and what was on their minds.

This was an interesting case of getting things backward. True, the new voters had not been questioned in depth, height, and width about their political positions, and some had even crossed state lines in that depraved condition. But politicians don't have to know who the voters are. Voters have to know who the politicians are. Any politician will want to know what people are concerned about. That is part of the job, and, beyond that, nobody running for office does it for the exercise. It is too expensive and demanding for that.

But the minute examination of the electorate has become depressingly familiar—the polling and the cross-polling, the calculation of how to make the appeal that is most productive in votes. Polling has become a malign influence on our politics. It may distort the political process by contributing to a band-wagon effect, by creating impressions that handicap candidates, and even by destroying candidates before they begin campaigning in earnest. A defeat may be softened because the loser got more votes than the polls indicated he would. A victory in a primary may be made equivocal, or turned into a defeat, because the victor did not get as large a margin as the polls said he would.

Muskie was an example. He became known as a man who had a big lead and lost it. On primary night in New Hampshire you could hear it said over and over again that Muskie went into New Hampshire two months before with a commanding 65 percent of the vote. His primary percentage—48 percent—was compared with that, to his disadvantage. For Muskie, it was the beginning of the end. Ask not for whom the public opinion polls; it polls for thee.

But did Muskie go into New Hampshire with a commanding 65 percent of the vote? There was a poll that said so, but even if it was accurate, it was irrelevant. Elections are held when they are held, not before, and not after.

The poll has the same appeal that other social science jargon has, but there is no evidence that opinion polling in advance of an election in any way improves the governing process. When the polls miss, the usual explanation is that they neglected to poll right up to the last minute, which happens to be election time anyway, or that they always said they operated within a 3 percent margin of error, which happens to be enough to decide many elections. Another justification is that they are meant to be a "useful tool" and no more. What is their usefulness? Even when the polls turn out to be accurate forecasts of what is to come, what is to come still has to come. We might as well wait for it.

If politicians want to use polls, nothing can stop them. Indeed, if news organizations want to use polls, nothing can stop them either, and nothing has. They get deeper into polling with each election. But it is a bad business, because it puts the emphasis in an election in the wrong place, on who is thought to be ahead, rather than on what the candidates propose and what their election might mean.

I never mention polls except to deprecate them. On election night anyone with that attitude could easily feel like Edmond Dantès in the Château d'If. However, with me, it appears to be considered only an eccentricity that comes with age, and in any event nobody is distracted from coverage of that momentous question: Were the polls right?

Politicians should be encouraged to stand for what they believe in, not to try to smell out the exact mosaic of attitudes and positions that will appeal to the greatest number. Politicians should also be responsive to the popular will. But if the popular will does not coincide with his own, each politician has to work that out with his own conscience, and the voters must decide how far they want their representatives to mirror them and their feelings. Government by poll, which is to say by statistical sample, is uninspiring and distressing.

Finally—and here is where the effect of polls on language is so profound—because they help to set a style of expression, public opinion polls have become one of the great institutional bores of our time. Ask not on whom the public opinion palls; it palls on me. In 1968 a Lou Harris poll on Hubert Humphrey showed that a majority of those questioned thought Humphrey was long-winded. What a revelation!

At a recent British by-election, a victorious candidate, a Scottish Nationalist, was interviewed by the BBC. The interviewer, bemused by polls, projections, swings, and other esoterica, asked: Would you say that the result was a success for you?

CANDIDATE: I won the seat, if that is what you mean by success.

I said earlier that anything that depersonalizes is an enemy of language and that the poll does depersonalize. It reached its logical conclusion—I *hope* it is the conclusion—in a study of voters' reactions to televised political advertising in the Nixon-McGovern campaign for the Citizens Research Foundation of Princeton, New Jersey. The authors, Thomas E. Patterson and Robert D. McClure, explained that their research was "rooted in a specific psychological theory of attitude organization and change—the attitude-belief model developed by Martin Fishbein. In operationalizing the Fishbein model," they went on, "measures of the following variables were obtained during each personal interview wave: issue and candidate image attitudes, beliefs about candidates' issue positions and image characteristics, salience of issues and images, and beliefs about the salience of issues and images to the candidates."

After operationalizing the Fishbein model, Patterson and McClure concluded: "We have a rather precise standard for judging the effectiveness of persuasive political messages. If a campaign communication has a positive effect, more voters will change their attitude-belief relationship in a favorable direction between one time and a later time [i.e., $p(a_ib_iC(t) < a_ib_iC(t+1))$] than will change their attitude-belief relationship in an unfavorable direction [$p(a_ib_iC(t) > a_ib_iC(t+1))$]."

The finding that an effective message wins over more voters [$p(a_ib_iC(t) < a_ib_iC(t+1))$] than it loses [$p(a_ib_iC(t) > a_ib_iC(t+1))$] must have stirred politicians all over the country. The use of the term interview wave unquestionably did the same for social scientists.

In addition to the damage the poll does to language, it discourages spontaneity and aggrandizes the predictable, whereas life is more fun when not everything can be foreseen. In the 1930s there was a Greta Garbo movie called *Queen Christina*. In it she played a seventeenth-century Queen of Sweden who liked to go out among the people, disguised as a young man, to see how the common folk were faring. One day she rode too far and had to stay overnight at an inn.

Along came the new Russian ambassador, played by John Gilbert, en route to the royal court at Stockholm, where he was to take up his post. He could not make Stockholm by nightfall, so he also stopped at the inn. Because the inn was crowded, the landlord told him that he would have to put him in a room that had only a double bed, which he would have to share with a young man. Did he mind?

The ambassador said he did not mind, and went up to the room occupied by Greta Garbo.

"Sorry about this," said the ambassador, "but this is the only thing they had available."

"That's all right," said Greta Garbo in her deepest and manliest voice.

"I'm tired," said the ambassador. "Think I'll turn in."

"Yeah, me too," said Greta Garbo, and took off her jacket, whereupon the ambassador, who happened to be looking in her direction, said, "Life is so gloriously unpredictable."

In those days, there were no polls.

There were no elections either, of course. I do not presume

to say whether that was good or bad, but it did have this to be said for it: there was at least no ethnic approach to the electorate.

Here is a candidate for mayor of New York kicking off his campaign. His name is John Marchi and he is a Republican member of the State Senate. A television reporter approaches, places himself in front of his station's camera, and notes that it is raining as Marchi's campaign begins. "Does that have any meaning for you, Senator?" he asks.

Marchi does restrain himself. He does not say, "Itsa rain. Thatsa good." All the same, a large, dutiful smile spreads across his face. "My people believe it means good luck," he replies.

That's a good reason to vote for a man.

The ethnic approach is not confined to politics. Excerpt from a letter sent out by the American Jewish Committee:

"Dear Friend:

"The energy crisis obviously confronts all of us as American citizens, and raises particular intergroup and interreligious questions of concern to the Jewish and Christian communities."

Probably what they wanted to head off was Jews getting gasoline on even-numbered days and Christians getting gasoline on odd-numbered days. It could have led to bad feelings, or, to use the technical term, divisiveness.

The tribal attitude did not come about because of the sheer perversity of immigrants and their offspring. There were many causes. Banding together within immigrant groups for protection, mutual help, and understanding has always been a factor in American life, and after the Second World War new forces pushed in the same direction. The countries of Western Europe recovered economically and politically, and Americans went to live in them, and there came to be no opprobrium involved in being associated with them. Many foreign products proved to be superior to their American counterparts and better adapted to American life, and with that foreign products took on a certain glamor (though it helped to sell them if they were called imported rather than foreign).

These developments coincided with the decline of the American city, which took some of the shine off the American dream, and with the war in Vietnam, which weakened the central loyalty of Americans to their country and led some of them to search for loyalties that were more immediate and closer to home. The ethnic connection lay to hand. Finally, there was the black revolt, an outburst that convinced other groups that they and their grievances were being overlooked and led them to use the same tactics.

So it happened that Eugene McCarthy, in his book *The Year of the People,* recalled hearing in the spring of 1968 that Robert Kennedy's organization had set up twenty-six committees to deal with twenty-six different kinds of Americans. McCarthy remarked at the time that he had heard of twenty-six different flavors of ice cream, but he had not known there were that many kinds of Americans.

So it happened also that President Nixon said that he was pleased to have Vice-President Agnew, with his Greek background, in his administration. This statement was made early in Mr. Nixon's first term. Later, Mr. Nixon was pleased to have Agnew, with his Greek background, out of his administration. But the point remains that it was a doubtful kind of appeal to make. True, Mr. Nixon was speaking to the Ethnic Groups Division of the Republican National Committee, which tries to offset Democratic pioneering in this area, but suppose Agnew were of Russian, or Scandinavian, or Polynesian background? What difference would it make? Mr. Nixon's own ancestry is Scottish and Irish. Should we be writing stories that begin, "President Nixon, who is of Scottish and Irish ancestry, today signed a bill authorizing the modernization of seven bankrupt railroads in the Northeast and Middle West"?

Agnew himself spoke to the Ethnic Groups Division of the Republican National Committee after Mr. Nixon did, and said that his background actually was Greek and English, thereby setting off a thrill of pleasure felt as far away as London, Manchester, and Leighton Buzzard, Bedfordshire. Agnew remarked also that his wife was of German, Irish, English, and French extraction, thereby making her an ideal politician's wife.

After Agnew was forced to resign, an NBC elevator operator said to me, "Well, I guess we Greeks won't be getting any more big jobs for a while." At about the same time another NBC employe explained that she had a vivid imagination because she was a Hungarian.

I suppose one should know these things about oneself, or cannot help knowing them, but what is the point? I find all this so depressing that I think we should change the election date in New York City so that the campaign never again coincides with religious holidays. In November, 1969, the contest for mayor became a contest over which candidate could wear his skull cap into more synagogues than the others. Prime Minister Golda Meir of Israel visited New York during the campaign, and Mayor John Lindsay, running for reelection and afraid he had lost the "Jewish vote" because of what some considered his excessive solicitousness about blacks, barely stopped short of proposing marriage to her.

A catalogue of ethnic stalking of public office in New York City alone would run into volumes, extending far beyond the well-known indigestion tour of pizza, Chinese egg rolls, and the like. In 1961 a candidate for president of the City Council sent out campaign literature printed in green ink, with a map of Ireland as the background and the counties of Kerry and Cork marked in. That's a good reason to vote for a man.

I know there are large numbers of people who do not agree with me about this. The idea of group rights, as distinct from individual rights, is spreading. As might have been predicted, it has been legitimized and given an imposing name—pluralism, the pluralistic society. There is much in it that is logical and understandable. If you are a member of a group that has been rejected, or at any rate not favored, it is natural to respond by insisting that the group is good, and then you take pride in it, and then you make a virtue of necessity and argue that clannishness is a good thing in itself.

It is understandable, and it is not for me to tell people who have suffered because of their name or skin color how they should react. Those groups are entitled to use place of origin and skin color in their own interest, as such personal characteristics have been used against their interest, but I cannot see that it makes any sense to encourage the ethnic outlook. It bases policies and attitudes on considerations that should be irrelevant.

Pluralism is, of course, the kind of word social scientists love, though it is giving way with surprising speed to a new entry, multi-ethnic, and the hyphenated American approach to politics is growing stronger as a result of its acceptance not only among politicians but among social scientists, who appear to welcome the fact that we are not becoming the single, integrated, melting-pot society that was envisaged for so long, and to revel in it because it gives them such good material. It also fattens the social scientific vocabulary. The pluralistic ideal becomes creative ethnicity, defined as ethnic groups learning about themselves and one another in order to interact constructively.

I am made uncomfortable when I hear the breakdown of voting results according to religion and race and national origin. Not because it is not a generally efficacious way to figure out how an election is going—its efficacy has been demonstrated—but because it helps to perpetuate divisions that we might be better off without, because it leads people to go on thinking of themselves in a particular way, as members of a particular group, which may have little connection with the issues the election is about.

I have another reason that seems to have been generally overlooked, which is that this exhaustive research, this pinpointing classification, tends to destroy the privacy and secrecy of the voting booth. You do not know how an individual votes, but you do know how an individual is likely to vote, because you do know how the group of which he is, electronic data procedurally speaking, a member is likely to vote. Still more, he knows how he is expected to vote. The consequence of that, it seems to me, is the promotion of excessive calculation among politicians. I think we are better off when we calculate less.

We in the news business contribute to this by the way we

break down and analyze the votes. We talk about the black vote and the Jewish vote and the Italian vote, and where they've gone and who got them. We discover a trend among unfrocked Catholic priests in northern Rhode Island, and there is no holding us. It takes some work to do this, and it costs a lot of money, and I have been thinking that it might be done more simply and at less cost. When people register to vote, they could indicate whether they intend to cast a Serbo-Croat vote, or a Coptic Christian vote, or whatever it may be. That would be entered on their registration card, and when they entered the polling place on election day they could be directed to an appropriate machine—a machine for Seventh-Day Adventist votes only, for example—and we could have our analysis ready much sooner.

This may sound like know-nothingism, and standing in the way of the social sciences, and opposing the advance of knowledge, but I don't think it is. Multi-ethnicity is much more attractive to those who are not mono-ethnic themselves, and pluralism is more comfortable for those who are on the inside than it is for those who are out. As for opposing the advance of knowledge, anybody who has ever done graduate work knows that a vast amount of pointless information is collected by academics. I do not say that they should not collect this information if they want to. I do say that it is part of an unfortunate and damaging preoccupation, and calling the society multi-ethnic does not change that.

That same preoccupation may be seen in that bit of charmless Americana, "the Polish joke," and now that a few million dollars a year have become available under the federal Ethnic Heritage Studies Act, I suppose we may look forward to doctoral theses on the subject: "The Polish Joke: Multiple Manifestations of Interpersonal and Intergroup Stress in a Pluralistic Society, 1962–63."

I went on the "Today" show one morning to say that I was tired of ethnic jokes and would like to hear no more of them. I mentioned Polish jokes, among others. Letters came in praising me for "sticking up for the Poles," and I was asked to go on again to tell about the record of Polish Americans in Pennsylvania in volunteering for military service in the Second World War. Since I had said that all that Polish jokes amounted to was that Poles were stupid, I was also accused of saying that Poles were stupid. So much for the influence of the electronic medium in shaping the nation's dialogue.

I am not suggesting that American humor be denatured, that the vigor and bite be taken out of it. I know that much of the humor in this country, for as long as anyone now alive can remember, has been ethnic. That was logical and unavoidable: the unintentional misuse of English by immigrants who understood it imperfectly often had amusing results. The difficulty that many of the newcomers had in adapting to the customs of the United States also gave rise to amusing situations, though these often had overtones of sadness as well.

The result was a robust kind of humor, sometimes endearing, sometimes cruel, but one that many people could recognize as having some application to themselves. Even today, some ethnic content in American humor is still inevitable. But the Polish and Italian and Hungarian jokes we have been hearing for so long are manufactured and mechanical and boring to a lot of us. They have been persisted in for so long that they have taken on a meanness of spirit. They appear to be substitutes for the jokes about "niggers" that are, happily, no longer heard in public. One is driven to suspect that many of those who so airily toss off the Polish jokes and the rest really believe them. It is not a laughing matter.

I think, as I said, that we are better off when we calculate less, but politicians (and who can blame them? See how British Prime Minister Edward Heath became just British Edward Heath when he impetuously called a general election at the end of February, 1974, sixteen months before he had to?) do not appreciate the glorious uncertainties of life. By and large they prefer the controlled and dependable. Spontaneity is all right, provided they can rehearse it first.

I am reminded of an incident involving a United States senator. It would be unfair to say who he is, because his notes were for himself and I saw them only because we were seated

next to each other in such a way that it was impossible for me
not to see them. He was on "Meet the Press" at a time when he
had some hope of being nominated for president. Accordingly,
he found it necessary to give himself some advice and to keep
that advice before him. He therefore listed these reminders:

"1. Candid. Straightforward.
"2. Thoughtful.
"3. Modest.
"4. Some very short answers."

Finally, if he should be asked about the political significance
of the defeat of Governor Ronald Reagan's proposal to limit
personal income taxes in California, the answer he suggested
to himself, in case it should otherwise slip his mind, was

"5. I don't know."

There is something dispiriting in the knowledge that politicians have to remind themselves to be candid. Also, I suppose
the adjuration regarding thoughtfulness was less to be thoughtful
than to appear it. But for modesty, the admission of ignorance,
and, still more, very short answers, we can only be grateful.

I would not, of course, claim that a politician's language will
always be more engaging if it is his own and spontaneous.

The following glittering performance opened the "Meet the
Press" program of Sunday, August 16, 1964. I was the moderator, and Lawrence Spivak was questioning Robert Wagner,
then mayor of New York:

MR. SPIVAK: Mayor Wagner, Attorney General Kennedy
said the other day, and I quote, "Under no circumstances
would I ever have considered or would I now consider coming
into the State of New York against the wishes of the Mayor."

If he seeks the Senate seat from New York, will it be
against your wishes?

MAYOR WAGNER: I saw the Attorney General a week ago
Friday and discussed generally the matter with him, and at
that time he said that he would want to think it over a bit more

to decide whether he would like to come in and seek the Democratic nomination for Senator, and we both agreed that, given that opportunity to think it over—and I would also have the opportunity to canvass a bit and discuss the matter with various people and those who have various political leanings within the Democratic Party—I will see the Attorney General in the next day or so and find what he has in mind also at that time explore the possibilities with him. I may say that there has been a certain amount of criticism of his candidacy. There has also been a good support among various factions. I emphasized, too, with him, that I felt to come in under the original support that he had, which he said was no part of his understanding in the matter, of some of the so-called political bosses was not the best way to come in.

MR. SPIVAK: Mr. Mayor, that is all very interesting, but the question was, if he seeks the Senate seat from New York, will it be against your wishes?

MAYOR WAGNER: I think I could better answer that, Mr. Spivak, after I have had an opportunity to talk to him and we, number one, find out whether he is interested, and then talk about some matters to make sure that, if he would be in, it would not in any way prevent what we have tried to do, and that is, make the Democratic Party a little more representative of the rank and file.

MR. SPIVAK: Are you saying that as of now you are neither for nor against him?

MAYOR WAGNER: True.

MR. SPIVAK: Certainly you have given a great deal of thought to the subject.

MAYOR WAGNER: That is true. I would be able to answer that question as to whether I would approve of his coming in after I have had a further talk with him.

MR. SPIVAK: Is there much question in your mind—there isn't in the minds of many other political observers—but that he would like to come into New York, would like to run for the Senate?

MAYOR WAGNER: I must say that since I have last talked to him, he has been away. There have been a lot of people apparently talking about this matter. I don't know whether they truly represent his thinking. I find oftentimes—I read about "sources close to City Hall," "spokesmen for the Mayor say this," when I have never said any such thing, and I would rather hear it from the individual concerned, directly.

MR. SPIVAK: We would like very much to hear it directly from you, too, Mr. Mayor.

MAYOR WAGNER: I am sure we will give it directly to you after I have had the opportunity to see him in the next day or so.

MR. SPIVAK: Almost everyone else has given us your reasons for refusing to endorse him, because that is exactly what you have done to date: you have refused to endorse him. Will you give us your reasons now, your own reason directly for refusing to endorse him, because evidently you have many restrictions in your mind about endorsing him, or you would have come right out for him?

MAYOR WAGNER: First of all, I think we should know whether he is a candidate or not. I think that is important, because if he is not a candidate then the party must seek another person as a candidate or find out whether he is in the field with those candidates who have already announced or are available.

Secondly, I want to clear up this point, that I have never opposed Mr. Kennedy's coming into this race because of any fear that he would then share in the power or take over the Democratic Party in the State of New York. I have never felt that way. I would like to have more people interested in running for high office here, more people who have ability to be available for important positions in the party, and I have never felt that I would be opposed to anyone running for the Senate because they might in any way interfere with my political position because—

MR. SPIVAK: You have admitted very little in answer to my

questions, but will you admit this, that if he does come in, there is a chance that you may oppose him?

MAYOR WAGNER: I would say that if he comes in, I think he would come in under circumstances that would be best for him and also good for the party.

Even this verbatim account does not give the true flavor of the exchange, because Wagner dropped innumerable "ahs" into his replies and slowed them still more, and these were thoughtfully excised by the monitoring service. When Spivak sank back, exhausted, and we went into a commercial break, Wagner, exhilarated, turned to me.

"I love this fencing," he said.

Wagner is a Democrat. We have a two-party system, however. Not to be outdone:

December 11, 1973. The Red Room of the State Capitol, Albany, New York. Governor Nelson Rockefeller:

"I will resign next Tuesday after fifteen years of service to the people of the state.

". . . after long and careful consideration, I have concluded that I can render a greater public service to the people of New York and the nation by devoting myself to the work of two by-partisan national commissions . . .

"Because I feel this so deeply, I'm resigning as governor in order to be able to devote my energies to the success of these commissions. My only regret is that my undertaking these tasks has been interpreted as a political maneuver to seek the Presidency . . .

" . . . above all, my deep gratitude to the people of New York State as a whole. By electing me four times as your governor you granted me a unique opportunity of public service. I thank you for this privilege."

According to the Citizens Research Foundation, Rockefeller and his family put up more money than any American had ever spent before to obtain public office. The Foundation calculated that Rockefeller's campaign spending from 1952 to 1970, while he ran for governor four times and for the Republican presidential nomination three times, exceeded $27,000,000. In Rockefeller's 1970 campaign alone, the Citizens Research Foundation said, $4,500,000 came from his family. His stepmother gave $2,803,500; his brothers and sister gave $1,448,533 altogether. More than $7,700,000 was spent in 1970, almost as much as by the state's other candidates for governor and its candidates for United States senator combined. This kind of thing tends to make the people's grant of unique opportunities for public service more likely.

Still, Rockefeller nearly convinced me that he was giving up his presidential ambitions. He did that with the reference at the beginning of his remarks to "long and careful consideration." Men interested in being president usually give "long and prayerful consideration."

Further, it appeared that Rockefeller would fail to speak of the people's hopes and aspirations, not what one would expect from a man with an eye on 1976. He caught himself in time, however. "No one is more aware of the people in all areas of this state, their hopes and aspirations, as well as their concerns," he said. True, he was speaking of his successor, Malcolm Wilson, but the requisite words were there.

Wilson, lieutenant governor for fifteen years, was ready:

"Your historic announcement today will soon place the executive leadership of the state on my shoulders. And with God's help, my total commitment will be to give the best within me to the responsibilities of that high office.

"Fortunately your decision is not to withdraw from public service but rather, as a private citizen, to devote your vast experience, your deep knowledge, your great courage, your total integrity, and your compassionate concern for all people to the critical issues which challenge all America.

"I know, Nelson, that I reflect the sentiments of all New Yorkers when I say that we receive your decision with profound emotion, with regret certainly, for your having given us fifteen years of achievement unparalleled by any governor in this nation's history."

The language of Rockefeller and Wilson on that cold December morning in Albany was wasted on an off year in a state capital. It belonged at a party nominating convention. That is where fulsome political language goes unbridled and unabashed. It can be frightful to listen to, for politicians still exist who will look out upon an audience and say that they would rather live in a modest cottage, surrounded by books, family, and friends, than occupy the most splendid post ever conceived by the mind of man, after which they would rather lie in the corner of a tiny country churchyard than in the tombs of the Capulets. In the meantime, they may sacrifice every other personal consideration in the quest for office, and lie, cheat, and steal in the pursuit of power, but the language is marvelous, and it is in place.

It was in the middle of August, 1972, only a week before it was to begin, that it came home to me that the Republicans were going to hold a convention. The confirmation came when a man addressing the Republican National Committee spoke of "these United States." You can go for four years without hearing that, and with the country known as it usually is—the United States. Come the conventions and "these United States" pops out once more.

It is a heavily laden political phrase. It makes its bow to state feelings, and conventions are organized by states and presidential elections decided by the electoral votes of states. It has a special appeal to states' rights people and has, over the years, charmed the South.

The oratorical flourish does not stop there. Individual states are often referred to as sovereign, which they are not, since they do not have armed forces and do not conduct foreign policy, two irreducible attributes of sovereignty. But it is a ringing word, sovereign, and it is stored away with "these United States" until the conventions make it legitimate to use it once more.

Conventions have a language of their own. They also have an atmosphere, a manner, which is less easy to define than to describe, though heavy-handed humor is one of its unfailing characteristics. At the Republican convention in Chicago in 1960, Wendell Corey, the master of ceremonies, began with a request to clear the aisles, followed by this: "Please, let's not look like a bunch of Democrats in Los Angeles." The hall echoed with laughter and applause, and the aisles were cleared.

A bit later on came another joke, this one from the national committeewoman from Illinois, Mrs. C. Wayland Brooks, about how before the Democratic convention in Los Angeles, Chicago had been thought to be the world's windiest city, but now Los Angeies was.

This did not compare unfavorably with a joke told at the Democratic convention by Senator Sam Ervin of North Carolina, long before his Watergate days: "I have a grandson who is four years old. In December, my little grandson came to my house on Sunday to have dinner with his grandparents and one of the neighbors was there, and the neighbor said to my little grandson, 'Jimmy, did you go to Sunday School this morning?' He said, 'Yes, I went to Presbyterian Sunday School.' The neighbor said, 'Jimmy, are you a Presbyterian?' Jimmy said, 'No, I am a Democrat.' "

Convention language as such begins to be heard before the daily session officially opens, when the delegates who arrive early are entertained. Thus, at the Republican convention in San Francisco in 1964, the actor Victor Jory: "We are proud to present a worthy representative of our own very wonderful Republican women, a very special combination, I might add, an active party official who also has a beautiful singing voice, Mrs. Trefinna R. Wilson, who is the Republican committeewoman of the Fifth District of the Second Ward of the city of Wilmington, Delaware, a wonderful contralto."

I don't remember how well Mrs. Wilson sang, but Jory's performance was wonderful, which is to say routine.

In any convention, the adjective heard most often is great. If entertainers are provided, they may be described as wonderful, even if nobody listens to them, which is usually what happens.* Everything else is great. If a wonderful entertainer is to sing

---

* See case of Mrs. Trefinna R. Wilson, *supra.*

"O Sole Mio," it is a great song, and the wonderful entertainer gives a great performance. If a display of great friendship kindles a glow in somebody's heart, it is a great glow. The convention is a great gathering.

Even the clergymen who pray at the beginning and end of each session are great. On the second day of the Democratic convention of 1968, Senator Daniel Inouye of Hawaii introduced Billy Graham:

"It is my privilege and honor* to call upon a great American, a great theologian, a great religious leader, to invoke the divine blessings."

No politician will put in an appearance without being heralded as great, and those of middle age and older have a better than even chance of being called statesmen as well. And anybody who presents anybody else to the convention will be overwhelmed by his great good fortune in doing so. The ideal introduction was delivered in 1960 by the Democratic national chairman, Paul Butler, for the keynote speaker, Senator Frank Church of Idaho. Butler had a great pleasure and privilege, plus great pleasure and personal pride, in presenting a great American who was a great, able, and outstanding member of a great deliberative body.

In 1968, at Miami Beach, after the mayor, Jay Dermer, had somewhat puzzlingly announced that he was there to "extend our heart and our heartbeat" to the delegates, the Republicans had a bout of baton passing. Senator George Murphy of California introduced from "the great state of Tennessee" Senator Howard Baker, who introduced "one of America's greatest public servants," Senator Edward Brooke of Massachusetts, who presented from the "the great state of Wyoming" Senator Clifford Hansen, who introduced to "the great convention of 1968" from "the great state of Oregon" Senator Mark Hatfield, for whom it was "a great pleasure" to introduce "a great person," Senator Charles Percy of Illinois, who introduced from "the great middle-western

---

* Privilege and honor go together at conventions.

state of Michigan" Senator Robert Griffin, who being last had nobody to introduce and remained silent.

At the Republican convention in Chicago in 1960 it fell to Mayor Daley, who though a Democrat was the host mayor, to make it clear at the outset that great would not be slighted and tradition would be upheld. Daley therefore referred to the great city, that being Chicago; the great year, that being 1960, the only year available to him at the time; the great convention city, again Chicago; our great country; the great convention, that being the one that nominated Abraham Lincoln a hundred years earlier; a great country, the United States; these great centers, the local urban communities; the great central cities of our nation, which include Chicago; our great beach, the beach of Lake Michigan; and a great people, this being the American people.

This great speech by Chicago's great mayor lasted two minutes and drew great applause.

In 1968 Daley was addressing his own party, but it made no noticeable difference. He spoke of the Democrats' great chairman, John Bailey of Connecticut; Illinois's great governor, Samuel Shapiro; and the great political gathering that was taking place in one of the greatest neighborhoods of Chicago—his.

He pointed out that Americans had created more great cities than any nation in history, that 1968 was a great time of change, that the United States was a great country, that Chicago was a great city, that Chicago was one of the greatest cities in the world, that it was a great convention, and that the United States was a great country.

Shapiro followed. He told the delegates that Chicago was a great city. He mentioned Illinois's tradition of having great governors, described the Democrats as the greatest force for unity in America and the greatest force for progress, order, and justice, called the United States the greatest nation in the history of the world, and ventured the prediction that men the convention nominated would be great Democrats.

Soon after Mayor Daley's 1960 speech, Senator Karl Mundt of South Dakota presented a gavel to the convention chairman, Senator Thruston Morton of Kentucky. Mundt inexplicably missed the opportunity to call it a great gavel, but he recovered and pointed out that it had been made by a professor at South Dakota's great agricultural college. Mundt then demonstrated how dangerous it is for convention speakers to leave the well-trodden ways. He told Morton that the gavel was massive in size, although massive does not describe size but solidity of composition, and that it was made of endurable maple, although maple furniture, while popular, is not everyone's favorite, and it was surely for Senator Morton to say whether he wished to endure it.

Gavels have a special place at conventions. They exemplify the core of cliché and sentiment. I have seen one presented to a convention chairman that was made from the tongue of a covered wagon, and another made from a purple beech tree planted at Monticello by Thomas Jefferson. The Virginia delegate who handed over the purple beech gavel said he hoped it would sound as a claxon. The trick with gavels is to make them from great and important pieces of wood, and unless Mount Vernon becomes available for the purpose, Monticello will clearly hold pride of place. At Chicago in 1968, Liv Bjorlie, national committeewoman for North Dakota, gave John Bailey a gavel made from timber removed from the Monticello mansion during its renovation in 1954. "This gavel," Mrs. Bjorlie said, "represents the foundation of our democracy." Bailey banged it on the table and pronounced it good.

At the Republican convention in 1968, local boosterism crept in. Three orangewood gavels were presented, to the temporary chairman, the permanent chairman, and the chairman of the Republican National Committee. In their acknowledgments they spoke of the great state of Florida (twice), the great orange industry (twice), and the great convention (twice), also known as the great event (once).

To conclude our consideration of great: Much time and effort could be saved if great were understood to occur before each noun to which it might conceivably apply. At conventions, to call something great is to damn it with faint praise, rather like the routine description of each candidate for the nomination as the next president of the United States.

In 1968 Gerald Ford sensed this. Montana, he said, was "one of our very great, great Western states."

Skipping lightly over the formal speeches and debates on the party platforms (though this slights such statements as that by John Bailey in 1968 when, almost visibly pulling himself together, he asserted his long devotion to the party by saying, "In convention assembled, I cast my vote for Roosevelt, Truman, Stevenson, Kennedy, and Johnson"; and by Catherine Peden of Kentucky in the same hall, "If we are to continue as the party of hope, we must refuse to play patty-cake opportunism"; and by Elly Peterson of Michigan to the Republicans in 1964, when she said, "I hold no brief for power-hungry politicians who would nibble away at our freedom," without telling why politicians hungry for power should be eating freedom instead; and by Lieutenant Governor Jared Maddux of Tennessee, who told the Democrats in 1960, "I would just like to know if Mr. Chamberlain's venerable umbrella is being dusted off in anticipation of another Armageddon, where this nation, speaking too softly and too gently and too humbly, might crucify the hopes and aspirations of free men upon the cross of timidity"), let us push on to the nominating procedure. It is not thought proper merely to say that somebody has been nominated. He or she has to be placed in nomination. Thus for the Republicans in 1960 we had Governor Paul Fannin of the great state of Arizona rising on the platform for the purpose of placing in nomination the name of a great American as president of the United States of America. That is the full orchestration. Fannin placed in nomination rather than simply nominating, and he placed a name in nomination, which compounded the redundancy, something that is always admired at conventions.

Another approach to nominating is the alliterative. In 1960 Mark Hatfield, then governor of Oregon, nominated, or placed in nomination, Richard Nixon, describing him as one who had demonstrated courage in crisis from Caracas to the Kremlin. Hatfield produced five hard c sounds—courage in crisis from Caracas to the Kremlin—and plainly exhausted himself in the process, for the best he could do after that was to say that Nixon also had earned the affection and respect of millions from Ghana to Warsaw, which was not alliterative and did not rhyme either.

Hatfield remains, nonetheless, unchallenged. Seconding Hubert Humphrey's nomination in 1968, Governor Kenneth Curtis of Maine fell well short with character, courage, and compassion. He would have had to add his own name, Kenneth Curtis, to equal Hatfield's record.

Another approach is the immaterial. When the Democrats met in Los Angeles in 1960, one of the Missouri delegates introduced the great governor of the great state of Missouri, James G. Blair, Jr., who then proceeded to point out that there were five states between Missouri and the Atlantic Ocean, and five states between Missouri and the Pacific Ocean; two states between Missouri and Canada, and two states between Missouri and Mexico. That led him to conclude that Missouri was the heart of the Motherland of America, which made it logical that Governor Blair should nominate for president a man from the heart of America, who was Senator Stuart Symington of Missouri.

The more habitual approach to nominating and seconding is the declamatory:

"History will record the greatness of his administration. As it is inscribed upon the permanent page, so it is etched in the minds and hearts of a grateful people."

"But his warmth and compassion and sense of justice are implicit in the entire range of his record in public life."

"Mr. Chairman, I proudly rise tonight to confirm a commitment that was wrought in the crucible of another era."

"It is the worst of times that calls for the best in men."

"Destiny has again marked this man. A man to match our mountains and our plains. A man steeped in the glorious traditions of the past. A man with a vision of the unlimited possibilities of a new era."

This last was said at the Republican convention in 1968, which also produced a man for all seasons and two legends in their own time.

The clergymen who open and close the convention sessions get into the spirit and sound as though *they* are making nominating speeches:

"We are assembled in trying times that test the souls of men."

After the nominations come the demonstrations for the various candidates, which, to the regret of almost nobody except the musicians and others who were paid to take part in them, are not what they used to be. The only memorable thing that ever happened to me during a demonstration came in Los Angeles in 1960, when I ventured out during the demonstration for Kennedy. The first person I saw was the actress, which is stretching things a bit, Zsa Zsa Gabor. She had met the governor of a southwestern state, and she was telling him that she had a soft spot for that state because she had once been married there. That did not make the state exactly unique, but the governor seemed grateful.

It is the roll calls that bring forth the strongest expressions of measured ecstasy. It is permissible for the chairman of a delegation to say merely that his state casts so many votes for so-and-so, and occasionally that does happen. Some chairmen are content to say that their states proudly cast, or are proud to cast, so many votes for so and so. Beyond that point there is no holding back. States may cast their votes in the proud tradition of the independent man. They may couple their pride with another emotion, so that Michigan may be proud and honored, Minnesota may feel pride and satisfaction and New Jersey pride and enthusiasm, while the Virgin Islands may do its voting proudly and unanimously, this being made easier by its having only one delegate.

States like to point out their distinguishing qualities during the roll calls—Virginia, mother of presidents; Arizona, most promising state of the union; Florida, the original and unequaled sunshine state, which may draw boos from California, the other original and unequaled sunshine state; the beloved island state of Hawaii, where East meets West in the spirit of aloha; the beautiful-sky state of Colorado, not to be confused with Montana, the Big Sky country; North Dakota, the only state with an international peace garden, which is also North Dakota, the state that is cleaner and greener in the summer, and whiter and brighter in the winter; Vermont, the Green Mountain state; Washington, the only state in the union named after George Washington; the District of Columbia, where the White House is; Tennessee, the great Volunteer State and home of Andrew Jackson (for Democrats only); Wonderful Wyoming, which may also point with pride to its grant of legal equality to women ("The first state to recognize you lovely ladies"); Montana, "the first state to send a woman to Congress"; Delaware, "the first state to ratify the Constitution"; Nebraska, "the football capital of the world"; and Guam, "where America's day begins."

States may boast of their worth to the party that is holding the convention. I have heard Vermont say it had voted Republican for one hundred and four years; Illinois that a hundred years before, it was the state of Abraham Lincoln; North Dakota that it was traditionally Republican; Kansas that it was the most Republican state in the union; and Mississippi that it was the fastest growing Republican state in the country. On another roll call, Mississippi settled for being the home of two past Miss Americas, but that provoked a crushing reply from Utah, the home of Miss Universe. At the 1968 Democratic convention, Pennsylvania reached for immortality as the state where Senator Edmund Muskie's father worked in the coal mines.

Rivalry is everywhere and arises over what may seem to the rest of us not fighting issues. One competition went this way:

Nevada—native state of Richard Nixon's wife.
Ohio—native state of Richard Nixon's father.
Oregon—neighbor of native state of Richard Nixon.

Another rivalry pitted Puerto Rico, "a bulwark against communism in the troubled waters of the Caribbean Sea," against the

Virgin Islands, "your pearls in the Caribbean and America's tropical playground." Later, evidently out of sheer exuberance, the Virgin Islands threw in that it was "the southeasternmost real estate under the American flag" and the "home of the world-record blue marlin."

The 1972 Democratic convention in Miami Beach was organized under the McGovern-Fraser rules that brought women, blacks, Chicanos, Indians, the young, the old, and the poor as delegates in unprecedented numbers. A vice-chairperson presided much of the time and California had a co-chairperson; Spanish was spoken from the platform ("Yo exhorto a los delegados a derrotar este asalto a la justicia Americano"), and at one point it was announced, "The Chicano-Latino caucus is now being held in the Dolphin Room"; the delegates were asked to get with it; and under the heading of sexual orientation there was a debate on a gay rights plank, with one proponent claiming to represent "20,000,000 gay women and men who are looking for a political party that is responsive to their needs" and another beginning her speech: "I am Madeline Davis. I am an elected delegate from the Thirty-seventh Congressional District in Buffalo, New York. I am a woman. I am a lesbian."

In this atmosphere, rivalry took a different tack and, as the roll calls went along, was measured in disdain for nonunion lettuce:

"The Oregon delegation, which boycotted nonunion grapes in 1968, and which now supports the United Farm Workers' boycott of nonunion lettuce . . ."

"New York's delegation, which supports the boycott of nonunion lettuce . . ."

"New Jersey, another state which boycotts nonunion lettuce . . ."

"New York, the largest state that continues to boycott lettuce . . ."

"New Mexico, which has a lettuce boycott . . ."

"Idaho, where we, the Chicanos, also boycott nonunion lettuce . . ."

"Colorado, which fully supports the United Farm Workers' boycott of lettuce . . ."

"The District of Columbia, whose delegation here will eat no lettuce until the United Farm Workers tell us . . ."

"The Oregon delegation, which has demonstrated support for the lettuce boycott by not eating lettuce served on the United Airlines plane, at this convention, throughout our state, and at the hotel . . ."

"The Arizona delegation, which supports the United Farm Workers . . ."

"California casts 131 votes yes, 114 votes no, 26 not voting. Oh, and we don't eat lettuce."

It is not unheard of for states, as they proudly cast their votes, to drum up a little business en route. Arkansas may recommend its razorback hogs, Idaho its potatoes, Kansas its wheat, Alabama its Birmingham 500 automobile race, Florida the Daytona 500, New Hampshire its granite, Delaware its Delaware-Marvelous chickens. And the competition for tourism can be fierce among South Dakota, home of Mount Rushmore; beautiful, wonderful, friendly West Virginia; North Carolina, the summer land where the sun doth shine; Minnesota, the land of ten thousand lakes; Colorful Colorado; Vermont, the eastern vacation capital; New Hampshire, the scenic land of America; Rhode Island, America's first vacation land; Michigan, the water, winter wonderland, and the arsenal of democracy to boot; Wisconsin, America's dairy land and the vacation land of the Midwest; New Mexico, the land of enchantment; and the great pine tree state, America's vacation state, the home of the Maine lobster and the Maine potato, a state eventually revealed to be Maine. Missouri once entered the lists as "the state with everything."

Gratifying as the opportunity to say such things may be to those who say them, the overwhelming majority of delegates never address the convention. They will, if there is nothing better to do, pay a certain amount of attention to the speeches, enough so that on certain key words—This great party, We will win in

November, Franklin D. Roosevelt (for Democrats only)—they clap hands and cheer. Given clues of sufficient clarity, they also boo. When there is a pause, they may cheer mechanically, on the assumption that the speaker expects it and that is why he paused.

Many words go by without being noticed. Nuclear holocaust does not cause a ripple. In the Jeffersonian tradition—no reaction. We say to the Communists we accept your challenge to peaceful competition—silence. We cannot shirk this challenge and we will not shirk this challenge—not a stir. Sterile, unsound, and doomed to failure, a description of the opposing party's policies—silence. This is no ordinary convention; this will be no ordinary election; for these are no ordinary times—nothing. We are proud of our record, but we will not rest on it or be content with past performance—nothing again.

A recurrent theme at conventions is We can, we must, and we shall. When the Democrats met in 1972, Governor Reubin Askew of Florida made it, "I submit that we can, I submit that we must, and I submit that we shall." The official proceedings of the convention note that he was applauded for this, and I am in no position to dispute this, since I do not remember. However, it is a rare speech that stirs the delegates. Except when something big is going on, the convention floor is a combination social hall and lounge. The delegates meet their friends, read papers and magazines, write letters, have their pictures taken with well-known politicians, and carry on conversations. One of the most popular spots for conversations is just below the speakers' platform. At times you wonder why they don't set up a table tennis tournament.

Those who are interested in convention language are better advised to stay at home and trust to radio and television than to try to hear it at the convention itself, as the following poignant passage shows:

"Delegate from the state of Nevada—'Mr. Chairman, we had been prepared to place in nomination for Vice-President of these United States the name of Lieutenant Governor Rex Bell, Nevada's favorite son and Silver Statesman of the Silver State, but now that Richard Nixon has been officially chosen as our standard-bearer in 1960 we are abandoning this plan in deference to our favorite daughter and your favorite daughter, Pat Nixon, a native of America's last Free State. Therefore, Nevada passes.'

"The Secretary of the Convention—'I wish more people could have heard that. If the people would please be quiet, you could hear some of these beautiful words being spoken.' "

4

Not to Worry, Gold Stick, Old Chap

During breakfast one morning in a hotel in the English south coast resort of Bournemouth, these words came floating across the dining room: "I do hope Nanny is able to stop Giles fiddling with himself before he goes away to school."

It would be pleasant to report that the other guests rose as one, applauded, and shouted "Hear, hear," or that a kindly psychologist happened to be present and sent the woman a discreet note explaining that the latest studies suggested there was no cause for alarm: "Perfectly normal, madam. Healthy juvenile curiosity about the self. Only to be expected." In fact, nothing happened. Breakfast went on. The Bournemouth hotel where Giles's fiddling was made public knowledge clung to such gentility as it could, and in such places the propensity of the British upper classes, or would-be upper classes, to speak as though nobody else is present, at any rate nobody worthy of notice, is well known. It must have evolved in the days when prosperous Britons were constantly surrounded by servants and there would have been no conversation at all if nothing personal had been said until the servants had gone.

The practice does surprise the stranger, however, on first encounter. I had been in Britain only a few days when, in a hotel elevator, I heard one of two women tell the other about her recent marriage. Her husband, on seeing her two dozen pairs of shoes for the first time, had said, "But surely these are not all necessary," and she had triumphantly replied, "Of course they are not all necessary." Hotel elevators, since they are enclosed and are likely to contain strangers, offer ideal sites for such pronouncements. In that same elevator, a woman looked at me, looked at her husband, and said, "Timothy, here is a man who is taller than you are." Timothy appeared to take this intelligence in good part, though whether he later gave way to despair can only be surmised. As with the outcome of Giles's fiddling, we shall never know.

The confidence with which such people speak, the disdain for others, and, among women working for airlines, for example, the disembodied voice cultivated at British charm schools lead many Americans to stand in awe of the British use of English. There is no reason for Americans to feel inferior to the British when it comes to language. The British are as intent on ruining theirs as we are on ruining ours. Americans should also understand that most Britons who come to the United States, sounding polished, are from the upper and middle classes. Lower-class British accents, which are seldom heard here, are appalling.

An American inferiority complex is without justification, if only because British English is fed by the stream of American English. The British leap at the trite and banal and make them their own with the same avidity as Americans. You cannot spend a day in Britain without hearing game plan, becoming operative, image, think tank, nitty-gritty, rapping, for real, and other afflictions that the United States has exported.

On August 17, 1973, Thorn Electrical Industries announced

in London that it was dissolving a partnership with GTE International. Thorn said: "The original expectation of broad market penetration of the United Kingdom market has not been met in the time-frame contemplated, and the two companies have now decided that their objectives will be better served by separately owned activities."

That could not be more authentic, even to the slightly off-line idea of serving an objective. At times, however, the Americanism undergoes a sea change. The British have taken over the personality weather forecaster, but he is an employe of the Meteorological Office, not of the television network. He is understandably cautious, but conversational, so that he may say, "I'm going to use a broad brush tonight and not be very exact," and he may note, "There's a bit of fog about," and instead of the old stand-bys, bright periods and sunny intervals, he may speak of gleams of sunshine or the odd chink of blue. But while he is sympathetic and homely, he does not smile, and when the weather belies his forecasts, he does not laughingly take personal responsibility for unexpected storms and icy patches on the roads or explain that his weekend, too, was ruined. This is just as well. Hearty humor about wintry showers, freezing fog, and gale-force winds would only make things worse.

Many Americanisms are distorted during export. A correspondent for British Independent Television News thought that the Conservative Party Leader, Edward Heath, talking to people outside Boots the Chemist in Nottingham, was on a whistle-stop tour. "Let them," the head of the British policemen's union said during a recent wage dispute, "put their money where their sentiments lie."

The British can be as stubborn about pronunciation as they are in their belief that Chicago and other places away from the East Coast constitute the provinces. They rejoice to think that Layonard Bairnshtine is in London or Manchester as a guest conductor, possibly with Eezock Shtairn as violin soloist. They still think kindly of American commanders of NATO, but to them General Lauris Norstad was Norshtadt, and General Alfred

Gruenther, who came from Platte Center, Nebraska, was given a Wagnerian pronunciation that might have put him on the German General Staff. The BBC may quote a comment from Washington by Markee Childs of the *St. Louis Post-Dispatch,* perhaps on the case of Spy'ro Agnew or that of John Air'lich'mann.

In 1972 the BBC, secure in its own view of American life, was convinced that the World Series was being played by the Pittsburgh Pirates and the Baltimore Creoles. Still, many Britons think it a mark of generosity to learn American names at all. My daughter was a student at Oxford at the time of the 1964 American presidential election. When word came in that President Johnson had won, one of her tutors said to her, "Better than thingummy, I suppose."

This last attitude intimidates some Americans, and their feeling of inferiority may be reinforced by the success of British plays in the United States. When American plays succeed in London, it is more likely to be put down to their "vigor" and "revelation of human emotion" than to their ideas or the high quality of their language, which are what British plays are usually credited with over here. Why this exaggerated respect for British plays persists, I—after six seasons of examining the relevant evidentiary material—cannot tell you.

Winston Churchill is credited with saying that the fact that the United States and Great Britain speak the same language is the most significant fact of the twentieth century. When I was reviewing plays, there were many nights when, for me, Churchill's significant fact had its drawbacks. Thus I saw *How the Other Half Loves,* which was about moronic married couples living in the suburbs and fighting, getting drunk, throwing food at each other, using electric toothbrushes that didn't work, having misunderstandings on the telephone, and putting antiperspirant in the soup. The child of the family played grocery with his father's shoes and left a tomato in one of them. Why it was thought necessary to supplement American mass production of comedies about moronic married couples in the suburbs I never did figure out.

One citation is hardly conclusive, but there was also *Not Now, Darling,* billed as a "romp," in which the audience could tell the leading actor was funny because he had a funny name, Arnold Crouch. Sample dialogue: "Mr. Crouch, where are you going?" "Out of my mind."

There was also *The Flip Side,* in which two married couples swap partners one night and nasal repartée all evening, and—I'll skip the names—there were comedies that relied on military officers going about without trousers, comedies of marital infidelity, comedies of mistaken identity, comedies of marital infidelity and mistaken identity combined, and more, many more.

Canada's English-speaking population one night opened a northern front by sending us a play called *A Minor Adjustment,* about a businessman who did not want his son to marry early and who, through his public relations man, hired a spirited girl artist to break up the affair. In the process the son became a hippie, and in the process we heard such jokes as "Try to pay a woman a compliment and she'll ask for a certified check" and "I know you're not kidding, boss, but I'd like to ask you a question: Are you kidding?"

Critics have no business feeling sorry for themselves, though it is an occupational hazard, but one reason I felt that I should not be so set upon by the British and the Canadians was that I was already receiving the attentions of American playwrights. Consider the plays that follow. They are not listed in any particular order, and, as you will see, there is no reason they should be.

Come Live with Me. About an American screen writer in London. Danish girl says, "I am Danish and I am finished." Drunken screen writer says, "God save the weasel. Pop goes the Queen."

Happily Never After. About two married couples. One husband throws up when he is troubled, the other complains that his wife is not reliable about taking birth control pills, while she explains that his ostentatious gargling with mouthwash is killing her love. Sample line: "Do you think when I'm up there sleeping, I'm sleeping?"

Love in E Flat. A young intern, jealous of his girl friend, bugs her apartment, while she deceives him into believing that she is pregnant and about to marry somebody else. Sample: "It is remarkable how inheriting a bank can make a man look like Richard Burton."

Lovely Ladies, Kind Gentlemen. Musical adaption of *The Teahouse of the August Moon.* The Americans bluff and innocent, and the natives, as it was compulsory to call them, quaint and innocent. The natives said "Okey-dokey," "Knock it off," and "Scram."

Another City, Another Land. About a hairdresser of integrity who conducts a hopeless fight against curls, waves, and wigs, and winds up on a street corner giving out religious tracts.

Lime Green and *Khaki Blue.* A double bill. In the first, a boy from Arkansas and a girl from New York come together, each intent on a first sexual experience. The boy is fixated on the color lime green. In the second, a woman of the evening remembers her innocence through an alcoholic haze and recalls a man whose eyes she thought were khaki blue.

The Mother Lover. A comedy about an aged woman and her son who hate each other. The son urges the mother to die, so that he will not have to support her, for then he and his wife, whom he also hates, could afford a live-in maid.

Something Different. A playwright re-creates in his house the conditions in which he wrote his only work—his mother's kitchen, complete with cockroaches and a large actress who impersonates his mother and comforts him by shoving his head into her bosom.

The Ninety Day Mistress. A sexually emancipated young woman picks up a young man and offers him ninety days of cohabitation. She is free with her favors because her father deserted her pregnant mother twenty-five years earlier. She and the young man fall in love. The father comes back.

The Song of the Grasshopper. A Spanish play, adapted, about a lovable ne'er-do-well in Madrid who lives in a house where rain comes through the roof and who smokes a pipe to show that he is happy.

A Time for the Gentle People. A former football star in Mississippi, now a drunken repairman in a tenement in Hell's Kitchen, sits fully clothed in a bathtub, quoting Shakespeare. His brother, the mayor of Biloxi, thinks his brother's name can help him become governor and has found him a job as a football coach. Should the repairman go back?

The Impossible Years. A psychiatrist is unable to control his own daughter. Psychiatrically oriented line: "He worships the ground your couch is on." Nonpsychiatrically oriented line: "Those cigarette butts will stay on the carpet until it dies of nicotine poisoning."

Great Scot! A musical about Robert Burns, who makes his poetic bent evident early by singing "As long as there's a star, the answer can't be far." A cow gives birth, offstage, sound only.

Anya. A musical based on the story of Anatasia. Dauntless but melancholy peasants, melancholy but dauntless aristocrats, stern but gracious royalty, devil-may-care cossacks.

Agatha Sue, I Love You. "A lot of people would like to change places with you." "Well, if you can arrange it, make it one of the Rockefellers."

The Happy Time. A musical with French Canadian characters who frequently advise each other that they are luckee and happee.

The Star Spangled Girl. A former Olympic swimmer gets mixed up with the editors of a left-wing magazine who have published an article on twenty-seven ways to burn a wet draft card. The AP is confused with the A & P, and ball point pens are ruined in an automatic pencil sharpener.

For Love or Money. A musical comedy about a family in Italy trying to marry off a son to an American girl. "Now we're cooking with mozzarella." Lyrics: "My heart is full of sorrow, We're almost on the morrow," "If you cheat at love's game, You take the blame," "While I'm in my prime, Let me taste that heavenly wine."

The Rothschilds. "They are ruthless men who will stop at nothing."

Two by Two. About Noah's Ark. When the flood comes, Noah sings "The God I Know Will See Us Through" in march tempo.

Soon. Rock opera. "I wanna know who puts the poison in the sea, I wanna know why the people still aren't free." Showed the influence of the environmental movement on the theater.

The Best Laid Plans. A playwright needs disturbed women as material to work into his plays. A girl pretends to a variety of delinquencies and captures his heart. "You are a narcissi." "What is a narcissi?" "A narcissi is a flower that doesn't like girls."

Ari. Adapted from the book *Exodus*. "We bagged that blockade runner." "Jolly good."

All the plays mentioned, British as well as American, were seen in New York, after I had ceased to work in Britain and after my attitude toward that country and its language was formed. Still, whatever I thought of the plays, I was glad to hear "Jolly good" in the last one. I had gone to London expecting to hear it shower down on all sides, but it was rarely used. I learned early that it was a mistake to look for such constants in the way the British use language. Instead, there were fads.

At this moment, for example, bloody-minded, once used only occasionally, is a fad. Bloody-minded is used principally in industrial disputes, but also to condemn the attitude of anyone who will not give way to your point of view. The high and mighty and the socially prominent use it to show that they are both democratic and with it. If they can work it in somehow, they will show that they are even more with it by referring to the place where they live as their pad.

Nonetheless, there are a few granitic eternals in the British language. One is the cough, one is the giving of leads, and one is the code. There are many coughs in Britain: the discreet clearing of the throat by the butler when he interrupts the master in some dubious activity or nodding over the family's deteriorating accounts; the cigarette smoker's rasp; the concertgoer's convulsion, which can drown out the entire series of trumpet calls in the *Leonore* Overture Number Three. I am thinking, however, of a businesslike bark, almost universal, and favored by a climate that makes practice possible all year round. Justice Potter Stewart of the United States Supreme Court said about pornography that he could not define it but he knew it when he saw it. The all-England hack is like that: people know it when they hear it, and it is a sign to any Briton within hearing that a countryman is present. It is a morale-builder and a reassurance.

This all-England hack, I believe, holds the explanation of that curious institution, the English Sunday. It is not now as determinedly gloomy as it was in the days when the Church of England flourished and Sunday Observance was one of the consequences, but even now many a visitor, walking the deserted streets, has wondered what is going on behind the curtained windows. The answer is simple: the generations have gathered for a family cough.

The second constant is the conviction, held by all shades of political opinion, that the world is looking to Britain for "a lead." This persists today, though less aggressively, but when I lived in England, from 1949 to 1957, it shocked Americans, who believed that supplying leads was their province. One of the first leads I ever saw given was handed down by Princess Elizabeth before she became queen. She made—or read—a speech in which she argued that there was much to be said for an old-fashioned view of the family and for family life, and advised her listeners not to be afraid of being called prudes. A well-known Sunday paper at once rushed into the streets with a special article headed: Princess Elizabeth Gives Us a Lead.

One difficulty is that while leads are given freely, they are less often taken, which has a way of provoking disagreements. Sometime in the 1950s, when John Foster Dulles was secretary of state, the American and British governments were extremely angry with each other about something in the Middle East and exchanged insults and acrimony. A member of the Foreign Office was asked about the situation. He was a diplomat of the old school. "Merely the projection of a long-standing difference of emphasis," he said.

His blandness notwithstanding, the British were highly displeased that they had gone to the trouble of giving a lead that was not being followed. However, as their influence diminished they became accustomed to doing this and soon drew satisfaction from having their leads ignored, because that showed how perverse and shortsighted other people were who didn't know a lead when they saw one. The British still give leads, but not in the manner of a great power. Their leads now are in such fields as showing self-discipline and setting disinterested examples. These have even less chance of being followed than the other kind.

I remember the Labor Defense Minister, Emanuel Shinwell, in the early 1950s doing something that displeased Winston Churchill, and Churchill snapping at him, "Oh, go and talk to the Italians. That is all you are good for." Now, their confidence sapped by economic troubles, the British warn each other that if things don't pick up they may well have a growth rate lower than Italy's. This is quite a comedown. They even warn each other that if they don't follow this or that policy, they will sink to the economic level of Portugal. This is a far cry from giving a lead.

It is also insulting to Portugal, which, at least until the 1974 coup, appeared not to mind being held up as an object lesson in abjectness. The British, however, do not stop even at Portugal. They warn each other that if they are not careful they may well have inflation on the scale of a banana republic. This implies that the British still believe it is in the natural order of things for them to be superior to Portugal and banana republics, though how long that confidence will last nobody can say. Why it is nobler to export Scotch and gin (and be a gin monarchy) than it is to export coffee, tea, sugar, spices, and bananas the British appear not to have asked themselves.

As a matter of fact, the British once seemed to me to want to become a worm and chair monarchy. I covered an exposition of British goods in New York at which they were selling worms. The worms, of course, did come from what Shakespeare called "this blessed plot, this earth, this realm, this England." No other worms could make that claim. The exposition also contained a pub called The Red Lion. Here the visitor was able to sit in a replica of a chair used by Mary, Queen of Scots. Why beer should taste better if the drinker is sitting in a replica of a chair used by a martyred queen was not clear. The British may have thought it would appeal to the much-publicized sentimentality of Americans.

One of the many fields in which the British thought they were giving the world a lead was in density of bonnie babies in proportion to the population. This homely phrase was refurbished at each election, general and by-, as we do with sovereign state and these United States. The party in power claimed that the babies of the country had never been so bonnie, thanks to the enlightened policies of the party in power, while the opposition party claimed that the babies' bonnieness, though undeniable, arose from *its* earlier period in office when reforms leading directly to bonnieness were instituted, and furthermore that they would be bonnier still if the opposition got back in. This rivalry did not end until the British became more interested in the bonnieness of houses, cars, and holidays abroad.

The third common denominator was the use of code. We were in a London theater watching a Sean O'Casey play in which he made fun of British landowners in Ireland when two Irishmen whom I took to be construction workers—navvies is the British word—and who had obviously stopped off en route to fortify themselves, commenced contributing their own anti-British lines to the performance. Soon the theater manager and the commissionaire came down the aisle. (Army sergeants from the First World War formed a corps of commissionaires to be employed as doormen-guards-receptionists.)

"All right, lads. Come along now," said the commissionaire.

The Irishmen understood the code—leave quietly or the police will be along and there will be trouble none of us want but which you in particular don't want. They rose and left.

What appears to be gentle treatment often isn't, if you know the code. You will see members of Parliament described as respected, highly respected, well loved, popular, colorful and flamboyant. The first four categories are self-explanatory, although well loved usually means, in truth, that the M.P. is old and has been around for a long time and is no longer effective. Colorful means that the M.P. works too hard at attracting attention, and flamboyant means that everybody would be happier if he went away. If a newspaper reports that a politician was tired while making a speech or appearing on television, the meaning is that the politician had been drinking. If the politician was very tired, he should not have been out in public at all.

This restraint about politicians, with which libel laws may have much to do, often is not matched among the politicians themselves. In the House of Commons, known in some journalistic circles as the Mother of Parliaments and when there is any disorder as the normally staid Mother of Parliaments, there are well-established measures of the response of members to a speech or statement—sympathetic noises in all parts of the House, cries of "Hear, hear," cheers, loud cheers, prolonged cheers, and waving of papers. There may also be hostile noises, groans, and shouts of "Resign." After this, individual initiative takes over with "Sit down," "Belt up," "Shut up," "Get stuffed," "Knock off," "Put a sock in it," "Disgraceful," "He's drunk" and "Cock-a-doodle-doo."

When I arrived in London in 1949 I was astonished by the hooting to which the Laborites in the House of Commons subjected Conservatives. Labor, of course, was riding high in those days, and at the beginning of that Parliament one of its members, Hartley Shawcross, had made a well-publicized remark to the Conservatives: "We are the masters now." Shawcross, a lawyer and one of the prosecutors at the Nuremberg War Crimes Tribunal, later became Lord Shawcross and prominent in the financial district, the City of London. He may have felt the same way there.

Conservatives are more vulnerable to hooting and to the salutations listed above because so many of them affect an upper-class stammer. Actually, it is not so much a stammer as it is the repetition of certain words—and and but, principally—and the frequent insertion of "Errr," said in a rather distant way. Whatever the reason for it—to give the impression that the precise word is being searched for, to show that haste is unseemly, to build up drama by making the audience wait—it does give those listening a chance to make their own comments.

The House of Commons prides itself on the level of its debates, and it can be cruel. Near the end of his career, the Labor politician Herbert Morrison made a speech on economic policy in which he said, "If it were just a little matter that didn't matter, it would be another matter." Groans went up all over the House, first because of the banality of the statement, second because Morrison was still hoping to become leader of the Labor party. He had only an outside chance and the speech killed it.

As a politically suicidal comment, it ranked with Prime Minister Harold Macmillan's comment on the Profumo scandal of 1962–63. "All got up by the press," said Macmillan, thereby propelling himself into the twilight of his career. Another consequential remark was Winston Churchill's in the 1945 election campaign that if the Socialist ministers in his wartime coalition cabinet came to power, Britain would have a Gestapo. Some years later there was the Laborite Aneurin Bevan's "The organized workers of this country are our friends. As for the rest, they are lower than vermin." You don't say that kind of thing in a two-party system and have much chance of becoming prime minister.

Stuck with their upper-class stammer, the Conservatives often dream of finding working-class candidates to run under their banner (though not for safe seats). At the first Conservative party conference I went to, in 1950, a man named Anthony Bulbrooks was introduced. He mounted the platform, thrust out his hands, palms toward the audience, and announced, "I work with these." The cheers were stupendous, and the trapper who found Bulbrooks and brought him in was probably paid a bounty.

There was nothing like it for years afterward until one of the more erratic spirits among the Tories, Quintin Hogg, came up on the platform with an enormous bell, which he rang while he shouted a message to Labor: "Ask not for whom the bell tolls. It tolls for thee."

You will hear Cockney and Midlands ("Ee, lad") and other accents at Labor party conferences, but not all the Laborites are horny-handed sons of toil, and expressions of pride in "our working-class movement" delivered in Oxford English by people born to privilege are a Bulbrookian equivalent. There are, also, few things as incongruous as the party leaders standing on the platform at the end of the conference, linking arms and singing "The Red Flag." After that, their revolutionary duty done, they —lawyers, academicians, managers, professional politicians, journalists, trade-union officials, businessmen—go home.

To me the most characteristic moment at Labor party conferences was the moment of the emergence of the composite resolution, which is pronounced with a long i and the accent on the last syllable. It was then said, when a number of resolutions had been brought together into one, that they had been composited. For party functionaires able to say this, it was the high point of the year.

Another part of the British code is the hyphenated name. Among no other people is the hyphen so imaginatively used. British hyphenation preserves the bride's name, though not as an early example of equality for women but rather as a signal that two dynasties had been joined. It results for the most part in prosaic names like Hornsby-Smith and Gordon-Walker, but rises to a higher level of inspiration with Finch-Knightley and Fox-Strangways and Lowry-Corry, and occasionally produces a national treasure like Buller-Fullerton-Elphinstone and Money-Coutts.

The British peerage pours new names into use because it needs regular infusions of recruits if it is to be kept going. Somebody who has been Reginald Edward Manningham-Buller all his life, for example, may disappear and reemerge, at the age of fifty-nine, as Lord Dilhorne. This keeps everybody alert.

Since 1964 no hereditary peerages have been created, only

life peerages, which become extinct when the new peer or peeress does; the title cannot be handed on. Among the life peers there is a tendency to keep their own names and so to become Lady Burton or Lord Sorenson, or whatever it may be. Sometimes they also keep their first names and insert a hyphen where none has been before. Thus Lord George-Brown made up for the loss of Manningham-Buller's hyphen, above. When the government of Prime Minister Heath created a new batch of life peers after dissolving Parliament and calling an election in early 1974, one of those ennobled was the politician Duncan Sandys. He became a baron and in this new eminence felt the need of a hyphen. He therefore changed his name by deed poll to Duncan Duncan-Sandys. (The y is silent and the pronunciation is Sands, which adds to the general good cheer.)

I think that if I were British I would try to enter into the spirit of the thing by hyphenating my name by deed poll and making it, perhaps, Edwin Deed-Poll, or possibly Edwin Hyphen-Newman. I was dismayed to meet in Ghana the wife of a British official who was entitled to use four names and three hyphens but used only two and one respectively. This undermines the system.

By contrast, there lived in England Admiral the Honourable Sir Reginald Aylmer Ranfurly Plunkett-Ernle-Erle-Drax, who fought at Heligoland, Jutland, and Dogger Bank in the First World War, and was a convoy commodore in the Second. I deeply regretted that I was never able to include his name in a broadcast, or those of members of the Montagu-Stuart-Wortley-Mackenzie and Hovell-Thurlow-Cumming-Bruce families. One hyphen down, Lady Jane Vane-Tempest-Stewart made some headlines as a debutante. I never got her name on the air either.

The Admiral and the Lady had an embarrassment of hyphens, but noteworthy names can be made with a single hyphen, as Sir Humphrey Dodington Benedict Sherston Sherston-Baker showed. For the British, the hyphen serves somewhat the same purpose as the accent. It is a bird call by which the species is identified. In British general elections, only the names of the candidates for Parliament are given, not their party affiliations. At the election of February, 1974, the son of a duke said that by the time he got inside the voting booth he often forgot which candidate was the Conservative. "In that case," he said, "I look for the name with a hyphen." If there was no hyphenated name, he said, "I look for a name such as Knox or Jones and vote against it."

There was a time when sons of dukes were expected to forget which candidate was the Conservative, and to forget everything else of consequence. Then, as they grew older and became dukes themselves, they were expected to potter about. Pottering about was considered a suitable occupation for someone in their position whose money came from land rather than commerce and who had the requisite breeding. Pottering ceased to be valued so highly when a more aggressive consumer society, imitating the American, took over. There used to be, for example, the tradition of genteel advertising, embodied by the notice that said, "If you know of a better toothpaste than Gordon-Moore's Satin Dental Cream, we should be glad to hear about it." I assume that people with hyphenated names would still lean to Gordon-Moore's, but advertising of such disinterested confidence is no more.

The British have a way of referring to certain well-known Americans, past and present, as Foster Dulles, Cabot Lodge, and Luther King, implying that a hyphen should be present. The hyphenated name has never caught on in the United States, but we do come close to it with a legacy of our own. This is the richness afforded society by the names of university and college presidents.

Take two well-known examples, one from the past—Nicholas Murray Butler, president of Columbia, 1902–45—and one from the present, Kingman Brewster, president of Yale since 1964. Both names could be hyphenated without difficulty: "Sir Roger Nicholas-Murray-Butler said today that he was leaving the family banking firm to found . . ." and "Anthony Kingman-Brewster, son of the former British Ambassador to Iraq, is joining the

Welsh commercial television company as an assistant producer."

But both names go well beyond hyphenability. Each is interchangeable within itself. Kingman Brewster. Brewster Kingman. Nicholas Murray Butler. Nicholas Butler Murray. Murray Nicholas Butler. Murray Butler Nicholas. Butler Murray Nicholas. Butler Nicholas Murray.

They are also interchangeable with each other. Nicholas Kingman Brewster. Brewster Nicholas Kingman. And so on and so on.

If you examine the names of American university and college presidents, past and present, you find this circular quality to a remarkable degree. In the Kingman Brewster style, there were, for example, Glenn Frank (University of Wisconsin, 1925–37) and Grayson Kirk (Columbia, 1953–68), though it should be noted that the field is so rich that while Kingman Brewster achieves interchangeability in four syllables, Grayson Kirk does it in three and Glenn Frank did it in two.

The Nicholas Murray Butler style of three interchangeable names represents the peak and occurs less commonly. James Russell Lowell (Harvard, 1909–33) was an early example, and among current presidents there are Lloyd Drexell Vincent of Angelo State University, Texas, whose name seems to me to mark him out for certain academic advancement, and Forrest David Mathews of the University of Alabama, and Bernard Tagg Lomas of Albion, in Michigan.

There is a third style in which an initial occurring either at the beginning of the name or in the middle comes into play. Thus R. Dudley Boyce of Golden West College, California, and Atlee C. Kepler of Hagerstown Junior College, Maryland, and Porter L. Fortune, chancellor of the University of Mississippi.

When I became aware of the unusual properties of university presidents' names, which I did at an early age, I noticed that some, even when they fell short of interchangeability, still had a striking quality. My favorite for sheer symmetry was Robert Maynard Hutchins (University of Chicago, 1929–45). For pyramidal symmetry it was Guy Stanton Ford (University of Minnesota, 1938–41). For rhythm and euphony, it was Dixon

Ryan Fox (Union College, Schenectady, New York, 1934–45).
One of Fox's predecessors, serving from 1802 to 1866, was
Elithalet Nott, a name well worth reviving.

Still, as noted, the peak is represented by the interchangeable
triple name, and to reach this peak there are five requirements.
The first is being male; the second is having an Anglo-Saxon
surname; the third is having an Anglo-Saxon family name,
usually the mother's, as a middle name; the fourth, displaying it;
and the fifth, living among people who do the same or at least
do not consider doing so a laughable affectation. These requirements met, a university presidency should not be far off.

I now append a short list of American university and college
presidents with interchangeable names, double, triple, and double
with initial, to show how high the incidence of interchangeability
is, and how widely scattered. The list is drawn, alphabetically
by state, from the Yearbook of Higher Education for 1973. Note
that I have not taken the easy way; there is nobody on the list
with James or Charles as first or last name; college presidents
named (at any point) Thomas, Stanley, Howard, Leonard,
Benjamin, Frank, Paul, Lawrence, Francis, Wallace, Albert,
Ernest, Willard, Frederick, Douglas, Martin, Harvey, Wesley,
Herman, Henry, Gordon, Glenn, Seymour, Lewis, Russell,
Oliver, Willis, Curtis—and such college presidents are legion,
or Legion L. Legion—have likewise been eliminated. Note also
that the names are interchangeable up, down, diagonally, taking
every other name, every third, fourth, fifth, and so on, at random,
and—for parlor game purposes—any other way you can think
of. In mixed clusters of three, especially when read or sung aloud,
they are often enchanting.

Levi Watkins	Alabama State University Montgomery, Alabama
Woodfin P. Patterson	Jefferson Davis State Jr. College Brewton, Alabama
Imon E. Bruce	Southern State College Magnolia, Arkansas

Cornelius P. Haggard	Azusa Pacific College Azusa, California
Cordas C. Burnett	Bethany Bible College Santa Cruz, California
Higgins D. Bailey	California College of Podiatric Medicine San Francisco, California
Brage Golding	California State University San Diego, California
Gibb R. Madsen	Hartnell College Salinas, California
Terrel Spencer	Imperial Valley College Imperial, California
Wiley D. Garner	Long Beach City College Long Beach, California
Leadie M. Clark	Los Angeles Southwest College Los Angeles, California
Burton W. Wadsworth	Victor Valley College Victorville, California
Rexer Berndt	Fort Lewis College Durango, Colorado
Dumont Kenny	Temple Buell College Denver, Colorado
Thurston E. Manning	University of Bridgeport Bridgeport, Connecticut
Cleveland L. Dennard	Washington Technical Institute Washington, D. C.
T. Felton Harrison	Pensacola Jr. College Pensacola, Florida
Culbreth Y. Melton	Emmanuel College Franklin Springs, Georgia

J. Whitney Bunting

Georgia College
Milledgeville, Georgia

Pope A. Duncan

Georgia Southern College
Statesboro, Georgia

Prince Jackson, Jr.

Savannah State College
Savannah, Georgia

Forest D. Etheredge

Waubonsee Community College
Sugar Grove, Illinois

Hudson T. Armerding

Wheaton College
Wheaton, Illinois

Beauford A. Norris

Christian Theological Seminary
Indianapolis, Indiana

Landrum R. Bolling

Earlham College
Richmond, Indiana

Byrum E. Carter

Indiana University at
Bloomington
Bloomington, Indiana

Glennon P. Warford

Ellsworth Community College
Iowa Falls, Iowa

Merne A. Harris

Vennard College
University Park, Iowa

Arley A. Bryant

Cloud County Community Jr.
College
Concordia, Kansas

Duke K. McCall

Southern Baptist Theological
Seminary
Louisville, Kentucky

Mahlon A. Miller

Union College
Barbourville, Kentucky

Dero G. Downing

Western Kentucky University
Bowling Green, Kentucky

Broadus N. Butler	Dillard University New Orleans, Louisiana
W. Ardell Haines	Allegany Community College Cumberland, Maryland
D. Deane Wyatt	Baltimore College of Commerce Baltimore, Maryland
Atlee C. Kepler	Hagerstown Jr. College Hagerstown, Maryland
J. Renwick Jackson	St. Marys College of Maryland St. Marys, Maryland
Randle Elliott	Bay Path Jr. College Longmeadow, Massachusetts
Wheeler G. Merriam	Franklin Pierce College Rindge, New Hampshire
Placidus H. Riley	St. Anselm's College Manchester, New Hampshire
Ferrel Heady	University of New Mexico Albuquerque, New Mexico
Prezell R. Robinson	St. Augustine's College Raleigh, North Carolina
Ferebee Taylor	University of North Carolina at Chapel Hill Chapel Hill, North Carolina
Laud O. Vaught	Northwest Bible College Minot, North Dakota
Garland A. Godfrey	Central State College Edmond, Oklahoma
Dolphus Whitten, Jr.	Oklahoma City University Oklahoma City, Oklahoma
Harris L. Wofford, Jr.	Bryn Mawr College Bryn Mawr, Pennsylvania

Lane D. Kilburn	King's College Wilkes-Barre, Pennsylvania
Mayo Bryce	Moore College of Art Philadelphia, Pennsylvania
Bertrand W. Hayward	Pennsylvania College of Textiles and Science Philadelphia, Pa.
Hilton M. Briggs	South Dakota State University Brookings, South Dakota
Powell A. Fraser	King College Bristol, Tennessee
Odell Horton	Le Moyne-Owen College Memphis, Tennessee
Spurgeon B. Eure	Southern College of Optometry Memphis, Tennessee
Lloyd Drexell Vincent	Angelo State University San Angelo, Texas
Fount W. Mattox	Lubbock Christian College Lubbock, Texas
Granville M. Sawyer	Texas Southern University Houston, Texas
Lyman B. Brooks	Norfolk State College Norfolk, Virginia
Lambuth M. Clarke	Virginia Wesleyan College Norfolk, Virginia
J. Wade Gilley	Wytheville Community College Wytheville, Virginia
Thornton M. Ford	Tacoma Community College Tacoma, Washington
D. Banks Wilburn	Glenville State College Glenville, West Virginia

Irvin G. Wyllie   University of Wisconsin–Parkside
                                Kenosha, Wisconsin

Tilghman Aley   Casper Community College
                                Casper, Wyoming

It happens rarely, but sometimes both the university and its president have interchangeable names. Note in the preceding list Dumont Kenny of Temple Buell College in Denver, and Wheeler G. Merriam of Franklin Pierce College in Rindge, New Hampshire. J. Osborne Fuller was president of Fairleigh Dickinson University in Rutherford, New Jersey, for some years until December, 1973. Fairleigh Dickinson could just as easily have been president of J. Osborne Fuller University or Dickinson Fuller of Fairleigh J. Osborne. The name of the town, Rutherford, might also be brought in, but that way lies madness.

There is another unquenchable and growing source of interchangeable and impressive names—foundations, another American phenomenon that, like universities, produces a sort of American peerage. Here we find, for example, W. McNeill Lowry, formerly vice-president for policy and planning of the Ford Foundation, now its vice-president for humanities and the arts. It is not necessary, however, to go below the topmost level of administrators. Far from it:

F. Paschal Gallot of the Miranda Lux Foundation, San Francisco; Tilden Cummings, Continental Bank Charitable Foundation, Chicago; Thorwald J. Fraser, Anderson Foundation, Boise, Idaho; Tecla M. Virtue, Phillips Foundation, Los Angeles; Royce H. Heath, Allen-Heath Foundation, Chicago; Emory K. Crenshaw, Frances Wood Wilson Foundation, Decatur, Georgia; Cason J. Callaway, Jr., Pine Mountain Benevolent Foundation, Columbus, Georgia; Alden H. Sulger, Stone Trust Foundation, New Haven, Connecticut; Lawton M. Calhoun, Savannah Foundation, Savannah, Georgia; Brannon B. Lesesne, Patterson-Barclay Memorial Foundation, Atlanta; and since it must be obvious that this can go on indefinitely, the following, hardly more than a smattering, given without affiliation:

Leighton A. Wilkie, Brice E. Hayes, Chapman S. Root, Sacket R. Duryee, W. Craig Keith, Danforth Helley, Delmar S. Harder, Campbell A. Harlan, Firman H. Hass, Miner S. Keeler II, Cleveland Thurber, Burrows Morley, J. Woodward Roe, Shaw Walker, Macauley Whiting, Hobson C. McGehee, Shields Warren, Girard B. Henderson, J. Seward Johnson, Moore Gates, Jr., W. Parsons Todd, S. Whitney Landon, G. Sealey Newell, Oakleigh L. Thorne, Campbell Rutledge, Hart Taylor, Schuyler M. Meyer, Jr., P. Mathis Pfohl, Malin Sorsbie, Stark S. Dillard and—to close—J. Clib Barton of the Doss T. Sutton Charitable Foundation, Fort Smith, Arkansas, and E. Blois du Bois of the du Bois Foundation, Scottsdale, Arizona.

Like E. Blois du Bois, though unlike J. Clib Barton, many foundation heads are heads of foundations that have the same name they do, suggesting that a name itself may have a powerful influence, that if you have an interchangeable name, the demands of good citizenship impel you toward foundation founding, if no university presidency is available, as a British name of weight propels one toward the House of Lords. However, since anyone whose name qualifies him to be a university president is simultaneously qualified to be a foundation head, inevitably there is traffic, and even competition, between the two worlds. Note in the list of university presidents the entry Landrum R. Bolling, Earlham College, Richmond, Indiana. After the list was compiled Bolling was named executive vice-president of the Lilly Endowment. Bolling was succeeded at Earlham by Franklin W. Wallin, who had been president of the Institute for World Order, Inc., a position he occupied while on leave from Colgate University, where he was dean and provost and, given his name, inexorably moving higher.

The best-known foundation head is, of course, McGeorge Bundy, of the Ford. In the days when Bundy was in the government, I used to have a fantasy about the instructions President Johnson gave him before sending him off on one of his numerous visits to Vietnam.

"Listen, McGeorge," Mr. Johnson would say, "I don't want

you wasting time out there. I don't want you talking to just any McTom, McDick or McHarry."

It was thanks to a 1953 movie called *The Treasure of Kalifa* that I became aware of another style in American names, less orotund but no less evocative, and identifying its owners as surely as a hyphen does. It has not entirely survived the changes in movie-making of the last couple of decades, but it did lie in the mainstream of American film-making in its time. That was when the male stars had one-syllable first names. Not ordinary, unimaginative names, but names that served a purpose, that punched, that revealed.

The stars of *The Treasure of Kalifa* were Rod Cameron and Tab Hunter. To pronounce those names was to know what manner of men they were. They were laconic, tough, informal, nononsense Americans. Their names also disclosed the nature of the film. It was an action picture, perhaps even an all-action picture, set in the great outdoors. The leading characters, busily engaged in all-action, barely had time to grunt. These were ideal parts for Rod and Tab.

See the utility of this fashion: Take the film *Back to God's Country*. This was another action or all-action picture, set in the frozen North, and it also had two laconic, tough, informal, nononsense Americans, Rock Hudson and Steve Cochran. Rock, however, was plainly the hero, because his name preceded Steve's in the billing. Rock, in fact, was "in" the picture, while Steve only "co-starred" with Marcia Henderson.

This, I agree, is easy. A man who was "in" a picture was more likely to be the hero than a man who was merely co-starring with Marcia Henderson. Let us suppose, therefore, that we did not know that the Rock came before the Steve. It would still have been possible to know at once that Rock was the hero: his name had only four letters while Steve's had five. Steve may have been laconic, tough, informal and no-nonsense, but he was not as laconic, tough, informal and no-nonsense as Rock. All of that the names made clear.

So far so good. But go back to *The Treasure of Kalifa*. Rod and Tab are both three-letter names, and their owners were billed together, on the same line. Who was the hero there? The answer had to be that both were heroes. They were more: they were tried and trusty friends. It is true that in the film itself their names were different, but it is pleasant to think of a scene in which they stand silently, one at each side of a corner of a house, gun drawn, unable to see the other side but knowing somebody is there.

This is the suspenseful dialogue:

ROD: Tab?
TAB: Rod?
ROD: Right, Tab, it's Rod.
TAB: Right, Rod, it's Tab.

Both men then emerge, holster their guns, and call each other "you old galoot."

There was, of course, a limit to the number of films in which the leading men could be friends, and for the most part the producers juggled plots and casts so that they did not have a man playing the villain who had the same number of letters in his name as the man playing the hero. But allowing for the worst, suppose that a producer had a four-letter villain already cast when he found no two- or three-letter hero available. Even in this extremity, the producer had a way out. His salvation was to use a hero whose four-letter name was less orthodox and more manly than the four-letter name of the villain. Thus in *The Great Sioux Uprising* Jeff Chandler triumphed over Lyle Bettger. But Jeff would hardly have had a chance against somebody named, let us say, Hook.

There is an additional point—that some names were works of genius. By way of illustration, a Biff could easily have given away two letters to, say, an Os and still come out on top. Nobody name of Biff's gonna get beat by nobody name of Os, leastwise not if they fight fair. Feller name of Lash LaRue, star of *Son of a Badman* (and not to be confused with Whip Wilson, star of *Crashin' Through*), might do it, specially with the help of his sidekick Fuzzy St. John and extra specially if Fuzzy's name gits shortened to Fuzz. Otherwise, cain't do hit nohow.

The ideal one-syllable name for an all-action film hero would have been Id, particularly when westerns began to be made with psychological overtones. We might have had Id Libido, playing a character whose life is warped because his Italian descent makes him the butt of jokes by crudely chauvinistic cowboys, shooting it out with String Greenberg as the first Jewish cowboy west of St. Louis and trying to show how tough he is. Both die in the shoot-out, which makes the point that we should all be brothers, while Dream O'Day, playing an heiress who wants to be useful and who runs a pioneering psychological counseling service in the Oklahoma Territory, mourns them both and sobs that she has failed. She is consoled by a Chinese laundryman who laughs at everything because that is expected of him but deep down understands all, including acupuncture. With the help of a gently humorous Catholic priest, Father Figure (played by the famous Irish actor, Spalpeen Gossoon), he makes her believe that continuing her psychological counseling service will be worthwhile. The curtain falls before she can become Oklahoma's first woman senator or fit in another appointment.

On the whole, it will be seen that when it comes to names, we can match the British at their own game, even without hyphens. What they do have that we do not is heraldry, the science of armorial bearings. Britain remains one of the few places left outside of crossword puzzles where queries of a heraldic nature arise in life's normal course. They are referred to the College of Arms, where the functionaries answer them with a straight face. (It is said that an American correspondent once called the College of Arms and identified himself as representing the *New York Heraldic Tribune,* but if so, this was plainly the work of a cad and it is no wonder the paper died.)

At the College of Arms, which is to say King's College of Heralds and Poursuivants of Arms in Ordinary, you can see and talk to the Richmond Herald—a man, not a publication, and to be addressed, once you get to know him, as Richmond—and the Garter King of Arms. (Somewhere here there lurks a joke about "My son the herald," but let it go.) Not, mind you, that Richmond Herald and Garter King of Arms are outstanding as titles go. On the whole, the best titles for all purposes are Gentleman Usher of the Black Rod and Gold Stick-in-Waiting, who are in the Queen's household.

They are known, less formally, as Black Rod and Gold Stick, and I can almost hear a conversation between them as they stand, concealed from each other, while on a security round in a dark and musty corridor of Buckingham Palace:

BLACK ROD: Gold Stick?
GOLD STICK: Black Rod?
BLACK ROD: Not to worry, Gold Stick. It's Black Rod.
GOLD STICK: Not to worry, Black Rod. It's Gold Stick.

Both men then emerge, lowering their Black Rod and Gold Stick respectively, call each other "old chap," wish each other "cheerie-bye," and depart.

I suppose I have a soft spot for Britain. It was there, through appearances on the BBC and the commercial network, that I achieved my first recognition. I was standing outside the NBC offices in London one day when a car went by, stopped, and reversed. The driver rolled down the window, put his head out, and said he knew me, that he recognized me as a television face. After some effort, he recalled my name. Then he reached for his wallet and gave me his business card.

"We do very good interior decorating," he said. "We would like to have your business. Drop in anytime."

Once you have grown accustomed to this sort of adulation, it is not easy to do without.

That ends this small and random sample of experiences with British English and some of its American counterparts. If you know of a better small and random sample, I should be glad to hear about it.

5

The Capacity
To Generate
Language
Viability
Destruction

The business instinct is by no means to be sneered at. I have had only one moneymaking idea in my life. It came to me like a flash (though not from Mr. Tash, the manager of a jewelry store in Washington, D. C., after the Second World War, and the inspiration of a radio commercial which began, "Now here's a flash from Mr. Tash—If you'll take a chance on romance, then I'll take a chance on you," meaning that he sold engagement and wedding rings on credit). It came to me like a flash one day when I was thinking about the growth of the population and the domination of American life by the automobile.

I fell to wondering, as any red-blooded American would, how some money might be made from that combination of factors, and I conceived the idea that because walking as a pleasure was becoming a lost art, a great deal of money might be made by setting up a pedestrians' sanctuary, a place where people could walk. I saw in my mind's eye the name WALKORAMA, or STROLLATERIA, or something of the sort, and a place that would require little in the way of outlay or upkeep—just some space, grass, trees, and quiet. Obviously it would need a parking lot so that people could drive to it and park their cars before entering the walkorama to walk, and I intended to hold on to the parking concession for myself.

Nothing came of it. It was a typically footless newsman's dream, like the little weekly with which to get back to real people, dispense serene wisdom, and go broke, in Vermont.

I do not, therefore, sneer at the men and women of business. If they were not buying time on NBC, the world might or might not be a poorer place, but I would unquestionably be a poorer inhabitant of it.

However, the contributions of business to the health of the language have not been outstanding. Spelling has been assaulted by Duz, and E-Z Off, and Fantastik, and Kool and Arrid and Kleen, and the tiny containers of milk and cream catchily called the Pour Shun, and by products that make you briter, so that you will not be left hi and dri at a parti, but made welkom.

This book was originally typed on paper drawn from a "slide-out pak."

"You're saked," the angry Amtrak chief said. "I caught on to you in the nik of time. I don't know what it was, but something cliked. If it hadn't, an entire trainload of knikknaks would have been lost. You make me sik," he went on. "There has been no lak of understanding of you here. You've carried on like a high muky-muk, with assistants at your bek and call, but you're driving us to rak and ruin. You'd have us in hok up to our neks. You were hoping that I'd blow my stak and crak under the strain, but I won't. Pik up your money, pak your things, and go. I want you cheked out in an hour, by four. You thought that you could duk responsibility, that you were dealing with a bunch of hiks, and that we were stuk with you. You were playing with a staked dek. Well, in sixty minutes, I want you out of here, lok, stok and barrel."

"Sok it to him, boss," a Uriah-Heep-like character among the employes murmured. "He has no kik coming. He just couldn't hak it." He gave a quaklike laugh and fed himself from a tube of Squeez-a-snak.

Dik Windingstad (for it was indeed he) hardly knew how to respond, so shoked was he, so taken abak by the Amtrak chief's attak, so roked bak on his heels. He felt like a hokey goalie hit in the face by a puk off the stik of Bobby Hull, and the tik-tik-tok of the stately clok as it stood against the wall sounded in his ears like the sharp reports of ak-ak guns. His heartbeat quikened. Then he thought sardonically to himself, "The buk stops here," and his mood changed. "We've had some yaks," he thought. "I must have upset the peking order."

He glanced down at his finely tailored slaks, never again to be worn in these precincts. "I'll go," he said finally. "But not with my tail tuked between my legs, as you'd like. Hek, no. Lok me out, if you want to. Mok me. Someday you'll take a different tak. Someday I'll get in the last lik. All I can say now is good-by and—for some of you, anyway—good luk. Please forward my mail to Hamtramk."

Dik spun on his heel and made traks. Amtraks.

In many such monstrosities, the companies involved know what they are doing. In others they often do not, especially when it is a matter of grammar. New York remains the business capital of the United States, and on a typical day there you may pick up the *New York Times,* or that paragon of eastern sophistication, the *New Yorker* magazine, and find a well-known Fifth Avenue jeweler telling the world that "The amount of prizes Gübelin has won are too numerous to be pure chance." I happen to know that this was a straw man Gübelin was knocking down because nobody had said it were pure chance. The sentiment in the circles I travel in was that the amount of prizes were fully deserved.

In the same advertisement Gübelin also gives us the following: "Sculpture II, an 18-carat white-gold ring with 24 diamond baguettes and two smoky quartzes, fancy cut, is a unique work of art to be worn on one finger, and without doubt rightly among the Gübelin creations that have taken the Diamonds-International Award." Turning the word rightly into a verb is no small achievement, but it should have been rightlies, so that the advertisement would read, ". . . and without doubt rightlies among the Gübelin creations that have taken the Diamonds-International Award."

Another possible verb is gübelin. "I have gübelined," he said, hanging his head, "and I no longer rightly among you, winners all of the Diamonds-International Award." He turned and walked falteringly toward the door.

"For a moment it seemed that the high priest, or Tiffany, was about to forgive him, but it was not to be. 'Go,' the Tiffany said, pointing to the outer darkness, 'go and gübelin no more.' "

The edition of the *Times* graced by Gübelin also had an advertisement from Wallach's, a men's clothing store. It was headed, "Portentious prophesies," and the first of these came from an "anthropoligist." It was, "Men will shrink to a height of two feet in another 2 million years." This may have been thought not portentious enough, because there was also a prediction by a dermatologist (correctly spelled) that in a hundred years or so men and women would go through life bald, and one from an astronomer that in a billion years or so the earth would be dry. Here was a portentious outlook indeed, men and women, members of a species that had been bald for 999,999,900 years, and had been two feet tall for 998,988,026, either seriously dehydrated or long since removed to other planets. (Among the earth's animals the camel had survived, being able to get his nose under the portent.)

There remained the question of what bald men and women two feet tall would be wearing while the earth was going dry. Wallach's had the answer in portentious prophesies by a designer and a hair stylist. The hair stylist said that men and women would soon be wearing gold and silver wigs for formal occasions, and the designer thought that reversible clothing might come in, so that a man could arrive at work wearing a gray worsted and, by turning it inside out, leave in a black dinner jacket. Here is the complete portentious outlook: bald men, two feet tall, wearing reversible thirty-four and thirty-six shorts for the most part, and bald women, two feet tall, wearing reversible dresses or pants suits bought from boutiques called Pocket Venus and Short Gals, while the earth turns into a desert littered with gold and silver wigs glinting in the relentless sunlight. Portentious isn't the word for it.

Most business language is not so evocative. It is simply wrong. Gulf Oil used to speak of "one of the most unique roadways ever built," which of course helped Gulf to be ready for what it so long claimed to be ready for—"Whatever the work there is to be done." TWA has long had it Amarillio, not Amarillo, Texas; B. Altman in New York advertises sweaters that are "definitly for a young junior"; Bergdorf Goodman makes it known that "an outstanding selection of luxurious furs are now available at tremendous reductions"; Cartier believes that a memorandum pad, a stationery holder, and a pencil cup make a triumverate; the Great Lakes Mink Association wrote a letter to a New York store, the Tailored Woman, referring to its "clientel," and the Tailored Woman was happy to print it in an advertisement, though I do not say that this is what caused the Tailored Woman to close down; the chain of men's stores, Broadstreet's, capitalizing on the growing interest in food, tried to sell some of its wares by spreading the word that "Good taste is creme sengelese soup in a mock turtleneck shirt from Broadstreet's," but the number of people in New York familiar with, or curious about, sengelese cooking must have been small, and even the later announcement, "We shrunk the prices on our premium men's stretch hose," did not keep Broadstreet's from disappearing from the New York scene. Hunting World, a New York shop, sells Ella Phant, "pride and joy of the Phant family," and says, "She's only 9″ tall, and every little people you know will love her and you will too." Perhaps that depends on the kind of little people you know. Every little people that some of us know probably would be more interested in the Selig Imperial Oval Sofa, advertised by the Selig Manufacturing Company of Leominster, Massachusetts, which noted that "an orgy of 18 pillows, all shapes and colors, make a self-contained environment." An orgy do a lot of other things also.

Business language takes many forms. Camaraderie: "Us Tareyton smokers would rather fight than switch." Pomposity: When Morgan Guaranty Trust announced that negotiable securities worth $13,000,000 were missing from its vaults, it said, "A thorough preliminary search for the securities has been made, and a further search is now being made." All it needed to say was, "We're looking for them"—if indeed it couldn't expect its distinguished clients to take for granted that it was looking.

Pseudo science: "You are about to try the most technologically advanced shaving edge you can buy. Wilkinson Sword, with a world-wide reputation for innovation, brings you still another advance in razor blade technology, the first third-generation stainless steel blade. First, a microscopically thin layer of pure chromium is applied to the finely ground and stropped edge. Then, another layer of a specially developed chromium compound is applied. This special layer of chromium compound adds extra qualities of hardness, durability and corrosion resistance. Finally, a thin polymer film is coated onto the edge. This coating allows the blade to glide smoothly and comfortably over your face." Shaving seems an inadequate employment for so distinguished a product of razor blade technology, but even technology cannot hold back the dawn, and the razor is going the way of the reaper and the cotton gin. We are now invited to use the Trac-2 shaving system, which apparently is to the razor as the weapons system is to the bow and arrow. Much more of this might make you want to use the first third-generation stainless steel blade, or even the Trac-2, to slit your throat.

Stainless steel I may not be, but I was the first third-generation American in my family, on either trac, to hear life jackets carried on airliners referred to as articles of comfort. It was on a flight from London to New York in 1966, and the stewardess began her little lecture by saying, "Because of our interest in your comfort, we will now demonstrate your life jackets." It was a wonderful notion, classifying the gadget to be used after a plane has gone down in the North Atlantic as part of the comfort of flying. Euphemistic business language can go no further. Only calling used cars pre-owned has, in my experience, equaled it.

The life jacket incident might have appealed to the novelist Evelyn Waugh. Waugh hated the modern world and wished that he had been born two or three centuries sooner, and he hated modern devices of transport and communication such as the automobile, which he refused to drive, and the airplane (about which more later), and the typewriter and the telephone, both of which he refused to use. This attitude was sometimes inconvenient. A new and lucrative British literary prize was about to be awarded at the time I met him, and he had some hope of getting it, and every time the telephone rang he had to wait for whichever member of the household was willing to have truck with it to tell him whether the hoped-for call had come. It never did.

In any case, in 1956 I made a short film with Waugh, for NBC, about the way he lived and the way he worked. I learned, among other things, that he wrote with a quill pen and professed to believe that American reporters could not function without frequent infusions of whisky and that all Americans had been dye-vorced (his pronunciation) at least once.

We did the filming at his house—actually, it was a house provided by his father-in-law—in Stinchcombe, Gloucestershire. He had there a number of paintings he had collected, including a series of four called *The Pleasures of Travel.* Three were nineteenth-century paintings about the various discomforts of going by stagecoach, ship, and train. The fourth, which Waugh himself had commissioned, showed an airliner with a wing on fire. The passengers had been having breakfast, and they and their orange juice were being thrown all over the cabin as the aircraft plunged to destruction.

The other members of the NBC crew and I were frequent air travelers, and we all laughed hollowly for Waugh's benefit, as I also laughed hollowly on hearing the life jacket described as an article of comfort.

When we left at the end of the day a couple of us asked

Waugh to autograph books of his that we had brought along. I had *Officers and Gentlemen,* which had just come out. Waugh, who clearly had never taken a course in psychodynamic salesmanship or human engineering, made an ungracious remark about people who received free copies of books. I said that I had bought mine. He then wrote on the flyleaf, "To Edwin Newman (who bought it!)," and below that, "Souvenir of Stinchcombe," with his name and the date. I was unable to make out Souvenir and asked him what it was.

"Souvenir," he said. "That's French for remembrance."

Remembrance, with its touch of sentiment, is the kind of word much used in the women's beauty industry, which employs the most complex of the business tongues. Consider the following:

"The poets talk about lips that are warm, soft and moist.

"Most cosmetic ads talk about lips that are Ravishing Red or Pizzicato Pink.

"We think women ought to pay more attention to the poets than to the ads.

"That's why Germaine Monteil created Acti-Vita Emollient Lipstick."

Now take Princess Marcella Borghese, who promised an iridescent gloss of pearlized blushing color in Apricot Shimmer, Copper Shimmer, and Rose Shimmer. A woman's crowning glory is known to be her iridescent pearlized copper shimmer gloss, but this lacks the artful combination of moods and suggestions of Germaine Monteil—love (warm, soft, and moist) and the laboratory (Acti-Vita Emollient), seduction and science, the rapturous and the pharmaceutical.

The women's clothing industry also must tempt and reassure at the same time:

"Some of us just can't jump into those clingy new clothes and come off looking like they were made for us. We need the right kind of help in the right kind of places." The help is provided by a body briefer from Natural Smoothie. It is a garment in direct conflict with the principle of the legitimacy of multiple body styles, referred to earlier, but there are also multiple style styles.

Advertising aimed at women must of course keep up with the drive for equal rights. In the 1930s and 1940s the only acceptable female response to a cigar was an infatuation crossing over into insanity with the man who smoked one. Later, a woman sitting next to the man she loved—loved, as already noted, because he smoked cigars—was permitted to drool and simper because she wanted a stogie herself, and at a time when there was no national consensus on whether a gentleman should offer a Tiparillo to a lady.

Soon thereafter the Cigar Institute, which studies these things, estimated that there were sixty thousand female cigar smokers in the United States, many of whom belonged to cigar-smoking clubs in which they sat around and puffed away and, one supposes, cursed Fidel Castro. The latest estimate of those for whom having a cigarette of their own now, baby, and coming a long, long way is not enough is more than five hundred thousand. And the president of the Cigar Institute of America, presumably for esthetic reasons, has come out against women smoking in the street, and not a moment too soon.

For other advertisers the best approach is the most direct. Thus Mitchum Anti-Perspirant's "Plan tonight to sweat less tomorrow." A corporate decision probably had to be made at the highest level not to say perspire, just as somebody must have authorized Winston cigarettes to taste good like rather than as, and somebody in a command role at Eastern Airlines, eyes teary with gratitude, must have said an eager "Yes" to "You gotta believe." That is how civilization moves ahead, through the pioneering of the visionary and the brave.

The national preoccupation with fetid armpits—and the profits therefrom; it's a $475,000,000-a-year business—suggest that had the product been available at the time, the Minutemen at Lexington and Concord and the other heroes of the American Revolution would have kept their antiperspirant, like their powder, dry, and that when the village smith's brow was wet with honest sweat, it was only because he was a boor and didn't mind offending others. With such an outlook Winston Churchill, who after all had an American mother, might have said, "I have nothing to offer but blood, toil, tears and antiperspirant."

The precursor of antiperspirants was Lifebuoy Soap, which shielded those who used it from B.O., which stood for Body Odor and was so dreadful an affliction that it has been spoken of only in initials, like V.D. and TB. It threatened the well-being of the nation at the same time that a number of manifestations of osis did. These were halitosis, which was fearlessly translated as bad breath; lordosis, too large a bottom, curable by corset; homitosis, which was bad taste in home furnishing; and gaposis, which meant that your clothes didn't fit as well or adjust as they should have because they did not have a certain brand of zipper. It had nothing to do with the dollar gap, and the credibility gap, and all of the other gaps that came along in various connections later on.

The nation survived B.O. and halitosis and such later dangers as tattletale gray, denture breath, morning mouth, unsightly bulge, and ring around the collar, only to find itself still, anticlimactically, perspiring.

When business turns its attention from customers to shareholders, the change in tone is drastic. Customers must be tempted and/or bullied; shareholders must be impressed and intimidated, wherefore the annual corporate reports. Something like six or seven thousand of these are issued every year, but the language is so nearly uniform that they may all be written by a single team, as paperback pornographic novels are written wholesale in porno novel factories. (I was about to say sweatshops, but I assume that for reasons already made clear, the sweatshop either is no more or exists only where perverseness bordering on un-Americanism lingers on.)

In the pornos, what counts is the detailed description of sexual enterprise. In corporate reports it is growth, which at the very least should be significant, and with any luck at all will be substantial. The ultimate for growth is to be dynamic. Whether it is, and whether it occurs at all, depends largely on growth opportunities; if they occur often enough, a consistent growth pattern may be achieved, brought about, perhaps, by an upward impetus that makes things move not merely fast but at an accelerated rate.

No company can grow, of course, without having a growth potential. To realize that potential, the company must have capabilities: overall capabilities, systems capabilities, flexible capabilities, possibly nuclear services capabilities, generating capabilities, environmental control capabilities, predictability capabilities. If all of these are what they should be, and the company's vitality, viability, and critical reliability are what *they* should be, the growth potential will be realized, and profitability should result.

There are, however, other factors that must mesh. Outlooks, solutions, and systems must be sophisticated, or, if possible, highly sophisticated or optimal. Innovative products are requisite; they, in turn, are the consequence of innovative leadership that keeps its eye firmly on target areas, on inputs and outputs, on components and segments and configurations. Innovative leadership does this because capabilities are interrelated so that requirements, unwatched, may burgeon. For example, after a corporation has identified the objective of getting a new facility into start-up, environmental-impact reporting requirements must be met so that the facility can go on-stream within the envisaged time-span.

Even this tells only the bare bones of the story. Multiple markets and multi-target areas may well be penetrated, but not without impact studies, market strategies, cost economies, product development and product packaging, and consumer acceptance. Product packaging sounds simple enough, but it may call for in-house box-making capability. Box-making in turn is a process; that calls for process equipment capability; and *that* calls for process development personnel.

If all this is to be done, management teams must be sound and prudent and characterized by vision, enterprise, and flexibility. In a surprising number of companies, the corporate reports assure us, management teams are.

Business puts enormous pressure on language as most of us

have known it. Under this pressure, triple and quadruple phrases come into being—high retention characteristics, process knowledge rate development, anti-dilutive common stock equivalents. Under this pressure also, adjectives become adverbs; nouns become adjectives; prepositions disappear; compounds abound.

In its report on 1972, American Buildings Company told its shareholders that its new products included "improved long-span and architectural panel configurations which enhance appearance and improve weatherability." Despite the travail concealed behind those simple words, the achievement must have been noteworthy on the cutting edge of the construction industry.

A statement by the Allegheny Power System was, on the other hand, hardly worth making: "In the last analysis the former, or front-end, process seems the more desirable because the latter, or back-end, process is likely to create its own environmental problems." This is an old story, for the front-end process often does not know what the back-end process is doing.

In its annual report for 1972, Continental Hair Products drove home two lessons. One was that "Depreciation and amortization of property, plant and equipment are provided on the straight-line and double declining balance methods at various rates calculated to extinguish the book values of the respective assets over their estimated useful lives."

Among Continental's shareholders, one suspects, sentimentalists still quixotically opposed to the extinguishing of book values may have forborne to cheer. But not the others, and they must have been roused to still greater enthusiasm by the outburst of corporate ecstasy which was the second point: "Continental has exercised a dynamic posture by first establishing a professional marketing program and utilizing that base to penetrate multi-markets."

For myself, looking at this array of horrors, I forbear to cheer. People are forever quoting Benjamin Franklin, coming out of the Constitutional Convention in 1787, being asked what kind of government the Convention was giving the country, and replying, "A republic—if you can keep it." We were also given a language, and there is a competition in throwing it away. Business is in the competition and doing nicely. In its favor, however, one must note that business lags far behind the leader in throwing away the language we were bequeathed. The leader, moving confidently and without strain, is the social sciences. It is in the social sciences that the true language viability destruction-generating capacity lies.

In the summer and fall of 1951 I worked for three months in Greece for the Marshall Plan, under which the United States helped to bring about economic recovery in Western Europe after the Second World War by providing billions of dollars of assistance in money, capital equipment, and technical advice. My job was to write stories about what was being accomplished in Greece, with the hope that these would be published in American newspapers, a hope only skimpily realized.

The resources of American social science were sometimes called in to help, and I remember seeing a report on how to reach the Turkish peasant, it being thought that this might help us to reach the Greek. The Turkish peasant had no radio (television was not yet a factor), he could not read, and he had no access to moving-picture theaters. The solution, arrived at after research and analysis, and possibly amid cries of "Eureka," was a van that would carry information films, a projector, and a screen on which to show them.

In Greece, an American university's applied social science research team examined the way opinion was formed in the villages and brought forth a concept and three subcategories. The team found that the priest, the schoolteacher, and the mayor were usually the only ones in the village who could read, and designated them opinion leaders. The rest of the population was designated opinion followers. However, the taverna in each village usually had a radio, to which people listened, and the taverna proprietor had the power to switch the radio on and off and to twirl the dial. Taverna owners were therefore designated opinion controllers.

That was one of my early experiences with academic jargon.

There have been many since, including, most recently, a series of surveys of cultural trends said to be transforming the American work ethic. The surveys found that those people most likely to be dissatisfied with their work were "By and large . . . those under 35, those who have high expectations of what their jobs will offer and those who seek psychological rewards from their jobs." The full implications of this finding, that those who wanted and expected most felt the greatest disappointment, may not be understood for some time.

The ability to use jargon is learned at an increasingly early age. From February 23 to 27, 1974, an organization called the National Student Lobby held its third annual conference. It took place at the Thomas Circle–Ramada Inn in Washington, D. C., and it seems to have been pretty much a prearranged affair, to judge by a press release received a few days before it began.

"Students To Site Grievances at National Conference," the press release was headed, thereby suggesting that the students in the National Students Lobby might be wise to lobby for courses in spelling if, as appears, it is not part of their curriculums. The alternative was to believe that these were grievances gathered from their usual locations, roughly midway between the liberal arts faculty parking lot and the Office of Course Relevance Certification, and placed so as to remain stationary at the Thomas Circle–Ramada Inn for some time to come. Students' grievances are not very cheerful to have around, but the Thomas Circle–Ramada Inn probably had no convention groups due in later that needed space for grievances of their own.

The same press release had Arthur Rodbell, executive director of NSL, saying, "A unique feature of this year's conference will consist of 'role playing' sessions in which six members of Congress will participate.

"In the first phase of these sessions," the press release went on, "students will practice their lobbying techniques on these Congresspersons, who will assume their normal roles. During the second phase, the members will switch roles: students will assume the Congressperson's role and the Congressperson's that of the students."

The press release then went back to quoting Rodbell: " 'This will help prepare the students for actual lobbying in pursuant days on Capitol Hill,' Rodbell commented."

After noting that the apostrophe in the second Congressperson's above has no business there and would go on having none even in pursuant days, one supposes that the students doing genuine lobbying in pursuant days would stay away from the congresspersons they were practicing with, since these congresspersons would surely spot the rehearsed techniques and discount them.

In pursuant days in New York City, where grievances are often sited, the objection was made by a union official that some Spanish-speaking school principals chosen by community boards could barely read or write English. The chancellor of the city's schools, Irving Anker, rose to the occasion with a notable example of candor and concrete expression. Among "some of the new supervisors," he said, "there may be a lesser demonstration of formal academic standards."

At about the same time, a letter arrived on my desk from the director of the Office of Information Services at Dartmouth College that offered a greater demonstration of formal academic standards. I have no wish to embarrass Dartmouth College, assuming that to be possible, but the letter is representative of much of the language coming out of academe these days, and something must be done to try to stop it. The director wrote about a press conference that was to be held to announce the results of a two-year study by nine eastern private universities and colleges of the financing of higher education. The nine institutions were described as a "diverse leadership group of schools" forming themselves into an "on-going consortium" as a by-product of the study.

A summary of the report and a press release were enclosed for my "prior background information," and I was told that the report contained "arresting conclusions of almost watershed quality," but no "easy panaceas," or hard ones either, I suppose. The letter concluded, "Looking forward to hopefully seeing you."

There may be something in the air in New England. In June, 1974, Hampshire College in South Amherst, Massachusetts, graduated its first class. The plans for the college were set out in December, 1966, as a "working paper," and so far as I know, the language has never been equaled. These were some of the positions taken: that social structure should optimally be the consonant patterned expression of culture; that higher education is enmeshed in a congeries of social and political change; that the field of the humanities suffers from a surfeit of leeching, its blood drawn out by verbalism, explication of text, Alexandrian scholiasticism, and the exquisite preciosities and pretentiousness of contemporary literary criticism; that a formal curriculum of acadamic substance and sequence should not be expected to contain mirabilia which will bring all the educative ends of the college to pass, and that any formal curriculum should contain a high frangibility factor; that the College hopes that the Hampshire student will have kept within him news of Hampshire's belief that individual man's honorable choice is not between immolation in a senseless society or withdrawal into the autarchic self but instead trusts that his studies and experience in the College will confirm for him the choice that only education allows: detachment and skill enough to know, engagement enough to feel, and concern enough to act, with self and society in productive interplay, separate and together; that an overzealous independence reduces linguistics to a kind of cryptographic taxonomy of linguistic forms, and that the conjoining of other disciplines and traditional linguistics becomes most crucial as problems of meaning are faced in natural language; and that the College expects its students to wrestle most with questions of the human condition, which are, What does it mean to be human? How can men become more human? What are human beings for?

Readers are encouraged to turn back and read that again. I'll be happy to wait before pushing on to the bluff and earthier Middle West.

I once made a speech under the auspices of the Educational Facilities Center in Chicago, an organization dedicated to improving teaching in primary schools, junior high schools, and high schools. From the program of the meeting I drew the following:

"Overview." What one of the speakers was offering.

"Authored." What one of the speakers had done to a book. If authored, why not authoring? Why not, "He playwrighted a play," and "She paintered a picture"?

"Select the sessions of your choice," in preference, apparently, to selecting the sessions of somebody else's.

Also:

"She is a member of a Junior High Humanities Team which employs an interdisciplinary process approach to education."

"Probed in this session will be what goes on between the teacher and child, showing the relativeness of communication skills."

"Participants will explore the concepts of communication, expressive arts and language skills, the technique of individualizing, and the place of language arts in the developmental stages of a total person. Dr. DuFault" (Nap DuFault, principal of Westmont High School, Westmont, Illinois, and professor of education at Illinois Benedictine College) "will treat both the philosophical as well as the practical day-to-day needs of preparing students for power through communications."

We may ignore the minor error in grammar in "both the philosophical as well as the practical." We may acknowledge— I certainly do, from what I saw—that these are good, worthy, and devoted people engaged in valuable work. I have no reason to doubt that this is true at Dartmouth and the other eight diverse leadership institutions as well. They do, however, reflect influences brought to bear on them for at least a couple of decades, and they are influential themselves. They have helped to carry us into a world in which speaking and writing have become communication skills, in which on-going consortia work out interdisciplinary approaches and people look forward to hopefully seeing each other, and in which the module is all. It is a world in which things that are good for society are positive externalities and things that are bad are negative externalities, in which unemployment is classified as an adverse social consequence, in which subjects are listed under rubrics rather than headings, rationing becomes end-use allocation, stressful situations arise in the nuclear or matrifocal family, and people in minigroups or, if the shoe fits, maxigroups are in a state of cognitive inertia because self-actualization is lacking.

The Committee for the Future, Inc., which describes itself as a non-profit, tax-exempt educational organization, proclaims that its purpose "is to discover, articulate and bring new options for a positive future into the arena of public discussion for action." When, as part of its process of public participation and planning, known as synergistic convergence, it brings together "leaders and pioneers—builders of new options for humanity," it serves them conviviality at seven o'clock and dinner at eight. Dinner is an old option, and so is conviviality, but in a new guise:

> In some secluded rendezvous,
> That overlooks the avenue,
> With someone sharing a delightful chat
> Of this and that,
> And conviviality for two.

I think it may be better to grunt unintelligibly than to use such language, for it is so impersonal and manufactured as to be almost inhuman. Not that there is any mystery about why it is used. Social science jargon is tempting because it sounds weighty, important, rather like the policeman's "I observed the perpetrator," followed, all being well, by "I apprehended the perpetrator." The Iowa chapter of the National Agri-Marketing Association recently called my attention to Iowa Agriculture Day. The letter was signed by the chairman of its Media-Awareness Committee. The jargon is catching, too. I work with a man who ordinarily speaks well and plainly, and sometimes with passion. When a program brought in letters from the State Department and two United States senators, he wrote me that we had achieved "penetration of significant audience strata."

At that, penetration of significant audience strata was child's play compared with what was recently visited on parents of children in the lower grades of the public schools in Dallas. Instead of report cards, they received coded reports, and to help them understand the code, a manual, twenty-eight pages long, called "Terminal Behavior Objectives for Continuous Progression Modules in Early Childhood Education." Later, a local advertising man was hired to simplify the manual and make it shorter.

A large part of social scientific practice consists of taking clear ideas and making them opaque. Carl W. Hale and Joe Walters showed their peer group the way in "Appalachian Regional Development and the Distribution of Highway Benefits": "It is thus probable that . . . highway development expenditures will conform de facto to the efficiency criterion, and will have their greatest initial impact on the periphery of Appalachia, where the more viable growth centers are located." Which is to say, money to build highways in Appalachia probably will be spent where it will do the most good, and at first in the growing towns on the edge of the region.

Lee Rainwater was quoted by Daniel P. Moynihan, a member of his peer group, in *On Understanding Poverty:* "The social ontogeny of each generation recapitulates the social phylogeny of Negroes in the New World *because the basic socioeconomic position of the group has not changed in a direction favorable to successful achievement in terms of conventional norms.*" Or each generation of American Negroes, like its predecessors, makes less money than whites.

For a social scientist to make obscure what he considers to be unnecessarily clear calls not so much for an imagination as for an appropriate vocabulary in which boundaries are parameters, parts are components, things are not equal but co-equal, signs are indicators, and causes are dependent or exogenous variables (and it may take a regression analysis to find out which).

To know oneself is to have self-awareness, communities being studied are target areas, thinking is conceptualization, patterns are configurations, and people do not speak but articulate or verbalize; nor are they injured: they are traumatized.

The jargon may, on rare occasions, take on a vigorous flavor, so that you hear of imperatives and of dynamic hypotheses. Usually, however, the words are leaden—archetypal, misspecification, disaggregates.

Once you've caught on to the technique, it's easy. For example, in the social sciences as in business language, inputs and outputs are everywhere. You do it this way: In a school, textbooks and students and faculty-student ratios are inputs; so are chalk and basketballs. Good citizenship and reading scores are outputs.

You can move on quickly to more complex constructions. Siblings are conflicted in their interpersonal relationships means that children of the same parent or parents don't like each other. Exogenous variables form the causal linkage that explains the poverty impact, the behavior modification, and the intergroup dissonance in the target area means that outside factors cause the poverty and the changes in people that lead to trouble in the neighborhood. A recommendation by a medical ethicist that a physician obtain an input from the patient's own value system means that the patient should be asked whether he wants the treatment.

These are, I confess, pushovers, and they leave us with healthy reserves, including the two all-purpose whizbangs, role reversal and interstitial. Versatile as these are, they should not be squandered. Role reversal and interstitial should be used when nothing else is available and the situation is desperate.

Luckily for those who give money to the various claimants (an act known as funding; with foundation offices in the buildings that tower over the harbor, New York is the Bay of Funding), there is a certain comity in the social sciences. Suppose, however, that the money ran short and the various centers and institutes saw their existence endangered? All would refuse to self-destruct and a great jurisdictional dispute would set in

over the precious lifeblood that enables all of them to measure
cumulative impact, which, next to things coming together in the
state known as inter, is the greatest problem facing society today.
Who would win, among the centers and institutes, the academies,
projects and programs for Contemporary Problems, Society,
Ethics, and the Life Sciences, Mental Health Research, Behavior
Modification, Study of Democratic Institutions, Study of the
Person, Child Study, Interracial Justice, Faith and Order, Critical Choices, Policy Alternatives, Policy Research, Human Relations, Inter-American Relations, and the rest?

Some might make a better case than others, but suppose they
all said they wanted to set up ongoing ad hoc mechanisms for
option assessment and constructive and creative response? Suppose they all wanted to draft programmatic proposals that could
later be implemented on the basis of a meaningful ethos able to
supply definitive answers to fundamental value questions and
identify dangerous fallout? Suppose—the ultimate horror—they
all claimed not only the same set of concerns but the same constituency within which an informed dialogue would resonate?
What price cross-fertilization at the interface then?

One thinks of priceless bits of natural eloquence, remembered for years. There was the boy in the West Indies who offered
me a shoeshine. I said no thanks. "All right," said he, a resourceful salesman, "how about a dus' off?"

I remember the concern of a porter in a New York apartment
building about a pothole in the street. "A person," he said, "could
break their bot' arms."

My own father, when he could tolerate his school-age sons
no longer, would fire a warning shot across our bows. "I'll hit
you so hard," he would say, "you won't know where it came
from." As a behavioral psychologist would say, it provided reinforcement.

On the other hand, Abraham Lincoln was on the side of the
social scientists when he said, "God must have loved the people of
lower and middle socio-economic status, because he made such a
multiplicity of them."

6

Is Your Team Hungry Enough, Coach?

Meaning no disrespect, I suppose there is, if not general rejoicing, at least a sense of relief when the football season ends. It's a long season.

I have an additional reason for watching football fade out without much regret. That reason is a protective interest in the English language. The phrase "pretty good," as in "He hit him pretty good," and "We stopped them pretty good," and "He moves pretty good for a big man," gets worked out pretty good from late September to mid-January. After which it should be given a pretty good rest, or allowed to rest pretty good, or at any rate left to basketball, where they hit the backboards pretty good.

Basketball, of course, cannot be played without referees, and generally they do the officiating pretty good, but not always. Said K. C. Jones, coach of the Capital Bullets of the NBA, explaining why he would not comment on the officiating in a play-off game against New York: "No sense in risking a $2,000 fine. To hell with it. They read the papers pretty good for our remarks."

After basketball, baseball. Al Downing of the Los Angeles Dodgers, who threw home run number 715 to Henry Aaron: "I was trying to get it down to him, but I didn't and he hit it good —as he would. When he first hit it, I didn't think it might be going. But like a great hitter, when he picks his pitch, chances are he's going to hit it pretty good."

Pretty good has its final flowering in football on the Sunday of the Superbowl, when opinion is likely to be general that one reason the winners beat the losers was that they stopped their running game pretty good. The losers might have been able to make up for this even though they were hurting pretty good, meaning that some of their players were injured, if they had got their passing game going pretty good, but they didn't, and that was that: the winners were the world champions.

When the majestic ocean liner the *QE 2* tossed gently in the balmy Atlantic, her engines dead, early in April, 1974, a number of American football players and coaches were aboard, showing films and giving chalk talks as part of the entertainment. One was Hank Stram, coach of the Kansas City Chiefs. Stram told a reporter that after emergency repairs the ship had "moved along pretty good" for thirty minutes. It is necessary to stay in shape during the off-season.

At the 1974 Superbowl, Pat Summerall, in search of a more analytical explanation, attributed the success of the Miami Dolphins' defense to their having "so many different variations," leaving us to suppose that the Minnesota Vikings' defense failed because their variations were uniform. Ray Scott, working with Summerall, told us that Larry Csonka "apparently is injured around his one eye." He may have had Csonka confused with the legendary fullback Cyclops, who helped the Giants defeat the Titans but, unlike Csonka, never played on a world championship team.

World champions—there's another point. Are they really? They are the champions of the National Football League, but they have not played any teams in other leagues. No doubt they could beat them—the others are minor leagues, after all—but that still would not make them world champions. American football is not played in other countries, and it is a little hard to be world champion in a game that is played in your country only. It is as though a Siamese claimed to be world champion in boxing Thai-style, or a Scotsman claimed to be world champion in tossing the caber. World championships require some international competition, and in American-style football there isn't any.

The same is true of the baseball World Series. It may be a series, but it is grandiose to speak of the world. Perhaps it is a harmless conceit, but the American and National leagues do not represent the world, even with two divisions each and a team in Montreal.

The teams aren't usually very good, either. In these days talent is spread so thin by expansion that some players doing regular duty swagger up to the plate with .189 batting averages and nobody thinks there is anything untoward about it. These players are often said to have a way of coming through with timely hits. When you're batting .189, any hit you get is likely to be timely.

Still, whether the World Series is played is determined not by the quality of the teams but by the annual occurrence of October, and again, whatever the quality of the teams, the series must end in seven games or less, which is the sports-page version of seven games or fewer. Equally inescapable is the pre-series analysis, in which the experts, paid and unpaid, compare the opposing sides, weigh their strengths and weaknesses, evaluate their physical condition, take note of the weather, calculate which side has more of that magical substance, momentum, and point out that the breaks can nullify any advantage, that anything can happen in a short series, and that you still have to win them one at a time.*

---

* In boxing there is a rough equivalent of this: They both only got two hands.

In this arcane atmosphere you may find yourself reading an explanation of why, although Team A's first baseman hits better with men on than Team B's does, Team B's first baseman has more rbis. The explanation is that the man with more rbis (runs batted in, or ribbies to the cognoscenti) had more chances to bat in runs because he came up fourth in the order whereas the other came up sixth. However, the man who batted sixth might have done better had he been allowed to bat in the cleanup position, and indeed he wanted to but allowed himself to be placed in the sixth position for the higher good of the team and an interest-free loan from the club owner.

Even for the most knowing, comparisons are difficult in a time when a manager may platoon left field with four players of different sizes, depending on the height of the outfield grass, but once the experts' analyses are complete, they interview the managers. The answers are purely ritualistic, but nobody minds. It is part of the great fall classic. I will omit the questions and give only the answers.

"Getting runs home is the name of the game, and my boys have shown all year that they can get the runs home."

"Pitching is the name of the game, and we have the pitching."

"I think our rookies will do pretty good."

"I think our veterans will do pretty good. Their records speak for themselves."

"The double play is the name of the game, and our guys can really turn it over."

"Hustle is the name of the game, and nobody is going to outhustle us."

"Pride is the name of the game, and we didn't come this far to lose."

"Kirilenko closed with a rush this season and got his average up to .219, and I look for some real power hitting from him."

"Frelinghuysen has good speed and good power. But we think we can handle him."

"Yes, I think so." (I'd better give the question here. It was "Do you think you can put it all together?")

Putting it all together was identified as the key to success a few years ago, and it has swept all other explanations before it. When the series has ended, it accounts for one team's coming out with the right to fly the championship flag while the other does not. Many things go into putting it all together: pitchers reach back and give it everything they've got; infielders go skyward after errant throws; pivot men in twin killings elude sliding runners (nobody has come up with a synonym for slide); outfielders swing potent bats and scamper to the farthermost barrier to haul in arching blasts, while on the side that did not put it all together outfielders also scamper to the farthermost barrier to haul in arching blasts but swing once-potent bats, now shackled; bloopers barely escape desperate grasps; balls are deposited in the distant seats; heady days of glory are relived; speed on the base paths pays off; somebody trots out his assortment of breaking pitches, to his opponents' almost total frustration; and it is found once more that there is no substitute for the high hard one when the high hard one is needed. And, when starters get into trouble, relief pitchers warm up and the announcers tell us, "There is activity in the bullpen." Ogden Nash once wrote a poem about a relief pitcher named MacTivity so that he could say, "There is MacTivity in the bullpen."

The interview before the World Series closely resembles the spring training season interview. Again it is a two-character affair. The sports writer is named Buck and the manager is named Al. Buck's first question is, "Well, Al, how do you think you'll do this year?" Al is not thrown by this. He says, "Well, I think we'll do pretty good. I think we'll do all right."

Buck follows that up like a hawk. He says, a shade aggressively, "Well, are you predicting the pennant, Al?" Al replies that well, they won it last year, and the other teams are going to have to beat them. He knows one thing: they are not going to beat themselves.

The interview has been under way for about a minute at this point, and nobody has said anything about the name of the game. This is now remedied. Buck asks Al where he thinks his main strength lies, and Al replies that scoring runs is the name of the game and his boys can get the runs home. Buck then says that some people think pitching is the name of the game, and Al says it is, it is, and he thinks his pitchers will do pretty good, but he still has one outstanding need, a reliever who can go at top speed for a full inning without tiring. He has such a man on the roster, a Cuban named Felix Miguel Arbanzas Lopez y Puesto, a real flame thrower, but there is some question about Castro's letting him out and the FBI's letting him in.

Buck asks about right field, normally occupied by High Pockets Kirilenko, a somewhat moody player who (as we know) closed with a rush last season and got his average up to .219. Al says that Kirilenko has good speed and good power, but because of that big .219 average Kirilenko is holding out for a share of the concession revenue, a commitment by the club owner to cover any losses he may sustain on his investments in the stock market, and the services of a hairdresser before each game.

If High Pockets doesn't get in line, Al will try the French Canadian rookie, Willie LaBatt. LaBatt has been up before, but he really shattered the fences in the Australian Instructional League over the winter, and he may be ready. Al also has hopes for his new first baseman, Cy (The Eel) Lamprey, who should be a ballplayer because he grew up in the shadow of Ebbets Field. In fact, Lamprey was lost briefly under the debris when they tore it down, but they dug him out and he looks pretty good.

The team will, however, miss second baseman Ron Larrabee, who had so much range to his left that he crashed into the first-base stands going after a grounder and broke his shoulder at a crucial juncture of last year's pennant race. Larrabee is therefore hobbled by injuries and not yet ready.

The interview is approaching its climax. Soon fielding is the name of the game, and so is base running. Buck's last question is whether pride isn't really the name of the game, and whether Al, who has pride, can communicate it to his players. Al replies that if he didn't think he could, he wouldn't be there, and while you never know in baseball, his team has a real good shot. Buck says, "You better believe it," and there, to the regret of all, the interview ends.

There is an alternative ending, more appropriate in some cases—for example, in Al's, since his team made it into the series last year. It is:

"Is your team hungry enough, Al?"

"I don't think a team can ever be hungry enough."

Regional differences in speech are easily accommodated by this last exchange:

"Is your team hongry enough, coach?"

"I don't think a team can ever be hongry enough."

In the closing days of the 1973 baseball season, I watched on television a game between the Pittsburgh Pirates and the Montreal Expos that was delayed by rain several times and for a total of more than three hours. At one point the play-by-play announcer, Jim Simpson, remarked that it was "raining pretty good." He must have been embarrassed because he immediately added, "It's raining pretty hard."

There is no way to measure the destructive effect of sports broadcasting on ordinary American English, but it must be considerable. In the early days sports broadcasting was done, with occasional exceptions such as Clem McCarthy, by non-experts, announcers. Their knowledge of the sports they described varied, but their English was generally of a high order. If they could not tell you much about the inside of the game they were covering, at any rate what they did tell you you could understand.

Then came the experts, which is to say the former athletes. They could tell you a great deal about the inside, but—again with some exceptions—not in a comprehensible way. They knew the terms the athletes themselves used, and for a while that added color to the broadcasts. But the inside terms were few, and the nonathlete announcers allowed themselves to be hemmed in by them—"He got good wood on that one," "He got the big jump," "He really challenged him on that one," "They're high on him," "They came to play," "He's really got the good hands," and "That has to be," as in "That has to be the best game Oakland ever played."

The effect is deadening, on the enjoyment to be had from watching sports on television or reading about them, and, since sports make up so large a part of American life and do so much to set its tone, on the language we see and hear around us.

There is one sports announcer who does not go where the former athletes lead him. That is Howard Cosell. Cosell is a phenomenon, or as some have it, phenomena. Nothing can shake him away from his own bromides, of which the supply is unquenchable. Cosell can range from a relative paucity ("Despite the relative paucity of scoring . . .") to a veritable plethora (Let's continue on this point of this veritable plethora of field goals") without drawing a breath, and there is every reason to believe that when he says "relative paucity" and "veritable plethora" he is not kidding; he means it.

Only Cosell would have described the mood of the crowd at the Bobby Riggs–Billie Jean King match as "an admixture" or remarked that for Riggs "It has not been a comedic night." Only Cosell would speak of a football team "procuring a first down," or say that a fighter was "plagued by minutiae," or that the cards of the referee and judges, made public after each round in a fight in Quebec, "vivified" the problem facing the fighter who was behind. During a Monday night football game nobody else would say, "The Redskins have had two scoring opportunities and failed to avail themselves both times," or that "The mist is drifting over the stadium like a description in a Thomas Hardy novel." At any rate, we may hope that nobody else would say it.

I am far from arguing that the language of athletes and former athletes never adds to the gaiety of the nation. Jake LaMotta, the old middleweight, interviewed long after his fighting days were over, told his questioner that he had no fear of the future because "I got too much growing for me." Another middleweight, Rocky Graziano, during his fighting days was pleased with his reception in the Middle West. He said, "They

trutt me right in Chicago." An old ballplayer, Joe Hauser, had
the same sort of genius. Near the end of his career, badly slowed
down, he was retired on what should have been a single to right.
He said with some bitterness, "They trun me out at first."

Joe Jacobs, manager of the German heavyweight Max
Schmeling in the 1930s, described his dreamlike condition when
a decision unexpectedly went against his man: "I was in a
transom." Before their first fight Joe Frazier said of Muhammad
Ali, "He don't phrase me," and was right on both counts, and
Ali spoke of not being "flustrated," which he rarely was. In one
of the disputes over rules at the 1972 Olympics, a United States
swimming coach spoke of signing "alphadavits." We would all
be poorer without this.

Mention of disputes over rules carries me back to the annual
fall classic. If a player is thumbed out, or given the heave-ho, by
an umpire, the precedent is more than a century and a quarter
old. This is on the authority of the New York Public Library,
which was inspired to do the research after I spoke on television
about the complaint by the former National League umpire
Jocko Conlan against abuse of umpires by players and fans.
Conlan wrote, "I don't understand why the fans boo an umpire.
I know a lot of it is humorous, and it's part of the game, and the
American way and all that. But why is it? Who started booing
the umpire and calling him a blind bat and saying, 'Kill the
ump!' "

The library could not answer the question directly, but it
did find out that the first player to be disciplined by an umpire
was named Davis, and that he swore at the umpire and was
fined six cents. This unpleasantness took place as soon as
humanly possible, in the first game between organized teams, the
New York Knickerbockers and the New York Club, on June 19,
1846. The scene was the Elysian Fields in Hoboken, New Jersey.

I look for the Boston Braves, or as they are also called, the
Philadelphia Athletics, to take this year's fall classic in six.

Although I have spent a fair part of my life in Britain, British
sports, unlike American sports, are of little interest to me. I am

impressed by the sustained violence of rugby, and I can appreciate that cricket calls in a greater range of complexities than baseball does, but I think you have to grow up with a sport to have much feeling for it.

British sports writing, on the other hand, can be fascinating, for several reasons—the literary tradition, the naïveté, and the fact that the British almost never win anything in international competition, which means that the writers have to provide in the word the excitement that is missing in the deed.

I remember, for example, during the 1972 Olympics, a British expert describing a fight and saying of one of the fighters, "If he hits him hard again, he will be doing much better." Of another bout, the expert said that one of the boxers would be in trouble if he let the other man "get to him too often." These were what are now known as insightful remarks.

When the British champion Lynn Davies was eliminated from the Olympic long jump competition, the commentator explained that his last jump was of a kind that Davies "didn't really want to make." British commentators help their viewers to understand the situation in ways that Americans do not.

Similarly, during the 1500 meters, a British runner, Alan Foster, was lying fifth when the British commentator felt called upon to point out that Foster was "more aware than anyone of what he can do." The viewers must have found this good to know.

In one of the boxing finals, a Cuban against a Mexican, the commentator noted that the Cuban had defeated the British entry and was "now looking for similar success." Again the insight.

I went to Britain in 1949. I had not been there very long before there was a light-heavyweight fight between Joey Maxim of the United States and Freddie Mills of Britain. British sports writers showed great restraint. Only one wrote that it was a duel between the Maxim gun and the Mills bomb. He may, of course, have been the only one old enough to remember the weapons of the First World War.

This restraint fooled me, but I quickly learned that British sports writers could let themselves go, though in a way we would hardly expect.

The between-rounds man for the BBC in those days, radio days, was W. Barrington Dalby. He entered on the cue "Come in, Barry," and reached the peak of his career one night when he said that one of the fighters was "a better puncher qua puncher" than the other. So far as I know, this is the only time Latin has been invoked to explain the course of a fight.

It was at about the same time that a boxing writer for the *Daily Telegraph* wrote that one fighter's immense courage had enabled him "to give perhaps a quarter of a Roland for an Oliver." So far as I know, this is the only time the *Chanson de Roland* has been invoked to explain the course of a fight.

The Roland and Oliver swapping might have led one to believe that it was the *Telegraph* that was preeminent among British papers in having an Old World approach to sports. Not so. The *Times* of London is a paper that, in referring to a man who had been left more than £2,000,000, thought it a fair comment that he was "not unendowed with the world's goods," and it once remarked editorially that "to plunge into a third world war would not be the best means of defending peace." This style spilled over into the sports pages, making the *Times* preeminent. It has since lost some of the old flair, but preeminent it still is.

You will appreciate why I speak of the *Times*'s old flair when I quote its pre-game story on the All-England soccer final in 1951. It begins plainly enough: The King and Queen will be there, the match is between Arsenal and Liverpool, it will be played in Wembley Stadium, it is the sixty-ninth such final. With that, however, the *Times* man is off:

"The teams will be birds of a strange plumage, indeed— Arsenal in shirts of old gold and white trimmings; Liverpool in white with red facings. But the disguises will in no way cloak the simple fact that once more the ritual of a Cup Final will have been set in motion."

Having reassured those who might have thought that the

new colors meant that the Final would *not* be played, he continues:

"A crowd 100,000 strong will be ranged around the curving, elliptical basin of Wembley, its clear rim far up, cutting the sky. Yet beyond that, and beyond exact computation, some millions will be there in spirit, linked by radio and television with this scene; for the Cup Final, like the Derby, the Grand National, and the Boat Race, is a sporting event of national interest that draws a whole people together."

Letting fly an "alas"—knowing precisely when to let one fly is among the most highly specialized techniques in all British writing—the *Times* man yearns for "Kennington Oval, first home of the competition, where once the crowds, removing the horses from the shafts of Lord Kinnaird's carriage, drew the great man in his vehicle to the entrance of the pavilion for one of his nine appearances in the early finals."

He admits, though, that Wembley also has its points: exquisite velvet turf, community singing, the solemn moments of "Abide with Me," the feeling for ritual, the controlled excitement. "Seldom," he writes, "has an afternoon passed there without its full share of dramatic upheaval."

By this time, perhaps, the reader could not be blamed for losing the thread. This the *Times* man is able to sense.

"Into this atmosphere," he notes quickly, "now sharpened by a North v. South motif, will stride Arsenal, twice winners of the Cup, and Liverpool, who have yet to lay their hands on the trophy." Rather reluctantly, he then mentions the teams' records, their personnel and playing styles, and their chances.

I concluded that the man who wrote the story was about to retire and didn't care that he had left himself nothing for next year.

The *Times* golf correspondent was somewhat less spendthrift, but in the same vein:

"Walton Heath with a blue sky, a hot sun, and cooling northeasterly wind before which the young birches bowed their heads in their new green liveries—what better conditions could anyone desire for the watching of golf?" The question was rhetorical, and the story went on:

"This was the second day of the *Daily Mail* golf tournament, the end of which would see a sad chopping off of heads before the final two rounds on the third day."

Which heads were chopped off, which were not? Only the most pedestrian sports writer would tell. Instead: "As the hours wore on with comparatively few low scores, it seemed that Walton Heath had the better of the argument and the qualifying scores would be high."

Here there is a diversion to describe a round played by Alf Perry, and presently, in the thirty-third line, we are informed that Perry's two-round total was one forty-two, which gave him a two-stroke lead over Ward. On line 84—after a detour in which the *Times* golf correspondent remarks that Ossie Pickworth of Australia was the man he most wanted to see and that he was not disappointed—we are told that Pickworth came in with a seventy-three and was only one stroke behind Perry. A good writer makes you feel that you were present. The *Times* man makes you feel that you played the round, carrying the clubs yourself, with rocks in the bag.

It is, naturally, in cricket, which has produced a vast literature of its own, that the literary allusion flourishes. Thus the *Times* cricket correspondent from Sydney, Australia:

"Once more your messenger enters to report a setback. But not, be it noted, with the sickening self-satisfaction of his ancient Greek counterpart whose probably sole delight was to catch the King in a moment of rare happiness and to tell him with sadistic prolixity that his summer palace was burnt to the ground and that his mother, in whose continued existence the King still fondly believed, was even now crossing the River Styx, then to leave the bemused monarch to the beard-waggings and breast-beatings of an ancient and admonitory chorus.

"No, the chorus will be controlled. But the King will recover, perhaps within the week. He has done so before. In short, our cricketers out here are like many fighters of repute. They

need to be knocked down first. It is partly a matter of tempera-
ment. Their performance against Queensland just before the
first Test match was too bad to be real. It is hoped by Australian
as well as English spectators that the same may be true of their
current performance at Sydney. After two days of play, M.C.C.,
with three batsmen gone, are still 479 runs behind an Australian
eleven's total."

That, of course, is cricket. Could a boxing writer hope to
measure up to that standard? Probably not. Still:

"Hopes and fears were nicely balanced in the chief contest
at Harringay last night, with rather less intense feeling intermit-
tently aroused by the efforts of the novices engaged in a heavyweight competition."

So! The novices engaged in a heavyweight competition
aroused only moderately intense feeling. Let us carry on:

"The interest in the two chief bouts also was nicely divided,
though, in the titular sense, it was clearly more important that
Terry Allen, the Islington flyweight, should win a world championship recently given up by Rinty Monaghan than that Danny
O'Sullivan, the bantam champion of Great Britain, should
acquire a European title as well."

Having brushed aside O'Sullivan's feelings in the matter,
probably biased, the *Times* man has established the relative
values of the two bouts. He continues:

"Both were confronted by sufficiently formidable foreign
boxers, and Allen's opponent, Honoré Pratesi of France, had
once outpointed him over ten rounds." Now he looses the dull
fact: "This time, in a tiring rather than punishing fight, Allen
won, and deserved to do so, on points."

This information digested, what of O'Sullivan? Granted that
it was not so important for him to win, we might nonetheless be
given a clue. That is not the way. There must be first a strictly
chronological account of the Allen-Pratesi bout, covering five
hundred and seventy-five words. Then:

"The fight between Danny O'Sullivan and Luis Romero of
Spain, a southpaw with a devastating punch in either hand, had

a hair-raising start. It remained hair-raising to round 13, when Romero was declared the winner." After three hundred words of another round-by-round account, there are two lines for the novices engaged in a heavyweight competition mentioned in what I would once have been unimaginative enough to refer to as the lead.

The main lesson to be learned from British sports writing in those days, two and more decades ago, was to suppress any inclination to unseemly haste. Here is a last example of how it is done, drawn from the *Sunday Times,* which was then unconnected, except in spirit, with the other *Times*:

"It being impossible even in this age of speed to be in two places at the same time, I devoted part of a perfect Saturday afternoon to the White City, and part to the Chiswick stadium.

"At the former," the story goes on, "the first London Caledonian games ever held in London provided food for all tastes. I confess with shame that I have never yet seen a Highland games meeting on its native heath. I intend to remedy the deficiency at the earliest opportunity. There was a most impressive opening ceremony, which did not seem in the least out of place, and the 'call to the gathering' made spectator, dancer, official and athlete alike feel that they were sharing in a common spectacle."

Three more paragraphs—equally absorbing—follow, and then it comes: "Later in the afternoon, E. MacDonald Bailey won the 220 yards in 21.1 seconds. If this time were to be recognized, which is unlikely, it would beat by one-tenth of a second the British record made by W. R. Applegarth in 1914."

It is hard to resist the feeling that Bailey should be ashamed of himself for intruding. Getting that reaction from one's readers was, in those days, the ideal for which to strive.

All of that came, as noted, in the early 1950s. It has changed since then, but not entirely. I remember a Wimbledon in the middle 1950s in which the *Times's* tennis man wrote of Frank Sedgman of Australia that he "bestrode the court like a colossus." One might hesitate to use such language about a tennis match, but a dozen years later there was this, about the South African, Barry Moore: "Moore, on the other hand, kept his head under his long fair locks, sideburns and mustachio that spoke of flower power and a psychedelic. Certainly it was he who gave the heartstrings a wrench of all the young female interflora on the sidelines. It was he who produced the squeaks of joy. And it was this energetic mind of his and an ability to change his tactics that pulled him through the final set when service was broken five times in seven games to leave the match in disorder."

The British seem so detached and serene to us that their true feelings often go unnoticed. In the days of austerity after the Second World War, when it seemed that economic recovery would never be achieved, nothing lifted British spirits as much as Randolph Turpin winning the middleweight championship from Sugar Ray Robinson. It was understandable in the circumstances, but for years now the national mood has been set for weeks at a time by the success or failure of Britain's footballers in the World Cup, and you can actually hear such an exchange as this:

INTERVIEWER: Could England fail to qualify for the World Cup?

EXPERT: It is treason to talk of England failing to qualify for the World Cup.

At the Olympics, the yearning for a British victory mingles with the remnants of a colonialist attitude, so that a French high jumper may be described as "a dark-skinned little man," or a Kenyan is said, patronizingly, to have "dignity on the track and in conversation," and there are references to "Japs," "great white hopes," and "the blacks who run for America."

In its purest form, British chauvinism expresses itself in a desire for Britain to win something. Anything. Thus the 10,000 meters in the 1972 Olympics, with the British commentator screaming about the British runner David Bedford, "The eyes of the world are on this man!" and the statement in the early stages, "The whole field, one suspects, is waiting for Bedford to make his move." When the race was over and Bedford, having had an off day, had come in twelfth, the commentator said, "Hmm. That was a curious run by Bedford. He never really made a positive move."

Pickings were so thin for the British in 1972 that a BBC commentator, otherwise bereft, spoke of one of the marathon runners this way: "Though he was born in Barrow-in-Furness, he is running for Australia, to which he emigrated. But if he does well, he'll give us some reflected glory."

Came the last day and one of the riding events, in which the British rider, Ann Moore, after doing poorly at the early fences, improved markedly. The commentator was beside himself: "Look at that—a great comeback by Ann Moore. That is what the Olympics are all about!"

This is reminiscent of a bit of folklorish nonsense in which the British sometimes indulge, when they say of an athlete that he is a Yorkshireman, i.e., dour, and therefore doesn't like to lose. We are left to believe that to athletes from other counties, not so dour, defeat is less unwelcome.

Inevitably, it is cricket that reveals the British at their most characteristic, for the game itself gives us the myths and legends and usages made concrete—the calm, the understatement, the greenness, the rules and rituals that in a larger context make it possible for so many people to live so close together without habitual mayhem and murder, and, finally, the clear understanding of what is "not cricket."

In British football, which we call soccer, a player kicking the skin or flesh off the legs of an opponent, or otherwise assaulting him, or using foul language to the referee, will "have his name taken." That carries an implicit threat of expulsion if the offense is repeated. In cricket it is not necessary to go that far. If a bowler is delivering the ball in such a way that it might well maim the batsman if it hit him, the umpire will "have a word with him."

Cricket also reveals the British sports writers at their most British. The cricket correspondent of the *Times* wrote not long ago that he had seen very poor performances by some players. "I will not name names this time," he added, "but if it should unfortunately become necessary, next time I will." Someone else's play, he wrote on another occasion when he did name names, "should be spoken of only in whispers."

One day in the summer of 1973 a BBC commentator remarked that a batsman had made an "abysmal" stroke. One of his colleagues became uncomfortable about it, and a discussion ensued over whether abysmal was justified. Eventually it was withdrawn and replaced by "indifferent," and no questions were asked in Parliament.

Indifferent is a useful word. It may be applied to what batsmen do, what bowlers do, and what fielders do. It strikes a suitably restrained note, providing condemnation without contumely, just as the crowd will often find the appropriate reaction to what is happening on the field in "a ripple of applause." There are some powerful hitters in cricket and some fiercely aggressive fast bowlers, but Britain is a moderate, temperate country in which a man captured by the police and about to be charged with the most appalling crimes is officially stated to be "helping the police with their inquiries." Cricket is a game to match. You rarely hear of a bowler helped by a strong wind. It is more seemly for him to have—and much more likely that he will have—"a slight breeze at his back."

In any case, superlatives are usually reserved for the weather. A glorious day is a day on which there is no downpour or steady drizzle.* A great day's cricket is a day on which the cricket has been exciting. This is not an easy thing to explain. A captain's innings (the captain is the playing manager) may not sound like a superlative but is meant to be, describing a situation in which a team's batsmen have failed to make runs and the captain,

---

* Fog may also be a problem, and is a greater one in football, which is played in the winter. During the football season you used to be able to count on seeing photographs of goalies peering anxiously out from the goal mouth, trying to make out what was happening downfield in the fog. The British have been cleaning their air, and these photographs are no longer so common.

when his turn comes in the order, scores well and saves the day. This may also be known as a real captain's innings. If the captain comes in and does poorly, it is not known as a captain's innings. This also is not an easy thing to explain.

I said earlier that cricket shows the British, and British sports writers, at their most characteristic. When cricket spread to Australia the attitude went with it. The following are excerpts from a column written by an Australian cricket correspondent after the Australian team's tour of Britain in 1972:

"As an old cricketer, I am a bit of a fogey when it comes to the privacy of dressing rooms, which belong exclusively to the players, and I have purposely not stayed at the same hotels as the Australians. If players on a tour as long as this want to let their hair down occasionally, they are entitled to do so in privacy and it would be more than odd if fit-to-busting young athletes did not want to go on the rampage occasionally with a few drinks and songs.

"Cricketers of any country are not parlour saints. The Australians did not emerge with flying colors from Scotland and Northampton. They were careless in their approach to both games and at Northants apparently offended the shop steward of the waitresses by helping themselves to cheese and biscuits.

"Manager Ray Steel, a splendid manager with discipline but no stuffiness, dressed them down in no uncertain terms over their playing approach. He did not mention the cheese and biscuits.

"My hackles rise when I think they are criticized unfairly and it often strikes me as odd how the bare one or two, who were possibly no plaster saints on the field themselves, are so eager to dip their pens in vitriol against Australians. You would think we are not of the same stock.

"Once again, I say I am proud of these young Australians, even if they do not ask for the biscuits and cheese to be passed."

But as I learned early from W. Barrington Dalby, British sports writers do go in for colorful writing of the more familiar kind. When Muhammad Ali fought the British heavyweight

Brian London in August, 1966, London was so inept that he aroused speculation about how he filled in his income tax form when he came to the blank for "occupation." The writers did considerably better than London, however. Some of them attributed the outcome to Ali's "killer punch," never seen before and not seen since, and the *Sunday Mirror* man gave forth this: "The 32-year-old bulldog was a dumbfounded spaniel at the finish."

There was no doubt that the thirty-two-year-old bulldog was knocked down, or at any rate had lost his balance. Most of the American writers at ringside preferred to be charitable and let slide the question of whether he could have continued. The British saw it in sterner terms. One had London "pawing impotently at the bottom rope like a man who had taken an overdose of sleeping pills." Another had him lying on his back, glassy-eyed. Still another wrote that London had been battered unconscious. One paper, a Socialist organ that earlier had been backward enough to refer to London as a white hope, used the headline, "London Is Blitzed!" Understandably, none went so far as to resuscitate "London Can Take It."

In the Ali-London fight, of course, the writers wanted to believe that Ali was an irresistible, even superhuman force. It helped the story. In other circumstances they react with less emotion and merely sigh and admit their mistakes. Thus the boxing correspondent of the *Times* of London on September 27, 1972: "I have never wished more deeply that I could have made a wrong prediction to the result of a boxing contest than last night at the Empire Pool, Wembley, when Bob Foster of the United States retained his world light-heavyweight title by knocking out Britain's champion, Chris Finnegan, after 55 seconds of the 14th round."

That was the sigh. Now the admission:

"I had just said confidently to a steward of the British Boxing Board of Control, I don't believe in Foster's right, when the American promptly struck home with a right and Finnegan was down on his back, carefully taking a count of eight, after looking for instructions from his corner before he arose."

This is candid enough, but I am not certain that the *Times* boxing correspondent is entirely trustworthy. He once wrote, after an unsatisfactory bout, that he had heard "cries from ringside spectators of 'rubbish' and 'now bring on the phantom raspberry blower.' " "Rubbish," yes, but "bring on the phantom raspberry blower"? Even in a nation of eccentrics, that defies acceptance.

British boxing writers probably deserve sympathy more than scorn. Historically, especially among the heavyweights, they have had to make do with very little. That is why every time Muhammad Ali fights they report that he was once knocked down by Henry Cooper, the former British champion. That is why, when Ali fought Jerry Quarry for the second time, the British announcer describing the fight for the BBC said almost disbelievingly that Ali was "toying with Quarry, toying with the man who knocked out Jack Bodell!" Jack Bodell had become British heavyweight champion two months before meeting Quarry in November, 1971, and was dispatched by Quarry in 1:14 of the first round, and then a month later by Manuel Urtain of Spain in 1:41 of the second round, after which he lost to Danny McAlinden of Great Britain, after which he retired.

Jack Bodell! The mind boggles.

Britain today is a very different country from what it was when I saw it for the first time in 1949. And yet—and yet—

"When Liverpool, the favourites, and Newcastle United, the unpredictable, meet at Wembley this afternoon they could fashion a Cup Final of raw endeavour and spirit. It might be elemental: lightning on the field and thunder rolling down the terraces from the dwellers of Merseyside and Tyneside as two great clubs and two deep rivers join headlong in open challenge.

"Emotion rather than any rich vein of skill may dominate the occasion, with victory in the end claimed by patience and the steadier nerves. A year ago the stadium shifted dramatically on its axis as Sunderland overcame all the odds to take the prize north-east at the expense of the powerful Leeds United."

That is from the *Times* of London, May 4, 1974.

The terraces down which thunder rolls are parts of all British football stadiums, areas where the admission price is low and there are no seats: everybody stands. Some of those on the terraces are rowdy to the point of violence, and in a game in Manchester in April, 1974, thousands of them burst out onto the field and caused the match to be cut short. I heard a soccer correspondent explain that this kind of behavior was not peculiar to big cities like Manchester. It was, he said, the same in Weymouth, mutatis mutandis.

Mutatis and mutandis are bosom companions of those with classical educations; so long as British sports writers use them, we will know that Britain's literary tradition abides. When the sports writers say mutatis mutandiswise, we will know that the past is dead.

7

Soup as What the Chef Made

I have a small reputation as a gourmet. It is undeserved, as will appear, but at a time of a boom in cookbooks it has led to my receiving a fair number of requests for my favorite recipe, if possible accompanied by an anecdote. The requests come from people who say they are putting together books of recipes by celebrities that are guaranteed not to bring on gangrene or the pip, and who would like to have one from me.

The reputation led on one occasion to my being invited to address a luncheon at which awards were being given for the outstanding cookbooks of the year. I don't remember which books won, but among the entries that remained in the memory were *Mazel Tov Y'all*, a peculiarly graceful mingling of languages that sounded like the salutation of a southern politician seeking votes in the Catskills, and *The Pedernales Country Cookbook*, a book conceived of before President Johnson decided he would not run again but published afterward, by which time it had hardly more appeal than a study of the musical tastes of Calvin

Coolidge. There was also *The "I Married an Italian" Cookbook*, by Bette Scaloni, who must have been terribly chagrined when she realized what she had done. I hope that at least it was hard cover and profusely illustrated.

So far as my qualifications as a cook go, I, like a lot of other men, lean to complicated recipes. Our cookery is based on the theory that the more ingredients a dish has, the better it is likely to be, so that any dish with sour cream, wine, the outer leaves of a head of lettuce, lemon juice, onion juice (what a job that is!), green pepper, monosodium glutamate, flour, curry powder, and dry mustard added to almost anything must have a stirring effect on those who eat it. The longer it takes, the better. Recipes that call for cooking over a period of days—"Allow the stew to simmer on top of the stove for 48 hours, stirring frequently"—are ideal. All this is still more the case if you use a lot of herbs. Men have faith in herbs. When I see them floating at the top of the pot, or flecking a chop, I know that success will soon be mine. Men also tend to make a lot of spaghetti, more than anybody can eat, especially at the beginning of their cooking careers.

I had two friends in college who were too poor for spaghetti and who made a dish using barley. They had no idea how much to cook and wound up depositing the surplus in brown paper bags on the doorsteps of people they didn't like.

But about the requests for recipes: I obliged only once, with a recipe for steak topped with a latticework of anchovies hugging—that's a cookery word, hugging—slices of olives stuffed with pimientos, and herb butter made with three herbs for the necessary excess. Magnifique! I wish I could remember its name. The other requests I declined because the reputation was cheaply won. It came about when I found myself living in Britain during the period of austerity after the Second World War, when greengrocers put out signs saying "Plums for All" and newspapers ran scare headlines like "Threat to Your Christmas Fruit and Nuts." Those were days when anybody whose gastronomic horizons went beyond cabbage, brussels sprouts, and cod was called a gourmet.

Not that I regret that time. It was rich in experience. I remember asking the flavor of the ice cream listed on the menu and being told, "Why, no flavor, sir," which turned out to be correct. And the waitress who, when asked for oil to put on hors d'oeuvres, replied, "The only oil we have at the moment, sir, is the oil we cook the chips in, and it's already been used, so it wouldn't be good." Or the waiter who, recommending rice pilaf, generously explained, "It isn't an English dish, sir, but it is very good." Or the waiter on the train between London and Penzance who, when asked what kind of soup was available, did not say, as tradition required, either that it was thick or that it was thin. He replied instead, "Soup as what the chef made."

Things were pretty bad in those days, as you will appreciate from the fact that newspapers printed recipes for carrot and turnip pie and for a dish called fadge, which I will not go into further, and from the fact that a line of frozen food was sold under the catchy name "Frood." This naturally had its effect on the confidence of the British, and even the food advertisements sounded intimidated. I remember a green pea boasting that it was "first choice for second vegetable."

It has changed greatly now, of course. London is a good place for food and drink, and has been for years. This has much to do with the foreign influence. (I don't mean that Britain is entirely transformed. My daughter went into an English restaurant not long ago, and she and her companion asked whether they might have some wine. The proprietor looked at them with annoyance. "We don't do ween and all that tackle," he said.) It might be added also that the British unduly handicap themselves with the names they apply to some foods—bloaters, pilchards, scrag end, bubble-and-squeak, toad-in-the-hole, nosh, fry-up, faggots, roly-poly pudding, stodge, black pudding, spotted dog. These things would not be acceptable even if decked out in slavering American menu prose. I inserted three of them in a TWA menu encountered on a transatlantic flight:

BRAISED SCRAG END BOURGEOISE

A classic dish. The scrag end is slowly simmered in a rich stock of natural juices accentuated by a bouquet of fines herbes, small onions, and spices. Served with Château Potatoes and honey-glazed carrots.

GRILLED STODGE CUMBERLAND

From the broiler we present a generous portion of succulent stodge topped with Hawaiian pineapple ring and sprinkles of orange rind. Enhanced with a tangy red currant Cumberland Sauce and accompanied by Duchess Potatoes and a fluffy Broccoli Soufflé.

BLOATER SAINT HUBERT

This French creation was a favorite of Saint Hubert, Patron of the Hunters. In preparing this dish, tender young bloater is cooked slowly in a zesty tomato sauce with white wine, shallots, and mushrooms. We serve it with Parslied Potatoes and Mixed Vegetables.

We have foreign influence in the United States, too, as may be seen from the free use of the word gourmet, which the dictionary defines as a connoisseur in eating and drinking, an epicure. A noun, in other words, which is used more frequently, in the United States, as an adjective. For example, foods that used to be known as delicacies, and which you would get at the delicatessen or fancy grocery, are now known as gourmet foods, and you get them at a gourmet store. Recently I saw a package of gourmet blintzes. I don't think that the blintz sees itself in that way. Maybe it could team up with knish lorraine. The two of them might go on the menu of an Israeli hotel in Jerusalem where gefilte fish came out carpe farçie traditionelle.

This use of the word gourmet is part of the increasing popularity of foreign words and phrases that are imperfectly understood, and you never know what you are going to run into when you enter a restaurant these days. I have come upon "restauranteurs" serving such exotic items as chicken soup a la raine; eminced chicken tetrazzini; lobster frad dabolo; o'grattan potatoes—made, one supposes, from an old Irish recipe; filet de mignon, perhaps from the opera by Ambroise Thomas; broiled filet of sole armandine, served, I imagine, with thin slices of the nut called the armand; bristling sardines, which may have been angry at being packed in that way; and for dessert, cake du jour. Some Americans think you can turn English words to French by adding an e, so that you have caramel custarde, and fruite, but cake needs stronger measures.

Similar to cake du jour in the way it weds two languages is the dish "eggs andalouse." A French restaurant on Forty-eighth Street in New York went that one better. It came out with eggs andalouise. I thought about this for a long time and concluded that the chef spoke with an Italian accent. One day a restaurant, or gourmet, correspondent asked him for the secret of this marvelous dish, and he replied that he got it from his Aunta Louise.

At another restaurant I was offered salaud de tomates, canapé d'anchovies, and egg in gélée, and invited to choose wine from a charto de vino. It reminded me of the liquor store in New York that proclaimed that it was selling wine of a fabulose vintage. And the place that called itself a saloon de thé.

A French restaurant in New York, or at any rate a restaurant with a French name, posts a menu du dinner. Quite by chance, it is not far from L'Embassy Coiffure and a drugstore that lists among the perfumes it sells Rêve Gauche.

The Loggia of the Polo Lounge of the Beverly Hills Hotel in Los Angeles mentions coffee, tea, and milk under breuvages, which is ancient French and possibly survives only in Beverly Hills (Les Collines Beverly). But the Loggia comes unstuck over coconut with a cocoanut milk mousse, and serves lucious apple slices with its Dutch apple pancake.

A restaurant on the roof of a Los Angeles office building offers Chef's Specials du Jour, and another establishment lists Beef French Dip, thoughtfully giving us the recipe: "Choice thin sliced beef, dipped in au jus. Set on a French roll." And wheeled in on an a la carte.

Another New York restaurant says it has "a complete salad and antipasto table, where you can help yourself to as much as you'd like as a compliment to your meal." The night I was there I helped myself to only a little, because there was some question about whether my meal deserved a compliment, but I did send my supplements to the chef.

Language is so misused, English as well as foreign tongues, that I sometimes think of asking for my steak media rare. Perhaps those of us who are troubled by these developments would be better off staying at home. We would miss the complementary hors d'oeuvres but we could, after all, avoid menu misspellings by having our egg's benedict and bar-ba-qued chicken at home.

My job does not permit this. It calls for much travel. That is how it came about that a visit to Lincoln, Nebraska, produced a restaurant that offered Maderia wine and quoted Louis Pasteur to the effect that wine was the most healthful and hygenic of beverages. Not surprisingly the restaurant served, if it said so itself, Food Supérbo. Said food defied pronunciation, if not eating. Another establishment, a block away, listed on its menu the Italianoburger, which was a hamburger on an English muffin with mozzarella cheese and pizza sauce. Why was the English muffin left out of the title?

As long as I'm complaining—and my friends say that as long as I am awake I am complaining, which isn't true because in November, 1963, I covered the first annual International Banana Festival in Fulton, Kentucky, banana rail-transshipment capital of the United States, and saw a one-ton banana pudding being made, in a plexiglass container, of bananas, custard, and ginger snaps, and did not say an untoward word—as long as I'm complaining, I will go on with my theory about how 98 percent of the members of the waiters' union became waiters. It was because they couldn't remember the jobs they originally wanted to get.

I say this in memory of the old, passé assumption that waiters in a restaurant would remember what the customers ordered. Waiters whose memories were unreliable wrote down the orders and did it in such a way that they connected the items in question with those who asked for them.

No more. The art of waiting has undergone a transformation, and its language has shrunk almost to nothing. If a waiter is new to this country, there is little for him to learn. He is taught to say, "Who gets the?" and then the names of the items on the menu after, or, if you prefer, subsequent to, "Who gets the?" With that, he is qualified. Not long ago I was in a group of five in a well-known New York restaurant. One person in the group ordered dessert, only one, and there was conversation between this person and the waiter about what it was to be. Nobody else took part in the conversation. One minute and forty-five seconds later the waiter reappeared with the single dessert. "Who," he asked triumphantly, "gets the sherbet?"

I cannot say with assurance that American restaurant food would be better if the spelling on menus were better or the waiters more conversant with their calling. But it would give diners more confidence, it would lend novelty to restaurant-going, and it *might* improve the cooking.

I have never been invited to address a luncheon at which awards were being given for the outstanding sex manuals of the year, but the language is much the same. Sex manuals are described as gourmet guides to lovemaking; as with cookbooks, consumer satisfaction depends on following the instructions implicitly; and if *The Joy of Cooking* tells you how to be happy at mealtime, *The Joy of Sex* offers between-meals snacks. Sex books are now as explicit and detailed as cookbooks, and have photographs intended to lead to coition as surely as photographs of Enchaud de Porc à la Périgourdine and Daube de Veau à l'Estragon are intended to encourage gluttony.

A bedroom is now to be thought of as a sindrome. In these days of sophisticated contraception it need not be in a condominium, but it is not complete without an illuminated stand next to the bed. The sex manual is placed on the stand so that the instructions may be followed as the lovemakers work their way through the foreword, chapters, footnotes, appendices, and index.

Ingredients:
Man (according to taste)
Woman (according to taste)

Bed, king-sized if possible

Mirror on ceiling, and also on wall

Incense

Flying trapeze

Whip

Champagne and four-course meal to be served during intermission

Artillery fire and pealing of Moscow church bells in Tchaikowsky's *1812* Overture, cued to play at moment of climax

Tape recorder in form of phallic symbol into which participants may dictate their impressions as act proceeds.

Sexual fulfillment is becoming as compulsory as the gustatory kind. Civilization demands it, though in dining, if not in sex, the pleasure promised by the language employed exceeds any that is realized in fact. This is also true of travel. It may be especially true of travel:

"There's nothing ordinary in it because there's nothing ordinary about India. The dark eyes of gracious people. The highest mountains in the world. 5000 years of history in art and architecture. Temples. A tomb dedicated to love. Places and things out of the ordinary because they're in India."

"This season, why go south again? Head east. To the Soviet Union. Warm. Friendly. Hospitable. Come and celebrate the gala holiday season with us."

". . . the impeccable service of all-Italian personnel dedicated to your well-being and comfort, uncompromising quality and attention to detail. With it all, a spirited atmosphere that only a zestful Italian flair can achieve."

"Once, just once in your life. A long ocean cruise with Holland America. We think you deserve it. So we give you everything the unforgettable is made of."

"Give that cold, shivering body of yours a break. Escape the wrath of winter and come to a warm tropical island. To a delightful Holiday Inn resort, where all the comfort, conveniences, activities and fun-facilities are ready for your sun-drenched island adventure."

"This is not a tourist's cruise, bound for the long-exploited, over-exposed harbors. This is an explorer's voyage through little-traveled waters into unfamiliar ports—each one affording a new, exotic experience. Vividly contrasting with the super civilized life aboard the *Renaissance,* so French in its cuisine, its solicitous French service, its gaiety aboard ship, its continuous round of diversions above and below decks."

"Elegant dining, elegant night clubs, elegant beaches, elegant opera, elegant ballet, elegant race track. Elegant people—the in-people, the beautiful people. This cornucopia of elegance is spilling out to all who take advantage of VIASA's incredible $220 minimum to Caracas—to the city in the country in the Varibbean. To the most exciting tropical resort that's always been there but is only now being discovered."

"Meet the spirited, hospitable people in Golden PRAGUE. Wander through medieval settings beating with the pulse of modern life. Listen to the music of Anton Dvorak in his native land and stroll the footsteps of Franz Kafka through the cobblestoned streets of Josefov. Wine and dine in romantic BRATISLAVA on the blue Danube . . ."

It has long seemed to this cold and shivering body, dark-eyed, gracious, spirited, zestful, elegant, spirited and sun-drenched though it is, that tourism, even on cruises that are not tourist's cruises and are not bound for long-exploited, over-exposed harbors, is out of hand. Every spring and summer, all over the civilized world—which is to say those countries that are obliged to advertise themselves as tourist paradises because their own citizens can't bear them and insist on going abroad as soon as vacation time arrives—every spring and summer, millions of people prepare for the experience of a lifetime. The French go to Spain, the Spaniards go to France, the British go to Italy, the Italians to Britain, others cavort in Kafka's footsteps to the tune of a Slavonic dance; there is a vast amount of churning around, and there is enormous competition for going somewhere nobody you know has been. The way tourism is expanding, people will soon be paying for the privilege of a hike along the natural gas pipelines in the Algerian desert, or for exposing themselves to tropical diseases in the Matto Grosso.

The director-general of the Vatican museums recently wrote to the *Times* of London:

"We have installed 21 television cameras with centralized monitors to keep the traffic situation under control (we shall have 35 in a short time). We are using 18 'walkie-talkies' and highly trained attendants manning them, for securing prompt communications. Five spacious galleries have been equipped to keep visitors at a stand-by position until difficult situations clear up in front of them. A complete public address system is being installed to keep visitors informed and interested in the surroundings, with messages in five languages, while they have to wait. A busy control room is operating to secure the safe flow of our visitors and to decide exactly when and where it has to be slowed down or stopped and resumed."

It seems to me that this is a lot of trouble, and expensive, and for the tourist nations self-defeating, and that there should be some easier way to do it.

Luckily, such a way lies to hand. It is an invention called the travel simulator. Everybody knows about those training devices the airplane pilot gets into and which lead him to believe that he is flying when he has never left the ground. The travel simulator operates on the same principle.

The travel simulator is an area, preferably at an airport, so that tourists are not deprived of the actual pleasure of going *there*. It could also be at a town terminal or at a specially equipped center financed by travel agencies, airlines, luggage manufacturers, hotel chains, and others dependent on tourist revenue. Wherever it is, the tourist must first call the airline on which he is booked to inquire about the flight departure, and be thanked for calling that airline, as though, having booked on TWA, he would be calling Northwest.

As the tourist enters the simulation area, he is given a check list on which he indicates the travel experiences he would like to have. Late departure of plane? There is a waiting room where he can sit, which is overheated and where the background music cannot be turned off. Flight overbooked? Tourist bumped? That can be arranged, and he can stay in the waiting room that much longer. If a sea voyage is preferred, it is a short step from motel beds that give you a mild shaking ("restful massage") for a quarter to a bed that can simulate rough seas and malfunctioning stabilizers. The seagoing passenger may, of course, choose the equivalent of the airliner passenger's overbooked flight—a strike in port.

Those who enjoy having their luggage lost have only to ask. Then, after checking into the hotel in the simulation area, they have no clothes to change into. That is, if they do check into the hotel. The clerks may have no record of the booking, and no rooms even if they do.

There are restaurants in the area. Tourists who like them overpriced, with uncooperative waiters, where Americans are made to feel unwelcome, have only to mark their forms accordingly. Women traveling alone can be turned away or, grudgingly, seated by the swinging kitchen door. No extra charge.

Hotels in the simulation area are either unfinished or getting a new wing, with construction work beginning outside your window at seven in the morning. Travel fatigue can be induced, as can digestive trouble—the makers of Entero-Vioforme may well be willing to underwrite the cost of this—and difficulty with the customs can be arranged when you return. ("Just think! You can be searched for dope!") Thanks to the magic of multi-media presentations, tourists can be taken on all-day jaunts of which the high point is an hour-long visit to a glass-blowing factory, where it is quickly made clear that you are grinding the faces of the poor if you do not buy. That is in the morning. In the afternoon there is a visit to a perfume factory, where those who do not buy are quickly marked out as wanting to bring on the poverty and resentment from which flow crime, war, and revolution. Unpleasant travel companions, specially trained and always on call, are thrown in as part of the basic package, as are fluctuating and un-favorable rates of exchange. A devaluation of the dollar and refusal to accept dollar traveler's checks—it's only fair—are counted as an optional extra.

In brief, the travel simulator gives the tourist all the thrills of travel without his ever leaving the airport. It does, nonetheless, take time, and in view of the demand for the service that is likely to arise, there are plans to provide a short course. In this the whole business would be telescoped, and tourists would be able to buy slides and journals of MY TRIP attesting to typical but exotic experiences according to the kind of conversation they want to have when they get home ("Really mind-stretching," "Wild," "What a gyp," "Was I ever glad to get home," "We had a ball," "There was this very nice hotel," "They told me to take my win-ter coat but I didn't need it," "I just went crazy," "The waiters came out with this very big tray," "We had seen that before," "I just have gone crazy here for a week," "I don't know how they live the way prices are there"). These and many more they could claim as their own, thus leaving them at no conversational dis-advantage against those who have had the real thing, i.e., the full simulated trip.

Veterans in the field will be eager to supply such accounts for an appropriate fee. For example, in November, 1973, I spent a few days in Moscow. The door of my hotel room opened onto a flight of four steps, the top one of which had its center part gouged out; it was ideal for provoking a fall. The door opened inward, so that when you wanted to open it from the inside you had to climb the four steps, and then, as you opened the door, go back down. Just inside the door there was a light for a dress-ing alcove. To light the alcove it was necessary to climb the steps, then come back. The light was turned off the same way, of course. The alcove held two wooden cupboards for clothes. The drawers in the cupboards could not be used because the cupboard doors could not be opened because there was not enough room in the alcove. Properly embellished, an account of all this, punctuated by nearly uncontrolled laughter and expressions of disbelief, can go on almost indefinitely.

If shorter reminiscences of simpler discomforts are needed, there was the time in Warsaw that I cut and bruised my knee on the footboard of the bed while getting up from the desk (I fall to the floor, holding my sides, while telling this one), and the bed in Jerusalem that seemed to be made of locally quarried stone. The essential point about such reminiscences is that they should have no intrinsic interest. All the foregoing qualify.

The idea of the travel simulator was born when I happened to find in Rome a leaflet the United States Travel Service had put out. The leaflet said: "Discover a new world of gastronomy. Visit the United States." It said that it was not true that Americans lived on coffee for breakfast, martinis for lunch, and frozen foods for dinner. It also explained that while the pioneers had had to use what they could find and borrow dishes from the Indians, these concoctions had since been refined. Being an American leaflet, it naturally misspelled the Caesar in Caesar salad. But no matter.

The Travel Service identified eight cooking regions in the United States. They were Gli stati dell' Atlantico Centrale, the Middle Atlantic States; Il Centro Ovest, the Middle West; Il New England; La regione dei creoli, that being Louisiana; Le Hawaii; La Pennsylvania Dutch; Il Sud, the South; and L'Alaska. The Italians were also told about drug stores. They were told that drug stores had developed so that their original function of selling medicines had become secondary, and that it was possible to take meals in them in an ambience without pretense (un ambienta senza pretese), which was a gentle way of putting it.

I soon had a vision of a tourist going to I Stati Uniti, and specifically to Gli stati dell' Atlantico Centrale, and to its greatest city, New York. Suppose that he had resigned himself to having gallons of ice water and ice cream forced down his throat, while legions of strangers told him their life stories and gave him their philosophies, and to being clubbed on general principles by any member of New York's finest who happened to catch sight of him, and that in search of a gastronomic discovery he took a city bus as transport to a native eatery. New York City buses have signs in them asking for contributions to the Legal Aid Society, the Visiting Nurses Service, the Greater New York Fund, the Boys Clubs of America, the Catholic Youth Organization, the Young Men's Christian Association, the Federation of Jewish Charities—and also give to the college of your choice. A visitor might get the impression that we are in pretty awful shape if he rode a charity bus. But suppose he took an illness bus, the kind in which the signs ask for help to fight cancer, heart disease, multiple sclerosis, cerebral palsy, hemophilia, tuberculosis, mental retardation, and mental illness, among others. Afraid? Sick? Lonely? one sign asks. Christian Science Can Help.

New York is a vast sanitarium. Some buses used to carry signs that said one New Yorker in ten is mentally ill and needs help. Taken literally, from a pocket Italian-English dictionary, that could have been interpreted to mean that there is one chance in ten that your driver is a mental case. Now there is a new one: Rape Report Line. 233-3000. A policewoman will help you. The tourist's appetite for a scoperto gastronomico is not likely to survive this. Still another sign may well convince him that *he* will not survive:

> There's so much beauty in the blooming Rose
> And through its life, Who knows where it goes?
> Some Roses will live over a season through
> While others will enjoy part of the dew.
>
> But even Roses with all their splendor and heart
> Will one day their beautiful petals fall apart.
> Man too, has his season like the Rose
> And then, one day, he also must repose.

The sign is placed by Unity Funeral Chapels, Inc., whose slogan is, We Understand.

The simulator is better.

8

The Vicious
Cycle of
Reality

There are millions of people who groan when they hear a pun. It is a standard response, and my impression is that they are simply envious or bent on denying themselves one of the delights that language offers.

I make no apology for punning. I have been at it for a long time, and a small, if anonymous, place in history belongs to me because of a pun. In December, 1945, I called a speech on Soviet-American relations by Secretary of State James F. Byrnes "The Second Vandenberg Concerto" because of its similarity to a speech made by Senator Arthur Vandenberg a short time before. This is reproduced in Ambassador Charles Bohlen's book *Witness to History*, though without credit to me. At the time of its conception it was printed in a number of newspapers and magazines, attributed to "a press room wag." A good wag is hard to find.

Sometime in 1960 I put forward "Pompidou and Circumstance" to identify the conditions in which a French government might fall. *Time* used this before I could, presumably getting it from a wag of its own, and leaving me with no more chance of claiming it than someone would have trying to take credit for the incandescent lamp from Thomas A. Edison.

To repeat, I make no apology for punning, and specifically for what follows. I am proud of it.

"Where have you been?" she asked.

"Out walking the dog," he said. "Looking for the old familiar feces."

"Your shoes are wet," she observed.

"Naturally," he said. "Nobody knows the puddles I've seen. That is why I am standing on these newspapers. These are the *Times* that dry men's soles." He took off his jacket and tossed it aside. "This," he said, "is so sodden."

"I'll never forget the time they brought you in frozen stiff," she said. "I was afraid you'd never come out of it."

He shrugged. "I thawed, therefore I am."

"I believe that dog has distemper or worms or something," she said.

"Maybe so," he replied, "but his bark is worse than his blight. By the way, I'm thinking of giving him to the Longshoremen's Union as a mascot."

"What kind of dog do they want?"

"A dockshund."

"I'm lonely," she said, and pointed to a button she was wearing that bore the words "Kiss me. I'm Irish."

"I'm hungry," he said. "Quiche me. I'm French."

She gave him instead a pastry consisting of thin layers of puff paste interlaid with a cream filling. He cut off a corner and ate it.

"Very good," he said. "Also the first square mille feuille I've had all day."

"Your French is getting better," she said. "I can remember when you thought the French for throw out the bag was cul-de-sac."

"O solecism mio," he said. "And I can remember when you

thought a porte-cochere was the entrance to a Jewish restaurant."

There was a moment's pause. Then:

"I had an apprentice French hairdresser once," she said.

"What did he have to say for himself?"

"Je ne sais coif."

"Having a man around the house does make a vas deferens," she continued.

"And having a woman around, too," he said gallantly. "You're a wonderful housekeeper. You keep everything polished."

"Maybe so," she said, "but I wish I could chamois like my sister Kate. I meant to ask you, did you watch the space shot at the office?"

"No," he replied. "To me the space program is a mere schirrade. I decided to go to a movie instead, the one in which Montgomery Clift plays the founder of psychoanalysis."

"What was his name again?"

"Pretty Boy Freud."

"I notice that in the early days of photography he had his picture taken with his coat on and looking furtive. Any idea why?"

"He must have been a cloak and daguerrotype."

She changed the subject. "I am glad we're out of Vietnam."

"So am I. It was time to let Saigon be Saigon's."

"What do you make of the situation between the Russians and Chinese?" she asked.

"Dogma eat dogma."

"You said a Maothful."

"Tell me, how was your trip to Washington?"

"All right," she said, "but the taxi driver insisted on talking. I felt that I was a cabtive audience."

"What was it you had to do there?"

"Deliver two messages."

"To whom?" he asked.

"One was to the junior Senator from Mississippi."

"Any trouble?"

"No. I was directed to a room where the Armed Services

Committee was meeting, and I simply went in and asked, 'Stennis, anyone?' "

"What was the message, by the way?"

"Just what you'd wish any politician during the festive season: a Merry Charisma and a Happy New Year."

"And the other?" he asked.

"That was more difficult," she said. "The nonferrous metals industry was holding a meeting and I had to find the one ferrous metals man who was there. Luckily I was able to go into the ladies' room and say, 'Mirror, mirror, on the wall, who's the ferrous one of all?' "

"Any luck?" he asked.

"Oh, yes," she said.

"What did you do about lunch?" he wanted to know.

"I had Chinese," she said.

"Not Korean?"

"No, though I do like Seoul food."

"Was the Chinese any good?"

"Not really. I sent back the soup."

"Any reason?"

"I told the waiter it had been tried and found Won Ton."

"You've done better."

"When?"

"That cold day at the Four Seasons when you didn't like the cooking and you told the head waiter, 'Now is the winter of our discontent.' But what happened after you sent back the Won Ton?"

"They brought me some consommé."

"How was it?"

"Much better. It was a consommé devoutly to be wished."

"I'd like to have a Chinese meal in Alaska someday," he said musingly.

"Why is that?"

"I'd like to try lo mein on a totem pole."

She was lost in thought for a moment, then blushed lightly.

"I don't think I've ever told you that I originally intended to marry a clergyman."

"Why didn't you?"

"Because," she said, humming softly, "I picked a layman in the garden of love when I found you."

It was his turn to hum.

"What are you humming?" she asked.

"The volcano's torch song," he said. "Lava, come back to me."

She pouted.

"This time of year seems to bring out the worst in you," he said.

"I know," she replied. "I'm often jejune in January."

"Sometimes I think you've never got over your regret at not being born a blonde."

"Not quite true. Actually, I dream of genealogy with the light brown hair. Wasn't it a shame about Father O'Reilly being mugged the other night after the ecumenical meeting?"

"He can't say he wasn't warned. Rabbi Goldstein was most explicit."

"What did he say?"

"Do not go, gentile, into that good night."

"And that didn't stop Father O'Reilly?"

"I'm afraid not. He left without further adieu."

"I thought that Father O'Reilly was going to give up the Church. I thought he had decided he preferred law to religion."

"Just the opposite. He said he'd rather be rite than precedent."

"Do they know who did it?"

"No, but they do know that the muggers were young and were laughing as they left."

"Jubilant delinquents?"

"Exactly."

"If the case comes to court, will you be a witness?"

"No, though I may put in a friend of court brief."

"That hardly seems necessary."

"It isn't, but if I don't submit one, it may be said that I'm amicus curiae yellow."

"And if they don't catch them?"

"Well, honi soit qui nolle prosse."

"I have to tell you that we got word today that we are over-drawn."

"Bankers Thrust."

"In spite of which I intend to spend some money tonight to go to hear Gloria Steinem speak."

"Women's Glib," he said. "Tote that barge, lift that veil. But isn't it your night for tennis?"

"My racket is being repaired. One of the strings broke."

"A gut reaction."

"I bought a book of British seafood recipes today."

"May I guess at the title?"

"Please."

"What Hath Cod Wrought?"

"No. It's *Cod et Mon Droit.*"

"By the way, the cod war between Britain and Iceland did end, did it not?"

"Yes, it was followed by the cod peace."

"I spent some money, too," he said. "I got us ballet tickets for *Giselle.*"

"There *is* nothing like Adam."

"I'm always embarrassed at the way people fidget when they play 'The Star-Spangled Banner' before the curtain goes up. We should have learned long ago that a short anthem turneth away wrath."

"I'd rather go to a movie than the ballet."

"Any one in particular?"

"Yes, that western with the Old Testament background—*Armageddon for the Last Roundup.*"

"To go back to cookbooks, you do get some strange ones."

"What do you mean?"

"Well, there was *Kurds and Whey,* the only book ever put out by the Kurdish Publishing Company."

"I did get the publisher's name wrong."

"You've heard me mention my friend Bales, the chemist?"

"Yes."

"He's lost his job."

"Whatever for?"

"The company wanted him to work on acetates, and he refused."

"Because he who acetates is lost?"

"Precisely. Even worse, when he was asked to explain himself, all he would say was, 'I have no retort.' "

"Is he looking for another job?"

"He's thinking of going into advertising, but he's hesitating. He says he feels it would be crossing the Young and Rubicam."

A sweet voice came from the kitchen. "Would you like some tea, Daddy?"

"Yes, my darjeeling, daughter." He turned back. "She sounds so sad these days. You'd think a girl pretty enough to be a model would be happy."

"It's modeling that's done it. It's turning her into a mannequin-depressive."

The sweet voice rose in anger. "It isn't. It's these hot, cross puns. Will you two never stop?"

They did.

So will I, in spite of having a reserve that includes Pilat project, buying cigars from the Good Humidor man, détente saving time, Gdansk, ballerina, Gdansk as advice to a Polish girl unable to make it with the Bolshoi, a worried Dutch conductor with the Concernedgebrow, a Middle Eastern psychiatrist known as the shrink of Araby, and a Japanese robot functioning shakily because of a recent frontal robotomy.

All the foregoing puns were invented. Of what follows, only the framework was invented. Everything else was seen or heard by me. Truth is stranger than fiction.

I hark back to a day when my wife and I went to a nuptual mass. We were not in the best possible mood for it because we were tired of the up-evils of daily life. Although we had not yet reached our autumn, or reclining, years, we wanted a cover for our chaise lounge but had not been able to arrange it. The delivery people never seemed to do enough pre-planning and were always flaunting the public.

I recommended to my wife that she calm her nerves by having her hair style changed at Mercede's Beauty Salon, which had done outstandingly well the day she had had her picture taken at the Select Photo Studio's. She followed my suggestion.

After the nuptual mass, we went to a café where the background music consisted of Tchaikovsky's "Variations on a Rococco Theme." There we met another couple and there also we fell to admiring the figure of a girl at the next table.

"It is possible," the other woman at our table said, "for the rest of us to have a figure like hers. Take up fencing. I have just bought a book of fencing instructions." She thereupon produced the book, called *En Guarde,* which proved to be an insightful essay on the value of the sport.

The meeting soon became one of those social engagements that drag on. Tchaikovsky's music gave way to a composition by Hector Burlio, culture was at fervor pitch, and when the male half of the other couple pulled out his imperial old bruyer pipe and began smoking, it was easy to see that we were in for a long session of badgering words back and forth.

After a while he put the pipe down, which I welcomed because I was feeling quasi, and told us about a friend who had carved out a notch for himself and reaped a veritable bonzana from investing in a company that restored richly designed Chinese objects d'art. Unfortunately, the bonzana was followed by a hollowcast because his friend took to drink and contracted multiple cirrhosis.

Our friend's wife was just back from Europe. She told us how much she enjoyed eating spaghetti a la dente in Italy, sauerbratin in Germany, and vichysoir in Paris, where she also visited Napoleon's tomb in the Invalidays.

At this point, the waiter, who had perked up his ears, came over, but our friend, not hungry, merely ordered a Puerto Rican

Libre, austensible successor to the Cuba Libre. We all ordered something to drink, and a man in the corner, possibly an Asian provocateur, came over and asked us to join in a toast to the unconquerable spirit of Britain, as revealed in Westminister Abbey. We did, and after saying that he believed that Britain soon would rise to new platitudes of achievement, the man retired.

The bruyer pipe smoker at our table, strongly patriotic, said it would be beggaring the question to deny that the American defense build-up, conventional and nucular, had given the western alliance new and powerful strength, and if he guaged things correctly, this was what Western Europe in the last resource relied on. He did not, of course, wish to appear chargined, but he thought that things had not been right since the days when Charles de Gaulle mistakenly thought of himself as another Joan D. Arc, intent on filling his countrymen with spirit de corps.

After that, there seemed to be no reason to go on with this fol de roy. My wife and I decided to escape from the vicious cycle of reality by going to a performance by the English ballet troop from Covent Gardens. I would have preferred the Comédie François but it was not in town, and anyway, we had received the ballet tickets as a free bonus gift.

We went and enjoyed it, possibly because we are homogenous types and have a good rappaport. Neither of us behaves aggressibly and if one wants to do something, the other is usually successible. As a result, we are evolving toward a better adjustment vis-à-vis our environment. You never know, of course, but at any rate, up to the present junction.

Index

A CIVIL
TONGUE

Acknowledgments

I owe thanks not only to my wife and daughter, to whom this book is dedicated, but to Jeannette Hopkins, who was the editor; Carol Bok, who did the research; and Mary Heathcote, the copy editor; and to NBC News. Much of what I have written is based on information and experience that I have gained as an NBC correspondent.

I am grateful to *Esquire* and *Change* magazines for permission to use, in altered form, material that first appeared in their pages.

Contents

After I,
the Deluge

When I was a lad, I did not serve a term as office boy to an attorney's firm. It was one of a number of omissions. I did, however, work for a while as a file clerk in a credit agency. Since I was sixteen years old at the time and had been graduated from high school, I knew a great deal and had opinions on a variety of subjects that I thought anyone else in the office would consider it a privilege to hear. I also thought that I discerned flaws in the way the office was run. One fine day I was advised to keep a civil tongue in my head. That meant "Be respectful to your elders," or less gently interpreted, "Shut up." Although I did not know the word at the time (nobody did), I prioritized my interests, even as Jimmy Carter many years later suggested that the Democrats prioritize their platform. Having a job was more highly prioritized than not having a job. Shut up I did.

I now take a civil tongue to mean much more than that. Mere politeness is part of it, though the temptation to place mere before politeness ought to be resisted. The alternative to a code of conduct is, if not chaos, certainly confusion and embarrassment, and language is conduct. Not that I am arguing for freezing the language. I would hate to take American English out of a cryogenic compartment in a hundred years and find, after the ice is chipped away and the language has thawed, that it sounds as it does now. I think I would put it back in.

How *does* it sound now? It does not sound civil.

"It's not nice to be a child molester," says a Connecticut penologist, "but if you're a junkie, you can find all kinds of peer support." That is the kind of support everybody wants. When I walk into NBC News in the morning and see another correspondent, I say, "Good morning, peer." "Peer greetings to you," the other is likely, in peer-shaped tones, to reply.

A Puerto Rican scholar writes, "Our children currently have no viable role models to emulate." Heroes they would have been called not long ago. And heroines. But that is too straightforward:

"Father, I cannot tell a lie. With my little hatchet, I chopped down the cherry tree."

"I'm proud of you, George. I was saying to your mother only last week that one day our son will be a role model for generations of Americans yet unborn."

A New York specialty shop advertises items "for all the giftees on your June list." I hope it spreads to Scotland:

"Wha hae ye there, lass?"

"Tis a wee giftie for the giftee."

"Aye, would some power the giftee gie us . . ."

The Mayor of New York, Abraham Beame, emits a Bicentennial comment: "Where else but in an American democracy could a boy of the Lower East Side, born in London to parents fleeing Russian discrimination, grow up to be mayor of a pan-ethnic city?" The merry, merry pipes of pan-ethnicity, and the usual tune.

Scientists investigating spontaneous glucagon secretion in the immediate postnatal period study groups of infants cross-sectionally and longitudinally. Cross-sectionally should not alarm anyone: it means at the same age. Longitudinally means as they grow older. A man is put in jail in Dubuque, Iowa. It isn't called the jail any longer; it's the law enforcement center. Time is served there longitudinally. When the soil-collecting scoop on Viking I on Mars fails to function, an anomaly team goes to work to set it right. No hits, no runs, no anomalies.

Washington churns out its usual nonsense. The chief of the United States Capitol Police posts a notice: "Vehicles will be parked chronologically as they enter the lot" (1975 models in this corner and 1973 models over there). The Undersecretary of the Treasury, Edwin H. Yeo III, is asked about additional loans to New York City: "If we find the reasonable probability of repayment is slipping away from us, then we'll have to respond in terms of extension of future credit." If they don't pay what they owe, we won't lend them any more. President Ford returns from a trip to China, Indonesia, and the Philippines in December 1975 and enunciates a Pacific Doctrine. It is never heard of again, but many Presidents believe that the right to enunciate a doctrine goes with the office. United Press International quotes an assistant to Vice President Rockefeller: "Ford not only let the Rockefeller juggernaut come down from New York, but has us in his stable now." The juggernaut, which had to lower its head to get in, is given the stall next to the Ford bandwagon. Both are let out occasionally to roll a bit, but not far.

The sports world makes its contribution. Don Rock, vice president of the National Hockey League, speaks disapprovingly of players who fester a grudge. The grudge may burst and spray those in range with rancor. A weather broadcaster in Marlboro, Massachusetts, calls small storms stormettes. Massachusetts come from a small Massachus. In Kansas City, Missouri, television viewers are told about "the heavy storm system that performed over our area last night." Music by Rossini. An airline stewardess urges her passengers to "have a nice day in Cincinnati or wherever your final destination may be taking you," and an investment company writes: "We have exceptional game plan capabilities together with strict concerns for programming successful situations." My final destination is taking me far away from game plans, capabilities, programming, and situations, there to have a nice day. A professor, Sam Schoenbaum of Northwestern, explains on ABC television why William Shakespeare was so eminent a playwright: "He had a tremendous commitment to his own medium, the stage." All the world's a medium, but the professor appears to believe that Shakespeare could have left the theater for television or Hollywood.

That is how the language sounds now. A civil tongue, on the other hand, means to me a language that is not bogged down in jargon, not puffed up with false dignity, not studded with trick phrases that have lost their meaning. It is not falsely exciting, is not patronizing, does not conceal the smallness and triteness of ideas by clothing them in language ever more grandiose, does not seek out increasingly complicated constructions, does not weigh us down with the gelatinous verbiage of Washington and the social sciences. It treats errors in spelling and usage with a decent tolerance but does not take them lightly. It does not consider "We're there because that's where it's at" the height of cleverness. It is not merely a stream of sound that disk jockeys produce, in which what is said does not matter so long as it is said without pause. It is direct, specific, concrete, vigorous, colorful, subtle, and imaginative when it should be, and as lucid and eloquent as we are able to make it. It is something to revel in and enjoy.

Unfortunately, it is also only a dream, for an ironic thing is happening in the United States. As we demand more and more personal openness from those in public life—unwisely, it seems to me—our language becomes more and more covered, obscure, turgid, ponderous, and overblown. The candor expected of public officials about their health, their money, their private lives, or what used to be thought of as their private lives, is offset in public matters by language that conceals more than it tells, and often conceals the fact that there is little or nothing worth telling.

We increasingly expect of those holding office an accounting of their financial holdings and their health. There are some who want a panel of psychiatrists to examine all who seek high office, to determine whether they can be trusted with public affairs and with their private ones. The way things are going, there will probably be a demand that those in public life give assurances that their sexual undertakings leave them without anxiety and ready to turn to affairs of state without lurid dreams that trouble their sleep. This demand will be strengthened by its having been reported that by the time Watergate reached its denouement, Richard and Pat Nixon had not slept together in fourteen years. During the furor over the liaison between Wayne Hays, chairman of the House Administration Committee, and Elizabeth Ray, a committee employee and Hays's mistress-turned-novelist, the Speaker of the House, Carl Albert, dealing with reports of orgies in his office, felt it necessary to say that he was sixty-eight and had not slept with a woman all year. (It was early June.)

I would be willing to get along with less information about this or that officeholder's tax return or bedroom activities if I could get him or her to speak more clearly about matters of public policy. When the press resolved to be thrilled by Henry Kissinger's bachelor exploits, I was less interested in knowing who his dinner companions were than in knowing what diplomatic agreements he was making and what obligations he was taking on for the United States. Early in the 1976 campaign the White House objected to press and television pictures of President Ford falling down while skiing. The obvious response is that the White House should not announce "photo opportunities" of the President skiing. A few months later it ruled out photo opportunities when he boarded a helicopter on the White House lawn because of unseemly publicity over the times he had bumped his head on earlier occasions. I must add, however, that I did not understand why there should have been any interest in the pictures. Skiers do fall down, just as tall men sometimes bump their heads on low airplane doorways. I have bumped my head, and my height—I stand seventy-three and a half inches nearer the stars—is not exceptional. It says nothing about my prowess as a news commentator. By the same token, Ford could be the greatest skier alive and that would have nothing to do with his ability to be President. When Betty Ford was asked what her reaction would be if her daughter had an affair, she replied that she would not be surprised.

I thought the proper reply was "None of your business." I certainly regarded it as none of mine.

It is easy to understand the insistence that public men and women tell all especially after Vietnam, Watergate, the resignation of a President and a Vice President, and various financial scandals and sexual escapades. What we ought to be demanding is that our leaders speak better English, so that we know what they are talking about and, incidentally, so that *they* do. The disclosure of such information as number of shares held, money in the bank, condition of kidneys, creates the impression that something is being done to protect us. For the most part it is an illusion. There is little salvation to be found in more psychiatry and less privacy. Some safety does lie in more sensible public attitudes, especially toward the public relations and advertising techniques now widely used by politicians. It lies in understanding that there can be many sources of leadership in the country, not the White House alone. It lies also in independent reporting by those of us in the news business, in greater skepticism on the part of the public, and in an unremitting puncturing of the overblown. In all of this, language is crucial. Let us go forward into a charismaless future.

A woman in Goshen, Indiana, told me recently that her daughter-in-law, for whom English is a second language, was sitting on the floor one day in despair, surrounded by housekeeping items to be kept, put in the attic, or given away. "So many junk," she said.

English, thanks to many for whom it is the first language, is in the same beleaguered position, hopelessly burdened by so many junk, which should not be kept, or put in the attic, or given away, but thrown away. If you drink, exclude vehicle use, says the California Highway Patrol. That should be thrown away. So should "In order to improve security, we request that, effective immediately, no employees use the above subject doors for ingress and egress to the building." The New York corporation that perpetrated that made ingress and egress sound as portentous as yin and yang. It should be egress from, and the company could have said entering and leaving. Or simply, Don't open these doors.

There are few other things to do with doors, even of the subject kind.* A young man writes to a Maine newspaper about an older man who "became an experiencing person in my life, lending an aura to my developing personality of absolute rapport and communicatory relevance." Evidently the older man was sympathetic and understanding. A civil tongue would have said so.

The Asbury Park, New Jersey, *Press* runs a story from Washington about a restaurant where important people go and where "dinner table banter transubstantiates into lunch." A small miracle, and without benefit of clergy. *Time* magazine reports Henry Kissinger's appearing "perceptibly relaxed." When Kissinger appears imperceptibly relaxed, reporters cluster around knowing that something is brewing. The *New York Times* writes an editorial: "Given the political balance in Congress, it is specifically up to the Democratic leadership in both houses to take initiatives that have so far been unimpressive." Why the *Times* wants the Democrats to recommend again courses already found wanting I am unable to figure out. The *Times* reports on a trial from North Haverhill, New Hampshire: "The Eames brothers contended that their mother, and not them, manages the theatre." Them were acquitted.

A Winston-Salem, North Carolina, budget proposal calls for money for "effective confinement and extinguishment of unwanted and destructive fires." Firemen unable to achieve distinguishment between unwanted and destructive fires and the wanted and constructive kind probably are destined to suffer languishment in the lower grades. Those of us devoted to a civil tongue suffer anguishment. The Winston-Salem budget also proposes "schedule adherence with emphasis on hitting checkpoints within the targeted time." That's making the buses run on schedule. It calls for "human interment space." Cemeteries.

When I entered the news business thirty-five years ago, I thought that I had taken an oath to preserve, protect, and defend the English language, as a President swears that he will preserve,

---

* Another possibility: Exclude door use.

protect, and defend the Constitution. I have tried to honor the oath, as have many others, in and out of news, but now it seems to me that American English, vigorous, adaptable, and resourceful, a treasure trove of wit, charm, and inspiration, may soon be lowered into a language interment space with a marker erected bearing the words Actuarially Matured. The interment unit diggers are all about us.

Late in 1974 the Secretary of Commerce, Frederick Dent, said that the rate of inflation in the second quarter of the year was 9.6 per cent, and this "validated the essentiality of President Ford's struggle to cut the inflation rate." A civil tongue would have said justified, but that would have cost Dent three words and nine syllables and, in the way of Washington, which would never say satellite photography when it could say technical overhead reconnaissance, commensurate self-respect. In March 1975, FBI agents and local policemen broke into an apartment in Alexandria, Virginia, because of a tip that Patricia Hearst was there. Later, Michael Morrow, assistant special agent in charge of the Alexandria FBI office, explained that the young woman who lived there would not open the door and "the only reason entry was forced was because of the totality of the situation." Patricia Hearst was not in the apartment, and the FBI stubbed its totality. It should have bitten its uncivil tongue.

A reporter asks Louise Lasser, of the television serial "Mary Hartman, Mary Hartman," what she knows about the boredom of being a housewife. "I don't know anything about the externalism of being in the kitchen," Miss Lasser replies, "but I certainly know about ennui." When I hear words like externalism, I also know about ennui.

The Supervisor of Reading in the schools of Ridgewood, New Jersey, asks parents to provide readiness experiences for their preschool children by encouraging them to reaffirm their perceptions on a tactile level. Parents are to model behavior that characterizes their values. They are never to model oral fragments, but they are to noun. Modeling oral fragments could mean posing for advertisements for chipped teeth, but doesn't. An oral fragment comes into being when you say, "Huh?" or "Wow!" You noun when you identify an object unknown to the child. In Ridgewood, New Jersey, you might say, "This is a supervisor of reading." Wow!

Nelson Rockefeller, when asked whether he would be nominated at the 1976 Republican convention, forswore the oral fragment. "I cannot conceive of any scenario in which that could eventuate," he said. Won't things improve when the younger generation of politicians takes over? No. Edmund Brown, Jr., asked whether his 1976 candidacy was really aimed at 1980, replied, "My equation is sufficiently complex to admit of various outcomes." Declining to ride to a money-raising dinner in a chauffeur-driven Mercedes, he explained, "I cannot relate to that material possessory consciousness," and used an unwashed Ford instead. Conspicuous inconspicuous consumption.

There are risks in writing a book in which you find fault with the language of others. It admits of various outcomes. On January 1, 1975, two months after the publication of *Strictly Speaking,* my first book on English, Meb Bolin, of Portales, New Mexico, wished me a Happy New Year and added, "May you survive the precarious position in which you have been placed by your book." It was precarious. I was obliged to agree with Helen M. Leonard, of Eau Claire, Wisconsin, that the phrase "as a matter of fact" was tattered, vacuous, redundant, and pompous, and that I should not have used it when interviewed by Bob Cromie on "Book Beat"; with Marjorie Driver, of Coon Rapids, Minnesota, that I said "It seems to me" too often on the Merv Griffin show; with Mary R. Livingstone, of Winchester, Massachusetts, that "quite a few," which I said on the "Today" show, means nothing; with Stephen C. Adamson, of Stoughton, Massachusetts, that if I said "I myself" on the Merv Griffin show, it must have been for emphasis but that "I" would have been sufficient. I acknowledged to Charles W. Laue, of Atmore, Alabama, that athletes' salaries cannot be infinitely larger than they used to be; to Bernadette Ellis, of East Troy, Wisconsin, that although I said "I don't think . . ." on the Phil Donahue show, I do think and should not deny it; and to

Esther Lafair, of the Center for Studies in Criminology and Criminal Law at the University of Pennsylvania, that in congeries the accent falls on the second syllable, not the first. To the brave belong Lafair, but I had been foolhardy.

In September 1975, I went to Tokyo to interview Emperor Hirohito before his visit to the United States, the first interview the Emperor had ever granted. Discussing it on the "Today" show, I wanted to say that everyone present had been behind a screen except the camera crews and me. I started to say it, but the sentence grew longer, with embellishments being dropped in, and by the end I could not remember how it had begun. Should it be I or me? I went for the fake elegance. After I, the deluge. My equation admitted of a form letter acknowledging error.

There could also have been a form letter *to* me about the title of my book. The Columbia, South Carolina, *State* made it *Strickly Speaking,* though on a best-seller list, which softened the blow. It was also *Strickly Speaking* at the Carnegie Public Library in Rock Springs, Wyoming; in an advertisement by Waldenbooks in the Newark, New Jersey, *Star-Ledger;* in the *Washington Post;* and at the Cecil County Library in Elkton, Maryland, a branch of the New York Public Library, the Minneapolis Public Library, the library in Townshend, Vermont, and the Thomas Jefferson Library System of Jefferson City, Missouri. A Jefferson City woman who asked for the book wrote to me that perhaps she had not spoken distinkly. The publisher of the book, Bobbs-Merrill, occasionally made it *Stricktly Speaking,* which showed a nice impartiality. Charles E. Lyght, a physician in Oklawaha, Florida, and editor-in-chief of the *Journal of the American Geriatrics Society,* ordered the book from a shop in Ocala and in return was promised *Strickley Speaking.* "Good old Strickley," Dr. Lyght wrote to me, "I remember him well."

I consoled myself that the misspellings merely proved the point I had been making. I was more troubled when a company librarian in Omaha, Beatrice Langfeld, wrote that when she asked the public library there how to classify the book, she was told under culture and cultural process, a subhead of sociology. Jane

Wyville, of Yuba City, California, told me that it was classified there under sociolinguistics. It is said that China simply absorbs its invaders. I do not want to be absorbed into sociology, still less a subhead of it. Sociologists are people who pretend to advance the cause of knowledge by calling a family a microcluster of structured role expectations or a bounded plurality of role-playing individuals. Among sociologists, a civil tongue is all but unknown.

A civil tongue should not pretend to command foreign languages that it doesn't. In *Strictly Speaking* a Latin phrase had Nehercule for Mehercule and ea for et. "Lapsūs typographici," Elizabeth Cummings, a Latin teacher in Harrisburg, Pennsylvania, graciously suggested. But as lapsūs go, typographici they were not. My daughter, who studied Latin, which I did not, and who received half the book's dedication, was less indulgent. She asked why I had not consulted her. She knew what kind of lapsūs they were. A librarian in Milton, Massachusetts, E. B. Pile, suggested that when I made certain British heraldic officers Poursuivants of Arms in Ordinary—they are Pursuivants—it was either a typo or a test of the alertness of my readers. I could have replied that poursuivants were British court functionaries who followed royalty around with teapots at the ready and that these matters were in the lapsūs of the gods. Instead, I took the blame myself. Quis custodiet ipsos custodes? Mrs. Pile had wanted to know. It was the sort of question to which, in the early days of television news, we used to respond, "I'm glad you asked me that" (Peropportune hoc rogasti), and then sign off (et tum audientibus valedicas).

Deane W. Malott, president emeritus of Cornell University, reprimanded me about "Boola Boola," the Yale fight song. I had written that boola boola was an adaptation of the Hawaiian hoola boola. "This," Dr. Malott said, in a sentence that was a role model of its kind, "is not correct." Hoola in Hawaii is hula, and boola does not exist because there is no "b" in the Hawaiian alphabet. My information on "Boola Boola" had come from Yale University. Quis custodiet ipsos custodes? Peropportune hoc rogasti. Lux et veritas.

Others in the audientibus were not so gentle. To the question asked by the subtitle of *Strictly Speaking*, Will America Be the Death of English? a reader in Huntington, Pennsylvania, unbidden, answered, "Yes," and predicted that I would be in at the kill. "As I read the book," she wrote, "I hastily jotted down at least 201 errors either in misuse of the introductory And/But when a subordinate conjunction should have been used or in incorrect punctuation." Frank Chesley of the *Seattle Post-Intelligencer* said that I used too many parenthetical expressions, and Florence Way, a retired teacher of English of Los Altos, California (California proved to be full of watchdogs of the language, watching me), complained that I relied too heavily on semicolons. She singled out a sentence with forty-four of them. I had thought it a brilliantly constructed apotheosis of the semicolon. David G. Lynch, of Cincinnati, said that he had read two paragraphs on page 157 over and over without finding a sequitur. It's a matter of knowing where to look. Ask the sequitary.

I wrote that President Kennedy delivered a speech in embarrassed silence. Herman Jervis, of New York, wished that more politicians would follow that course. Linda Wechsler, of Granada Hills, California, suggested that I follow my own advice and eschew more words than are needed. I had written, "No other politician will put in an appearance." Mrs. Wechsler recommended "No politician will appear." I replied in embarrassed silence.

I received gratefully a letter from Mrs. Robert O. Wright, in Peoria, Illinois, who liked the book and was afraid to say more. Miriam Nelson Brown, of Sayville, New York, gave herself a B-minus for her letter and added, "I have had this graded to save you the trouble." Jane Robison, a professor of English in South Carolina, suggested that any errors in the book probably had been planted there by me for the pleasure of teachers like her, an idea that escaped my professors years before. It reminded me of the time I interviewed the actor Dustin Hoffman in a glassed-in restaurant. As word spread of what was happening, young women gathered outside to stare in. Hoffman got up and went to the window. "Where were you when I needed you?" he shouted.

Those who complain about the misuse of English are widely

regarded as quaint and to be pointed out to tourists. Yet we are not such an exotic growth. After *Strictly Speaking* was published, I heard, as might have been expected, from teachers of English and of Latin, and from authors and editors, but also from judges, lawyers, doctors, members of Congress and of state legislatures; from employees of Congress, the CIA, NASA, the Federal Communications Commission, and a variety of other federal, state, city and county agencies; from foundation executives, retired people—some of them in old soldiers' homes—housewives, businessmen, airline pilots, newspeople, brokers, secretaries and accountants. There was a letter from Lois DeBakey, professor of scientific communications, Baylor College of Medicine, Houston, Texas, who tries to dissuade physicians from writing "There were four deaths, only one of which lived more than two months," and to persuade them to say swallowing instead of deglutination. A clergyman, Monsignor Charles J. Plauché, of Saint Francis Cabrini Church in New Orleans, wrote to say that he thought his days as a pastor were numbered. Unless the trend in language was reversed, he expected to become Coordinator of the Faith Community Dimension. Monsignor Plauché is probably right. Community is rampant, and I am surprised not to have been placed in the media community dimension. Particularly endearing are references to the intelligence community. It is as though the head of the CIA raps on the door of the director of Naval Intelligence to ask what sort of day he had and borrow a cup of sugar.

Letters cheering me on in the struggle for the language* have come from people in their nineties and from students, among the latter one in the ninth grade who spotted a mistake in an article about me in *People* magazine. So age is not a factor in concern for the language. Nor is it a concern only to the highly educated, or the effete Northeast, or to city folk. I have heard from Palouse, Washington; Decatur, Georgia; Morristown, Tennessee; Nakomis, Florida; Potsdam, New York; Jamestown, California; Brunswick, Maine; LaPorte, Texas; DePere, Wisconsin; Health Springs, South

---

* Though not validating its essentiality.

Carolina; Wallingford, Pennsylvania; Rocky Mount, North Carolina; Rocky River, Ohio; Fort Branch, Indiana; Kemenick, Washington; and Alpena, South Dakota. Some of the most impassioned letters have come from people who were not born in the United States, who worked hard to learn English and to use it well, and who were puzzled and pained by the language's decline. Others came from Canada, Australia, and Britain, and some from readers with APO and FPO addresses whose precise whereabouts could not be known. Hundreds volunteered material for a second book. Much of that material I have used. *A Civil Tongue* is my response.

Such support is immensely gratifying to an author, but I understand that it came to me because I was, so to speak, standing proxy for the English language. Some of my readers wrote to newspaper, magazine, radio, and television editors calling their attention to infelicities and asking, "What would Edwin Newman think?" The editors appeared not to consider this a pressing question.

I have been, as a consequence of all this, invited to join the Queen's English Society, which was formed in 1972 by some people in Britain who "felt very concerned about the decline of literacy since the War." The society offers its letterheads to members "to give weight to their communications with the press or BBC." I wish the Queen's English Society well, but I did not join it and I would not join a comparable organization here. There is no office of state to name it for, and a very good thing that is. The assertion of authority in these matters rarely succeeds. Besides, if American English is burdened with so many junk, the United States Government is the burdener-in-chief, with a large part of the gross national product devoted to the purpose. In this, policy is bipartisan, all branches join in, and checks and balances and the separation of powers are ignored. Beyond that, societies, committees, and the like are almost invariably a source of deplorable English themselves. If American English is to be saved, it will, in my view, have to be saved by individuals, or by small guerrilla groups that refuse to accept nonsense, send back unclear and pompous letters with a request for a translation, and insist that organizations they are part of speak plainly. This cannot be done on orders from above. It requires rebelliousness, buccaneering, and humor, qualities that organizations are short of.

Fortunately, practitioners of a civil tongue do exist. A reporter asked the head of the AFL-CIO, George Meany, for his analysis of the elections of November 1974. What was the people's mandate? Said Meany: "I don't believe in this mandate stuff. A guy runs for office and gets elected. All of a sudden he's got a mandate. Two less votes and he's nothing." A good mandate is hard to find.

A more cautiously phrased example of the civil tongue in action came from William Bateman, executive vice president of the Chase Manhattan Bank. When asked about the difficulties faced by real estate investment trusts, he said, "We're not anxious to see anything with the name Chase Manhattan in bankruptcy anywhere." Bateman should have said eager, not anxious, but the understatement was pleasant.

A civil tongue knows when to remain silent. Over the years, heads of state and heads of government have convinced themselves that their countries will lose prestige, and so will they, if they do not claim the right to deliver tedious speeches whenever possible. At the United Nations the consequence is that everybody assures everybody else of the need for peace and justice and progress, and archives result. In September 1974, Prime Minister Pierre Trudeau of Canada decided not to speak because he had nothing sufficiently important to say. Trudeau's gesture was little noticed. It should have made him immortal.

As little noticed was a gesture two months earlier by Norris Cotton. On July 3, 1974, President Nixon spoke in Caribou, Maine, about the visit he had just made to the Soviet Union. A reporter asked Cotton, then a Republican Senator from New Hampshire, for his reaction. "I cannot comment directly on the speech," Cotton said. "I was taking a nap and I missed it." He was, to be sure, about to retire from politics and had nothing to lose, but this may have been Cotton's greatest public service. He lighted a way that others, if they but will, can follow. NBC News correspondent Welles Hangen, missing since the fighting in Cambodia in 1970, had an unrivaled gift for the succinctness that is part of a civil tongue. Each year NBC correspondents tour the country in a group, appearing in public and answering questions from members of the audiences. In 1961, when India invaded what was then Portuguese Goa, Welles was NBC's correspondent in New Delhi. During that year's tour somebody sent up a one-word question: "Goa?" Welles gave a one-word answer: "Gone." At the Democratic convention in 1976, a reporter asked Amy Carter, eight-year-old daughter of Rosalynn and Jimmy, whether she had a message for the children of America. Said Amy: "No."

In the summer of 1960 I went to Sauk Center, Minnesota, for a television story about a festival honoring Sinclair Lewis, who was born there. One day a local resident said of a task that was facing us, "It's more than the horse can pull." We city boys thought that amusingly bucolic, but in seven words it's hard to say more. During an American Federation of Television and Radio Artists strike against NBC in April 1967, I was on the picket line, shortening my life inhaling the carbon monoxide fumes on Sixth Avenue,* when an NBC executive, a friend, walked by. "Bolshevik scum," he said cheerily. It made the day. In May 1960 the Big Four (Eisenhower, Khrushchev, de Gaulle, Macmillan) meeting in Paris broke up when Francis Gary Powers and his U-2 aircraft were shot down over the Soviet Union. I was NBC's Paris correspondent at the time, and when the conference ended I was among the reporters questioning Charles E. Bohlen, one of Eisenhower's chief advisers. A reporter asked Ambassador Bohlen whether the U-2 would be used again. Bohlen looked at him with mild impatience. "It is a blown instrument," he said. Five words. A complete answer.

---

* Officially it is the Avenue of the Americas, and there is an equestrian statue of Simón Bolívar at the northern end to prove it. Most New Yorkers say Sixth Avenue. It is hard to imagine anyone getting into a taxi and saying, "Fifty-second Street and the Avenue of the Americas, and hurry!"

I remember, decades ago, listening to Claude Pepper, then a senator from Florida, defending his vote on a civil rights issue that split him away from other Southern Democrats. Pepper has not been one of the most memorable of twentieth-century politicians, but he has always been an effective speaker. "I will not vote to stultify the Constitution of the United States," he said. Plainly phrased, but eloquent.

American English, drawing on so many regional differences, so many immigrant groups, and such a range of business, farming, industrial, athletic, and artistic experiences, can have an incomparable richness. Instead, high crimes and misdemeanors are visited upon it, and those who commit them do not understand that they are crimes against themselves. The language belongs to all of us. We have no more valuable possession.

Foreigners often have a peculiar talent for using English in an original way. After an earthquake in the North of Italy in the spring of 1976, a local resident described the scene. "Dogs were complaining," he said, "and animals were shouting." I am trying not to shout but I am complaining. Civilly. Most of the time.

A One-Way Streetcar
Named Détente

The rangy Texan had a sprawling ranch of his own, and his parents lived in a sprawling red brick building in a sprawling retirement community he often visited, so he felt not out of place on the sprawling game reserve where he had gone to pick off a trophy or two among the game animals with which he hoped to establish an adversary relationship. He wondered who his companions on the safari would be, and he had not long to wait. There was a hesitant, almost furtive knock at the door. Throwing it open, the Texan recognized a former Greek strongman.

"How are you, old buddy?" the Texan asked rangily.

"Not so well," the Greek replied.

"Anything specific? Any symptoms?"

"Well," the Greek said, "when I flex my muscles, nothing happens. They don't bulge."

Two military men followed in his wake. One was Admiral Isaac Kidd, known to the columnist Jack Anderson as the bluff head of Navy matériel; the other, Juan Velasco Alvarado, known to the *New York Times* as Peru's feisty army strongman. Kidd at once said something bluff about naval vessels. "When they break," he said, "I fix them." Velasco tried to say something feisty, but he was still bemused by his forcible retirement in August 1975. He looked about spiritedly, then fixed his eyes on the Greek and said, "I can lick any strongman in the house."

"You have the advantage of me, sir," the Greek replied. "I am a mere shadow of my former self. A few years ago it might have been different, before the foundations of my repressive regime tottered."

Velasco softened. "What happened?" he asked.

"The commonly accepted explanation," the Greek said, "is that I was chosen because my associates thought I would be a pliable figurehead. However, I turned into a firm, strong-willed ruler and sometimes lashed out at my cowed subordinates. The result was that after high-level discussion, far-reaching debate and last-ditch negotiations, followed by a spate of rumors, I was assailed as one who would turn the revolution to his own ends, arrested in a predawn raid, and toppled by my disgruntled fellow plotters."

"Was it a bloodless coup," Velasco asked, "or were lifeless bodies seen?"

The Greek hung his head. "Bloodless," he said.

"Mine was too," Velasco said consolingly. He changed the subject. "I also take on erstwhile boy wonders. Any of them here?"

"Cut it out, Velasco," Admiral Kidd said. "Any erstwhile boy wonders who would come here are aging prime ministers by now, or aged former prime ministers. You wouldn't go after them."

"I suppose you're right," Velasco said, "but I might make an exception for the Kremlin's aging leadership."

The Texan intervened. "The Kremlin's aging leadership is not coming," he said. "Its members were last seen in public reviewing the troops on the anniversary of the Bolshevik Revolution, standing on top of the refurbished Lenin Mausoleum wearing overcoats and heavy capes against a cold rain. The Chinese, who never spoke of the aging Kremlin leaders because of frail eighty-two-year-old Chairman Mao, described them as the Soviet revisionist leading clique, whose naked policy of colonial expansion was evidence of the new Tsars' feverish quest for world hegemony.* They also predicted that rightist deviationists would be smashed in their bourgeois headquarters by the torrent of the revolutionary mass movement.

"That shook the Kremlin's aging leaders," the Texan explained, "because they had themselves just finished administering a resolute rebuff to bourgeois falsifiers who seize upon any fabrication in their blind hatred for the future of all mankind. The aging leaders therefore went to the beautiful former imperial capital, Leningrad, where they could be protected by the vaunted power of the KGB."

"Is anybody ailing coming?" Velasco asked.

"Probably not," the Texan replied. "Reservations were made for an ailing chief of state and his aides, but they were canceled."†

---

* The Soviet and Chinese governments have a way of insulting each other that is peculiarly their own. You seek hegemony, the Chinese will tell the Russians. You seek hegemony, the Russians will tell the Chinese. In the 1950s some of us on the outside thought that the two governments might be seeking hegemony together, but their paths parted. Ever since, according to the Chinese, the Russians have been looking for hegemony high and low and in every nook and cranny, while according to the Russians the Chinese are obsessed with hegemony and think of nothing else except, in lighter moments, inciting a third world war. An unnamed Pakistani has told the *New York Times,* "The Indians have been bitten by the bug of wanting hegemony of the subcontinent." The *Times* found an Indian to deny it. The hegemoniacal debate goes on.

† Aides are used by aideworthy people not only for the obvious purpose—providing aid—but for the sake of journalists who find aides handy for hanging unattributable quotations on. *Time* magazine knows the location of more Washington aides than any other news organization and even used one to hang an unattributed murmur on: " 'That was really rough,' one of Ford's aides murmured."

When a politician acquires a number of aides, he has an entourage. Entourage members open doors, are brisk but friendly, and look as though they are standing by to be consulted on difficult questions. This

"Is there at least somebody coming from an ailing UN agency?"

"No."

"Why not?"

"Because the ailing agency is pulling in its belt and can't afford it."

"Explain something to me. I read in one of your papers about the ailing Daniel P. Moynihan. Is that a person or a position?"

"In a sense it is both, because although there is a Daniel P. Moynihan, it is also true that if there weren't he would have had to be invented."

"Is that because diplomacy is too serious a matter to be left to the diplomats?"

The Texan nodded.

"Moynihan has nonetheless left it to the diplomats."

The Texan nodded again. "An oversight," he said.

Here we leave the rangy Texan, the bluff head of Navy matériel, and the former Greek and Peruvian strongmen, though they will be back with further adventures at the end of this chapter. I want to pause here to consider how our ranches came to be sprawling and our language in politics and foreign affairs so burdened by clichés that thought about them is almost ruled out.*

---

is not so easy as it sounds, because if the entourage member ever seems to be at loose ends or superfluous, he runs the risk of appearing to be a hanger-on. The hanger-on's position is not official; he is not on the payroll, or even on a per diem; and his hold is precarious. One rarely hears the term hanger-on without mere before it. That implies contempt, and nobody turns up at somebody's campaign headquarters and says, "I'm applying for a job as hanger-on." However, for the hanger-on of accomplishment, there is always the possibility of promotion if an opening should turn up in the entourage.

* By the same process, the dust jacket of *Strictly Speaking* credited me with having anchored NBC's coverage of various events. "I missed your broadcasts and would be much obliged if you would send me a diagram showing how you anchored the coverage," wrote Jacob L. Fox of Chicago. "A weighty assignment, no doubt," wrote Conrad Teitell from his law office in New York. Very weighty.

In foreign affairs, for example, it has long been almost impossible to go beyond the question of whether, in its relations with the Soviet Union, the United States is on a one-way street or a two-way street, and whether it even knows the difference.

I used to think that glory awaited the politician who took the next logical step and said that détente must not be allowed to become a dead-end street, but President Ford may have put an end to that possibility. Soon after Ronald Reagan pronounced détente a one-way street—connecting the New Hampshire and Massachusetts primaries—Ford announced that détente was "only a word that was coined" and that he would not use it because it was no longer "applicable." Instead, Ford said, "I think what we ought to say is that the United States will meet with superpowers—the Soviet Union, China and others—and seek to relax tensions so that we can continue a policy of peace through strength."

Because in diplomacy détente means a relaxation of tensions, it appears that everybody was so busy looking for hidden significance in the President's remark that nobody thought of asking him who the other superpowers were. There were none. It is my guess that there was also no hidden significance. Ford was tired of hearing that he had been seen on a one-way street consorting with a foreign word of doubtful reputation. It is only a step from being seen on a one-way street in such company to being accused of détenting on the old camp ground, which would be sacrilege. However, nobody can say, "Seeking to relax tensions so as to continue a policy of peace through strength is a one-way street." Ford outwitted his rival.

Jimmy Carter, coming late to these matters, pronounced détente a two-way street but also asked that if we travel down the nuclear road we do so with our eyes wide open.* Open eyes are advisable on all thoroughfares, and Carter was not thought to have made an original contribution to arms control theory and practice.

---

* Look down, look down, that nuclear road, before you travel on.

Leonid Brezhnev, although he was also taking part in détente, was not having the problems that Ford was. For one thing, the Soviet Ministry of One-Way Street Construction has been in existence for a long time and is the most experienced ministry of its kind in the world. There is no equivalent in the United States. We have not even had any proposals to divert money from the federal highway fund for the purpose, whereas the Russians divert money from one of their dearest projects, toiling masses transit. So in his keynote speech to the Congress of the Soviet Communist party in Moscow, Brezhnev was able to say, "We make no secret of the fact that we see détente as the way to create more favorable conditions for peaceful socialist and Communist construction." From Ford's point of view, Brezhnev might have done better to keep it a secret, since the President's critics insisted that all of that construction, the nature of which the wily Brezhnev did not specify, came down to laying out and paving you know what.

I must say that all this left me puzzled. If peace and security lie at both ends of a two-way street, as they must—after all, if both nations are going in the same direction on a two-way street, they might just as well be on a one-way street—why bother to leave your end for the other? Moreover, if eyeball-to-eyeball confrontations are to be avoided, the one-way street seems to be the place to avoid them. On a one-way street, all traffic moves in the same direction, and unless somebody is walking backward no one's eyeball can come flush against anyone else's. Simply stated, a one-way street is not what Henry Kissinger would call a context of confrontation, and that is the context eyeball-to-eyeball requires. The confrontation states of the Middle East, subsidized by their oil-rich neighbors, follow a confrontational strategy, and are the owners of some of the most bellicose eyeballs now on view. Yet they sedulously avoid one-way streets. So do the developing nations Kissinger himself has said constitute "a rigid, ideological, confrontationist coalition of their own." They know that it is on a two-way street that even an innocuous bilateral meeting may turn sinister—a turn to the left on a two-way street—when the eyeballs are barely in range. That is why they are often seen lounging on two-way street corners, looking for trouble. Multilateral eyeball-to-eyeball confrontations are, by definition, impossible.

I hope that this information will be reassuring to Senator Lowell Weicker of Connecticut. Weicker has been worried lest a mistaken policy on energy result in our being confronted with a confrontation. Not if you take the right road. It should also reassure our allies in Western Europe, who want arms standardized in the North Atlantic Treaty Organization and who, because they don't want to buy everything here while we buy nothing there, would like the transactions carried out on a two-way street. They should forget the streets. A broad avenue of cooperation is what they should have in mind.

Because of the preoccupation with streets, broad avenues of cooperation have not been much talked about of late, but they lead, all being well, to the broad sunlit uplands of peace and plenty to which, at the end of many of his speeches, Winston Churchill used to see humanity advancing. It always came as a shock to me when, sitting in the House of Commons press gallery in the 1950s, I would hear jeers going up from the Labour side as Churchill approached his peroration and took off. Some of this was simple partisanship: they were Labourites and Churchill was the leader of the Conservatives. But it was also caused by their knowing what was coming—oratorical flourishes, an inspirational ending, an attempt to equal some of the great phrases spoken ten and fifteen years before. Churchill was more effective away from the sunlit uplands and when he was at his most concrete. "Jaw, jaw," he once said about talking to the Russians, "is better than war, war." An argument cannot be put better than that.

A few years later one of Churchill's successors as prime minister, Harold Macmillan, tried a variation on it. "There ain't," he said, "gonna be no war." Coming from a man of his fusty appearance, it was brilliantly effective in turning debate on foreign affairs into the channel where Macmillan wanted it. Language is a marvelous servant for those who know how to use it. In 1958 a revolt in Algeria by French colonists and military men who wanted Algeria to remain French restored Charles de Gaulle to power in Paris. De Gaulle went to Algiers and, from the balcony overlooking the Place du Gouvernement-Général, where all the huge rallies had taken place, spoke to those who had brought about his return. *"Je vous ai compris,"* he told them. "I have understood you." Applause, cheers, exultation. The phrase could not have been more carefully chosen. The unspoken part of it was, "Yes, and you're not going to get what you want." What de Gaulle did say quieted the storm. A few years later, Algeria was independent. Was it fair? Perhaps not. But as an effective use of language, it has rarely been equaled.*

I remember some effective language being used on me at that time. During the uprising I went to Radio Algiers to broadcast to the United States. American policy was not popular with those in revolt. A soldier with a rifle blocked my way. *"Vous êtes Americain?"* he asked. I said I was. *"Prenez la porte,"* he said, literally "Take the door" and unmistakably "Get out."

Four years later I was in Vietnam talking to a South Vietnamese colonel about the strategic villages and hamlets plan. This involved placing the peasants in fortified areas from which they would go forth to the fields in the morning and to which they would return to be sealed off from the Communists at night. The colonel, later killed in mysterious circumstances while trying to seize power, said, "They're not locking the Communists out. They're locking the Communists in." It was a precise measure of what was happening, and a precise explanation of why the plan failed.

Talk about contexts of confrontation and two-way streets,

---

* De Gaulle, by the way, could speak English. When he visited the United States at the end of 1959, I went along, as NBC's Paris correspondent, to help in the coverage. There was a reception at the French Embassy, and as I approached de Gaulle I saw one of his associates nudge him and tell him I was there. He looked down at me and said, "I am very happy to see you here." Whether he spoke in English because he was in Washington and thought it fitting or did not want to provoke me into speaking French, I never knew.

its banality apart, makes discussion of foreign affairs and politics empty. It substitutes stereotypes for thought. It reduces discussion to an exchange of catch phrases. We are caught between one-way street slogans on one side and communiqué language on the other.

In November of 1974, President Ford went to Japan, a visit that, whatever else it may have achieved, produced a compendium of communiqué language not surpassed before or since. The communiqué contained—here you proceed at your own risk and probably would be well advised to have a companion—friendly and cooperative relations, harmonious relations, constructive relations, cooperative relations, the totality of varied relationships, a close and mutually beneficial relationship based on the principle of equality (it's only the beginning, folks, only the beginning), a common determination, an enhanced scope for creativity, the maintenance of peace and the evolution of a stable international order, peaceful settlement of outstanding issues, sustained and orderly growth, contributions made in the light of responsibilities and capabilities, an effective and meaningful role, dedicated efforts, coordinated responses, intensified efforts, close cooperation, growing interdependence, global economic difficulties (about halfway there now), the constructive use of human and material resources, an open and harmonious world economic system, constructive participation, a stable and balanced international monetary order, more efficient and rational utilization and distribution of world resources, enhanced cooperation, further international cooperative efforts, a new era of creativity and common progress, constructive participation in multilateral efforts, the well-being of the peoples of the world (hang on), a steady improvement in technological and economic capabilities, a common concern, sound and orderly growth, new challenges common to mankind, broad cooperation, mutual understanding and enhanced communication, the expansion of cultural and educational interchange, the spirit of mutual friendship and trust, frank and timely consultations, potential bilateral issues, pressing global problems of common concern (nearly home), many diverse fields of human endeavor, major foundation stones, an indispensable element, a new page in the history of amity, and a promise to go on striving steadily to encourage a further relaxation of tensions in the world through dialogue and exchanges with countries of different social systems. (Author! Author!)

The Tokyo communiqué somehow left out resolute action, which governments often promise to take at the end of meaningless meetings. Otherwise it is the Sistine Chapel of communiqués. It said what was to be said on the subject forever, and no more communiqués need be issued. Instead, the most-favored-nation technique used in trade could be applied. We would offer any friendly country the same terms that were given to Japan—harmonious, constructive, stable, rational, enhanced, steady, broad, frank, timely, mutual, and the rest. New pages in the history of amity could be turned over at will.

It will be recalled that we left diplomacy in the streets and our minds in the gutter. Let us say that an eyeball-to-eyeball confrontation has taken place, possibly on a street temporarily closed for repairs. In the classic case, it will turn into a head-to-head summit, though this requires some contortion and agility on both sides and, when aging leaders are involved, as they often are, cannot always be arranged.

The *New York Times* columnist William Safire spotted one head-to-head summit at which four eyes were looking at each other but only two eyes met. This may happen with experienced politicians, who appear to be considering the immediate situation but actually have already sized it up and have one eye on the future. It may also be caused by that scourge of American life, irregularity, which leads the mind to wander. The irregular one may be looking at you and apparently concentrating on what you are saying, but his mind is on something else.

Sometimes there is an intermediate step between confrontation and summit, between eyeball-to-eyeball and head-to-head. This is taken when one of the parties to the confrontation says challengingly and perhaps with a slight sneer, "How about a little poker? Diplomatic poker, I mean." The other is nothing loath (sometimes, indeed, he is ailing Prime Minister Nothing Loath) and the game is on. The principal problem in arranging a diplomatic poker game used to be finding a suitable location, since the participants may bring along as bargaining chips intercontinental ballistic missiles, advanced industrial bases, and burgeoning farm production, and much space is needed to stack them. This is no longer a problem, since it is widely understood that the game will take place either in "the gray area between foreign policy and overt commitment" that Henry Kissinger spoke of in a speech at the University of Wyoming at Laramie, or the "twilight area between tranquility and open confrontation" that he identified in a speech to the Institute of Strategic Studies in London.* Almost everybody knows where to find the gray area. It is out-of-doors, under a heavy cloud cover, and on an intersection between a one-way street and a two-way street. The twilight area is the next area over. Sometimes disputes arise over which is to be used, but the twilight area is open for only a couple of hours a day and has to be booked in advance, so the gray area gets most of the games. Visibility is not good in either.

In spite of its menacing ring, eyeballing is not always hostile. In December 1974 the Democrats held a midterm convention in Kansas City. Members of Senator Henry Jackson's staff chose groups of ten to fifteen delegates and led them off the floor for what one of Jackson's assistants called "an eyeball-to-eyeball"

---

* As Kissinger's reputation declined, so did his language. It became harder for him to convince Congress and the people that his policies were correct and that he was still a miracle man as advertised, and he began to use the language he heard around him. Discussing his warning to Cuba against further military activities in Africa after the intervention in Angola, Kissinger told the Senate Foreign Relations Committee: "We should not look at the immediate situation in terms of planning a new move in any time frame that is now immediately foreseeable." In the speech at Laramie, however, he foresaw a time frame in which the United States might "become an isolated fortress island in a hostile and turbulent global sea." An isolated island, as noted elsewhere, is a peculiarly lonely place to be, but for the United States to become one would require more cooperation than Mexico and Canada are likely to offer. The global sea, a perfectly round body of water, has so far been produced only under laboratory conditions.

with the Senator. That meant that the delegates were allowed to be close to Jackson and to converse with him without an intermediary and to judge the stuff of which he was then made.

This kind of eyeball-to-eyeballing, though often amiable, should not be confused with eyeballing, eyeball analysis, or eye contact. The baritone Sherrill Milnes has told an interviewer that he is able to sing a score after eyeballing it. The action here is unilateral. The score does not eyeball back. Eyeball analysis takes place when archeologists dig up artifacts and look at them with the naked eye. However, most archeologists consider it infra dig and prefer to use instruments, even though it was *on* an infra dig that one of the most important infrastructures of an ancient civilization was found.

Eye contact comes from television, and it occurs when a broadcaster is courageous enough to look up from the script and into the camera lens. This requires that the broadcaster have confidence that when he looks down again he will be able to find his place in the script or, lacking such confidence, be willing to risk it. You will hear it said of someone particularly adept at this, "Boy, has he got eye contact!" In the elections of November 1974, Governor Francis Sargent of Massachusetts, though he lost to Michael Dukakis, exhibited, according to the *New York Times,* "a folksy, grinning, hand-shaking, hugging style that won him the admiration of professional politicians, who said that he could lead a parade and make 'eye contact' with everyone in the crowd." Sargent, of course, with no script to follow, could concentrate on eye contact alone, and it must have helped, since late in the campaign he came from a long way back and almost won. This may start a new form of competition for votes among politicians, in which they no longer make promises or issue position papers or even make speeches, but simply go out and look citizens squarely in the eye. "Come to the speakin'," Lyndon Johnson used to tell voters when he campaigned. "Come to the eyeballin'," he would be saying now.

In television, a broadcaster need never look down at his script at all if a Teleprompter with a script on it is placed in front of the lens. However, one not skilled in its use may appear to be peering, mesmerized, into space. This does not count as eye contact. Sometimes the Teleprompter is placed above the lens, which calls for still more skill in looking up while not appearing to look up. A viewer sent me a drawing showing my eyes virtually all whites and pupils disappearing northward. This also would not count as eye contact.

It does not count as dialogue, either, that being what a politician who cannot think of anything else to issue clarion calls for issues clarion calls for. "We need," he says, "a dialogue."* This means that he is being constructive. Rhetoric is used when a politician wants to dismiss some argument or proposal as not constructive, and to convey a tone of tolerant contempt. "This," he says, "is rhetoric." Calls for dialogue are not dismissed as rhetoric. If they were, political life in the United States would come to an end. Dialogues recently recommended to us would have engaged developed and developing nations, producing and consuming nations, labor and management, President and Congress, East and West, North and South, and would have been meaningful, true, patient, honest, responsible, and conducted in a conducive atmosphere. There would also have been a natural gas dialogue at the request of the Pennsylvania Chamber of Commerce.

The *New York Times* asked for a dialogue on oil in an editorial in which it had the oil-consuming nations biting the bullet of pride and moving toward a common energy policy, while the oil-producing nations bit the apple of wisdom and planned to meet at the summit. Biting an apple smacks less of hysteria than biting a bullet, and this, as well as their possession of oil, explains why the OPEC countries have lately been so successful. In February 1975, twelve Senators and seventy Representatives asked President Ford for a serious, unemotional dialogue on getting the United States out of Indochina. They should have asked for eighty-two dialogues.

---

* This information has only recently been declassified: A dialogue consists of meaningful initiatives followed by a constructive response.

It is curious, this devotion to dialogue. An Army officer involved in the clemency program, Major General Eugene Forrester, told *People* magazine that he and his nineteen-year-old son had had "extremely volatile dialogue over Vietnam." He apparently meant that they had shouted at each other. A television executive made a speech in which he urged upon his listeners the virtues of a mutual dialogue together. The dialogue umbrella is broad. An interior decorating company in Lawrence, New York, is called Dialogue International Limited. An associate director of the Jewish Defense League, Dov Fisch, announced that the League would be sending some of its members "to engage in dialogues with Soviet diplomats as they emerge from the mission. We used to call it harassing," Fisch explained, "but harassing is illegal." Would that dialogue were.

Since editorials are unsigned, I do not know who composed the *Times*'s call for a dialogue on oil. It may have been Leonard Silk, a member of the paper's editorial board, who asked about a meeting between rich and poor nations in Paris, "Will Paris Talks Produce Dialogue?" How could they not? Or it may have been correspondent Charles Mohr, who in an article from Johannesburg reported that Prime Minister John Vorster of South Africa had "conducted a growing dialogue with some domestic black leaders." Mohr added that Vorster did this even though "Superimposed on the entire situation is the dead weight of an ideology of racial separation that has handcuffed many politicians and convinced many South Africans that there is no need to disengage from what one concerned Afrikaner had called 'an insufferable status quo.' " No one can disengage from a status quo when he is handcuffed by an ideology's dead weight, unless he gets help. This is exactly what a growing dialogue is intended to provide.

Other evidence suggests that the *Times*'s editorial on oil was written by a reporter named Steven R. Weisman, who in a review of a book called *The Real America* wrote that "it merits full recognition as a major contribution to the nation's political dialogue," one reason it merited that recognition being the fact that its author, Ben Wattenberg, had "limned a remarkable portrait of the American people." I did not know that anyone any longer limned, even columnists, and even while making a major contribution to the nation's political dialogue, which needs all the major contributions it can get. Limned?* I thought it had gone the way of lambent and plangent.

In February 1975 *Time* magazine had this to say about disagreements in Washington over energy and the economy: "For all the rhetorical smoke, the President and the Democrats are not that far apart on many other aspects of the program." Rhetorical smoke was used by American Indians when sending up signals that needed no answer, i.e., required no dialogue. *Time* may, however, have had a different source of the phrase in mind, the well-known saying, Where there is smoke, people are far apart.

King Hussein of Jordan said in April 1976 that any political changes in Lebanon should come about not through violence but through dialogue. Hussein was in Washington at the time as the guest of President Ford, which was appropriate because Ford is unusually fond of dialogue. Soon after taking office he called for a new dialogue with the nations of Latin America, though most of those nations were not aware that the old dialogue had ended, or even begun. Later, Ford called for a deepening dialogue with the nations of Latin America. Until then I had thought that a deepening dialogue took place between two men who talked to each other while digging a hole.

When Ford was involved in two shooting incidents late in 1975, he said that he did not want to cut down on his public appearances because he wanted to continue his "dialogue with the American people." Plunging into a crowd to shake hands is not a dialogue. Nor is making a speech. There has to be someone talking back. The twelfth annual America-Israel Dialogue was held in Jerusalem in June 1976. The former Israeli foreign min-

---

* In the course of his limning, Wattenberg, relying heavily on attitudinal surveys, found that "The dominant rhetoric of our time is a rhetoric of failure, guilt and crisis." Attitudinal surveys often lead to platitudinal conclusions.

ister, Abba Eban, said, "We must talk in full mutuality." That's a dialogue. Dialogue offers an excellent example of what is happening to the language. It is a word with a specific meaning in books, plays, moving pictures. That meaning is being lost, as governments embark on a policy of dialogue and the editorial writers follow along, urging a policy of dialogue on those governments that unaccountably don't already have one.

The State Department, announcing the appointment of an official to represent consumer rights and interests within the Department, promised "to take those steps necessary and feasible to promote and channel these rights and interests with respect to the maintenance and expansion of an international dialogue and awareness." Somebody was paid to write that. Before Morocco took over the Spanish Sahara, the Moroccan foreign minister went to Madrid to discuss the issue in, as he put it, "a spirit of dialogue." That is better than going in a spirit of monologue, but we are seeing dialogue taking on a mystical, magical quality, as though it meant more than a couple of people talking to each other, and as though a dialogue in itself were a solution.

Dialogue has become so ubiquitous that when, in October 1974, the Guards units in Whitehall in London returned to the saddle after three weeks on foot because their horses had had sore throats, it occurred to me that the sore throats had been caused by too much neigh-saying in the equine dialogue.

The deepening dialogue with the nations of Latin America that President Ford hankered after should be distinguished from the discussion in depth. The deepening dialogue is conducted on land, the in-depth discussion in water. On December 31, 1975, the White House announced that Prime Minister Yitzhak Rabin of Israel would visit Washington on January 27 so that he and President Ford could "discuss in depth the situation in the Middle East." The White House deputy press secretary, John Carlson, did not say what the depth would be, and speculation was, as it so often is, rife. Would Ford and Rabin duck their heads beneath the surface of the White House pool and exchange signals? Snorkel?

Don divers' gear* and go full fathom five into the Potomac? Would each board a submarine, have the skipper pass the order, "Take her down," and communicate by radio? Would they, mocking the dismay of the security men responsible for their safety, descend to a level that, so far as was known, had been reached only once before? (This was when federal officials carried out what one of them—he did not permit mention of his name—called "a very, very in-depth study" of the condition of New York City banks at the time the city was threatening to default on its debts. The officials were brought back by easy stages to avoid the bends.)

In the event, Rabin and Ford did none of these things— perhaps Carlson was misinformed—and I concluded that they had at most a shallow discussion. It was hardly worth Rabin's while coming over.

What has happened to some of our other old favorites since last we met—major, constituency, controversial, parameter, hopefully, and the rest? All have extended their reach. Thus, controversial. *Time* reported that "the delegates to an unusual General Congregation that is charting the controversial future course of the Jesuits voted to change policy on the papal vow." Evidently the Jesuits decided earlier that their future course would be controversial and the delegates were arranging it.

When President Ford went to Japan in 1974, his trousers aroused some unfavorable comment. Mrs. Ford, who did the President's packing, said that she had followed instructions in "a booklet on clothes and accessories" put out by Brooks Brothers. Brooks Brothers' manager in Washington, Robert Mallon, denied this. "We supplied the coat only—the coat only—plus the ascot and shoes," he said. "The controversial trousers belong to the President." The White House later explained that the controversial trousers had been left over from "an inauguration." Ford undoubtedly hoped that he would hear no more about them, and wore nonpartisan trousers from then on.

Nonetheless, there are politicians who might have envied

---

* Gear is always donned. It is never put on.

Ford the trousers and their grip on public attention. The mayor of Utica, New York, Ed Hanna, employs a public relations firm to advise the press that he is "available for interviews upon request," that he and "his frenetic populist regime have been flailing at tradition," that the heart of his plans for Utica is "the La Promenade re-development project," which would have an art center, antique shops, a crafts unit, apartments, and unusual boutique stores, and that in Mayor Hanna's view, "The phonies and the bluebloods and the politicians, who gave this city the name 'Sin City,' have been draining this lousy town too long." A press release describes Hanna as "New York State's Most Controvertial Mayor." This is not quite right. He is not the most controvertial mayor. He is the only one. For Mayor Hanna, man of the La Promenade project, controvertial is the le mot juste.

As controversial has extended its reach, so has alleged. When a House committee decided to publish a report on United States intelligence activities, White House press secretary Ron Nessen said, "Under the agreement, the President should have had a chance to review the classified material in the report before it was leaked to the public. The President views with the most serious concern the leak of the alleged contents of the report." A leak of alleged contents is itself only an alleged leak until it is determined that the contents are the genuine contents. As alleged. The New Haven, Connecticut, *Register* began a story from Hamden, Connecticut: "It doesn't pay to allegedly attempt to remove auto parts from Chet's Auto Parts, Inc., 87 Welton St. Two young men found that out this week." Crime doesn't allegedly pay.

Convince to, as in *New York* magazine's "Phyllis convinced Ford to join her on an expedition to a ski resort" and United Press International's "Five bandits convinced a Brink's armored car driver to open his truck door by pointing a 50MM anti-aircraft gun at him,"* has expanded in three ways. First, people may now be convinced not to.

---

* A .38-caliber revolver was known as a convincer in the gangster talk of the thirties. Imagine how convincing an antiaircraft gun must be.

"Kansas City, Mo. (UPI)—Democratic National Chairman Robert Strauss said he doubted if reform delegates could have been convinced not to walk out of a weekend meeting to plan the party's December miniconvention."

People may now also be convinced into.

From an article in the *New York Times* travel section by a senior editor of a large New York publishing house:

"Here is where we will make love," Antonio said. "Now you will take off your suit."

"Listen, Antonio, I told you no," I insisted. "Do you really think I'm saying it just so I can let you convince me into saying yes? I'm not like that. I say what I mean and I mean no."

He shrugged his shoulders. "It is time to eat now. Give me the plastic bag."

From the resignation expressed by Antonio, driven though he was to eating a plastic bag in frustration, we may conclude that people may not only be convinced into doing something, they may also be convinced out of it.

Lengthy brief, as in "The defense attorney submitted a lengthy brief in support of his motion," has not done well. The prosecuting attorney of Allen County, Ohio, Lawrence S. Huffman, closed a moving picture theater in Lima, Ohio, as a public nuisance on the ground that it showed obscene films. The order was overturned in court, and Huffman asked the United States Supreme Court to reverse that. He submitted a lengthy brief in which the statement of facts covered nineteen pages and the legal arguments eighty-three more. The Supreme Court told him to make his lengthy brief less lengthy and more brief or it would not listen to his argument.

Constituency, as in "He is building a constituency among the poor and disadvantaged," has lost standing also. It now takes supportive before it, or broad-based. Broad-based constituencies are extremely difficult to build because they are made up of people who are continually on the move, usually in wide-bodied comfort on American Airlines or on TWA's widebody 1011 service between New York and Los Angeles.

Confrontation, referred to earlier, appears to be strong, but the expert eye can detect a slight crack, a fraying. This appeared with the first mention of direct confrontations, which implied that there could be confrontations of secondary and tertiary kinds. C. L. Sulzberger has written in the *New York Times* about a friendly confrontation between the Swedish and Yugoslav versions of socialism. All this threatens so to cheapen confrontations that no self-respecting government will want to have one.

Somewhat the same thing is happening to parameter. Although at times the entire nation appears to be running in a hundred-parameter dash, parameter is shrinking or narrowing and may eventually disappear. Jules Power, executive producer of ABC's "AM America," wrote that "There are fairly narrow parameters as to what one can and cannot do" in the Soviet Union. The journalism review *More* sighted narrow parameters in this country, these being the parameters of debate over energy policy in the United States. The Institute for American Strategy accused CBS News of reporting in a partial and slanted way and so of "narrowing the parameters of public debate" on national defense. That is impossible, but CBS denied it anyway.

David Halberstam, writing in the *Atlantic,* recalled Edward R. Murrow's becoming a tough-minded correspondent on the domestic scene after the Second World War and creating tension that "quickly marked the parameters of freedom within broadcasting in the 1950's." By 1960, according to Halberstam, Murrow saw broadcasting becoming "more and more a vehicle for manipulation rather than a vehicle for broadening the parameters of vision." Murrow opened the door of the vehicle and got out, and the flags flying at the parameter line were taken down.

Parameter was not around in Murrow's time. He would not have used it if it had been. It is true, of course, that in those days the parametric pressure was not so strong as it is now. Now the State Department, according to its public announcements, thinks nothing of looking within itself for action parameters and finding them along with improved linkages and a broad spectrum, which make up an impressive bonus.

The *New York Times* reported that labor and management were working out the economic parameters of a settlement. Later, President Ford welcomed those parameters as falling "within the parameters of what we would call a defendable agreement." (The Council of Economic Advisers mans the parapets.) The *Times*'s business page one day set out the parameters for the new magazine *People*—among them that it have single-copy sales only, reach a high female audience with reasonably high demographs, and have a good pass-along audience. Reasonably high demographs means that the magazine's readers fall within an age group, usually the early twenties to the mid-forties, that does a good deal of buying. It will be recognized at once as a parameter. (Demographic increments, which sound somewhat the same, are not parameters. Demographic increment is a social science term for an addition to a population. Demographs within demographic increments would vary.) In a good pass-along audience, those who have read the magazine pass it along a straight and narrow path to people who have not. It is the domino theory of circulation.

Hopefully—as in "Hopefully, this afternoon the fog will lift and we can get out there with a helicopter" (from the United States Coast Guard in New Orleans); "Hopefully it is a shorter-range evil" (President Ford); "I am happily and hopefully going to shut off their federal funds" (Madalyn Murray O'Hair, opponent of prayer in the schools); and "Hopefully the dead man will float to the surface* after about ten days" (author unknown)—has hopelessly infected other words heretofore immune. I have, for example, seen an advertisement for a California Riesling that was "regretfully available only in very limited quantities." That is the hopefully disease spreading, but no variation is likely to approach the majesty of the announcement by the president of the Green Bay Packers, Dominic Olejniczak, when discussing the hiring of a new coach. "We hope," he said, "to have an announcement before the end of the week, hopefully before that."

This has been rivaled in my experience only by an application

---

* With the body badly decapitated.

of the foundation stone of American English, "Y'know." A friend in Detroit told me he had heard a colleague say, "Y'know, you never know."*

Inoperative, as in Ron Ziegler's announcement in April 1973 that his earlier statements on the Watergate affair were inoperative, has reached the construction industry. I live in midtown New York, near a site where a big new building recently went up. Projects of that size have public address systems for transmitting instructions, and one day I heard this: "Please use the inside elevators for going up in the building. The outside elevator is inoperative."

Unfortunately, I was not there when the announcement was made that the elevator was, in the Washington style, once again operational, which is Washington's way of saying that something is ready. Operational is just beginning to wrinkle from exposure to the elements. Its future is certain. It will be a cliché.

So will presence be a cliché. Presences are usually military. The United States had one in Thailand for twenty-six years, until in 1976 the presence became a thing of the past. Presence is a Washington word, so the British have picked it up. Said Lieutenant Colonel Robert Ward, commander of the First Regiment of the Queen's Dragoon Guards, stationed in Northern Ireland: "The first aim is to reassure the local populace of a maximum presence here."

We came, we saw, we established a maximum presence. The leaders of the victorious faction in the Angolan civil war told an assistant to Senator John Tunney of California, "We have no desire for a permanent Soviet or Cuban presence." They probably would have preferred to say that they did not want the Cubans and

---

* Hopefully has its academic supporters, who say that it is the equivalent of the German *hoffentlich*. However, Nicholas Christy, a professor of medicine at the College of Physicians and Surgeons of Columbia University, wrote to me that *hoffentlich* means it is to be hoped. The German for hopefully, he wrote, is *hoffnungsvoll*. Which leads me to say *hoffnungsvoll* that Americans, *hoffentlich*, will stop misusing hopefully.

Russians to stay but wanted to assure Washington on this point, since Washington obstinately believes that presence makes the heart grow fonder. They therefore put it into language the United States Government would understand.

As new clichés make their way in, often used incorrectly, serviceable old words make their way out. Ambivalent, which means having conflicting feelings—feelings, for example, of love and hate—is shoving ambiguous, which means uncertain or doubtful. Ambiguous should shove back. Consensus is coming in, and majority and agreement are going out. We are being told about a fair consensus, a strong consensus, a growing consensus, a solid consensus, a general consensus, a broad consensus. Jimmy Carter said about certain campaign issues, "You'll never get anybody to agree on them. You won't even get a consensus on them." A consensus is an opinion collectively held, and it either exists or it doesn't. It cannot be fair, meaning partial, and it must be general or it wouldn't be a consensus.

Consensus has obvious appeal. It is new and pompous, its meaning is not well understood, and its use makes public discussion less specific. It was bound to flourish. Consensus is not quite the biggest of the new clichés, however. Global is, and as it comes in, world and worldwide go out. Henry Kissinger speaks of maintaining a balance of global stability (balances of instability are notoriously hard to maintain) and of global peace. Kissinger also points out that "In the global dialogue among the industrial and developing worlds, the communist nations are conspicuous by their absence." Since the communist nations take up a large part of the globe, if they are absent the dialogue isn't global.

The commander of NATO forces in Europe, General Alexander Haig, sees the West confronted by a global Soviet military capability and wants the western nations to develop the ability (not capability?) to manage global Soviet power in a global sense. James Schlesinger, when he was Secretary of Defense, put it more succinctly. He worried about the global military equilibrium with the Soviet Union. (If you don't have it, there goes the globallgame.)

The United Nations General Assembly convokes a global conference on the consequences of the misuse of land. The consequences of that misuse, I am sorry to say, go under the name of desertification. A new book about multinational corporations is called *Global Reach*. A *Publishers Weekly* reviewer says that the heads of these corporations are global oligopolists and have global vision. Very broad parameters. In the press, the migration of wealth from one part of the world to another—after oil prices were raised, for example—is described as a global challenge, and there is much concern about global fallout, though how anything can fall out of the globe I do not see. Ronald Reagan accuses the Ford Administration of lacking a coherent global view, and Governor Edmund Brown, Jr., of California, known for a certain shyness, deprecatingly describes something he has said about the limits of natural resources as "a bit global." Later, Brown's organizers in the Oregon primary hold a strategy meeting in Portland in the Global Delicatessen, which, I take it, sells the world's wurst.

The Canadians, ever on the alert, ask: Can one of Canada's most successful international companies get global recognition with a name change? Their answer is yes, by changing its name from Northern Electric to Northern Telecom. An easier way would have been to broadcast on Canada's Global Television Network. As the old saying goes, it's a small globe.

Global was a cliché once before. During the Second World War, Franklin Roosevelt talked a great deal about global interests, global considerations, and global repercussions. The playwright Clare Boothe Luce, then a member of the House of Representatives, disagreed with much of what Roosevelt was saying. It was, she said, globaloney. It took global thirty years to recover.

The Canadians may find the corporate name change from Northern Electric to Northern Telecom counterproductive. That is another new cliché, used in place of self-defeating, unwise, misjudged, and foolish. Counterproductive is altogether larger than any of these, and more nearly official. In the medical world it has already spawned countertherapeutic. It sounds major.

Major itself is colossal. I have already mentioned major contributions to the nation's political dialogue. These might be encouraged by being made tax deductible. "Did you make any major contributions to the nation's political dialogue last year?" the question on the income tax form would say. "If so, write brief summaries of them in the space provided and attach receipts showing to whom they were made and your estimate of their value. When possible, estimates should be accompanied by documents, receipts, etc."*

The *New York Times* continues to be the great, or major, discoverer of the quality of majorness almost everywhere it looks, wholesale. Picking my way through the *Times*'s major jungle of major news stories of the day, past major tests, major enemy categories, major groups of prisoners, major western embassies, major roles, a major witness, a major theme, major social issues, major highway construction, a major setback, a major argument, major gains, a major realignment, major social and psychological implications, major rail lines, major fields, major bills, major elements, major progress, major states, a major war, major nationalist groups, major help, a major producer, a major case, major differences, major industrial powers, a major operation, major disasters, major banks, a once-major voice, a major spring season, and a major incident that might spark potentially explosive material, I came to two stories in which the *Times* surpassed itself. One came from Watergate days and contained a major task, a major event, major trials, major players, and major solid cases to be made against major figures. In the other story the *Times* showed what it could do with limited space in a front-page précis: "The first major revision of the city's new fire code for high-rise

---

* The Internal Revenue Service would have in mind here evidence that a contribution has been noticed and discussed and so deserves to be deemed major. Mention in a column by David Broder or Joseph Kraft or Evans and Novak would be considered conclusive proof. So would serving as the basis for a question on "Meet the Press" or the "Today" show. Being discussed by an aide to a candidate, and without attribution, would not by itself be enough.

office buildings, designed to remove a major cause of fire deaths, went into effect yesterday with the vast majority of buildings in noncompliance." The detailed story ran on a non-outside page, and in it the major revision and vast majority of buildings were joined by a major violator and a major factor. The *Times* is a major violator. I often wish it weren't. If a major boycott were imposed by the *Times* copy desk for one day's editions, the news would be fit to print, but couldn't be.

President Ford sent a message to Congress on energy in which he said,

"I have a very deep belief in America's capabilities. Within the next 10 years, my program envisions:

"200 major nuclear power plants.

"250 major new coal mines.

"150 major coal-fired power plants.

"30 major new refineries.

"20 major new synthetic fuel plants."

That was 650 majors. In major competition, that is known as throwing down the gauntlet, or as the galloping major.

Presidents have obvious advantages in these matters, but what counts is playing the game. The *Book-of-the-Month Club News* has described the publication of a book as "a major event," even without the assurance that the book would become a major motion picture. There is a Conference of Presidents of Major American Jewish Organizations. In November 1974 a Major Interdisciplinary Symposium on the Human Condition was held in Palm Coast, Florida. In February 1975 the San Francisco Board of Education voted to end public school sports as an economy measure, and Erv Delman, president of the San Francisco Coaches' Association, said, "This is catastrophic and major."

On December 10, 1974, the twenty-fifth anniversary of Chiang Kai-shek's arrival on Taiwan, the *New York Times* reported that "Few noticed and those who did averted their eyes as a major milestone in the history of this embattled island passed by today without commemorative speeches, editorials or public recognition of any kind." It is easy to see why the *Times* considered this news. A minor milestone might be expected to escape public attention, and the most it can hope for in the end probably is to be installed along the road to recovery in a once thriving hub of commerce, but a major milestone trudging by cries out not for averted eyes but for recognition.

"Who is that shrieking out there, Sergeant?"

"I believe it's Major Milestone, sir."

"Very well, Sergeant. Let him in."

"Yes, sir." (Salutes smartly and turns.) "Advance, Major Milestone, and be recognized."

The British, possibly because they want to go on being considered a major power, are making major their own. In early 1976, Iran had a budget deficit and began delaying payment for goods bought overseas. A British government official, asked about this, said that Iran had not done anything as serious as canceling a contract. "What we're looking for," he said, "is a major 'no' on a project that would point to a central government direction not to spend any more money." In a world in which people avert their eyes as major milestones pass by, a major no that points should not be impossible to find. It may well be found watching the march past of the major milestones and warning them away from paths down which they should not go.

Major milestones usually forage off the country, and they sometimes set up more or less permanent camp in the hope of becoming turning points. When they do, they may run into competition, especially in Washington, where most of the country's turning point production is concentrated. When President Ford signed his proposed budget for fiscal 1977 he said that he hoped it would be a turning point for the American people. More precisely, that is what he *would* have said a few years ago. However, the President knew that an unadorned turning point is ignored in Washington.* He therefore placed a major before it. Even then, Ford felt his phrase inadequate, since major turning points are claimed by people who are not even in the govern-

---

* "Why, it's just a little old turning point, son. We get 'em here all the time."

ment. When the Kentucky legislature defeated an attempt to rescind ratification of the Equal Rights Amendment, Liz Carpenter of ERAmerica, an organization in favor of ratification, said, "This represents a major turning point across the country for the equal rights. amendment." Ford therefore made his a very major turning point.

Nelson Rockefeller has helped to bring about the state of affairs in which major is routine and a turning point insignificant. In June 1975 a commission headed by Rockefeller and charged with investigating the CIA handed its report to President Ford. Rockefeller told reporters that the report would show that "There are things that have been done in contradiction to the statutes, but in comparison to the total effort, they are not major."

Senator Church of Idaho, chairman of a Senate committee investigating the CIA, objected that he had "hard evidence" that the CIA had been involved in murder plots, and said, "I do not regard murder plots as a minor matter."

Rockefeller replied that when he used the words "not major," he meant only the number of times the CIA broke the law,* not the seriousness of what it did. "I made no comment on seriousness," said Rockefeller. "I talked about magnitude." Magnitude means great size or extent, great importance or significance. Something of magnitude might once—come to a turning point, O Time, in thy flight—have been called major.

In the creation of old favorites, which is done by aging them prematurely, *Time* magazine has unrivaled resources. The tone is set at the top, as may be seen in the "Letter from the Publisher" in the issue of February 10, 1975, when the publisher, Ralph P. Davidson, wrote about a Middle East news tour by fifty-three United States businessmen, journalists, *Time* editors, and others.

After blinking at the distinction drawn between *Time* editors and journalists, I noted that the fifty-three tourists were citizens traveling at their own expense through an arena of world events. What kind of citizens? A practiced *Time* reader would know at once: Influential and concerned. What kind of arena? Crucial.

---

* A free translation by me of "done in contradiction to the statutes."

The "letter" contained no surprises. The tourists were given an opportunity (unique) to learn (firsthand) about a region (vital) by posing questions (hard) to Middle East kings, emirs, prime ministers, and presidents, to whom, during a round of interviews, dinners and seminars (busy), they were given access (well merited).

Were the tourists impressed? Deeply.

On the war-ravaged Golan Heights, how did the possibility of renewed fighting seem to them? Ominous.

And the current peace? Fragile.

The coffee in Saudi Arabia? Bitter.

The nations of the Persian Gulf? Rich.

No more?

Croesus-rich.

Another letter from the publisher described the cover story on the entertainer Cher by a contributor (prolific) who explored Hollywood's star syndrome (glittery), then drew on his experience (wide) for a story about the singer (slinky), who was interviewed on a day off (rare), while others made comments (candid).

A *Time* quiz:

In J. Edgar Hoover's last years as head of the FBI, what kind of head was he? Aging.

Could he have been otherwise described? Yes, durable.

What sort of gleanings from the FBI files did the aging but durable Hoover offer President Johnson? Juicy.

For which Johnson had what kind of appetite? Voracious.

Actress Sarah Miles was given a bash in a Madrid night club. What kind of bash and what kind of night club? Lavish and swank.

The annual increase in family budgets that would be brought on by President Ford's energy proposals was, according to one estimate, what? Whopping.

If a soldier is old, what else is he likely to be? Grizzled.

So goes *Time,* whopping and not ungrizzled itself, and still devoted to bbl. for barrel, bu. for bushel, and gal. for gallon. Roll out the bbl., don't hide your light under a bu., and a,b,c,d,e,f,g,h,i got a gallon in Kalamazoo.

Now that we know what *Time* can do, we are better able to judge what we can do ourselves. You will remember that we left the rangy Texan, the bluff head of Navy matériel, and the former Greek and Peruvian strongmen on a sprawling game reserve preparing to go on safari and having just learned that reservations for an ailing chief of state had been canceled and that if Daniel P. Moynihan did not exist he would have to be invented. Since then, sitting before a crackling log fire while Christmas slipped quietly into Bethlehem under the wary eye of Israeli guards, they have been discussing who else was going on the safari. The former Peruvian strongman spoke first:

"Listen," Velasco said, "is there any chance that we will see beetle-browed and pantalooned Kurdish leader Mulla Mustapha Barzani?"

"None," the Texan said. "He has slipped across the Iraqi border into Iran."

"Who told you?"

"Kurdish sources."

"Well placed?"

"It goes without saying."

Velasco persisted. "What about black-robed bearded prelate-president Archbishop Makarios, who once fled his island nation?"

"He won't be here either."

"How do you know?"

"Greek Cypriot sources."

"Familiar with his movements and in a position to know?"

"What do you think?"

"Piebald Robert Mardian of Watergate fame?"

"No."

"Pipe-smoking Harold Wilson?"

"I don't believe he can get away."

"But he no longer heads the deficit-ridden British government."

"True, but Britain is strike-plagued."

"What about the bewigged Speaker of the House of Commons?"

"Same problem."

"The steely-eyed Georgia peanut farmer, Jimmy Carter?"

"Ironing out differences."

"Crusty old George Meany?"

"Busy with a list of bread-and-butter Democratic liberals he would like to take to the woodshed."

"Why?"

"Because they broke with him on the all-important trade bill."

"Crusty sixty-five-year-old Christian President Suleiman Franjieh of Lebanon?"

"My understanding is no crusts of any description."

"The ambitious but sorely troubled Shah of Iran?"

"Dealing with his once burgeoning oil revenues."

"Short, blunt Teng Hsiao-p'ing?"

"Is he the same as tough, pragmatic Teng Hsiao-p'ing?"

"I believe so."

"Purged by his powerful enemies."

"On what charge?"

"Peddling sinister revisionist trash, and stirring the right-deviationist wind."

"What about a straight-talking foreign minister? The country doesn't matter."

"At the moment there aren't any."

"This is a damn dull safari," said the bluff Kidd.

"It'll perk up. It's only a matter of time," the Texan said. "Politically potent Italian Communist Party chief Enrico Berlinguer is coming."

"The spare Sardinian?"

"That's right."

"What's keeping him?"

"Maybe he ran into a papal motorcade," Velasco said.

"I doubt it," the Texan said. "The more likely explanation is that, as a spare Sardinian, he is much in demand for Sardinian dinner parties and has had trouble breaking away."

Kidd and Velasco stared out the window.

"I've never seen a military formation like it before," the Peruvian said, "if it is a military formation. One group is marching in the usual way, but the other seems to be falling over to the side."

The Texan, all business, went to the telephone and dialed the operator. "Hello," he said, "I'm a rangy Texan and a long way from home, where I am socially prominent. Get me an informed neutral source."

There was a pause, and then the Texan explained what they had seen. There was another pause, after which he said, "I understand," hung up, and turned to the others. "Perfectly simple, once you realize what it is. One left-leaning delegation and one crack regiment, arriving together to provide a façade of unity in this strife-torn continent."*

Velasco spoke. "That's how you know so much," he said to the Texan. "Sources."

"That's right."

"Have you ever met a neutral source?" Kidd asked.

"Only once."

"What was he like?"

"There wasn't time to find out," the Texan said. "He was a prestigious but self-effacing scholar, as many sources are, and he effaced himself before my eyes."

The former Greek strongman intervened. "I'm surprised that you did not recognize a left-leaning delegation on your own," he said. "Had you never seen one before?"

"Never," the Texan said. "Individuals, yes, but not delegations. And the left-leaning individuals I saw were otherwise perfectly ordinary. I'd like," he went on pensively, "to see some queer, soft, left-leaning eggheads who went to Harvard. Hard-driving, tenacious Woodward and Bernstein established their existence in *The Final Days.* Of course, they are exceptional reporters who know where to look when the rest of us don't."

---

* A reader suggested to me that politicians, journalists, and others who lean left may do so because of a faulty metatarsal arch. It was a stunning insight.

Ize Front

I n January 1976, before any of the presidential primaries, Howard "Bo" Callaway, chairman of President Ford's campaign committee, said, "The White House is so concerned about perceptions of a politicized White House that the President and those around him just totally unpoliticized the White House." After a number of Bo peeps of this kind, the President semirepoliticized the White House by bringing in Rogers Morton as a political counselor. Later, Callaway was put out to pasture, or pasturized.

The chairman of the Democratic National Committee, Robert Strauss, did not speak of unpoliticizing anything, but these were only healthy political differences, normal in a two-party system. In a discussion of who should have access to the Democratic convention floor, Strauss announced, "We're not going to depoliticize a political convention."

Toujours la politicizesse.

At a meeting of intellectuals to discuss UNESCO's attitude

toward Israel, Professor Seymour Martin Lipset of Stanford University said that the problem was "the politicalization of UNESCO."

Toujours la politicalizesse.

To ize a word is one thing. To wise it is another. Senator Birch Bayh of Indiana, campaigning for the Democratic nomination for President in October 1975—possibly on the theory that the early Birch catches the worm, which in this case it didn't—put forward the notion that a President can help the economy by sounding cheerful. One of our troubles, he said, was that "energywise, economywise and environmentalwise, we have become obsessed with the problems."

Affecting cheerfulness is not a notion with a history that commends it. During the Great Depression, prosperity spent an unconscionably long time just around the corner, and although Franklin Roosevelt's "We have nothing to fear but fear itself" has become a staple of television programs around inauguration time, the Depression was not beaten until the beginning of the Second World War. I can remember being panhandled when I was a boy in New York in the early 1930s and seeing the "Hooverville" huts of the poor and homeless along the banks of the Hudson. Happy talk did not help then any more than it helped Bayh.

If he were President, Bayh said in that same speech, and Federal Reserve Chairman Arthur Burns held back recovery by keeping money tight, "I'd create a structure to do an end run around him." Burns might of course have chosen to do a little running endwise himself, possibly tackling the structure before it got past the line of scrimmage. Moreover, if the other members of the Federal Reserve Board, joined by Federal Reserve bank presidents across the country, were to group themselves around Burns wedgewise, what could the structure—probably ad hoc, anyway, and rickety—have done?

Because Bayh abandoned his campaign for the nomination, we will never know the answer to that, though I would be inclined to put my money on Burns. Structures are nothing these days in Washington, where it is restructuring that counts. I am less in the dark about why Bayh tacked that wise onto energy, economy and environmental (it should have been environment) instead of saying, "We have become obsessed with the problems of energy, the economy and the environment," which is the same length syllablewise and more direct. Those who use wise as a suffix are convinced that they are saving time, because they are using one word instead of two. The program notes for a concert by the Chamber Music Society of Lincoln Center in New York had this: "Dvořák was a late bloomer, compositionwise."

If Dvořák was a late bloomer anythingwise, it was composerwise, but it is a small point.

"Been up to much lately, Antonin, compositionwise?"

"Quartetwise, it hasn't been bad, but symphonywise it's slow, and operawise . . ." His voice trails off. "I'm low," he says, "selfconfidencewise."

The misconception that time is being saved accounts for a wise to the word. The ize to the word comes about for another reason, which is that ize is thought to have a businesslike ring or, which in some cases is just as good, to sound technical. The *Wall Street Journal* reporter who covered Bayh's campaign in Boston spoke of the Democrats as "a factionalized party." No time was saved, since he could have said factional or, better still, factious. But he must have thought that factionalized carried more authority, which explains its appeal. What those who use ize overlook is that it is usually unnecessary, and always dull—it is a leaden syllable —and that it imposes monotony on the language by making so many words sound the same.

Not many can resist the temptation to ize. The *New York Times* said that a politician who went from agent to advisernegotiator for Mayor Abraham Beame had metamorphosized. It worked out fairly well but was a mixed metamorphosis. An adviser to Governor Hugh Carey of New York complained that members of the state legislature did not understand the urgency of New York's financial problems and so carried on as before. Said he, "They overstrategize themselves."

That over was significant. What is wanted in New York is the right amount of strategizing. A state senator sent me a copy of a proposal by an advertising company that wanted the $135,000 state contract for letting people know—"our objective is to generate measurable response"—about food stamps. After recommending radio announcements "because they offer access to the broadcast medium," meaning that if you put your announcements on radio they will be on radio, the company promised: "We will also strategize with the client on ways to optimize usage of the spots by broadcast management." The company got the contract. For linking strategize and optimize—somebody must have conceptualized this—it deserved to.

The Department of Public Instruction of the state of Iowa, conducting a survey of job prospects for those without a bachelor's degree, asked cooperating businesses to maximize the accuracy and validity of information supplied by keeping it as localized as possible. If they did, then the need for vocational training could be prioritized. Social and behavioral scientists never look back. Ize front.

I have been told that a television news broadcaster in Alabama announced that a deputy sheriff, killed in the line of duty, would be funeralized the following day, and there is, unfortunately, no reason to doubt it. United Press International, in a story about the Kennedy political tradition, remembered an occasion when John Kennedy prophecized. The Reverend Allison Cheek, one of the first women ordained in the Episcopal Church, said after celebrating communion, "I will not let the church inferiorize me again." Some believe that in the last analysis we are all humble, or inferiorized, servants of the Lord, but that covers everybody and takes away the sting. In other circumstances being inferiorized is no fun. I was covering the Turkish elections in 1957, relying on interpreters, as everyone else was. Then the BBC sent in a correspondent who spoke Turkish. It seemed to the rest of us that the BBC was hitting below the belt, but we were indubitably inferiorized. President Roy Amara of the Institute for the Future, an institute for the future in Menlo Park, California, prophecized not long ago, "Most of the influences on us today are rigidized for the next five years, and on a current momentum course that is irreversible." Five years carry the current momentum course to the point of no return, where it sees what the fates have in store if it continues. It reverses.

There is no limit to the bountiful imagination with which Americans ize. Sometimes I seem to hear thousands of voices raised in song:

> I fell in love with you
> First time I looked into
> Them there ize.

Americans annualize weekly and monthly costs and put out form letters that are personalized. Vulnerabilized to disease or traumatized by injury, they may be hospitalized. Because of the 1960s and 1970s, some of them have been cynicized and some radicalized. They privatize their houses with window shades and accessorize their spacious master bedrooms with oil paintings. As it happens, when the opportunity arose recently to accessorize my own spacious master bedroom with oil paintings, I could not seize it because I was making beautiful happen to my window treatments with Levolor Riviera blinds from Levolor Lorentzen, Inc., of Hoboken, New Jersey. Some days in New York, I wish I could make clean happen to my window treatments.

The publicity director of a publishing house received this letter from the assistant secretary of a large insurance company:

"Dear Mrs. C._____:

"We have finalized the structure of the program for our meetings in 1976, and unfortunately, the decision has been made not to utilize the services of an outside speaker. The decision on this was by no means unanimous, but by those whose final decision prevails. Perhaps sometime in the future we shall be able to put to use your services."

I knew what Mrs. C.'s feelings must have been. Many NBC program structures over the years have been finalized without putting to use my services. This sort of treatment is not without purpose. A British business slogan summed it up: Treat 'em mean and keep 'em keen.

Those in the government and academic world ize furiously. An art critic wondered what would happen to photography as a result of its museumization. The State Department has promised to utilize and vitalize ongoing machinery in dealing with the environment. A candidate for the Park Commission in Framingham, Massachusetts, offered analization of the park department's participation records. He was elected, but if the offer of analization was the reason, it would be interesting to know what the voters thought they were voting for. Maybe they could be psychoanalized.

During the 1974 campaign President Ford, verbalizing cuff-offwise at the airport in Greensboro, North Carolina, told the Republicans gathered there, some of them hard-nosed professionals, "Really, I look in your eyes and I plead with your hearts, and I beg with your mind, that you maximize your efforts." Maximize your efforts. A stirring call to arms.

It is often assumed that hardness of nose means that the owner of the nose is on the political right, or conservatized. It is not an infallible sign. C. L. Sulzberger of the *New York Times,* a connoisseur in such matters, gazed upon Helmut Schmidt, the Chancellor of West Germany, and declared him hard-nosed. A few weeks later Craig Whitney, chief of the Bonn bureau of the *Times,* examined Schmidt's nose and confirmed Sulzberger's finding. What neither appreciated is that a hard nose may help to keep the head level and sometimes above water. Complications arise not from a nose's obduracy—a hard nose turneth away wrath—but from its going where it is not wanted. Such a nose is not sensitized.

I once had a brief hope of being thought hard-nosed. One rainy day in Washington in 1946, I was at the airport covering President Truman's return from a trip, and another reporter mistook me for a Secret Service agent. I said nothing and concentrated on looking alert and rugged of nose. The hope faded when a real Secret Service agent told us, me included, to move back. My nose, which responds to flattery, wanted to continue the masquerade, but I knew that my hard-nosed days were over and that nothing lay ahead but being a two-fisted, shirt-sleeved newsman with a tough exterior concealing a heart as big as all outdoors.

An economist has pointed out to me a study (not his) in which the following appears:

"The definition of net wage rate in equation (2) suggests that wage-rate changes are best parameterized by changes in u." This is the first parameterized that has come to my attention. The study is dated October 1974. O Pioneers!

What is u? I do not know. I can tell u that the same study speaks of "an estimate which suffers from truncation bias." On a hunch, truncation bias means too small, pint-s, if I may say so, ized. A strange new language is emerging from the field in which this study was made. English is being econometricized. It is not for the better. Here is a passage from the study "Tax Effects on Job Search, Training, and Work Effort," by Jonathan R. Kesselman, published by the Institute for Research on Poverty at the University of Wisconsin:

"Basic Properties of the Model
"The assumed form of utility converts the problem to a two-stage maximization. For any given amount of leisure consumed, the worker wishes to choose the *income*-maximizing combination of search and work times. This determines his budget constraint in income-leisure space. Subject to this constraint, the worker chooses the *utility*-maximizing bundle of income and leisure.

"The income-maximizing choice of search time for any given leisure time is determined:

$$\delta Y/\delta S = 0 \longleftrightarrow HvW' - W = 0 .$$

"We call this the optimality condition for job-search. Let us interpret this condition under laissez faire (or any program other than a wage subsidy):

$$W(S) = HW' \text{ with } u = 0 .$$

"A worker is spending the optimal time on search when a marginal hour will earn him the same amount at work, $W(S)$, as at search, HW'. Because v enters both sides of the equality, its value does not affect the result. Search optimality is not dependent on the marginal utilities, owing to the assumed utility form (6). The second-order condition for (7) to be a maximum rather than a minimum solution is:

$$\delta^2 Y / \delta S^2 < 0 \longleftrightarrow HW'' - 2W' < 0 \,.$$

"Before proceeding to the second stage of the maximization, we examine two properties of the income-maximizing budget constraint. The slope is readily established."

Since, as Kesselman says, the slope is readily established, it need not detain us. We move ahead to the point at which, Kesselman says, we may "conventionally assume the utility function to be twice differentiable and concave:

$$C = W^2 U_{YY} - 2WU_{YL} + U_{LL} < 0 \,.$$

"We shall later state the stronger second-order condition needed for an internal tangency in the presence of the convex budget constraint. Let us designate income the numeraire good. Then the first-order condition for the worker's utility-maximum will be:

$$U_Y = U_L / W \,.$$

"This is the familiar first-order condition of the standard labor-supply model."

It does have a certain familiarity about it. It is living beyond your numeraire good that is the problem.

A historian, Richard Morris of Columbia University, has told other historians that during the American Revolution the Tories were fifth columnists and that they should not now be heroized. I was not aware of any mad rush to heroize the Tories for the Bicentennial, but hasty izing does sometimes have to be undone, or neutralized. Hugh M. Bowen, associate professor of applied psychology at Stevens Institute of Technology in Hoboken, New Jersey, has pointed out that, in Britain, prostitution has been de-illegalized. There is already a movement in the United States to have marijuana decriminalized.

Obviously, if ize were avoided in the first place, no one would have to de. It may be stated as a rule: ize before de. Africa, for example, could not have gone through decolonization if it had not been colonized first. Also, ize before re. "Since 1967," an Israeli journalist told the *New Yorker,* "we have been reghettoized." And fy before de. When the French Communist Party became openly less dependent on Moscow, a French analyst explained, "It is de-Russifying itself, but not de-Stalinizing." When the Viking I space robot landed on Mars in July 1976, John Leonard of the *New York Times* wrote about the prospects for demythifying the planet. They were bright. Demythifie on you, John Leonard. But there are exceptions to the rule, especially where covert activities are concerned. Governments are ripest for destabilizing when they have not been stabilized to begin with. Thus the CIA destabilized the Allende government in Chile, and the leader of the Portuguese Communists, of all people, saucily complained that reactionary forces were trying to destabilize Portuguese politics. This was prestabilization destabilization, de taking place before our very ize.

The terms were unknown to me at the time, but I went through heroization and deheroization in short order in 1941, just after I went to work in the International News Service bureau in Washington, and years before my—the Canadians are no slouches at izing; this is the *Toronto Globe and Mail's* word—televisionization. I was in the Senate press gallery, much impressed with everything, including myself for being there, when Senator John Overton of Louisiana, an ally of Governor Huey Long, rose to attack the columnist Thomas Stokes. Stokes had written an exposé of the misuse of federal money by the Long machine, and had received a Pulitzer, or, as Overton prophetically put it, had been Pulitzerized. He repeated the word a number of times with deep sarcasm. He waved his arms and his face grew red. He seemed dangerously angry.

Soon after Overton finished, I left the gallery and entered one of the elevators reserved for Senators and the press. Stokes was in the car also. One floor down, Overton got in. The car was small, and Overton and Stokes were cheek (Overton's) by (Stokes's) jowl. I saw myself getting a scoop as Overton flung himself frenziedly on Stokes, and I—more than a reporter, a hero—pulled them apart.

"Hello, Tom," said Overton.

"Hiya, Senator," said Stokes.

"Goodbye, scoop," said Newman to himself. "Goodbye, hero."

I was also deheroized with great dispatch when I returned to the United Press Washington bureau near the end of 1945. I made the rounds, saying hello to those who had stayed on through the war, and I was exceedingly glad when the night-side editor, known to be dour and demanding, welcomed me with great warmth. I was congratulating myself on the reputation I had obviously made in the bureau three and a half years before, when the night editor spoke again. "Now," he said, "at last we can get rid of some of those damned women."

Rapid heroization and deheroization is my lot. In the spring of 1976, George Washington High School, in New York City, decided that it would have a Hall of Fame of graduates and would hold a dinner to celebrate it. The actresses Jean Arthur and Paulette Goddard were among those chosen, and Henry Kissinger, and Alan Greenspan, Harold Robbins, the novelist, and Senator Jacob Javits, and the baseball player Rod Carew. So was I. I sent in my check for the dinner. It came back. Enough members of the Hall of Fame were willing to attend and be goggled at, but other alumni, not famous, who would have had to do the goggling, no.

Prolonged observation—by me, not of me—has led me to the conclusion that the most widespread izing now going on among Americans is optimizing. Americans are insisting on freedom to optimize, and this may become an inalienable right. It is being popularized.

I learned from a report by the Central and Southern Florida Flood Control District that optimization techniques play a large part in water resources management. These techniques require, among other things, optimization models, conceptual visualization, parametric analysis, inputs, overall methodologies, the inclusion of all viable pathways in the system evaluation schemes, statistical deterministic models, statistical probabilistic models, and, of course, minimization and maximization, the Damon and Pythias of our time.

Congress optimizes, as indeed, since it speaks for the American people, it should. A House-Senate conference committee considering an oil bill reported that the bill was designed to optimize production from domestic properties. This was to be done through a pricing system intended to give the President "a substantial measure of administrative flexibility to craft the price regulatory mechanism in a manner designed to optimize production from domestic properties subject to a statutory parameter requiring the regulatory pattern to prevent prices from exceeding a maximum weighted average." Here is a standard to which all free men will repair.

Not all congressional language is of this kind, though the amount is unquestionably increasing. My mind goes back to the late 1940s and the English used by Ab Herman, administrative assistant to Senator H. Alexander Smith of New Jersey. Herman would hand a press release to another staff member with the instruction, "Give it the backdrop," meaning "Put in the background. Put it in context." Another instruction was "Bulletproof it," meaning take out any mistakes. This admirable brevity may have been a product of his days as a professional baseball player before good velocity took over.*

It almost seems that everybody optimizes. William D. Lawson, class of 1949, running for the Cornell University Board of Trustees, thought that he deserved support because, he wrote, one of his principal interests in the business world (he was assistant general manager of Du Pont's fabrics and finishes department) was long-range versus short-range optimization. He thought, Mr. Lawson wrote, that this was probably the most difficult problem that faced a university, partly because the educational needs for a satisfying and contributing life tended to cyclize. Mr. Lawson was not

---

* See page 86.

elected and had to look for a satisfying and contributing life elsewhere.

The Engineering Division of the Travelers Insurance Companies of Hartford, Connecticut, optimized in a pamphlet on product quality and safety: "The question arises, 'If one has optimized a stable design and a well-directed manufacturing operation, why is a quality control program necessary?' The primary answer is *people*. Since no perfect human being exists at this time, errors can and do contaminate the manufacturing cycle. To minimize these errors, the total manufacturing cycle must be policed to assure product/design integrity." The Travelers missed a significant point. It said that people cause errors, even with a well-directed manufacturing operation and optimized stable design. That is precisely why no perfect human being exists at this time. Because of the difficulty of policing the total manufacturing cycle, which remains stubbornly privatized, none is likely to any time soon.

Many foreigners have written that the American character has been shaped by the fact that we are still a young country, rich in ideals and resources, and with the frontier only recently closed. This explains why so few Americans pessimize. However, I do not want to exaggerate this aspect of the American character. Many of those who do not pessimize nonetheless nonoptimize, so that the absence of pessimizational activity does not necessarily imply the presence of optimizational activity.

Non, which is becoming as popular at the beginning of words as ize is at the end, has many uses. It can be vaguely neutral. After President Ford went to China a committee of the National Press Club declared that his press secretary, Ron Nessen, had given "a disastrous non-performance." Said the committee: "Nessen lunged to his nadir." A nadir is a nonzenith. Strictly speaking, it is an antizenith. Without the disastrous and the nadir, non-performance might almost have been taken as noncommittal.

However, non may also be discriminatory and pejorative, as in the case of those who are nonsmokers, nondrivers, and nonwhite. The other identity dominates—smoking, driving, and being white are the affirmative acts, and they define the relation. Being non means being classified according to what you do not do and are not. In the United States, not driving a car is roughly equivalent to not existing, and people who do not drive find that they often have trouble paying by check because they cannot produce a driver's license. A few states issue nondriver identification cards, and in one state a legislator proposed a non-driver's license. The proposal may have been inspired by generosity of spirit, though it sounded as if those who did not drive would need licenses to be permitted not to. This may be coming.

There is a movement among those encouraging the teaching of Indian languages and literature—at South Dakota State University, for example—to refer to Indians as Native Americans and to other Americans as non-Native Americans. This is a narrow view of nativity, and would make people nonnatives of the country in which they were born. Perhaps they could be given resident aliens' visas.

Politically, non may imply a favorable judgment. Americans for Democratic Action refers to certain Senators and Representatives as non-Southern Democrats, though Southern Democrats are not known to the ADA as non-Northern Democrats. Being non-Southern is the desired characteristic. During the oil embargo in 1974, being non-Arab was a considerable recommendation in itself.

Sometimes non is used to be reassuring. Nonlethal gas is thought by those who use it in police and military actions to be almost benevolent. Walt Disney's amusement parks, according to a writer in *Signature,* offer nonperilous adventure. Night clubs recruiting dancers will specify nontopless so that prospective employees will know that they need not go about half-naked. Though non-Southern means Northern, nontopless does not mean bottomless. A night club offering that kind of dancing, perhaps called the Bottomless Pit, would probably state it more plainly. Its dancers would go about dressed to the nons. Non may also be used evasively, as in the case of the liquid that goes into tea and coffee and is called aerated nondairy creamer. One blanches to think what aerated nondairy creamer would be called on the basis of what it is rather than what—dairy cream—it is not.

I mentioned earlier the State Department's promise to utilize and vitalize ongoing machinery. The stated purpose was to strengthen an ever broadening dialogue on the environment. Ever broadening dialogues, which go from the particular to the general to the global to the cosmic and then to horizons not yet dreamed of, are intended to enable nations to deal with each other on the basis of what Secretary of State Kissinger called non-belligerency, including, he specified, the non-use of force. Each side monitors the other closely to be sure that force is what it is nonusing and— Kissinger again—pursues energetically all signs of noncompliance. If neither side has reason to say to the other, "You noncomplied," or if one does noncomply but gets away with saying that it will nonrecur, both may find themselves on what Senator Henry Jackson, in the kind of language that helped to end his campaign for the Democratic presidential nomination, called a nonadversary basis.* They may also find themselves, if the dialogue has not ceased to broaden, non compos mentis.

A nonmember is as different as different can be from a non-chairman member. A nonchairman member is a member. He is simply not the chairman. This may be easily grasped in the following *New York Times* dispatch:

"Albany, April 6—Governor Carey's office is actively considering† withdrawing the nomination of Herman Schwartz as chairman of the Commission of Correction and renominating him as one of the two nonchairman members of the prison watchdog agency."

A nonmember is neither a chairman nor a member, and would not be expected to show up for meetings at all. In fact, nonmembers should be careful about the meetings they do go to. Rabbi Arthur Hertzberg, president of the American Jewish Congress,

---

* Someone may have written this phrase for Jackson under a non de plume.

† To be distinguished from inactively considering.

complained because remarks he made at a meeting in Israel were picked up and reported. "I took it," he said, "to be a nonpublic meeting."

Nonmembers should not be confused with, for example, nonminority group members. A nonminority group member is a nonmember of a minority group but a member of a nonminority—formerly called a majority—group. To remain a nonmember, it is useful to be a noncommunist and noncontroversial. This helps the nomination of a nonmember to get through. The time may be coming when, to retain one's position as a nonmember, it will be best not to be a nonlawyer. This is because Chief Justice Warren Burger has proposed that nonlawyers be appointed to small-claims courts in place of judges, I presume after they have spent some years in non-law school. Burger's idea has been to this point what the British call a nonstarter. Burger might have been wiser to submit the idea first to a nonprofit, nongovernmental research organization for analysis—nonpartisan, of course—before making it nonprivate.

To be a nonmember, it helps to be also a nonpolitician who is a noncandidate for public office. There are, as always, exceptions. In 1976, Hubert Humphrey remained a noncandidate against heavy odds. Equally, being a nonpolitician is not an infallible guarantee of retention of nonmember status. In early 1976 the *New York Times* reported that Daniel Patrick Moynihan, "who enjoys an image as a nonpolitician," might run for the Senate. The *Times* added that Democrats who definitely did want to run "for the most part cultivated an antipolitics image." This could have discouraged Moynihan, for the others, being anti to his non, were more negatively charged against politics than he was. None of this made much sense to me. Since the antipolitician and the nonpolitician would lose anti and non status, respectively, immediately upon election, their appeal was fleeting. Nor was it suggested that if Moynihan went to the Senate his place at Harvard should be taken by a nonscholar, though nonscholars are occasionally invited to lecture at universities to let in a breath of nonstale air. Nonetheless, a candidate who was in favor of politics, which might seem logical for someone seeking political office, evidently stood no chance at all. He would offend the nonvoters.

When political news is heavy, NBC likes to have as many employees on hand as possible. This is why an NBC memorandum once described the news assignment desk as being in a nonvacation, full-staff configuration. If you do intend to take a nonvacation, your place of work is the best place to do it. Configuratively speaking.

The appeal of non is nondifferent from the appeal of ize. It sounds technical, which is why doctors often speak of nonemergency rather than elective surgery. Beyond that, non suggests not that something is being done but that something is not, which perhaps makes it easier to swallow. The Superior, Wisconsin, *Telegram* quoted Chancellor Karl Meyer of the Superior campus of the University of Wisconsin on his attempt to limit reductions in the university budget. If the cuts were smaller, the *Telegram* reported Meyer as saying, it might be possible to save the jobs of some who "would otherwise be non-retained." If not, Meyer would be the old family nonretainer.

Any teachers on the Superior campus who have been non-retained may be able to find jobs in New York State with the Project on Noncollegiate-Sponsored Instruction. The Project is designed to obtain college credits for those who have taken courses from corporations, volunteer groups, state agencies, and other organizations and institutions classified as—need I say?—nonacademic.

Although non can sound neutral and even faintly reassuring, as in nontopless and nonlethal, de cannot. De is almost brutal. It means that something is being removed, or got rid of, or abandoned. The hunger to use de is almost as great as the hunger to use ize and non. When Sam Jaffe was a television news correspondent he also worked undercover for the FBI. Jaffe covered for CBS the trial in Moscow of Francis Gary Powers, the U–2 pilot shot down in 1960, and when he returned to the United States, Jaffe said, he was debriefed by agents of the FBI. When Richard Nixon went to China in February 1976, Secretary of State Kissinger said that details of the debriefing would be decided on Nixon's return.

In both cases there was a misunderstanding. If debrief means anything, it means to withdraw instructions, usually those given to a lawyer, and it is a thoroughly unnecessary term. The FBI was not debriefing Jaffe, and the State Department was not debriefing Nixon. Jaffe and Nixon were the ones who had the experiences and were giving the summaries. They were doing the briefing. The FBI and the State Department were asking questions, at most. But government people who think of themselves as debriefers do not look at things that way. For them the active role in the transaction is theirs. The others are merely debriefees. Hardly has their man deplaned—which is another misnomer; the plane is being cleared of people, not the other way around—than they are all over him, debriefcases at the ready, to find out what he knows.

Debriefing also may follow quickly on deshipping, detraining, or decarring, and sometimes word will be passed that the debriefee has been wrongly classified. Debriefing is intended for friends. The harsher process of deprogramming is substituted for non-friends and friends who have been indoctrinated by nonfriendly forces. In particularly stubborn cases deprogramming is accompanied by threats that those not yielding up their programs fast enough will be defunded. There is a distinct difference here from debriefing, for those who are defunded must first have been funded (Funded in 1876. A Hundred Years of Service). They will also be threatened with being delisted, that is, taken off lists they would like to be on,* and in some countries they may be threatened with captivity in rooms that have been delamped, which is not the same as being delighted and carries an implied threat that the captives may shortly become defunct. They realize that continuing to hold

---

* Project Equality, a religious group that devotes itself to equal employment opportunity, may delist companies from its *Buyers Guide* after conducting or not being allowed to conduct "validation reviews of selected facility implementation." Members of Project Equality are then informed of the companies' "delisted status." I've got, KoKo might have sung, a little delist.

out in a defunded condition, when they don't have a fund in the world, will only generate diseconomies for them. This is a disincentive to continued defiance. Debriefed, deprogrammed, and dejected, they desist.

The supreme comment on de came from Harry W. Hiscock, of Rochester, New York, a private in the Marine Corps who was shot in the hand as part of "hazing" by a drill instructor at Parris Island, South Carolina. "They talk about motivation around here," the private said. "Well, ever since what happened, I've felt very de-motivated."

The private was assigned to a medical rehabilitation platoon whose doctors hoped that the second knuckle and other parts of his hand could be rebuilt, and, one supposes, his motivation with them. They could not be, and Hiscock was given a disability pension. The Marines talk a great deal about motivation. Private Lynn McClure, of Lufkin, Texas, twenty years old and said to be mentally retarded, died of brain damage three months after being beaten with "pugil sticks." Pugil sticks are poles tipped with padding that are used in bayonet training. According to other recruits who took part, when McClure did not want to fight and said that he was injured the drill sergeants ordered the others to beat him. One of those who did the beating told the *Los Angeles Times:* "Just to beat on this guy gave us the feeling that the drill instructor liked this and that we were really showing motivation."

McClure was in the "incentive section" of the "motivation platoon." It cannot be argued that if the Marines did not speak of motivation McClure would be alive. But motivation is one of those fashionable words that smack of psychology and pedagogy. It enables those who use it to conceal from themselves what those they are motivating are being motivated to do. It camouflages reality. We are all safer when language is specific. It improves our chances of knowing what is going on.

A faculty member at a university I had better not name received a memorandum from a high administrative officer of the institution: "Having prioritized available funding, your request for staff-support facilities cannot be actuated at present. Student throughput* indicators show marked declining motivational values in subsequent enrollment periods in elective liberal arts choices." My correspondent thought that meant his request had been turned down.

I have written of certain syllables that mean a great deal to people in government and the academic world—ize, de, dis, ive, re, fy. Ful is another. To say that something was impactful rather than that it had an effect sounds official. News people like it too. It makes *them* sound official. A correspondent for the Public Broadcasting Service asked the head of an agency whether the resignation of a colleague would be majorly impactful on the agency's work. The PBS correspondent should have been deprogrammed at once but wasn't.

I have been told of an executive in an advertising agency who wrote to a client: "This will enable us to direct the most maximally impactful advertising toward the small and medium size dog owner." And the least maximally impactful toward the large size dog owner.

Ive has many applications also. The chairman of President Ford's election campaign, Rogers Morton, said that a Cabinet "ought to be made up of competent people who are qualified to do the job but who are totally supportive of the President." A doubtful thesis, as Vietnam and Watergate demonstrated, but doubtful or not, Morton could have said "who support the President." Perhaps "totally supportive of" is thought to denote a higher level of loyalty, but that is not the reason for using it. It has a quality much loved in Washington. It is ponderous. "The issues," an expert has proclaimed, "are promotive of apathy." So are words like promotive and endorsive.†

To combine dis and ive is especially esteemed. The lieutenant

---

* The meaning of throughput here is obscure. It may refer to students' intentions. A State Department definition of throughput—jazzily spelled thruput—may be found on page 96.

† Benjamin DeMott, reviewing a novel by Alan Lelchuk in the *Atlantic,* wrote, "Mr. Lelchuk is never endorsive of fatuity." Endorsements of fatuity, except in election years, are rare.

governor of New York, Mary Anne Krupsak, said that opponents of the Equal Rights Amendment ran "the most distortive political campaign ever to unfold." The Librarian of Congress, Daniel Boorstin, in an address to the Association of American Publishers, spoke of "the displacive fallacy." I do not know what Boorstin meant, but it is clear that dis and ive unite as smoothly as de and ize, although more often than not de ize have it.

Ive is particularly in vogue with economists. Democrats on the Joint Congressional Economic Committee have sometimes called for more stimulative fiscal and monetary policies, with the Republicans replying that economic recovery required that Congress refrain from further stimulative measures. In January 1976 the Council of Economic Advisers, though recommending a deceleration in the growth of federal spending and concerned about renewed imbalances and sectoral distortions, argued that some stimulative measures were needed so that the country could return to high levels of resource utilization.

There is not a more depressive word in existence than stimulative, unless it is disstimulative, which I have not yet seen but which cannot be far off. In the meantime, a writer for the *Montreal Star* has produced this: "Fiscal and monetary policy, it has now been shown, is not, by itself, enough to stimulate or disstimulate the economy."

These syllables—dis, ative, ization—sound learned. They are the stuff of reports. They turn any paper in which they appear into a document. Not the least of such syllables is ee, a syllable drawn from the French and with a long and honorable history, as in fiancée, devotee, and refugee, but seized upon by governments and academics to enable them to speak more stuffily and so with greater self-importance. People invited are now called invitees. I expect schoolchildren soon to be called educatees, and one to whom money is owed a debtee.

When Portugal's colonies became independent, thousands of people left them. They were refugees. That was not, however, their official designation. To the Portuguese government, which must have thought refugee old-fashioned, they were returnees. It is the fate of returnees to be among those most likely to be debriefed and to be made, willee nillee, debriefees. Sometimes, to become returnees they must first become escapees, a word government agencies use—misuse—to mean those who escape.

"To what do you attribute your escape?"

"I am a fast runnee."

If the question is phrased in a more up-to-date manner—"To what do you attribute your successful escape?"—the answer is the same.* In this country some debriefees have been detailees. Detailees are people the CIA details to other duties, meaning that they are slipped into other government agencies. When they get back they are expected to tell all:

"What are you doing, Empson?"

"Debriefing a detailee, sir."

"Why is it taking so long?"

"It's all the confounded detail, sir."

"Can't you speed things up?"

"I will ask the debriefee to be brief, sir."

It fell to me to speak at a luncheon in honor of those who in 1975 completed twenty-five years with NBC. They were called new quarter-century club honorees. There is a phrase to quicken the blood and spark the imagination. At that, the honorees could have been worse off. After appearing on the "Today" show one morning, two representatives of the Golf Hall of Fame, in Augusta, Georgia, generously gave Gene Shalit and me copies of the Golf Hall of Fame Diary. A little later, they sent us two more copies and a letter of apology because the originals had not included the names of the 1975 enshrinees. If needs must, it is better to be honored than enshrined. It is better to be a retiree than an enshrinee, though it may expose you to such pronouncements as this one from the Home Insurance Company of Boston: "This change does not apply to the spouse of a retiree or active employee already deceased."

Rather than enshrinees, protectees be, which is what a spokes-

---

* See page 164.

man for the Secret Service—how can you have a spokesman for a secret service?—made of President Ford and his family. Enshrinement sounds so (here I acknowledge my debt to Representative John Murphy of New York, who could not bear to call a final paragraph final) conclusionary.

Using excess syllables makes words longer. That is often the purpose; it is an attempt to impress, and it goes on all over the country. No region wants to be left out. In Washington the House committee deciding whether President Nixon should be impeached studied not evidence but evidentiary material. Ality and icity also extend and inflate. A recent university graduate wrote to the public relations department of a large corporation in Redwood City, California, "My purpose in writing you and applying for a position with your firm is ultimately a selfish one: I need a professional context in which to give a more mature, enlightened and constructive shape to my rhetoricality." He suggested "that you revolutionize your rhetoric to the point of giving greater credence to the multiplicity of language forms." His language form was one to which the company did not give credence, and he was not offered a professional context.

In New York the Chase Manhattan Bank closed a branch on Times Square not because it had lost money but because of continuing unprofitability. At a meeting of the board of directors of the Transit District of Orange County, California, at which one of the members spoke of "the growingness of the Transit District," the board considered a market plan containing this sentence: "A communication objective built around the concept of trialability has been developed. . . . If trialability is achieved, that, in itself, will contribute to the education of the population."

It is debatable whether education of the population should be in the hands of anyone who believes that trialability is a word, or of anyone who believes that growingness is. It is already in the hands of some who have strange ideas about such matters, among them Sheila Huff, research associate at Syracuse University; Albert Shanker, president of the United Federation of Teachers; and a group of teachers in and around Appleton, Wisconsin. Ms. Huff wrote for the May 1974 issue of the *Harvard Educational Review* an article called, "Credentialing by Tests or Degrees: Title VII of the Civil Rights Act and *Griggs* v. *Duke Power Company*." With this diploma, I thee credential. She passed the torch to Shanker, who wrote, "One of the major functions of the schools has been to act as a credentialing agency." The teachers in Wisconsin, out on strike, informationally leafleted other teachers about their grievances. Leafleting and credentialing may also go on among the religious. The *Anglican Digest,* reporting on the death of the bishop of Western North Carolina, noted that he had been consecrated in 1948 and priested in 1936. I wonder when he was postulanted and noviced. A Texas museum has announced juried exhibits. Pilots flying from London to New York will announce: "We have just overheaded Shannon." The trappings of office include, for some office trappers, a chauffeured limousine. Democrats accused other Democrats of wanting a brokered convention. Instead, they got a credentialed one. Said Frederic A. Bennett, assistant security director for the Democrats at Madison Square Garden, "To our knowledge, no one, absolutely no one, got into the Garden this week who was not properly credentialed." It was my sixth Democratic convention but the first at which I was among the credentialees. A laxative has proclaimed itself chocolated, which reminds me of the days of austerity in Britain after the Second World War, when some foods were so scarce that you might find yourself being served baconed scrambled egg, which apparently meant that the bacon had been swirled around the pan before the eggs were cooked much as Vermouth is swirled around the pitcher for an extra dry martini. A correspondent with an APO address told me about some people who came home and found their house ramshackled. They must have been gone a long time. During the Montreal Olympics, ABC Sports told us about horses in the equestrian competition that had not done much eventing, and about swimmers who medaled. I now expect athletes also to trophy, ribbon, and cup, champions to title, and professionals to purse.

One other syllable ought to be mentioned, for it may be joining non and someday may even displace it.* That syllable is un. The makers of Seven-Up use it, advertising the drink as the Uncola. Un has also been used by manufacturers of handbags who wanted to stop saying that their products were made of plastic or imitation leather or, in one case, genuine imitation simulated leather. Unleather, they called it, and it certainly was. This opens new possibilities—uncowhide, unfur, uncotton, and fire warnings telling us not to walk but to unrun to the nearest exit.† All things considered, it may be wise to note the location of the nearest exit now.

----

* I hope that I am not falling prey here to the displacive fallacy.
† Jesse Unruh, the California Democrat, may move on to new political triumphs.

4

A Real Super Player
with Good Compassion

Afew years ago, after the relief pitcher Mike Marshall was
traded to the Los Angeles Dodgers, he found himself room-
ing with another pitcher, Andy Messersmith, when the team
traveled. The effect on Messersmith was profound. "I'm a better
student of hitters since Mike joined us," said Messersmith. "My
studiology of baseball is better." Marshall is a Ph.D. who worries
more about facing variables during a game than about facing
batters; probably the studiology he elicited from Messersmith was
to be expected. Though this be madness, yet there's methodology
in it. It is only part of a larger movement in which the language of
sports grows more pretentious.

Sports are being overcome by the All-American urge, the
urge to complicate. Much of the news on the sports pages these
days has less to do with the games played than with the circumstances in which they are played, and under whose auspices, and
with what guarantees, and with what ancillary income arrange-

ments, and whether they will be played at all. Athletes are growing what in the military would be called administrative and logistic tails—lawyers, agents, advisers, publicity specialists, all of them experts in turning fame into money.

When contests do take place, they are less an end in themselves than a means by which the players go on to other things. The principal purpose of winning the figure-skating gold medal in the Olympics, so it appears, is to have a professional career. Mark Spitz's seven gold medals in swimming in the 1972 Olympics were worth a fortune, though Spitz as an entertainer—or, a more nebulous category, a personality—could barely stay afloat. Cogito, ergo swim. In the spring of 1976, Larry Csonka, who had jumped from the National Football to the World Football League, jumped back, the World etc. having globally failed. He signed with the New York Giants, and one reason he chose them, Csonka explained, was that the promotional—outside income—possibilities were greater in New York than anywhere else. In that same spring the Oakland A's traded outfielder Reggie Jackson to Baltimore. Jackson did not want to go because his outside interests were on the West Coast. So was a 1975 batting average of .253. How can a player with a .253 average have outside interests?

Obviously athletes should think about the future and should bargain, individually and collectively, for the best deal they can get. I hope that they are better protected than some of the celebrated athletes of the past, especially fighters, who sometimes found that more of them was owned by others than existed. There were cases in which 150 per cent of a fighter's contract was sold. Distribution of 150 per cent of the purse did not leave much for him.

Still, the almost endless haggling and legal dueling that have become standard are tiresome. Most sports stories now provide about as much entertainment and excitement as the briefs filed in railroad bankruptcy cases. A topheavy structure of complication, negotiation, and protocol is being reared on the competition that actually does take place and on the frequently modest talents of those competing. As a result the language of sports more and more resembles the language of politics and diplomacy—a new reciprocity, for politicians and political writers have traditionally borrowed from sports to show that they are not stuffy and that they have the common touch. An election year can hardly begin before somebody is designated the front runner, and there is talk of staying up in the pack, and this candidate makes a grandstand play, and that candidate picks his spots, and So-and-so has momentum but has only faced the second team* and it may be different when he goes one on one with Such-and-such on his home ground.

After Ronald Reagan beat President Ford in the Indiana primary, the Republican chairman in Michigan, William Mc-Laughlin, pronounced the contest for the nomination "a real ball game." That made it a doubleheader, because Representative Morris Udall was at that same time pronouncing the Democratic contest a whole new ball game, and even predicting that he would be in the play-offs. It wasn't and he wasn't. Before the Pennsylvania primary Senator Henry Jackson said that it would be well to come first in the preferential voting there "but the name of the game is delegates." Soon thereafter the name eluded the Senator, going through to Jimmy Carter, who gathered it in on one hop, while remarking in Portland, Oregon, on May 19, "The name of the game is delegates," and Jackson was relegated to the bench.†

When the United States lent Britain $3,750,000,000 in 1946, a reporter at Secretary of the Treasury Fred Vinson's news conference told Vinson that he had been sitting in left field and had not heard Vinson's answers. "Well," said Vinson, a right-handed Secretary, "I'm a pull hitter." The military, too, borrow from sports. During the North African campaign in the Second World War, the British commander, General Sir Bernard Montgomery, assured his men that they would hit the German commander, Field

---

* On the night Jimmy Carter won the Illinois primary, I asked him whether it was not true that, with Hubert Humphrey and Edward Kennedy out, he was facing the Democrats' second team. He sidestepped and swung around me for an easy score.

† Sometimes rendered as regulated to the bench.

Marshal Erwin Rommel, for six. That is the cricket equivalent of a pronouncement by Harry Dent, Ford's Southern delegate coordinator, after the President visited Mississippi: "He knocked it over the fence." The temptation to borrow from sports overcomes judges, also. In Santa Fe, New Mexico, two prosecutors claimed the right to work with a county grand jury. "Neither of the two players," said Judge Edwin Felter, "shall decide which thereof shall carry the ball." Football huddle talk by a quarterback: "Whereas their left defensive end is consistently out of position, I shall now hear closing arguments against a quick opener off right tackle, and if none be forthcoming, I shall issue a writ of mandamus for said play forthwith."

The results of this cultural borrowing are not always happy. James R. Dickenson of the *Washington Star* covered a news conference held by Vice President Nelson Rockefeller and reported: "Rockefeller leaned nonchalantly on the podium and made no effort to field the inevitable question. He just stood and let it go by him." Anybody leaning on a podium, which is a low dais of the kind orchestra conductors stand on, would not be in a position to field anything. He would not be standing. He might be doing a one-arm push-up. Politicians do sometimes lean nonchalantly on the party platform, but that is different. The platform is pleased to be noticed at all.

I assume that Rockefeller was leaning on a lectern while standing on a podium while making no effort to field the inevitable question, which was whether he would try for the Republican nomination if Ford did poorly in the early 1976 primaries and dropped out. Rockefeller, of course, had gone after the nomination before—he "made a real good try on that one"—and had shown second effort. "He always gives a thousand per cent."

Now the traffic is flowing in the other direction. When Csonka —who, like all other players, including Rockefeller, is some kind of player—signed with the Giants, no details were announced except that he had signed a "multiyear" contract. That was instead of a uniyear contract for players in less demand. When Joe Frazier and George Foreman signed for their June 1976 multirounder, sportswriters were proud to attribute their information about the contract to "a highly placed boxing source." A boxing source bobs and weaves, feints with a left, and then throws a right that delivers the goods. A boxing judge, Harold Lederman, replying to a letter to a newspaper from the referee Barney Felix, wrote that Felix's words in reprehension of the sport were an unexpected animadversion that shocked him deeply. He felt strongly compelled to express his complete and utter incredulity. When I look at the language of sports, I often am myself.

Lederman's letter may have been ghost written by Howard Cosell, who speaks of teams in a poor field position situation, and of a back who will run unmolestedly down the field, thereby enabling his team to perpetrate a major upset, which may revivify the fans' interest or, if they are on the other side, lead them to give vent to their vocal discontent, rather as Muhammad Ali did before the George Foreman fight in Zaire, when he rendered himself, so Cosell told us, into a hoarse frenzy. During the Ali–Jimmy Young fight in April 1976, Cosell noted that Ali attemptedly delivered a number of punches. Young attemptedly blocked them. On another night, during half-time of a football game, Cosell announced, "I am variously bounded and circumscribed by Senator Edward Kennedy and John Denver." Kennedy was, geographically, on one side of him and Denver on the other.

Unfortunately, Cosell is not alone. Early in the 1975 professional football season, during a game between the New York Jets and the Kansas City Chiefs, Charlie Jones of NBC noticed Joe Namath raging about a call of offensive pass interference and announced that Namath was holding a détente with the officials. Actually, it was a démarche accompanied by an aide-mémoire, ending in a tour d'horizon. Luckily, the officials did not declare Namath persona non grata and ask for his recall.

On NBC, Jim Simpson described David Knight, a wide receiver for the New York Jets, as "a young man not of any specific speed and any specific size, who makes a living by knowing how to run the patterns." It is because Knight is of no specific size that, after he catches the ball, he is so hard to tackle. Simpson also told us, before a Miami-Baltimore game, that Miami was driving for its sixth consecutive play-off in a row. Many sports broadcasters now believe that consecutive is shorthand for consecutive in a row, just as eight straight wins seems incomplete to them alongside eight straight wins without a loss, and they would rather not take the easy way. All credit to them. All credit also to NBC, which told me one late summer day that college football had made its first full-fledged debut of the season, in a game in which one side beat the other closer than expected. And to CBS, which reported on what had to be the most westernmost football game played in the U.S. (It was in Hawaii.) Having to be most westernmost is a distinction and not to be spoken about in reprehension.

Sports broadcasters often have a shaky grip on grammar and on the connection between words and meaning. I learned one night from NBC that Dock Ellis, a pitcher formerly with the Pittsburgh Pirates, was "looking ahead to a low-profile image with the Yankees." A low-profile image is not unlike a poor field position situation and involves keeping an ear to the ground. From Brent Musberger of CBS, I learned during a game between the New York Jets and the Dallas Cowboys that "Tom Henderson found an opening and blocked Greg Gant's would-be kick." The would-be kick was disappointed at failing to fulfill its potential and promised to be satisfied with being a pass or a run next time. ABC, during an Ivy League football game, told us that one team's chance of winning had diminished completely, a clear infraction of the law of diminishing returns (when a team runs back punts and kickoffs for less yardage as the game goes on). In golf, *Sports Illustrated* noted that "a twosome of Bobby Nichols and Lee Trevino talk no more than most pairs—except that Lee does it all." Well, Jim, Howard, Brent, and *Sports Illustrated,* maybe Nichols came to play.

The newspapers are not far behind. The *Pittsburgh Post-Gazette* ran a photograph with the caption "Jimmy Connors gets an unidentified kiss from a local fan." The *Post-Gazette* was trying to say that the woman's name was not given; the kiss, apparently, was standard. A sportswriter for the Lake Charles, Louisiana, *American Press,* covering high-school football, called a team capitalistic. He meant that it turned its opponent's fumbles into touchdowns. Thus the class struggle in Louisiana.

Class attitudes are expressed in a more patrician way in the sports pages of the *Times* of London:

"The weather was a little cooler at Cheltenham yesterday, which helped to make us all better-tempered; and crowds at Cheltenham (the ground nearly full again) need to be good tempered, because handsome though the setting may be, the facilities are on the primitive side. I have not visited the gentlemen's lavatory tent this year, but am assured, by my friends, and indeed by my own nose, that the Ladysmith tradition is preserved. When, in the members' bar, I asked for some water with my whisky, I was told: 'There's a tap round the corner.'

"Still, Cheltenham is Cheltenham, and as one jolly round pink gentleman said to me, pressing a glass of champagne into my hand, under the impression that I was his godson: 'If you want real discomfort here, you have to come to the Gold Cup.' "

And so on. Seven lines later, he begins his account of the cricket match.

I am, I know, mixing up the sports, but I can hardly be blamed. Nowadays a long fly, arching skyward,* will chase an outfielder to the distant wall at the same time that a shifty guard, using a solid pick from a stalwart seven-foot center, drives the middle, a slap shot eludes the masked goalie's desperate lunge as he sprawls on the ice and the red light flashes on behind him, and a tennis player dueling on court does not give the shirt off her back but sells it as advertising space. In these days of short skirts, women players' underpants could carry a plug for, perhaps, radial tires. Women likely to be eliminated in the early round and hence

---

* I am not quite right about the long fly. It arches domeward, because stadiums are increasingly roofed over. With so many Latin-American players in the major leagues, we can imagine the shouted instructions: Look domeward, Angel!

not good investments might be required to carry public service messages: Vote!

Most Americans get their sports news on television, and the broadcasters like to make things crystal clear. So we are told about the team with the worst record in baseball won-and-lostwise, about the football player who incurs a penalty and is the guilty culprit, and about the players who have good success in spite of being plagued by physical injuries. Ralph Kiner has explained why a team may not use a squeeze play to get the man on third base home. The squeeze, he said, might not succeed successfully. The players have the same uneasy feeling that success may be failure. Dave Kingman, outfielder for the New York Mets, expressing his gratification after hitting two home runs off Andy Messersmith, post-studiology and with Atlanta: "I have had terrible success against him in the past."

Just as good success is desired, so are good power and good speed. Maury Wills has described a player as having good running speed. "I knew it was hit good," said Mike Schmidt of the Philadelphia Phillies, "but the ball doesn't carry good in the Astrodome." It carries bad. When James J. Braddock died, there were stories about the fight in which he lost his heavyweight championship to Joe Louis. In the first round Braddock knocked Louis down. Louis got up. Braddock: "I thought if I hit him good, he'll stay down." It did not work out that way. Braddock was a brave man, a light-heavyweight, really, who returned to fighting when he was unemployed and on relief and went on to win the heavyweight championship. He was a longshoreman and uneducated. Tom Seaver of the New York Mets is a college graduate: "Cedeno hit the ball pretty good." Budd Schulberg is a novelist. Said he, after the Ali-Foreman fight, "The fight turned out pretty good."

Good has long been indispensable to sports language:

1. "I guess he means good" (Manager Joe Frazier of the New York Mets about an umpire);

2. "Apparently somebody's controlling the Commissioner pretty good" (Manager Billy Martin of the New York Yankees on Baseball Commissioner Bowie Kuhn);

3. "He ran the curve good" (O. J. Simpson of ABC Sports on Dwayne Evans in the men's 200-metres at the Montreal Olympics); and

4. "Evelyn Ashford comes from behind very good" (Wyomia Tyus on the women's 100-metre dash at Montreal)

I believe that a change is in the making, but good has a few seasons left.

"I think we'll have a pretty good year," says the coach who knows that doom awaits but doesn't want to damage morale in the interim.

"We'll have a good season," says the coach who thinks his team may go all the way but prefers not to say so.

Now, the coach who is full of confidence or, in the words of Tom Landry, coach of the Dallas Cowboys, whose confidence factor is up: "All the players have real good attitudes, we have some real good prospects, including one boy who is going to be a real good kicker, and I think we'll have a real good season."

During the 1976 baseball season Reggie Jackson, after his first game for the Baltimore Orioles, reported that it felt good, because he was moving good and taking the pitches good. The pitches Jackson took did not come from Mickey Lolich, because Detroit had traded him to the New York Mets of the National League. After his second victory for the Mets, Lolich acknowledged that he was old for a pitcher—thirty-five—but, he said, "I still throw pretty good." When Gus Ganakas, basketball coach at Michigan State University, suspended ten players, he did not give up hope of getting them back on the squad. "I feel good compassion between us," he said. Bad compassion, Ganakas must have sensed, had been the downfall of many basketball coaches.

Since sports language has moved into politics, good has followed. Governor Hugh Carey of New York has spoken of a particular development as a good probability. Other kinds are the poor probability and the probability that is out of the question. During the 1976 primary campaign the *New York Times* reported that when Senator Henry Jackson mentioned Daniel P. Moynihan as a possible Secretary of State, he usually drew good applause.

Good applause is well meant and honorably intended. Bad applause should be rejected out of, so to speak, hand.

Politicians aren't the only good guys. Advertisers are also. We have it from Bill Cosby that "Ford-built means a lot of things that are good-built." In a television commercial for Manischewitz wine, Sammy Davis, Jr., announced, "I'm into wines pretty good," and Coca-Cola has a drink called Mr. PiBB, with the advertising slogan "It goes down good." Faced with an objection to the slogan, a Coca-Cola executive replied that the company was aiming at a target audience and liked to think it could relate to the "young even at the cost of using a phrase that is a 'put-on.' " The executive did not say who pays the cost. Coca-Cola doesn't.

Politicians and advertisers may discover that they are on the scene too late. A new generation of broadcasters has already moved beyond good to better things. Consider the former quarterback John Unitas. Unitas has three things to say about a player: He did a fine job. He did a real fine job. He did a super job. About entire teams, or categories of players such as offensive guards, he also has three things to say: They do a fine job. They do a real fine job. They do a super job. No mention of good.

Good shots are disappearing from golf. If a player hits a nine-iron shot to the green, the broadcaster will say, "That was a real fine shot." Sometimes, because he believes the audience is confused about the ball and the green and thinks the game on the screen is water polo, he will say, "That was a real fine golf shot." In exceptional cases, "That was a super shot."

Super is branching out—Colonel Arvid E. West, Jr., commander of cadet basic training at West Point, said of the first women cadets, "They're doing super—but it won't last." Not with real super waiting to be waved in. Moreover, winner of the 1976 Masters tournament Raymond Floyd has blazed a new trail. Before the final round Floyd was asked how he had slept. "I slept terrific," he said. There is always something grander beyond the horizon. In 1974, when the World Series was under way, in progress, and continuing in California, Vin Scully said on NBC about Reggie Jackson: "Granted he has a strong arm velocitywise, it's not so accurate." This entire nation knows what is meant when an outfielder is said to have a strong arm, but velocitywise adds a new dimension to our studiology. The California pitcher Nolan Ryan noted one day during 1976 spring training that he had good velocity. He understated it. Ryan has real good velocity. He is very fast.

I sometimes wonder—this may be regarded as a digression—whether there is not another accomplishment players must have if they are to last in the major leagues. This is the ability to spit with good velocity when the television camera is on them. It seems clear that a method of communication has been worked out between the television crews and the players. This is not necessary when a player is close enough to see the red light that means the camera is transmitting a picture on the air, but when he isn't, I suppose his instructions come from somebody in the television crew, perhaps by Navy semaphore flags. As soon as he gets the message, he shifts his tobacco or chewing gum and lets go.

Another possibility is that there is no arrangement* between the television crews and the players but that the players themselves have designated somebody in the dugout who is not otherwise occupied to watch the cameras and to wigwag to any players who may be in the camera's view. Perhaps this assignment is given to injured players as a way of keeping them involved in the club's fortunes. Whatever the method employed, it rarely fails. Camera on player or coach or manager, and out comes the oyster. Why does it? Spitting is thought to be a sign of virility, unless it results from a cough or a cold.

Twenty-three spittoo.

All is not lost in sports broadcasting. It is a matter of getting the right people on the job. It is easy to find someone, almost always an ex-player or ex-coach, who will say, "They're a very physical team"† and "I think they're up for this one," or a whimsi-

---

* Or prearrangement, which comes even earlier, as preplanning comes before planning and prerecorded programs are recorded before recorded programs are.

† This is why there are physical injuries.

cal one who will refer to the end zone in football as royal soil,*
the linebackers as the containment committee, and the referee as
the chief of the spheroid shylocks. Those who tell you that teams
deck other teams, or slam, squeeze past, down, clip, rout, outlast,
skin, rock, or thump them, while notching another win or upping
their mark to whatever the mark is upped to, are thick on the
ground.

I learned early about clichés of sports. In the fall of 1941 I
was a member of the Washington bureau of International News
Service (later to be merged with United Press in United Press
International). That puts it grandly. I was a copy boy, a position
that would now be called at NBC News a desk assistant. I hope it
makes a difference. When passes were available for sports events
that INS had no intention of covering, copy boys were able
to use them. This meant that you could sit in the press box and
pretend to be a reporter, and then call in a brief account of the
game in case the desk man in charge wanted to use it.

That fall I was given the credentials for the football game
between George Washington and, as I recall, Georgetown. It was
a game of no interest between teams of no distinction whatever,
and it ended in a scoreless tie.

I telephoned.

"What was the score?" the desk man asked.

"There was no score."

"Struggled to a scoreless tie, did they?" the desk man said.

I looked at my notes. Struggled to a scoreless tie was what I
had written. The desk man saved me the embarrassment of admitting it or the trouble of finding a substitute. "I don't think we need
it," he said.

My experiences were not always that unhappy. Once I was
given a ringside seat for a heavyweight fight. A new man in the

---

* Royal soil used to be pay dirt, and backs would tote the pigskins
into pay dirt, leaving would-be tacklers in their wake like so much
flotsam and jetsam, who used to play opposite defensive ends for the
Naperville, Illinois, Rapiers.

bureau, who outranked me, which was not hard to do, asked for the seat. I was moved back twenty or thirty rows. During the fight one of the boxers broke the other's nose. Blood spattered onto the suit of the man who had taken my seat. Those were days when I thought not merely twice but repeatedly about the cost of having a suit cleaned. Justice, it seemed to me, had triumphed. Copy boys were not to be pushed around.

Sports reporting is full of manufactured good cheer and catch phrases. I prefer natural eloquence, even when it goes wrong. Mendy Rudolph, who used to be a referee in the National Basketball Association, has become a color man* and analyst of NBA games for CBS. Rudolph has assessed two teams as very equal, and on another occasion, during a game between the Phoenix Suns and the Kansas City Kings, he stunned the play-by-play announcer, Don Criqui, by asking him, "That basket—how round is it?"

Criqui: How round is it?

Rudolph: Yes. How round is it?

After a while Criqui deduced that Rudolph was asking him the size of the basket, what its diameter was. It turned out to be eighteen inches. The Rudolph-Criqui exchange was the most interesting part of the game.

The words, "Let's reminisce about tomorrow night's fight," were uttered by a former fight manager, Vic Marsillo, who had a radio show in Newark, New Jersey. They tell us what sports broadcasting could be, and such colorful language should not be confused with poor grammar—"Our listeners may wonder why they can't run the ball easilier" and "He pursuited him very good on that play." Or with pomposity—"He is bigger, from the standpoint of physical proportions," and "The Jets maintain their hands on the football." Boxing managers, a strange and wonderful tribe, may be the great hope.

Here I must apologize for a mistake in my first book on

---

* Color men and color women supply quips, statistics, historical references, and, it is fondly believed, a dash of personality.

language, *Strictly Speaking*. I attributed the remark "I was in a transom" to Joe Jacobs, who was the American manager of the German heavyweight Max Schmeling. I thought that Jacobs had said it after Schmeling lost a decision to Jack Sharkey at Yankee Stadium in 1932. Harry Markson, who promoted fights in Madison Square Garden for many years, wrote to tell me that Jacobs was not the author of that mighty line. According to Markson, it was the heavyweight King Levinsky, who accounted for his poor showing against Joe Louis with the explanation that he had been in a transom. There were stories at the time that so intimidating were Louis's person and reputation, and so deep in consequence Levinsky's transom, that his manager, his sister Lena Levinsky, known with sports-page inevitability as Leaping Lena, had to force Levinsky into the ring at the point of a gun. The fight lasted two minutes, twenty-one seconds.

Markson sent along some lines, spoken by managers of his acquaintance, that in natural eloquence rank with Levinsky's. Managers usually refer to their fighters as boys, and one, on hearing that another manager's fighter had run out on him, thought he should say something kind about his own, who had stayed with him in good times and bad. "My boy," he said, "has always been fatal to me." Another came in one day to tell Markson that his boy was suffering from a crink in his back and a throbble in his side.

"Will he be able to fight tonight?" Markson asked.

Said the manager, "It's problemental."

Having apologized, I think I should explain how I came to attribute to Joe Jacobs a remark made by King Levinsky. I can explain by summarizing a news story:

A prisoner on trial on charges of attempted murder and armed robbery walked out of the Queens House of Detention for Men yesterday morning in place of another inmate who had completed a fifteen-day sentence for petit larceny but was, he said, asleep at release time. It was the second such erroneous release in the past ten months at the jail.

Correction Commissioner Benjamin J. Malcolm ordered an

investigation by his department's inspector general. "It would appear to me," Malcolm said, "that there was slippage."

That's how I came to make the mistake. Slippage.

More riches than are suspected lie in the language of sportswriters, if only they could be mined. I have been told of a game that sportswriters play to pass the time and that could enliven baseball broadcasts. It consists of asking a question not concerned with baseball and answering it with a line usually delivered by baseball announcers:

"How is your husband feeling, Countess?"

"The Count remains the same."

"Why are the flags being raised for the President's inauguration?"

"It's an obvious bunting situation."

"What will we do with this messy pile of Greek books?"

"Homer here will tie it up."

It's catching. I tried a couple.

"What happened to the handle on this jug?"

"He really broke that one off."

"I could swear we had another bottle of wine."

"That one is gone."

We have seen how sports language, as in good speed, spreads to politics, as in good applause. A basketball coach worries about being outsized and outquicked. Jimmy Carter's national campaign manager, Hamilton Jordan, had the same concern. "In every area," Jordan said during the 1976 primary campaign, "candidate's time, money, and staff depth, we are in danger of being out-resourced." If that was so, Carter must have had inner resources. I once spoke to an organization of young businessmen with an extensive educational program. In one of the courses the organization advised its members, "Nationally-known resources are available throughout the week for face-to-face discussions." At the Republican convention in Miami Beach in 1972, I had dinner in a restaurant where another of the diners was Rogers Morton, then Secretary of the Interior. Morton came over to say hello and was introduced to the others at the table. One of them was the young daughter of an NBC producer. When Morton left she said in delight, "I met a Secretary!" What might she have said if she had met a Resource? For that same 1972 convention E. Howard Hunt, one of the Watergate burglars, had plans for kidnaping unfriendly demonstrators. The "human resources side" of his work, he called it. The demonstrators would have been out-resourced and out of town.

The mingling of language in sports and public affairs may also be seen in the well-known political epithet, left-leaning. Sometimes, when a pitcher picks a runner off first base, he will explain, "I caught him leaning." This means that the runner, possibly the well-known base stealer Art Theft, defying the rifle-armed catcher Art Sleuth, was leaning toward second base, hoping to get a real good jump and steal second. The pitcher whirls and throws to first, and the runner, leaning the wrong way, that is, right, and delayed in returning to first base, is tagged out.

There are occasions, however, when it works the other way. If you are leading off a base but leaning left when the ball is hit, you are going to be slower getting to the next base. This may, in sports language, cost you. In political language it should have been costed out beforehand. In baseball, as in politics, there are times to lean left and times to lean right and times to lean not at all.

Pitchers lean, also. A left-handed pitcher, or southpaw, may lean left, or south, against a left-handed batter and deliver the ball from as far to the side as he can. This leads the batter to pull away from the plate—put his foot in the bucket is the term that swims back from youth—whereupon the curve, which is what the canny left-hander has delivered, sweeps over for a strike. A canny right-handed pitcher may use the tactic on a right-handed batter. For either pitcher the effect is compounded if he throws side-arm, which makes the lean more pronounced. The ball he delivers then goes under the terrifying name of cross fire.

For the batter, there is an advantage in being a switch hitter, one who faces a left-handed pitcher batting right-handed and a right-handed pitcher batting left-handed. The pitchers then, lean they ever so determinedly, will find that it avails them naught.

Many pitchers found themselves in this position when facing the distinguished switch hitter of the New York Yankees, Mickey Mantle. "What did it avail you?" they would be asked as they trudged off the mound, and the reply they gave was, "Naught."

Nowadays the conversation is much the same after they face Pete Rose of the Cincinnati Reds, who not only switches but crouches fiercely. "Say not the struggle naught availeth," pitchers are implored after facing Rose. You know the reply. However, there are few switch hitters. For most batters the task remains the same. It is to dig in their heels, stand up like men, and turn back the challenge from both extremes. There is a lesson here for all of us.

In the dear, dead days not quite beyond recall, the Brooklyn Dodgers had an ambidextrous pitcher named Pea Ridge Day. Day was something like Ring Lardner's celebrated infielder who couldn't hit but couldn't field either. Leaning left or right, he had trouble getting them out with either arm.

Washington language does in sports what it does in Washington—makes things sound more complicated. After the New York Knicks of the National Basketball Association lost one night to the Detroit Pistons, New York's coach, Red Holzman, complained about the officials. "They lived up to their capabilities," Holzman said. "They did exactly what I thought they would." Said Moe Finkelstein, football coach at Thomas Jefferson High School, in New York City, after his team went through a season undefeated, "This year, we won every game in a different way and had to use all our capabilities."

Capability came, as far as I can trace it, from the world of business,* where companies with even the faintest hope of being viable and major recognized the need for overall capabilities, systems capabilities, generating capabilities, in-house capabilities, phase-in capabilities, and, in a changing world, flexibility capa-

---

* I do not mean to imply that capability is a new word. The British architect and landscape gardener Lancelot Brown (1716–1783) used the word so often he has gone down in history as Capability Brown.

bilities. People on public payrolls in Washington phased it in in-house.

President Ford had barely taken office when he sat down with television reporters, one of whom asked him whether he had the brains to be President. On the man-bites-dog principle, Ford would have had to say that he didn't. No other answer would have produced news. Ford chose the harder way. "My feeling of security, my feeling of certainty grows every day," he said. "I feel very secure in the capability that I have to do the job." He could have said, "Yes, I can do it," or even "Yes," but either was too meager for Washington. When it came out that the CIA had been told to pass $6,000,000 to certain Italian political parties, Ron Nessen announced that Ford was angry because he thought that such disclosures "undermine our capability to carry out our foreign policy."

I have asked myself to the extent of my capability to put questions that I am willing to answer, why ability does not serve. It is for the same reason that serve no longer serves and is being replaced by service, as in the case of an organization that offers to service you with facts, statistics, and graphics. President Ford told a group of mayors early in 1976 that his administration wanted to give them the ability and the capability to deal with their problems. The mayors, who had been prepared to settle for either, must have been overwhelmed.

Nobody is more devoted to capability than the CIA. It had, according to the Senate Intelligence Committee report on assassination plots, a stand-by assassination capability (useful for knocking off old stand-bys who outlive their usefulness) which involved incapacitating, eliminating, terminating, removing from the scene, and altering the health of those on whom the capability was to be demonstrated.

The stand-by part is important. It will be remembered that in the opera *Rigoletto,* when Rigoletto wants the Duke of Mantua killed because the Duke has seduced Rigoletto's daughter, Gilda, he has no stand-by assassination capability of his own and turns, therefore, to Sparrafucile, an assassin for hire. However, Sparrafucile, at the urging of his sister, Maddalena, who has been charmed by the Duke, agrees not to kill the Duke, provided somebody else assassinable turns up at his country inn, and to pass off that body as the Duke's. This proves to be Gilda, who sacrifices herself so that the Duke ·may live. It will be seen that Verdi and his librettist, Piave, even in 1851—and before them Victor Hugo, who in 1832 wrote the play *Le Roi S'amuse,* on which the opera was based—were arguing that a stand-by assassination capability was essential if the work was to be well and carefully done.

Stand-by assassination capability is an element of covert capability, which conflicts with yet another capability, that of oversight. If the CIA has covert capability and Congress has oversight capability, which will be the more capable? This will depend on whether Congress's oversight capability includes veto capability. If it doesn't, Congress's oversight capability will merely lull it into a sense of false security, a sense on whose behalf, if we are to believe the columnists and editorial writers, lulling is incessant.

It will come as no surprise to anyone familiar with Washington that capability was quickly deemed to be insufficient. In his State of the Union message of January 1976, President Ford asked for an intelligence capability that would be effective, as though effectiveness were not what capability implied, and he asked that it be responsible and responsive as well. Ernest Gellhorn, dean of the College of Law at Arizona State University, and senior counsel to the Rockefeller Commission on CIA activities, wanted the oversight capability to be permanent and well staffed. Statements of this kind alarmed the columnist William Safire, who demanded that we "put the spotlight of pitiless publicity on oversight's lush patronage." Otherwise, he said, "We are condoning the concealment of a dagger of venality beneath a cloak of reform." This was precisely what Sparrafucile did and explains the false sense of security into which Rigoletto was lulled.

If the federal system is to thrive, capability cannot be confined to Washington. The Illinois Board of Education, for example, anticipates having model-creating and coalescence capability:

"The purpose of this project is to develop the capability for institutions of higher learning and community agencies and organizations to coalesce for the development of community services and create a model for services that would maximize the available resources from a number of institutions and provide communication and priority needs and responses to the educational needs of a given community."

In the world of the social sciences, the compulsion to create a model is all but universal.

"We're creating a model."

"*We're* creating a model."

"Our model is coalescing, and maximizing."

"Our model provides communication and priority needs and responses. It has the capability."

Capability exists beyond given communities and even as far afield as Rhodesia, in southern Africa. There the government spokesman, Edward Sutton-Pryce, said that Rhodesia had developed and was producing a combat vehicle with "counterambush and countermine capabilities." This last describes a condition in which the mine goes off under the counter.

I do not mean to leave capability in southern Africa, especially because a new species of it has turned up in Washington, this being unprecedented capability, a quality the Army claims for its new main battle tank, the XM-1. The XM-1's unprecedented capability is to take a hit and survive. Add agility, cross-country mobility, and a new compartmentalization design, and the Army believes that the XM-1 will have great battlefield survivability. If the flag is to continue to fly o'er the rampartmentalization we watch, survival capability at the preoverrun figure of $1,024,000 per tank seems not too much to ask.

President Ford has said that American ballistic missiles are more accurate than the Soviet Union's, and "much more survivable." That sounds as though the missiles could be more readily survived by their intended victims if they were used, but that is not what Ford meant. Survivable retaliatory capability is what he meant. He was using shorthand.

What has the State Department been doing while the Department of Defense develops tanks of unprecedented capability? The State Department has been tailoring a centralized focus for consumer interests and fashioning a viable blueprint for consumer participation,* with a capability that rests on inputs, outputs, and thruputs. An input is simple enough: It goes in. An output comes out. And a thruput? Just tell it, please, State Department, in your own words:

"Information inputs from consumers, thruputs between initiating parties and potential users, and outputs from the Department properly occur in varying degrees and at varying levels in this process. Inputs are directed toward existing or prospective programs, and can be solicited or unsolicited. Thruputs—a critical element in the Department's mode of operation—are manifested by interaction between the international community and the U.S. public and private sectors. Outputs are designed to educate and/or reply to the consuming public."

Thruputs may be critical elements in everybody's mode of operation, but most of us don't realize that we are launching them. Here is a perfectly balanced interactive thruput:

"Good morning, John. How are you?"

"Well, thank you. And you?"

A thruput of the kind the State Department has in mind is more complex:

"Hello, operator. This is the U.S. private sector. The international community, please. International community? U.S. private sector here. Let us go forward together in hard but friendly competition, with the peoples of the world reaping the benefit in lower prices and higher standards of living, secure in the knowledge that the quest for peace through mutual understanding goes on." Since interaction is required, the international community

---

* In 1972 there was something that sounded like this in the Nixon Administration. It was called Operation Responsiveness, and it tailored a centralized focus and fashioned a viable blueprint to enable federal agencies to help in Nixon's reelection campaign.

responds by speaking of removing artificial barriers to trade and of stimulating the free exchange of ideas, thus realizing the higher aspirations common to all mankind. The thruput is complete. In sports terms, they were shadowboxing. Neither laid a glove on the other.

Anything more in the State Department's own words? Yes, the Department had a few linkages left over from the nuclear arms negotiations with the Soviet Union. Wherefore:

"The introduction of the 'consumer communications channel,' as monitored by the Consumer Affairs Coordinator, will provide the linkage to enhance the effectiveness of these ongoing efforts."* The announcement also spoke of utilization of professional public opinion analysts to input consumer attitudes throughout the Department.† It concluded: "A special effort is being made by the Department to assure that Federal Register Items are clear, as brief as possible, free from jargon, and timely."‡ For this relief from jargon, much thanks.

I have not asked Representative Brock Adams of Washington whether he would stand with the State Department on input/output/thruput, but my guess is that he would. At the beginning of 1975, Adams became chairman of the House budget committee. At the beginning of 1976 he told a reporter, "My input quantum jumped tremendously in the past year in the ability to get things

---

* Linkage is what the second baseman provides in the continuum of a short to second to first double play. Ongoing efforts are needed in any sport, but especially in baseball. It's a long season.

† Forty-four per cent of the fans in the park thought the manager acted wisely in using a pinch hitter, 33 per cent thought he was foolish to do it so early in the game, and the remaining 23 per cent either had no opinion or were listening to a broadcast of the game on transistor radios and did not want to be disturbed. One fan who was shouting, "Get that bum outa there," was recorded as abstaining.

‡ We all know about the player who does not get many hits, though the ones he gets are timely, coming when his team is at bat. They are free from jargon, not being called bingles or safeties, and also as brief as possible, usually getting the timely one only as far as first base, where he remains while the next three men go down in order.

done."* Having an input quantum to be reckoned with is the successor to that wistful favorite of yesteryear, making a meaningful contribution,† and for a politician it can be a call to arms: "My opponent tells you that he can do more for this state than I can, but my input quantum was impacting the national decision-making process when the people of this state needed it. Where was his?"‡

I have assumed that an input quantum impacts the decision-making process rather than being inserted in it. This may be quite wrong. Inserting inputs seems more logical and, although this has the dysteleological effect of keeping the inputs from ever becoming outputs, so does outserting them. Outserting is already taking place at the Ford Foundation, in New York, where an executive told me that in the same mail delivery that brought him notice of a meeting of college and university administrators devoted to creative retrenchment§ he received a requisition which, in the course of a job description, employed outsert, as in, he assumed, "First outsert the plug from the wall." When enough people outsert themselves, we may be in the presence of an outpour, this being what the Secretary of Housing and Urban Development, Carla Hills, believed might come about if the trickle of suburban families back to the cities could be encouraged. Encouraged Mrs. Hills believed it should be, so that the cities would "attract a heterogeneous people mix and . . . broaden their opportunities for leveraging funds." Are you a heterogeneous person? With leverageable funds? Welcome to our mix.

Outserting a plug from the wall leads, naturally, to an outage. Outages defy climatic differences. The Associated Press reported

---

* Input quantum sets me humming Stephen Foster's "Camptown Races":

"De input quantum sing dis song, Doo dah! Doo dah!
De input quantum's five mile long, Oh! Doo dah day!"

† I know I can help this club.

‡ When did he ever get the most valuable player award?

§ First we have to contain their offense. Then we can think about scoring some points of our own.

one in Bethel, Alaska, where fire destroyed the municipal power plant, and United Press International reported more than one in Panama City Beach, Florida, after Hurricane Eloise passed through. UPI also reported an outage that hit Sacramento, causing the state legislature to stop work and many state employees to be sent home, which was a shame because the Sacramento Municipal Utility District had, until then, an excellent inage image. On December 24, 1974, the University of Pittsburgh, known to itself as the Cathedral of Learning, posted a sign announcing an elevator outage. This suggests that the principal justification for the university's regarding itself as a cathedral of learning is that it is in a high-rise building. High-rise buildings, by the way, used to be tall.*

I have no evidence that the University of Pittsburgh has gone this far, but there are places where two or more signs, taken together, are known as signage. The Sisters of Providence, of Holyoke, Massachusetts, announced in a newsletter completion of a study of the signage needs of the area. That was in October 1974, and the Sisters may have established a precedent. A year later, after moving to its new world headquarters in East Hanover, New Jersey, the National Biscuit Company advised its employees that increased signage was needed in the building and that signage would also be added above the cafeteria counters. Countersign capability.

Signage and outage I expect to arrive in baseball shortly, probably shepherded by Howard Cosell, who said during a football game that the New York Giants faced the problem of the stoppage of O. J. Simpson. (The blockage by the Buffalo linemen made the problem more difficult.) The catcher will be flashing signage to the pitcher, and the third-base coach to the runners, and the umpires will be giving the ball and strike and fair ball and foul signage, and declaring "Outage at first" unless the runner is viable. When players misbehave, they will be output of the game. A manager will send signage to the bullpen for a relief pitcher to

---

* It's a high-rise fly, about fifteen stories up, just inside the left-field line. The left fielder is under it, and he has it.

input after outserting the starter, against whom the opposition has been registering thruputs almost at will, five in the first inning alone, which is a large quantum to overcome. In the first inning there were five thruputs, six successful impactions of bat on ball, and two slippages. Two potential thruputs were left on.

It is my observation that in Washington, and elsewhere, there are far more inputs than there are outputs. This means that a large number of puts are disappearing somewhere in the process. God knows where they'll eventually turn up. It came to pass in the city of the input quantum that a job was available at the Federal Communications Commission, where employees who were interested were invited to submit their applications on Form A-136, "Application for Position Vacancy," rather as rookies and free agents are invited to a team's training camp. Applying for a vacancy rather than the position itself seems pointless, but it is of no moment: any government agency would rather say position vacancy than vacant position. The job was that of Word Processing Supervisor in the Word Processing Center of the Office of the Bureau Chief of the Broadcast Bureau, a noncritical sensitive position requiring security clearance, in which incumbent has total management responsibility for the operations of the Word Processing Center, so as to achieve maximum utilization of personnel and equipment, and timely, accurate, and cost-effective accomplishment of Word Processing Center objectives within the constraints established.

I am an experienced reporter, but I did no digging and thus no investigative work to learn what word processing centers are. I thought they might be printing plants or offices where all government statements are emulsified.* Not so. My knowledge of them I owe to a government employee in Washington who sent me a

---

* A story was told just after the Second World War about American and British correspondents waiting for the Italian government to issue its *épuration* law, the law under which collaborators with the Nazis would be dealt with. There was a delay, and some of the correspondents wondered aloud what the purifiers were doing. An American reporter, Homer Bigart, had an explanation. "Putting in the loopholes," he said.

copy of the FCC vacancy announcement. On request, he then sent me job descriptions. My next letter had a plaintive tone. "Is there anything available," I asked, "that explains what word processing is?"

"A word processing unit," my benefactor wrote back, "is a typing pool. Happy New Year."

Less pretentiously, the typing pool used to be called the bullpen. In baseball, the bullpen coach speaks on the telephone to the manager in the dugout, telling him which of his relief pitchers has good stuff, which one looks ready, and how long he thinks any of them can go. A comparable junior executive in the Word Processing Center could tell the Word Processing Supervisor whether Ms. Bright was at the top of her form and could deal with a tricky memorandum, or whether he should call on Mr. Hapgood, slower at the keyboard ("He doesn't have good speed") but steady and experienced and not likely to be rattled. Hapgood probably could use another day's rest, since he has lately been processing out of rotation because Mrs. Ewen came down with a sore arm and had to miss a couple of turns, but Hapgood's stamina is legendary and he is a sure bet for the Word Processing Hall of Fame.

Among the Word Processing Supervisor's subordinate incumbents, there is one who has the duty of correcting inadvertent errors in grammar, I suppose while letting the deliberate ones go. Others process a large volume of documents, including correspondence, memorandums, reports, agenda items, etc. Still others are known as specialists in document creation. I had long wondered where the documents came from for archives, for presidential libraries, for leaking, for losing and pilfering, for tugs-of-war between executive departments and congressional committees, for publication in the *New York Times;* for photostating and microfilming; for classifying and, once in a great while, declassifying; for filling large buildings, smaller temporary structures, and briefcases; for circulating within and across departmental lines; for keeping from scholars until a stated time has passed. The existence of the document creators solves the mystery. Richard Nixon was able to claim ownership of 42,000,000 documents when he left the White House. It was not an abnormal number. Since then, twenty-five tons of papers, packed in 1660 boxes, from the Reagan Administration in California have been given to Stanford University, which shows what can be done with fewer resources at the state level.

Government employees are not thought to be among the nation's most industrious workers. This surely maligns the document creators. It also maligns those word processors who wait, pad and pencil at the ready, for the heady order: "Take a document."

Some Enchanted
Citadel

A concept was delivered to me one day, by mail, with nothing on the envelope to indicate what lay within. The top page of the enclosure bore these words:

WESTERN INSTITUTE OF AVIATION
A Concept

and I closed the door and lowered the blinds before reading further. I reproduce here only the Introductory Statement:

"Aviation services and their impact now have great dimensions. With appreciation of the facts—including that only great things can have great faults and that perfection takes some time—oversimplification can be misleading. Improved communications are vital if aviation is to attain the full measure of its possible greatness.

"We trust, that by joining together the many specialist groups who make the system work—who have treated technical problems as opportunities—and who have achieved, for a majority of people, a quality of service that tends to satiate the recipients to a point approaching apathy, we may treat the opposition so as not to inflame the anti-aviation enthusiasts, but to convert them.

"Toward finding better ways to work out our problems, we offer the Western Institute of Aviation for broadening the base of understanding, evolving a means of lifting up our eyes and objectives and, hopefully, realizing our mutual interdependence in optimizing aviation services to people through the synergism of our efforts."

That concept was passed on to me by the director of airport planning in a large western city, whose help was being solicited but who had been satiated to a point beyond apathy.

Another concept reached me on an otherwise ordinary day in a letter from an instructional television center in a large city in Texas. It was the concept of human possibilities, which is a concept to reckon with. I was flattered to be told about this concept because the writer of the letter said that he was looking for extraordinary people in various fields who were using their potential to the fullest and who were willing to be interviewed on film for an instructional television course in the humanities.

Egomania drove me on:

"Here is the question we would like to ask you in a brief interview:

"Can you isolate a single moment in your life as *the* most fulfilling?

"Or put another way:

"What moment(s) did you feel most successful as a person?

"If you are familiar with the psychologist Abraham Maslow, you will know we are talking about 'self-actualizing' people, people who are being fully human.

"We hope the question intrigues you. Your answers can greatly help our students explore their own self-expectations."

Glowing, I reread the letter, only to find that I was not sufficiently extraordinary for the purpose, since, although I self-actual-ize madly, I do not use my potential to the fullest but only to the full. Reluctantly, I declined.

In public relations and in advertising, a concept is an idea that has become important. An expert in the field can spot the precise moment when the transformation takes place. It was, for example, the moment when the golf glove incorporated Iso-massage action to relieve tiredness in the hand, the better to grip Strata-bloc woods with cycolac inserts, and irons built with true-temper step-down steel shafts. Calling ideas concepts is itself a concept, and the greatestest thing of its kind since a conversation became a dialogue.

The potency of concepts is now widely recognized. A New York furniture store changed its name to Interconcepts. A public relations company put this advertisement in the *Wall Street Journal*: "Somewhere is someone who knows that our business is not a matter of placements, releases and contact. Someone who knows that professional PR, like professional advertising and promotion, is really a matter of strong, creative marketing communications concepts. Concepts that establish a singular identity for a company, a product or a service. Concepts that impact upon marketplaces, and hopefully industries as well." Marketplaces may profit from being impacted on by concepts, but hopefully industries have nothing in stock but good will, which they pick up for a song, usually Jerome Kern's "Look for the Silver Lining," from companies going bankrupt. They spend much of their time in wishful thinking, and the fact is that concepts are wasted on them. They need the attitude expressed in the song written by Jay Gorney and Ralph Harrison, Junior, for the thirtieth anniversary of the publication *PR News*:

What's the most exciting profession in our land?
It's PR, PR, PR.
What is most important for our people to understand?
It's PR, PR, PR.
What needs education
In our wonderful nation?

What, in our country, is destined to expand?
It's Public Relations!

CHORUS:
Yes, we are
Mighty PRoud to be in our PR.
Yes, we are
All doing our job well up to par
We live and love our thriving profession
One which can help overcome recession
Yes, we are
All PRoud to be in our PR. . . .

That shows how a song can arouse enthusiasm. This was part of the plan when President Ford launched the Whip Inflation Now, or WIN, campaign shortly after he took office. Dedicated enemies of inflation were to show it no mercy by wearing lapel buttons that said WIN, and the coup de grâce was to be administered by a song by Meredith Willson, composer of *The Music Man*. The song said that the nation did not need inflation and that you were going to pass it by and so was I.

The campaign foundered early, probably because the buttons lacked the killer instinct, and so Meredith Willson's song never had the opportunity to turn the tide. There was a faint echo of WIN across the Atlantic, where the British, aping the American craze for acronyms, came up with NORM, the National Optimism Revival Movement. When appearing in public, NORM's members proposed to smile, thus helping Britain out of its economic difficulties. NORM had no more effect than WIN did, but it was run by a resident of Leighton Buzzard, Bedfordshire, from a shed in his garden, and cost less.

I have never heard of a song about advertising, but otherwise the difference between advertising and public relations, so far as language goes, is nonmajor. Both set out to do the same thing— create desires and expectations, make people want something, leading them to believe that the world is more exciting than it is. Advertising language is more extravagant, but public relations and advertising are so close that they could be billed with nothing more than 'n' between them, like listings for macaroni 'n' cheese, chips 'n' dips, soup 'n' sandwiches; for neighborhood taverns called Surf 'n' Turf, Beef 'n' Bottle, Booze 'n' Board; for combination service stations and cafés called Tank 'n' Tummy; for houses or boats that bear the owners' names, like Dot 'n' Dave; for real estate developments called Hill 'n' Dale; 'n' Bell 'n' Howell's—pardon, Bell & Howell's—trade-in offer known as Switch 'n' Swap.

You may not think it to look at it, but 'n' is a concept. Actually, 'n is a concept. One letter and one apostrophe, taken together, suggest friendliness, informality, and no high prices. The second ' is always left out. I put in the second ' only to be 'n'noying.

There was a time when someone who wanted a home looked at apartments and houses. Now the choice is among concepts. I had a choice between, on the one hand, one of America's most exciting living concepts (a bold concept and landmark for our times, where the facilities created a total concept of leisure and an ambiance that would become synonymous with my way of life and an integral part of my exciting lifestyle) and, on the other, the world's most splendidly complete lifestyle in an enchanted citadel (a luxurious retreat with a unique vantage point, where life takes on a new richness and serenity, and where life is a banquet and you are the guest of honor because of a concept of service that frees rare and discerning people from the mundane task of providing for their own security and comfort).

Had I been willing to move to a suburb, I could have bought a condoflex with the fabulous Westchester lifestyle. Texas tried to attract me by designating the Dallas/Fort Worth area a metropolitan complex and calling it the Metroplex. In Florida I could have had lifestyle living, which I have not seen offered anywhere else. However, I stayed in New York and chose the landmark for our times because it had one more concept than its rival, the citadel (which thereupon became disenchanted), and because I was looking for a two-concept apartment at the time. Wiᴛ ᴐne concept facing south.

Concepts abound in Washington and, as befits the welfare state we are becoming, are often comforting. In December 1975 the head of the United States Consumer Product Safety Commission, Richard O. Simpson, wrote to President Ford that he did not want to be considered for reappointment. Simpson's term had run out in October, and he had not been able to learn what the White House intended to do with him. "I have been singularly unsuccessful in these attempts at communication," he told Ford, though he would hardly have been in a position to know whether his lack of success was singular. "I can only conclude, therefore, that for reasons as yet undisclosed my candidacy is not viable and that there is no specific timetable for resolution." The nonviable candidacy with no specific timetable for resolution is far preferable to being fired. It is a concept.

The CIA has in its arsenal a dart gun with silencer attached which it calls a nondiscernible microbionoculator. It is a concept that reflects the CIA's generosity to its potential victims. We all have our pride, and almost anyone the CIA felt it necessary to render nonviable would prefer being dispatched with a nondiscernible microbionoculator to being shot with a dart gun. Concepts lend dignity while obscuring intent.

ABC television now and then repeats programs, calling them special encore performances, though the calls of "Encore!" are supplied by the network like the laughs on a laugh track. Physicians, when treating mental patients who are not separated from other mental patients, may say that they are receiving milieu therapy. It sounds like something W. C. Fields might have invented:

"Do you practice milieu therapy everywhere, Doctor?"

"No. Only within these purlieus."

"How do your patients react to it?"

"They tell me they feel like a milieu."

To produce a concept, someone, somewhere, must conceptualize, a considerable, even electrifying advance on having conceived. There is a scientific term for two persons conceptualizing the same concept simultaneously. It is synchronicity. Such a phenomenon brought forth the twin concepts of acoustical perfume 'n sonorous design. Acoustical perfume is a background noise intended to sound like the noise produced by a ventilating system. It is used in large office spaces as a substitute for partitions, and is played just loudly enough to permit private conversations. The noise that does come out of a ventilating system is not suitable for the purpose because it is not a concept. Also, the president of the company that sells acoustical perfume says that noise is too negative a word for the environmentally oriented. Handsome does as handsome is.

Sonorous design is produced by Muzak, the background (and sometimes the foreground) music company, which recently passed its forty-second birthday, to my intense regret. Muzak calls its employees "specialists in the physiological and psychological applications of music" and estimates that they apply it to 60,000,000 people a day. I speak as one who does not want to have music applied to him, physiologically or psychologically, but those of my persuasion are being borne under. The chairman of the board of scientific advisers of Muzak, a Ph.D. in industrial psychology, has said: "Among the interrelated matters of a time and place, Muzak is a thing that fits in. The things that go together, including the Muzak, are synomorphs." Synomorphs, so far as I can tell, are forms that have the same shape, like a bun 'n burger. It hardly matters. "Muzak," the good doctor of industrial psychology continued, "helps human communities because it is a nonverbal symbolism for the common stuff of everyday living in the global village. And," he sped on, "Muzak promotes the sharing of meaning because it massifies symbolism in which not few, but all, can participate."

If Muzak is in the global village, I'm getting out and trying the global city. If they have it there as well, the global wilderness beckons. As for massifying symbolism, I don't know what it means, if anything, but my instinct tells me to be against it. I suspect, however, that mine is a losing cause. Consider the words of the director of music programming and recording for Muzak: "Our music is classified by a system of stimulus progression—some is more stimulating, some less. We put together 15-minute segments

with the maximum stimulus in the last part of the segment." She
has also said, "We at Muzak avoid using ... any ... kind of
music for the purposes of entertainment. Ours is functional music,
sonorous design to humanize man-made environments."

Muzak does indeed avoid using music for entertainment. On
the other hand, a man-made environment is by definition human;
you cannot humanize it. But that is by the way. The term sonorous
design is used to describe noise imposed on people for reasons
of profit. This is public relations language, with a touch of social
science, transcendent. Like acoustical perfume, it is a concept.

Concepts must be fought with concepts, which can be messy,
but then war is a dirty business, and it is a military axiom that new
weapons bring forth counterweapons. If you place something that
blocks noise between the noise and you, you are employing a
concept known as decibel buffering. If somebody could devise a
portable decibel buffer (to be marketed commercially as Porta-
buff) that could be pointed in the direction of the Muzak, the
target of sonorous design would have a fair chance. I would never
go out without one.

One night in January 1976 I was surrounded by conceptual-
izers, though I did not fully understand the significance of concepts
at the time. It was at a dinner marking the thirtieth anniversary of
PR News, at which I delivered—here I had no quarrel with the
press release—a witty talk on public relations parlance. For the
occasion, I looked at the language of *PR News* itself and found
it to be almost impeccable. Almost, so that my examination was
only slightly, to use the language of *PR News,* resultful. That did
not augur—in *PR News* it was spelled a-u-g-e-r, which is a tool for
boring holes in wood—that did not augur well for my speech. But
I did find in *PR News* a report of a conference that had been
provocatively themed; it was devoted to issue solving. Issues may
be resolved; they cannot be solved. Somebody at the provocatively
themed conference was reported as having "reminded that 'we
must communicate truthfully and continuously.' " I would like
an occasional respite from communication so that it is not continuous. I would also like reminded to be followed by an object.

As it happened, I ran across a provocatively themed press release from the Chilton Book Company, of Radnor, Pennsylvania, publishers of a book, *Shake Down the Thunder!*, about Frank Leahy, the late football coach at Notre Dame. In the release Leahy was referred to as The Coach—upper case—and the other coaches as the other coaches—lower case. After suggesting that if the Roman Catholic Church were ever to create a Saint of the Gridiron—upper case again—it was likely to be Leahy, the release went on: "He brought more honor than a mortal should bring to football and Notre Dame." How much honor should a mortal bring to football and Notre Dame? Alas, there was no answer. Still, I was glad to have seen the press release for *Shake Down the Thunder!* Before I saw it I thought that The Coach was not Frank Leahy but The Head Coach in the Sky, who decides who wins, loses, and ties on Saturday afternoons.

A provocatively topicked release came from the publishing house of E. P. Dutton. It was written on behalf of a book about the American economy, and the headline read: *"Powerful new financial colossus foreseen."* Between the headline and the lead, somebody must have told the author of the press release that a colossus was, at the least, likely to be powerful. She shifted ground. The American economy, she wrote, will soon be dominated by a giant colossus, a giant colossus being different from a medium-sized colossus, and still more from the colossus that is a thirty-four short.

My employer engages in public relations, sometimes with provocative results. One NBC press release about a dramatization of *Robinson Crusoe* summarized the plot for those not familiar with it: "It focuses on Robinson Crusoe, of a middle class English family, who turns away from a chance to lead a relatively quiet life in England as a businessman in order to become a sailor. His days on the high seas end when his ship breaks apart on a reef off the coast of South America. That's when his greatest adventures begin, first as a man with a friend—a native he saved from certain death and named Friday."

There was hardly any need for the dramatization after that, though I may have assumed too much knowledge of the book.

WVUE-TV in New Orleans, Channel 8, advertised "a strange and eerie adventure on a hostile planet," which was the movie *Robinson Caruso on Mars*. Singing his heart out. Still, I wanted to watch Crusoe saving Friday from certain death. It is the most extreme kind of death one can be saved from.

PR News, it seemed to me, was not provocatively themed itself when it told of the prestigious PR Professional-of-the-Year Award. Awards that are not prestigious or at least coveted are rejected out of hand by those selected to receive them. There was a time when prestigious awards meant a great deal. I knew a man who had received the prestigious Emmy Award and the prestigious Overseas Press Club Award and the prestigious Peabody Award. He had not received the prestigious Du Pont Award, but all the same, on the strength of the three he had received, he was feeling his oats, a sexual perversion so rare that it has not yet been given a name, and he got into serious trouble because of it.

The reason prestigious awards have fallen in public esteem is that their winners are usually given only plaques, medals, or statuettes, which now seem relatively modest. When *Candide* was playing on Broadway, it was billed, with pride, as the "most admired and awarded musical." Clemson University, in South Carolina, points out in a leaflet that its library building has been "awarded for excellence in architectural design." Giving away hit shows and libraries is the sort of openhandedness one expects from Americans, but Clemson did not say to whom the library was awarded, and the producers of *Candide* did not specify the recipients, so the claims of both must be treated with reserve. Talk is cheap.

What else had I to complain about in *PR News?* There was a reference to a meeting in Nairobi of African mediamen. That would make me a North American mediaman. I didn't like the sound of it.

"Hello there, North American mediaman. What are you up to these days?"

"Trying to raise some money, sir. Can you help?"

"You know the old saying, my boy."

"What saying, sir?"

"Media borrower nor lender be." (Exits, humming "Media Me Tonight in Dreamland.")

There are few words more annoying than media. I entered the news business thirty-five years ago, and at the proper time I would like to leave it. I do not want to make my exit from the media. Others may. I do not. Calling the news business the media is a concept. There is enough of that sort of thing at large without people in news contributing to it.

I was suffering from pronounced ennui (pronounced onwee') one day in the recent past—June 9, 1975, to be precise—but it passed so quickly that I did not have time enough to report it to the Smithsonian Institution's Center for Short-Lived Phenomena. (If you want more information, the address is 60 Garden Street, Cambridge, Massachusetts 02138, but hurry. If you have trouble with delivery, you may be able to get help from the Institute for Democratic Communication, at the School of Public Communication, Boston University, 640 Commonwealth Avenue, Boston, Massachusetts 02215. If you'd rather do it yourself, the Institute for Local Self-Reliance, 1717 Eighteenth Street, Washington, D.C. 20009, can advise you; so can Action for Independent Maturity, Fulfillment Department, P.O. Box 2400, Long Beach, California 90801, and so can the Self-Help Institute of the Center for Urban Affairs at Northwestern University, Evanston, Illinois 60201. If you would like to be joined by others without regard to race, creed, or color, apply to the Center for the Study of American Pluralism, University of Chicago, 6030 South Ellis Avenue, Chicago, Illinois 60637. If you can't make up your mind how to proceed, try the Institute for Mediation and Conflict Resolution, at Automation House, 49 East Sixty-eighth Street, New York, N.Y. 10021.) What brought on the ennui was a news conference held by President Ford. Not that I expect presidential news conferences or gubernatorial news conferences, held by gubernators, or conferences held by those who have won what has become known as the mayorality, to be scintillating bits of entertainment. That is not what news conferences are for. They are part of the interface process, which reaches its ultimate expression when all parties turn the other cheek.

At the news conference Ford was asked whether he would run for the presidency in November 1976. He replied, "There is no doubt of my intention to run," which made it sound as though he had sat himself down before going out to meet the reporters and asked himself what his frame of mind was. What happened next seemed to me more characteristic of the media than of the news business. "Are you getting closer to a specific announcement?" a mediaman asked. The answer to that could hardly have been no, since American elections fall on fixed dates and Ford had already said that he would run. The President replied, "We are getting closer and closer to an announcement." The reporter, who before the answer may have thought that Ford could make time stand still, desisted. He had his story. And what a story: The President acknowledged that he was getting closer to an announcement. All concerned had interfaced.

Ford is not alone, of course, in playing these games. Many politicians announce that on such-and-such a date they will make an announcement. That gives them two news stories, plus speculation about what their announcement will be. Sometimes they announce that on such-and-such a date they will announce the date on which they will make an announcement. That gives them three stories, plus the speculation. President Ford, though he did not use the White House as a bully pulpit, which is non-denominational and suitable for clergymen who are overbearing, got more than that.

In politics, some of those doing public relations work are now known as media consultants, meaning that they tell the candidates how to deal with mediamen and mediawomen and the precious media they guard. One such, Tony Schwartz, a New York advertising man, has said that the best political commercials do not tell the viewer anything but rather "surface his feelings and provide a context for him to express those feelings." According to Schwartz, this invites the viewer to take part by providing meaning for the advertisement out of his own experience and emotions, and so is not manipulation but partipulation.

"Where have you been, dear?"

"At the media stand, buying a paper."

"Where are you now?"

"In what was formerly the recreation room, rumpus room, and family room, now known as the media room."

"What are you doing?"

"Watching television."

"What is it?"

"A commercial for Mo Udall."

"Have any feelings surfaced?"

"He makes me uncomfortable. I think he's partipulative. He won't get my vote."

Being in the media has, for some newsmen, the virtue of sounding more scientific and more technical, pulling them out of radio and television and into the electronic media, where they become electronic journalists. For the same reason a newsman may avoid the word expertness in his copy, preferring expertise, and, when entering a foreign country and being asked the purpose of his visit, reply reportage. I have used both myself, expertise not in years, but reportage as recently as September 1975, when I was sent to Tokyo to interview Emperor Hirohito before his visit to the United States. It was the first news interview the Emperor had ever granted, and while he did not say anything memorable—constitutional monarchs should not—I thought it no small thing to be taken to the room where the interview was to take place by the palace master of ceremonies and to be handed over, for the journey across the room to the Emperor, by the grand master of ceremonies. I had arrived in Tokyo without a visa, and at the airport, filling out a form that asked my business in Japan, I wrote reportage. I thought it sounded important and might help to get me through. As things worked out, I had to write a short biography of myself, explain why I had no visa—thoughtlessness was the answer—and promise in writing never to do it again. I should have been asked to promise never to say reportage again.

I do promise never to say media, except as the plural of medium, because, for our purposes, media conveys nothing; on the contrary, it conceals and misleads. There are, after all, many kinds of media. Money is a medium. Language is a medium. By themselves they are inert. Money makes no decisions of its own, nor does language. News is an active business in which news organizations compete with each other and every news item competes with every other item to get into print or on the air. Those in the business make decisions constantly, and if they consist of nothing more than throwing press releases in the waste basket, that is still significant. Most press releases are thrown away. Media would not do that. They would transmit them. Beyond this, all news organizations are not equally reliable, competent, enterprising, or unbiased. Even within individual news organizations— NBC, for example—the work is not uniform. All this the term media obscures. The American people ought to understand this in their own interest. If they did, they would have fewer illusions about what we do, fewer groundless expectations, and fewer disappointments. They would be better able to judge what we give them, and they might demand a better job from us, and get it.

Competition in news isn't only trying to get a story first. It may be getting a story nobody else has. It may be interpreting a story more intelligently or provocatively. It may be writing it more clearly or more sharply or more amusingly. Early in 1946 I was a member of the Washington bureau of the United Press and was assigned to cover the State Department. One day the second in command of the bureau, Julius Frandsen, said to me, not without kindness, "I never want to see indicate in a lead again." Indicate is a weak word. It has no place in a lead, but it is the sort of word you find yourself using almost automatically when you cover the State Department: "Secretary of State Dean Acheson indicated today that the United States was considering . . ." It has to be guarded against. Frandsen, the calmest, most deliberate, and, in consequence, one of the fastest newsmen I have ever known, did not want weak leads going out on the UP wire. That would only have meant, for papers taking both the UP and AP services, that the AP story would have the better chance of being printed. The competition is real and it is earnest. On September 27, 1974, the AP led a story this way: "Washington—A Senate Appropriations subcommittee has acted to ensure that former President Richard M. Nixon is not provided household servants at government expense." This was UPI's lead on the same story: "Washington— The chairman of a Senate subcommittee says the government shouldn't pay for shining Richard Nixon's shoes."

Victory tends to go to the wire service with the stronger, or catchier, lead. People who read the news, or listen to it, or watch it, ought to know that so that they can, when necessary, discount some part of what they are told. Calling news organizations media, which carries no hint of competition, does not help them to know it.

Competition on television may take other forms—who has the better pictures, the more appealing anchormen and anchor-women, the snappier gimmicks, the more attractive set, the more striking visual effects, even whose weatherman grins more bravely at the lame jokes that suggest that he is responsible for the weather rather than for transmitting the government's forecast. Some of this is bunk, and television has few sights to offer more painful than the local anchorman taunting the sports broadcaster because one of his predictions went wrong ("You didn't look so good on that one, Al") or smiling determinedly and congratulating him because one came out right ("And here's our fearless forecaster, who was right on the nose again"), but it does not make news any less a business. It merely shifts the competition away from the news itself. It is true, of course, that the weatherman, who merely transmits a forecast others made, is a medium. So are television news broadcasters who do not write their own copy, who read whatever is put in front of them, and who bring no independent judgment to what they do. I think it is significant that publicity stunts and staged incidents are dismissed as media events. Nothing is dismissed by being called a news event.

News itself is competitive. What is news at nine o'clock in the morning may not be one or two minutes later. You can go into a studio to do a news show and, in the few minutes before going on the air, change the script because of breaking news—change stories, eliminate stories, add others. On a program like NBC

Nightly News, with a tight routine, with film and tape set to roll, commercials fixed, camera moves planned, and complex timing, a decision by the producer to change the show while on the air makes great demands not only of the broadcaster, who is out front where he can be seen, but of many people behind the scenes.

News is also an accidental business. Not always, of course; you can foresee some of what is coming, and one NBC News executive made himself famous by saying of a presidential inauguration parade, "I believe that this is what may be called a predictable event." Nobody was putting anything over on him. A good assignment editor, looking ahead, makes news as predictable as he can. To the extent that this can be done, news resembles public relations and advertising, in which effects are calculated and campaigns staged. But for those who are in it—perhaps I should speak only for myself—news is at its best when it is most accidental, for that is when it is most challenging. I don't have the same feeling walking to the studio to a daily television news program that I did when running to the studio to interrupt the broadcast of the 1973 World Series to announce that Spiro Agnew had resigned as Vice President or when it fell to me to announce on NBC radio that President Kennedy had been shot in Dallas. Even on a horrifying story—the murder of President Kennedy, the murder of Martin Luther King, Jr.—there is satisfaction in doing it well. Perhaps there is more satisfaction than comes from other stories, because the story is more important, and it is important that it be told accurately and without theatrics. This is nothing we choose, but for a newsman or newswoman, what is tragic or sad almost certainly provides better opportunities for demonstrating ability than happy events do. That is one thing that differentiates news from public relations and advertising. Public relations usually, and advertising always, tries to create expectations of happiness.

On the last night of the 1964 Democratic convention, in Atlantic City, New Jersey, President Johnson was speaking. It was the climax of the affair, the king acknowledging the affection of his people. I was on the floor of the convention hall, standing near some members of the Mississippi Freedom Party delegation. They, blacks and whites, most of them poor, had come to Atlantic City to challenge the regular Mississippi delegation. A compromise had been worked out and some of them were seated. On the last night the entire delegation was on the floor. As President Johnson spoke about freedom and liberty, a black woman in the Freedom Party group began to cry. I told the NBC producer in charge of our coverage. Should he cut away from the President? If he did, why to this one person out of the thousands in the hall? Again, if he did, what did it show—that she was weeping for what she knew about the United States, or the President, or the Democratic Party, or Mississippi? Or was she simply overwhelmed by being where she was?

There was little time to think, and there was no textbook, or study of the "media," setting out what should be done. News judgment is an amalgam of experience, knowledge, wisdom, workmanship, and competitive urge. His amalgam told the NBC producer to cut to the woman. I hope we will never get to the day when that is called media judgment.

During the Viet Cong and North Vietnamese Tet offensive in 1968, some unusual film came into NBC. (The Associated Press also had stills of it.) It showed a man, dressed in shorts and a sport shirt and identified as a Viet Cong, being taken along a street in Saigon to the chief of the South Vietnamese national police. The police chief, without a word, drew a revolver, put it to the man's head, and shot him dead. Somebody at NBC had to decide what to do with that film. If you use it, are you implying that this kind of thing is going on wholesale? Suggesting that there should be sympathy for the unarmed underdog shot down in cold blood? How much do you show? The look on the doomed man's face as he realizes what is about to happen? His face as the bullet strikes? His head hitting the pavement, the blood running out of his head, the blood running down the gutter? Where do you cut off? The decisions are made according to the news judgment of the person, or persons, making them. That is circular: those who decide decide. But that is the way it happens.

A few weeks after the Tet offensive, President Johnson decided not to run again. A medium would simply have transmitted what he said, which was that he was stepping aside to demonstrate the genuineness of his desire for peace in Vietnam, to show that his offer to negotiate was not being made for political advantage. As a journalist, I had an obligation to point out that Johnson had barely beaten Eugene McCarthy in the New Hampshire primary a few weeks earlier, that he was evidently about to lose to McCarthy in Wisconsin, that Robert Kennedy had entered the contest for the nomination, that Johnson could not go anywhere in the country except to military bases without hostile demonstrations, and much more. Nor would a medium have been in the fix that I was in that night. We had been given an advance copy of the speech with the warning that the President would say something that was not in the text. We were led to believe that he would announce a trip. He was almost at the end of the prepared text when I realized that he was about to announce his withdrawal from politics. The director, who was not listening, began to remind me, through the listening device in my ear—it's called a Telex—how long I would speak, where we'd switch to when the speech was over, that sort of thing.

I was trying to take notes on what the President was saying, also coming to me on the Telex, drawing my hand across my throat as a signal for silence and trying to convey by grimacing and by clutching my head that the stage manager and cameramen should tell the director to be quiet. I was also shouting, "Shut up!" into my microphone, which made three voices talking at once. Eventually the director was prevailed upon by the producer to stop talking, and later he performed heroically in improvising the changes that had to be made. Directors often do perform miracles, but they don't always listen. At the 1964 Democratic convention in Atlantic City I was covering the announcement by the credentials committee of its decision in the seating of delegates from Mississippi. I was to broadcast from the room where the announcement was being made. As it began, the director came through on the Telex with a reminder of the time allotted me, switch cues, and so on.

"Don't talk to me now," I said into my microphone, trying to hear the announcement.

He went on.

"Don't talk to me now," I said again. I said it a number of times.

Governor David Lawrence of Pennsylvania, the committee chairman, grew tired of the competition. He looked down at me. "Tell them," he said, "that I agree with you."

It was not one of my happiest moments, but these are small things. News is a great business. I count myself lucky to be in it. My vendetta against the term media arises not only for the reasons already given but because it implies a go-between, one who takes orders and carries messages, one who is employed by others for their purposes. There is no suggestion of the quality we need most, which is independence.

When I hear somebody say media, I think of a phrase heard long ago from somebody whose English was ungrammatical but eloquent: "I ain' in dat." My difficulty arises from the fact that so many people won't believe that I ain'.

Independence may be a prerequisite of the news business, but public relations and advertising encourage a cheerful dependency. In the glamorous life I lead, public relations persons are always ready to do my bidding. Three spades, they will cry out for me, and four diamonds, and, on occasion, he passes. They ply me with gifts, both free gifts of the sort offered by savings banks to new depositors, and the other kind. I still have to buy some things for myself, however, and here I am much affected by advertising. I try to do as I am told. For example, I like what I wear to communicate my personal fashion statement, direct, definitive, and pertinent, and the result is that I buy my clothes where European influences are adapted for the American man of status, with an ultimate sense of quality and understated elegance, expressed in a peak lapel, deep center vent, suppressed waist, and higher armholes. My waist sometimes demands freedom of expression, but what is made for me there is styled to underscore my élan and to project my personality—which varies, with my ties reflecting the variations: adventurous plaids when I am adventurous, discreet patterns when I am discreet. Even the fabrics are au courant. The fall scenario calls for young wools, and later, when the weather is colder, much of what I wear is fur-lavished. Some of my other costumes are buttery-soft leathers that are an extension of my own body, which is buttery soft itself. Saks Fifth Avenue, for one, sells a magnificient—m-a-g-n-i-f-i-c-i-e-n-t—glacé leather trench coat collared and lined with natural muskrat. Unnatural muskrat is a muskrat of doubtful sexual proclivities and would not be welcome on any coat of mine.

When riding the seven-ten to the Hamptons, or holding forth in the board room, I wear clothes cut to cope with a man's pace, and with that certain offhand sense of style and nonchalance that lets me know I've arrived. Sometimes they let me know I've arrived before the train is at the Hamptons, but I've learned not to get off without looking at the station's name, or at my wrist watch, which is united with its bracelet in an unbroken contemporary line and gives me the kind of timekeeping dependability that inspires my eternal loyalty. My luggage, which confers quality status, contains a wraparound that is a long drink of stretch terry to soak up the sea après swim.

It is a heady life. Gifts I buy at Tiffany's; where else would one find whisperweight earrings designed to go into one pierced ear and out the other? Used cars I do not drive. I do not even drive cars that have seen prior service. Nor, among new cars, will I settle for one of Detroit's mass-produced status symbols. I insist on a personal statement of automotive comfort, the epitome of automotive elegance, a luxury performance car at a realistic price, made with unhurried European craftsmanship, with rack-and-pinion steering and a negative steering-roll radius, and powered by a highly responsive four-cylinder, twin overhead cam engine that is coupled to a five-speed overdrive transmission. I regard the coupling of the four-cylinder engine and the five-speed transmission as indispensable. It is, moreover, a thing of beauty. You can watch it without feeling that you are a voyeur at all.

About my apartment this has been said: "The overall grandeur of this space is memorably enticing. The magnanimity of leasehold improvements is so well-designed, it would likely appeal to anyone." I cannot speak for anyone else, but well-designed magnanimity has always appealed to me, especially since it became tax deductible.

In the luminous retreat that is my apartment, the bedrooms are filled with what I am assured is Old World charm, despite the fact that the curtains are made of a Redi-Prest blend of dacron polyester and rayon, and the multicolored comforter fluffed with lightweight polyester fiberfill. There is also New World charm, thanks to new concept furniture, fabrics, and wallpaper. Life without concepts, as we well know, would be empty. Sheets and pillowcases I have drawn from the Mixed Emotions collection, a responsive range of coordinated bed and bath fashions that differ in mood from pattern to pattern and from color to color and yet intermingle beautifully, with an impact that can be serene or startling. My preference is for the unexpected. It sets off my casually cool and tasteful pajamas.

The bathrooms have finely crafted switch plates, door pulls, and towel bars that offer charisma for the commonplace. In the reception rooms the high-pile texturizing of the carpeting gives special shadings and diffuses footprints (which has proved to be a mixed blessing). The silver is in an elegant, tastefully restrained pattern that gracefully complements both formal and informal appointments. The kitchen has been described as the gourmetest in town, and because it is, I once opened there a packet of gourmet couscous manufactured by the Ferrero Company of Vitrolles, Bouches-du-Rhône (Mouths-of-the-Rhône), which exports to the United States Le Vrai Couscous Extra (the Real Couscous Out of the Ordinary). You may want to know how the broth for the couscous is prepared:

"Take a nice chicken or a little bit of mutton, or still better the two sorts of meat together, cut it into pieces and parboil it. Put

it into your pot with the necessary water. Salt and join hot pepper
(the pungent sauce with red pimento, grinded in a cup, can be
served separately), join the chick-peas, a tuft of pot-herbs, onion,
garlick (if you desire), and all possible vegetable according to
the seasons.

"The broth must be very perfumed and can be favoured with
spices. Pour the cooked couscous into a deep plate, undo the balls,
which eventually could have been occured, in stiring with fresh
butter. Serve the couscous, vegetable and meat, broth, in 3 different plates. Each companion will accomodate the couscous according to his taste, i.e. more or less of the broth and of the pungent
sauce, as well as the vegetable of his choice."

I joined the chick-peas, was occured, and have not been the
same since.

I drink a gin that is the quintessence of an exceptionally
well-mannered martini ("Not too cold for you, sir, I hope," I
have heard it say) and occasionally shift to a happy vodka, which
may burst into song on the way down, but with a limited repertoire
because Russian songs tend to be moody—"None But the Lonely
Heart," "The Volga Boatman," and that sort of thing. Usually the
vodka manages only Moussorgsky's "Song of the Flea," and I am
growing tired of its great peals of bass-baritone laughter. My
liqueur hails from the land where love comes first and the liqueur
comes second. It is appreciated for its glowing color and a flavor
that is, quite frankly, romantic.

I don't smoke. However, some of my friends will not entertain
the idea of giving up cigarettes because they have found smoking
a cigarette to be a rare and pleasurable private moment. Some
smoke a cigarette with a filter based on a new design concept; for
others the cigarette is a proud smoke, boastful even. But now and
then all shift to a cigarette with a long, lean, all-white dynamite
look (their hands tremble when they light up). A few use a cigarette that is alive with pleasure, and the fact that if they continue
smoking it may still be alive with pleasure when they are not
bothers them not at all.

Living in a total concept of leisure calls for little outside entertainment, and I confine my moviegoing to major motion pictures, though I notice that lately there are few of any other kind. I see some major motion pictures on the television sets in hotel rooms. On one trip alone I saw a major motion picture (it was actually a Major Motion Picture) about the wicked, wacky thirties, one that told The Story of a Girl's Love, a Boy's Courage and a Rogue's Reckless Daring, and one in which Sinbad battled the creatures of legend in the miracle of Dynarama. Dynaramite! After a while you can spot major motion pictures as quickly as Hollywood does. Harold Robbins's *The Pirate* could hardly help becoming a major motion picture since it was, according to its publisher, Simon and Schuster (a richly editored house), "richly charactered." This brought the producer requests for jobs from many character actors, including one who had played the part of engine corrosion in an antifreeze commercial.

When I read, I find myself drawn to a magazine that is a brand-new media option for advertisers, with a unique new up-scale audience mix made up of magazine imperatives, who account for 43.6 per cent of the new cars purchased by men, 53.5 per cent of the radial tires, and 53.5 per cent of the air trips. Some of the magazine imperatives apparently have radial tires but not cars, but it is a group I feel I should be identified with. With books, I tend to wait for such events as the publication of the Avon spectacular, Joyce Verrette's *Dawn of Desire,* which received major advertising and promotion featuring floor displays plus a media mix of major TV, buses, newspapers, and magazines, which is only right for a blazing, tumultuous novel of a love as old as time, as timeless as forever. Still, I am broad-minded and will also read a book that is destined to become a classic. There are not many of these.

Tennis is a passion of mine. I step onto the court, clad in a red-and-green-striped white cotton tennis shirt. My shorts are the same colors, with terry side panels. After my victory I slip into my color-coordinated sweater and shake my good-sport-coordinated opponent's hand.

Women? Here it is simply a matter of what happens in a setting of overall grandeur and an exciting lifestyle. The grandeur and excitement attract women who use cosmetics that give off a deep, throaty purr of luxury. This means, to begin with, a fragrance evoking a season of lilacs and plums, the vigor of cypress, the charm of amber, lingering, opulent, and stunning, and that says exactly what the woman wearing it wants it to say, unless, of course, she wants it to tell a man to go away, which perfumes do not regard as their mission and find it difficult to do. Alternatively, it may mean a perfume that has little, light oriental tones (for mystery), new floral blends (for youth), and what professional perfumers call green notes (for sparkle), resulting in a scent that whispers, "This woman is sure of herself yet mysterious, sophisticated but young and sparkling."

It's an odd effect, a woman standing there, her lips brushed with extraordinary gel lipgloss, which gives them sheer, glistening color, her superluscious creme eyeshadow in a long-lasting, non-creasing color, and her nails like iced porcelain thanks to a two-phase color-coordinated system that adds a new, highly reflective quality to perfect frosts, her makeup an extraordinary coup for skin with both oily and drier areas because it blots and moisturizes at the same time, while from her come fairly complicated whispered messages. Those hearing them for the first time may be upset, and the hard of hearing often ask for a repeat: "What's that again? I didn't quite get what you said." It's a sure party pickup.

Such a woman knows that for the admiration she thrives on she needs in-depth skin care with an extract in which natural ingredients and soluble proteins blend to make her skin look young and resilient. The extract goes on under moisturizer and makeup and accompanies her on her travels, though the purring cosmetics sometimes do not. The airlines have asked her not to transmit while in the air. On her legs she wears Frivole, the pantystocking with the high-rise panty top on a sheer stocking, ideal for wear in a high-rise building. When she walks, her feet are encased in trendy wedges, in which a classic moc-toe is deftly outlined with fine stitches and punctuated with a goldtone ornament. Or she may wear a quintessential dress moc with a welted front porch and heels stocked knee-high to a grasshopper. She may also be shod in burnished brown and lickety licorice black consummate spring walkers replete with all the newsworthy blandishments, among them high points traced with moccasin welting, contrast stitchery, and gilting here and there.

She is an American woman in the Bicentennial era. And the only revolution going on is in her head. It starts with a concept. Of luxe. And luxe is what she's always yearned for. No one can dictate fashion to her any more. There are no more absolutes. In the spring she welcomes the dash of pantsuiting that explores all possibilities, and a crisp butcher's coat that wraps over slacks expresses her adventurous attitude and shares her limitless potential. When she likes to feel utterly original a dash of silk chiffon makes her evenings sing, and if the chiffon is set afire with yellow and orange tiger lilies in a bed of reeds on a beige ground, she will be both tigress and temptress. To prepare for the beach, where the summer/she is the most sensuous creature under the sun, jeweled with stones and shells, she uses a soap that won't de-fat, deterge, or denature the skin, thanks to its mild heavy-molecular triethanolamine-base formulation.

I am as grateful to heavy molecules as the summer/she is. It is not generally understood how these stable configurations of atomic nuclei and electrons remain bound together by electromagnetic forces. It is an accomplishment taken altogether too much for granted. Also, a skin without terge is a horrible sight, and we can all be glad that we are spared having to see it.

Paradigm Lost

I know of a condominium in Pompano Beach, Florida, which in the plans given to prospective buyers identifies the kitchen as a culinary center, the bedroom as a sleeping chamber, and the dining room as a place de dinner. La Plage Pompano would have been an appropriate setting for a dish served to me and others in the Athens of America at a book-and-author luncheon sponsored by the *Boston Herald*: Crepes à la sea food. Both the *Herald* and the condominium may have acted on the basis of technical advice from the Biltmore Hotel in New York City, where, for the benefit of visitors drifting over from the United Nations, a sign outside a men's lavatory announces not only Gentlemen but Monsieurs.

The Culinary Institute of America, in Hyde Park, New York, is also a place de dinner of sorts. It was founded in 1946 "to provide educational opportunities for individuals seeking successful and rewarding careers in food service hospitality." Those seeking unsuccessful and unrewarding careers evidently are encouraged to look elsewhere. The Institute has a Rabelais Grill with a different grill-type menu, and an Escoffier Restaurant which, by deduction, must have a restaurant-type menu that the grill-type menu is different from. Those who want to make reservations are invited to use a Maitre d' Tel Hot Line. The Maitre probably can tell you what the soup d' jour is and assign you to a t' ble, but you do not ask him for a d' ble room. That might annoy him and might make L' Institut a crisis-type setting. Not everybody is at his best in that kind of setting, but George Washington was at Valley Forge, and so was William M. Birenbaum. In the spring of 1976 Birenbaum was chosen by the search committee looking for a new president for Antioch College, Yellow Springs, Ohio. Inez Smith Reid, professor of political science at Barnard College, in New York City, was chairwoman of the committee. Birenbaum, she explained, was "a populist-type leader" and an "experienced chief executive with a strong track record in crisis-type settings."

When Washington ran the revolutionary-type war that made the country independent, compiling a strong track record may have been easier. The country did not yet have what Jimmy Carter has called a heterogeneous-type American population. Nonetheless, I have always had the average amount of respect for Washington, first President, first in war, first in peace, first in the hearts of his countrymen, and, according to Byron, Cincinnatus of the West. Some small flaws, no doubt, but who, Mesdames and Monsieurs, is without them? It was not until the nation reached its Bicentennial that I learned that there was more wrong with George Washington than most of us realized. The diagnosis was made by Louis G. Heller, professor of classical languages and Hebrew at City College of New York, and James Macris, professor of English and linguistics at Clark University, Worcester, Massachusetts. The father of his country stood in need of massive remediation. He was weak in punctuation and spelling.

Remediation appeals to those in education for the same reason that a place de dinner appeals to condominium promoters in Florida. An unnecessary abstruseness is introduced, a hint of complexity. There is a suggestion that what is being discussed is, in the case of remediation, beyond the understanding of most, and in the case of the place de dinner, beyond their pocketbooks. For remediators and developers of places de dinner, substituting the soft and the bloated for the concrete and specific makes the heart beat faster. It is a declaration of importance and is increasingly characteristic of life in the United States, where fringe benefits become collateral entitlements and toilets personal convenience rooms, where children in school are told not to ask to leave the room but to request a health break, and where an excuse becomes first a rationalization and then a legitimizing tactic.

Aboard an American Airlines flight from New York to Los Angeles, a stewardess asked, "For your meal preference, would you like beef Stroganoff, chicken, or fruit plate?" I had already had a large preference, and abstained. Frontier Airlines, which surely used to offer free soft drinks, now offers complimentary soft beverages. This is hardly the language of the frontier:

"What'll it be, pardner?"

"Make mine a soft beverage. No chaser."

When I lived in Britain in the 1950s, somebody in the Labour government came up with the phrase (he probably did not realize that it was a concept*) parity of esteem. He wanted graduates of technical schools to enjoy parity of esteem with university graduates. They did not then and do not now, and it is easy to see why. What teacher would want to teach children when he could remediate them massively instead?† It is as unlikely as somebody volunteering to his quietus make with a bare bodkin.

---

* See Chapter 5.

† The director of the Field Services Division of the New Jersey Department of Education, Catherine Kavrilesky, has said that teachers will be held responsible for any students who cannot read. "If we go into a school district and find a teacher who has a classroom filled with kids who can't read, we are going to expect to find the reason," Ms. Kavrilesky said. "If the reason is incompetence, we expect that teacher to undergo remediation, and if remediation fails, we expect to see that teacher dismissed, tenure or not." Remediation, if it means anything, means applying a remedy. Remedies cannot fail. Or could not, before American educators got hold of them.

There has to be some explanation for the fact that, as we become more and more open about ourselves, speak ever more freely about sex, see homosexuality come out of the closet and homosexuals become a public pressure group, demand and get more and more intimate information about our politicians, and— men and women alike—use language in what once would have been called polite society that no polite society would tolerate, our language in other parts of our lives becomes less and less frank, more and more covered and obscure. Both developments have the same source and the same purpose. We are calling attention to ourselves, in the one case with arresting four-letter words (which soon cease to be arresting because of overuse) and in the other with pumped-up job descriptions and titles.

I once used the term "garbageman" in a broadcast. It was at the time of the strike by garbage collectors in Memphis, Tennessee, in 1968, in the course of which Martin Luther King, Jr., was killed. I soon received a letter from a woman who told me that her husband was one of the men I had referred to. "My husband is not garbage," she wrote. "Please don't call him that again." I wrote back saying that no such thought was intended, and I did not use the term again. The point, though—which I had the good sense not to offer the woman who wrote to me—is that respect should not come from titles. It should come from an understanding of the work being done and the value of the person doing it. It should come from reality, not from camouflage.

We should not, for example, scorn those who collect and dispose of our garbage. We should be grateful to them. Our cities would not be habitable without them. We could have less garbage for them to dispose of if we reduced "packaging," but that seems to be beyond us. Indeed, instead of cutting down the packaging of things, we have taken to packaging ideas. We even package the absence of ideas, emptiness. It gets the gaudiest packages of all.

Remediation is, as these things go, a package of moderate size. The first time I ran across it, it took me some time to realize that it had nothing to do with mediating, still less with mediating again. It appeared in the November 1974 issue of *Change,* an education

magazine, which contained an article by David L. Kirp and Mark
G. Yudof about admission quotas for students in colleges, universities, and graduate schools. While discussing "the task of making
up for past discrimination," Kirp and Yudof wrote this: "In many
cases, the burden of remediation to overcome past deficiencies
is staggering." Kirp and Yudof could have spoken of the burden
of remedying past deficiencies. They did not have to use remedy in
any form: In many cases, the burden of overcoming past deficiencies is staggering. Educators prefer to remediate. Charles G.
Walcutt, graduate professor of English at the City University of
New York, wrote, "The colleges, trying to remediate increasing
numbers of . . . illiterates up to college levels, are being high-
schoolized." High-schoolized colleges will need remediation themselves, or, getting into the spirit of the thing, remediational
activities. This last phrase appeared in a letter from the Southeast
Mental Health and Retardation Center in Fargo, North Dakota.
Remediation-type activities will no doubt be next.

I should have been ready for remediation because, three
months earlier, I had been introduced to reinforcer emission. This
came about through an article, "Reinforcement Practices of Black
and White Teachers in Integrated Classrooms," in the August
1974 (a vintage year in its way, 1974) issue of the *Journal of
Educational Psychology.* Credulous fellow that I am, I thought it
had something to do with teachers being held in strategic reserve
to be dispatched from room to room to repel boarders. It had
nothing to do with that. Instead, the teachers were reinforcing
the children by a process of emission, and the study covered not
only the number of reinforcers the teachers emitted but whether
they tended to be of the traditional distant kind—promotion next
term, or possibly skipping a grade—or proximity reinforcers such
as material rewards and close personal contact.

In other words—and if only it were—the subject was how the
teachers encouraged the children. The educational advantage in
saying emitting reinforcers rather than encouraging children—or,
for that matter, calling a teacher a facilitator or enabler, a teaching
period a module, and a classroom a learning station—escapes me.

That there is an educational disadvantage does not. Stuffiness and fake erudition are being substituted for reality and clarity. No child goes home after school and tells her mother that during a module in the learning station that day the enabler emitted a reinforcer in her direction. "And it was a proximity reinforcer, too, Mommy!"

I remember a teacher in junior high school—an elderly, determined woman, Miss O'Connell—giving my hair a yank one day when I was disrespectful. This was not so much reinforcing as enforcing, but it fell into the proximity category. It kept me in order for the rest of the module.

The father of a child about to enter a junior high school in Los Angeles sent me a circular he had received from the school principal. It explained the seventh-grade curriculum and it contained this sentence: "We are planning an articulation visit to all our feeding elementary schools in the near future." He thought this meant that parents could talk to teachers.

When New York City was, in 1975, somewhat belatedly trying to remain solvent, the chancellor of the city's schools, Irving Anker, said, "I am reluctant to effectuate economies through the closing of schools, even for one day. I also have a question about the legality of such action." Anker could have said, "I hesitate to save money by closing schools. Also, it may be illegal." If he had, he might have lost his professional standing. He might, for example, have been shunned by the coordinator of research of the department of education of an eastern state who wrote to thank someone for sending him "summarizative descriptions of law and citizenship programs."

Despite his thanks, the research coordinator had some doubts about the worth of the law and citizenship materials in his dissemination program due to—he meant because of—their lack of evaluative data, and he was troubled by the fact that the programs would require as instructors professional law personnel—lawyers, one assumes. He thought that this would "serve to delimit the installation possibilities in a local education agency." I suppose he meant limit.

It is no joke when the coordinator of research in a state education department does not know the difference between limit, to confine or restrict, and delimit, to demarcate, to establish boundaries, but what is more important is that this language is repellent. I mean this literally: it will drive people away from education. The least harm it can do is put about the wrong idea of what eloquence and lucidity are.

What must conversation among these people be like?

"What are you up to these days, Anker?"

"I am effectuating economies. And you, research coordinator?"

"I am reading summarizative descriptions of law and citizenship programs, but I fear that they will not be suitable for a dissemination program because of their lack of evaluative data and their requirement of professional law personnel."

In 1974 a summer program of the New York City Board of Education became the subject of a report by the Youth Services Administration. The writer, possibly expecting his work to be seen by Irving Anker, warmed up by assuaging unforeseen difficulties and facilitating goals. He spoke of employees who had been robbed after drawing their pay checks, listed precautions that had been taken against this, and concluded, "These precautions appeared to be quite successful in dissuading potential individuals with larcenous intent." This is a new way of looking at the well-known occupational group, the perpetrators. Perpetrators are potential individuals who have not been dissuaded. Undissuaded, they perpetrate and run the risk of being observed ("I observed the perpetrator") and apprehended ("and apprehended same").

Dissuading potential individuals is more likely to succeed if it is begun early. The Community Health Care Center of the University of Minnesota asked for $35,000 from the Governor's Crime Commission to buy dogs: "The major objective of the project is to assess the extent to which early education via the use of pets, in empathy, responsibility, and regard for behavioral consequence are instrumental in deterring potentially delinquent

9-year-old boys from committing delinquent acts." If the project backfires, Minnesota may find itself facing not only the boys but an unusually large population of potentially delinquent dogs, leading in turn to more money for assessment, perhaps a deficit, a period of fiscal restraint, and a program of cost avoidance.

Recently, in New York, a policewoman dissuaded a potential individual by disarming and arresting him and breaking his nose when he resisted. The incident was investigated by police captain Irving Liebman, who said, "This is strictly a kosher case. There's absolutely nothing wrong with what she did."

Then the captain emitted a reinforcer: "The entire incident," he said, "was commendatory of female police officers." In fact, it wasn't. It may have spoken well of the policewoman, Arlene Egan, but told nothing about other policewomen, any more than an act of bravery by a policeman tells something about other policemen. Probably it was the climate of the times. Captain Liebman simply wanted to say commendatory. Kosher was better.

When Captain Liebman said commendatory, he was speaking one of the more exotic forms of education language, that of the honorary degree, which flowers every spring when heads of university honorary degree committees, with no apparent embarrassment, address to those receiving the degrees such reinforcers as these:

Like one of Horatio Alger's youthful heroes, your rise from obscurity to power has been swift.

You set an example not only for musicians in your devotion to the discipline of your craft, but for everyone with the vitality and harmony of your being.

You bind rifts in the fabric of your city, disproving Yeats's apocalyptic vision that the center cannot hold.

Not one to be awed into silent inactivity by the promises of pure technology, you have dealt with the implications of science with a calm logic and with consistent attention to its human role.

Your histrionic versatility is such that as an actress, in roles sometimes sophisticated or fiery, sometimes naïve or demure, your technical achievement cannot be categorized.

Those are the genuine article. Emboldened by such precedent Captain Liebman could have said to Arlene Egan: You have opened new paths for female police officers, and you have not flinched from danger. Your methods have been worthy of an ancient ethnic tradition.

Now for a thrust:

"The major thrust of Youth Services Agency's recommendations to maximize the quality and efficiency of services rendered revolve around the necessity for more phone channels. Two additional phone channels would compensate greatly for both communicative and space difficulties and such implementation is strongly urged as an immediate necessity."

Revolve should be revolves, and such implementation is also urged as an immediate necessity, but no matter. A revolving major thrust is hard to match. It is as rare in our part of the world as a whirling dervish. However, the nonrevolving species is spotted fairly often. It was seen at the 1975 convention of the American Booksellers Association, where a press release noted that the major thrust of the convention was to "foster dialogue." I had thought that it was to foster reading.

The report on the Board of Education program concluded with the Youth Services Agency's opinion that the program "should be considered for expanded allotments of enrollee personnel and more supportive measures from its own direct funding source." This is packaging again—the equivalent of wrapping paper, decorative tape and bows, boxes within boxes, tissue paper, all of it having to be peeled away and discarded to get at the recommendation of more workers and more money that lies within.

Major thrusts are fairly widely distributed in the New York City government. In the fiscal year ending in June 1974, 862,000 potholes were repaired, and although the number to be filled in the next fiscal year was about the same, one Budget Bureau official felt able to say that whereas "Potholes were a major thrust before" they were no longer, and it was time to look elsewhere for new productivity gains. The number of potholes does seem extraordinary; it might have been easier to drive the unpotholed parts of the streets down to pothole level rather than build the potholes up.

Two sources of strength of the United States are that it is large and has distinct regions. I was about to say that it is also varied, but it isn't. The educators, packaging relentlessly, make us all one. Where New York calls for supportive measures from direct funding sources, the Metro School Board of Nashville, Tennessee, discussing curriculum planning, states its intentions thus: "Programmatic assumptions will be specified, competencies identified, a rationale developed and instructional objectives stated. Pre-assessment, post-assessment, learning alternatives and remediation will be an integral part of instructional modules within the framework of program development."

Four hundred miles west, it is argued in a paper on "The Need for a University of Arkansas Continuing Education Center" that "the continuing education program should never be finalized. Rather, it should be a flexible, chameleon-like product, ever responding to the changing needs of the people of the State. However, broad programmatic thrusts might be articulated, thus providing parameters for decision-making and increasing the benefit yield." The need, changing or otherwise, of the people of Arkansas for a chameleon-like product of any kind may be doubted, and the belief that the articulation of broad programmatic thrusts provides (or emits) parameters for decision making ("Sir Gawain thrust his sword programmatically toward the villain, and as it caught the light it seemed to shower parameters on the loyal Arkansans, who were gathered expectantly near a backlog of decisions") is a delusion. Many a thrust has produced not a single parameter, for the reason that parameters are artful dodgers and refuse to be rounded up. The benefit yield is something else. It may well be increased by programmatic thrusting, but without the parameters who would want it?

It is not generally understood how elusive parameters are; nor is it understood that thrusts may be dangerous. I was in Madison, Wisconsin, in September 1974 and saw, in the local paper, the *State Journal,* an interview with the new dean of the Department of Home Economics of the University of Wisconsin, Elizabeth J. Simpson. (Not that it is called Home Economics any longer; it has become Family Resources and Consumer Sciences.) The dean was discussing her previous job, in the Office of Education in Washington, and she said that much of her recent work had been in "conceptualizing new thrusts in programming." The dean is a brave woman. Beware the conceptualized thrust. I saw one that had gone berserk and it took six strong men to hold it down.

The spirit that turns home economics into family resources and consumer sciences is everywhere. When the University of Miami had a deficit of $560,000, its president, Henry King Stanford, was undaunted.* "We will divert the force of this fiscal stress," Dr. Stanford said, "into leverage energy to pry improved budgetary prediction and control out of our fiscal and administrative procedures." Dr. Stanford meant that he intended to cut some

---

* He could, in the way of university presidents, as easily be Henry Stanford King, Stanford Henry King, Stanford King Henry, King Stanford Henry, or King Henry Stanford. There is a requirement, not statutory but widely acknowledged, that university presidents have interchangeable names, three if possible. This lends dignity to their institutions. Those who wish to pursue this matter further may consult my earlier work, *Strictly Speaking,* Bobbs-Merrill, New York 1974, pages 117–122. They will also find their own research rewarding. A New York lawyer has written to me that he saw a university presidency ahead for his grandson, MacLaren Marshall Richardson. Another lawyer, Spencer Agassiz Gard, of Iola, Kansas, wondered why he was not a university president. He may be certain that a university will be constructed around him before the decade is out. Lounsbury Danforth Bates, who also wrote, is the librarian of the Harvard Club in New York and not a university president. However, Bates is known as Biff, which may be the reason.

The ideal university president's interchangeable name was that of Nicholas Murray Butler, who was president of Columbia from 1902 to 1945. Among those I mentioned as following the Butler tradition was Forrest David Mathews of the University of Alabama. Mathews became Secretary of Health, Education and Welfare, and in May 1976 received from Columbia University the Nicholas Murray Butler award, in silver. Whether the award is given for something more than having a name like Nicholas Murray Butler's I do not know and I would like to think not, but by the time Mathews received it he was calling himself F. David Mathews. Not the same. Not the same at all.

costs. When Betty Friedan taught at Yale, the students complained that she lectured too much. Ms. Friedan declared herself open to change, whereupon, so one student put it, the seminar was "restructured toward interaction." He meant the students were allowed to talk more. Says a member of the Federal Communications Commission, a former law professor, about regulation of children's television: The First Amendment "does not mean that we can make judgments on the basis of majoritarian sentiments alone." Fair enough. The minoritarians have their rights too. The woman in charge of publications in a rehabilitation hospital in New York State ran across "fostering interfamilial meaningful relationships with counselees recovering from cardio-vascular-pulmonary malfunctions." She deduced that it meant counseling families of heart attack and stroke patients. Edith P. Lewis, editor of *Nursing Outlook,* passed along to me a sentence she received in the line of duty: "Finalization of the implementation of the program which, it had been decided by the faculty, would facilitate forward movement toward goal achievement was made operational in the penultimate semester." In American society the penultimate is mightier than the sword.

Not long ago an appeal for money reached me from an organization at Princeton University that was looking for viable solutions to the complex and pressing problems of peace. Without them, I was warned, our very survival will continue to be imperiled, which is logical: Them as ain't viable won't last long. The older generation does tend to live in the past, but we used to look for solutions to problems and were pleasantly surprised on the rare occasions when we found them. Solutions are no longer sufficient; viability is required. Viable has moved into the legal profession: "The consent under Section 341(f) might be a viable solution if the corporation was subject to the capital gain tax under Section 1378(c). However, the development of such a situation would be very likely to be unusual." That would make viability very likely to be unusual, as well.

And if not viability, effectiveness. A statement of policy from the Committee for Economic Development said that a new generation of complex problems demanded fresh and effective solutions. A solution not effective would not be a solution. Nor need a solution be fresh. Old solutions do the job, and have the advantage of experience.

I mentioned money two paragraphs above. In the context it seems rude. Among restructurers toward interaction and those who look for grants for technical training because "a quality void in technical capacity constrains achievement," money is too bald a word. They prefer funds, or better still funding, because it sounds like something continuing. Again, they would rather not say continuing. Ongoing is preferred.

Ongoing has a mesmerizing quality. City College of New York wanted to have a communications center which would "train students to work within their immediate communications environment" and would have an ongoing placement service. How that would differ from a placement service was not made clear. Perhaps a placement service finds jobs for its clients while an ongoing placement service finds jobs for those who have demonstrated sufficient motivation to achieve in an appropriate employment setting. (Hands across the border: the part of the last sentence that begins with "demonstrated sufficient motivation" drifted down with a cold air mass from Winnipeg, Canada.)

A preparatory school I know sends questionnaires to the parents of applicants. Why, one question goes, have you chosen us? One father replied, "We feel that [name of school] offers an optimal synthesis of the traditional education in the fundamentals of learning and innovative education in creative involvement." The parent who brought this forth probably had his child accepted with a scholarship and was himself invited to revise the school's catalogue.

In the field of education the competition in producing nonsense is intense. What does the scientific method in the social sciences do? The answer, from a social scientist: "It supplies knowledge that can be transmitted from person to person *qua* knowledge, here called 'intersubjectively transmissible knowledge,' or, briefly, 'transmissible knowledge.' " A bridge over the river *qua*. The *Individualized Learning Letter,* which is published in Huntington, New York, and goes to school administrators, has told of the working draft of a report whose recommendations "seek to free learning and teaching from the shackles of time, place and age, and to breach the real and imaginary walls that tend to make intermediate and secondary schools isolated islands for adolescents." The island that is not only an island but is isolated as well must be an extremely lonely place to be. But that aside, time, place, and age are not shackles. They are inescapable conditions of life, which would be unimaginable without them. Does it make no difference where you are? When? Whether you are five or fifteen or fifty? If education is in the hands of people who consider time, place, and age shackles, and who would like islands no longer to be isolated, I prefer that their knowledge not be transmissible and I would blow up the *qua* bridge to bring that about.

Bernice L. Neugarten, professor of human development in the Department of Behavioral Science at the University of Chicago, has written that "if the young-old do not form a strong age-group identification of their own, they may well become major agents of social change in moving toward the society in which age is irrelevant." If the young-old do form a strong age-group identification of their own, I would like to know what it is. ("We are the young-old. We are naughty but nice and sometimes have to be cruel to be kind.")

In January 1976 George Millar, principal of Tunn High School in Palo Alto, California, asked to be reassigned. "I have been here six years," Millar said, "and that is probably long enough for a person to be principal of one school. As a change agent, my utility as principal is probably done." A change agent who stays too long in one place may grow young-old before his time.

I expect to cling to the belief that age matters. In many aspects of our lives it is the controlling factor. One need only be young or old to appreciate this. There cannot be a society in which age is irrelevant.

There is much at stake in understanding this. The use of language that is at bottom nonsense leads, as might be expected, to the advocacy of nonsensical ideas and, by the law of averages alone, to the adoption of nonsensical ideas. At the least, the language and the ideas go hand in hand. Let us return, for another demonstration, to Nashville, home of country music and the Metro School Board. In the discussion of curriculum planning mentioned earlier, the Board announced that it intended "to facilitate the development process, with the ultimate goal of creating a flexible model for an interdisciplinary approach to teaching" that would "correlate subject areas whenever meaningful to make learning experiences a related integral whole."

A related integral whole was not the educational ambition of William C. Pratella, superintendent of schools in Mount Vernon, New York. He wanted—but let him tell it: "We will present all the subject areas—no established curriculum area will be neglected —and teach them as a unified whole to reveal their inherent interrelatedness."

This is as practicable an idea as making all the world kin. All the subject areas do not make a related integral whole, or a unified whole, except in a sense so loose as to be meaningless. Nor would it be a good idea if they did. Education is a voyage of discovery that may take you in many directions. That's half the fun of it. It is normal for young people to be tugged this way and that by new ideas* almost as soon as (phrasing courtesy of a high-school principal in Evansville, Indiana) they are mainstreamed into the classroom situation. Talk about making education a unified whole is sloganeering, churned out to create the impression that something complex and abstruse is taking place. It is done for self-preservation and self-promotion. The American Federation of Labor, when it was made up of craft unions only, practiced job-conscious unionism, meaning that its members were principally interested in protecting their jobs. So it is with educators who speak of revealing the inherent interrelatedness of established curriculum areas. By mystifying the public they protect their jobs

---

* This concept need not be expressed so starkly. From a discussion of imaginal education methods in a paper of the same name: "Since new data inconsistent with operating images can challenge those images, it is clear that learning is a perpetual dynamic of re-imaging the 'real.' " This won the package-of-the-year award in 1976.

and avoid the danger that they will be (educational language again) excessed.

Nor is this unusual. Few of us pump out the smog that educators do, but it is also true that few of us spend our lives risking all. I have not often gone to see the head of NBC News and said, "I have prospered enough. Excess me." If I did, I would be told in a kindly manner, "Excessing is not our way here, Newman. We fire people."

Avoiding being excessed may require obedience to behavioral objectives. I realize that I should pause here to define behavioral objectives, but it is not easy to do. The term appears to have as much reality as inherent interrelatedness does. I have a paper prepared by an education organization in Massachusetts that advocates setting behavioral objectives for students, teachers, and parents. It is full of such phrases as learning sequence, learning outcomes, the instructional process, a variety of media and methods, and effective diagnosis. It reaches its peak with the claim that teachers who adopt behavioral objectives will be able to "provide students with a pharmacy of learning alternatives matched to the objectives and tailored to the individual characteristics of each student."

Where pharmacies of learning alternatives exist—usually at the back of the drug store, past the lunch counter and the toilet articles—students are sent in with prescriptions to be filled. They are watched closely for side effects, and if there are any the prescription is changed. It is a perpetual dynamic.

Because many people who sent me material for a second book asked that the source not be revealed, I can only say that "A Note on Grading in Economics 596 and 597" came to me from Texas, where an institution of higher learning was offering these courses for credit toward a degree of Master of Arts in Manpower and Industrial Relations. As I read the Note, it struck me that those offering Economics 596 and 597 were setting behavioral objectives, perhaps without knowing it:

"Do you realize, Miss Compton, that you have established behavioral objectives?"

"Oh, doctor!"

The Note put it this way: "These tests . . . are . . . intended to provide us with information as to the effectiveness of our instructional system with respect to the achievement of our objectives. They will also serve as an index, for your use, of how well you have learned the treated material." That would be, in short, that through the tests the teachers and students would know what the students were learning. In short it never is.

Using the Socratic method, the Note establishes that the final examination will consist of a series of multiple-choice-type items, and then, pursuing itself relentlessly, asks, "What is a creditable performance on the final examination?" It answers: "While we are reluctant at this time to set a hard and fast benchmark on this matter, our present inclination is to set the standard at somewhere in the neighborhood of the 90% correct level." Somewhere in the neighborhood of is a soft and loose benchmark.

As an alternative (obtained at the pharmacy) to the final examination, students in Economics 596 and 597 were told that they could submit an instructional module. The module referred to here is not simply the period with a facilitator in a learning station mentioned earlier, but "involves the selection or construction of a technology which, when implemented, is likely to be effective in moving the student population in the class from the condition of not having what you want them to have to the condition of having what you want them to have." At West Point it might be the very module of a modern major-general.

I often wish that my correspondent in Texas had told me which university offered Economics 596 and 597. It would be rewarding to drop in and hear the exchange.

"Good morning, student population in the class."

"Good morning, type-teacher."

After this promising beginning, the teacher says that he is tired and cannot remember whether the class has already been moved to a condition of having what he wants it to have. There is a bedlam of cries from the student population, some haves, some have-nots. Others are silent, too much talk about the instructional module having given them throat modules. The teacher, a son of the Ould Sodule and mindful of the maxim, Spare the rodule and spoil the child, says he will codule them no longer, and all go back to work, including a set of twins who are as alike as two peas in a podule.

When I was in school and teachers were trying to move me from the before condition to the after, and without benefit of modules, which had yet to be discovered, behavior meant conduct, whether you were good or bad. "Edwin's behavior has been better this term," the report card might say, "but he still sometimes talks in the corridors and sulks when he is corrected."

Years later I heard an ingenious application of the word in a calypso sung by a performer known as Growler, which told of his being fended off by a woman: "She say, 'Growler, have some behavior.' " Growler's behavioral objective evidently was not achieved.

If only educators could be told to have some behavior, with the language of modules and the like put off limits to them. But they will not be denied. They are demon lovers. Princeton University's Center of International Studies has a World Order Studies Program in which, among other problems, behavioral problems are studied. Thus: "The behavioral aspects of world order studies include problems associated with the relation of the diverse national attitudes of the world's societies and cultures to the common denominator of values necessary to a viable world order, and the creation and development of linkages between domestic and international order."

It is not often that one finds viable and linkages* so close to each other, and with a common denominator of values hardly a step away, and it is only a matter of time before the linkages will have to be viable, and the common denominators and values as well. However, advanced thinkers are finding viability inadequate or—this has arrived—not adequate enough. When Senator Lloyd Bentsen of Texas dropped out of the contest for the Democratic

---

* Not to be confused with causal links.

nomination for President, the *New York Times* said that he had never been a genuinely viable candidate. Governor Hugh Carey has called for a New York City that is "strong, viable and revitalized." If it's viable, it doesn't have to be revitalized.

The leaflet on Princeton's World Order Studies Program, a credit to the Ivy League, contains frames of reference, frameworks of action, normative aspects, the global community, normative implications, allocative institutions, political dimensions, resource utilization, and critical concepts, all being examined for the welfare of humankind.

Scene in the World Order Studies Program supply room:

"I need a critical concept, Jenkins."

"No trouble, sir. They're right here. They arrived this morning and we put them on the shelves at once. Any particular kind?"

"Yes, it should be a concept that is critical to the political dimensions of the problem."

"Would you like it sent?"

"Please. I also need a normative aspect, Jenkins."

"Sorry, sir, we're out of them. The demand has been heavy. I can give you a normative implication. There are a few of them left."

"Why weren't more aspects ordered?"

"I don't know, sir. That's a matter of resource utilization, and I'm only a clerk, sir. I have no allocative function. I can tell you that the implications come in a larger carton."

"All right, if that's all you have. Let me have one."

"What size, sir?"

"What do you mean, what size?"

"Broad or narrow, sir. Broad implications or narrow?"

"Broad, of course. Do you ever get orders for the other kind?"

"I'd rather not say, sir."

The appeal of this language lies in its slipperiness. It sounds as though it means something, especially to those who do not look at it closely. It serves as a fence that keeps others outside and respectful, or leads them to ignore what is going on because it is too much trouble to find out. For those inside, either effect is useful.

Language is used in this way in art, especially in painting. A press release issued by the Artemisia Gallery in Chicago was passed along to me. It said:

"Susan Michod's paintings have to do with multiplicity, ambiguity, and the layering of meanings. The basic drawing of the forms implies and denies a perspectival structure. This duality, also operating in the systematic use of color, value and pattern, pits three-dimensionality and flatness against each other. The slight wrinkling of the surface and fabric-like feel add elements of realistic illusionism to the formalist game-play. All of these elements are subservient to each other and the resulting complexity produces a shifting non-relational surface.

"The lack of dominance and the resulting non-hierarchical structure is a visual metaphor for a philosophical attitude about complexity, existentialism, feminism, and the absence of absolutes in our culture."

It is sad to see three-dimensionality and flatness pitted against each other. Both are known to be merciless and have reputations for stopping at nothing, and the presence of multiplicity, ambiguity, and the layering of meanings can only spur them on. But I suppose that that is the name of the formalist game-play.

The Artemisia press release is a child's primer compared with an article, "Formative Hermeneutics in the Arting Processes of an Other: The Philetics of Art Education," in the magazine *Art Education*. Its author was Kenneth R. Beittel, professor of art education at Pennsylvania State University. Here are some samples:

"The divided voice of the artist is taken up for and with him, the path unseen by the artist is allowed to announce itself, the past of the artist more strangely and as 'othered' enters his present and future, and his meeting with 'the other' is nonallergically extended and present 'face to face.' "

Now take a deep breath and go on.

"In terms of arting, where the reference condition is not fixed or even known conceptually but rather something coming to being, what can we hope through our formative hermeneutic movement? To make the 'otherness' of the arting process more other, more 'objective' in a newer sense and less 'subjective' in the older sense, so that the arting process itself speaks more purely?"

A further observation by Professor Beittel: "This is the very effect, then, that would strengthen the formative hermeneutic impact within the ongoing arting process. Here is no intervention, but an advent, in which the witness-as-sharer turns to co-agent. It is a shared adventure. . . . Thus, artist, witness and aborning work stand in relation: artist-witness, artist-work, and witness-work. A trinitarian co-agency, co-sharing, co-creating, transcending but not usurping autonomous otherness, but as in-relation, as in-between, is what is involved. While I believe this makes interpretation even harder, that is not a restriction to be imposed where the truth of being is the first concern. And, since anyone who has experienced essential being feels called upon to speak, the problem becomes that of how to speak."

The problem is, indeed, how to speak.

An invaluable piece of information appeared in capital letters, EXCESSIVE ANGER IN THE HOME IS DESTRUCTIVE TO SELF-IMAGE DEVELOPMENT, in a press release put out by Harper & Row for a book called WHAT EVERY CHILD NEEDS, by Lillian and Richard Peairs. I think of myself as EDWIN NEWMAN, and where possible in bold face as well as capitals, so my attention was caught at once. What every child needed, it turned out, was a positive creative image, a positive verbal image, a positive intellectual image, a positive ability image, a positive behavior image,* a positive physical image, and a positive social image. The only kind the child was thought not to need, evidently, was a positive image image, a serious flaw in the argument, for the absence of a positive image image may lead to what psychiatrists call identity diffusion, a state characterized by a lack of concept of self and a lack of concept of others,† which is as many concepts of the kind as it is possible to get along without.

It is sad to meet someone who lacks a positive image image.

---

* Growler did not have this.

† In dealing with this, formative hermeneutics may help.

I have heard more than one cast-down adult say, on being asked why he went about drooping and woebegone, that it was because he did not have a positive image of his self-image. "My self-image is fine," they would say. "I'm proud of myself. But I doubt that my self-image is justified."

In February 1976, on "Meet the Press," Helen Thomas of United Press International mentioned President Ford's "image portrayal problem." Ford had a positive creative-verbal-intellectual-ability-behavior-physical-social self-image. The problem Ms. Thomas referred to was that, at the time, some others doubted that his self-image was justified.

In June 1976 Leslie H. Gelb of the *New York Times* wrote that Henry Kissinger was suffering from bad imagery. Criticizing a Secretary of State for lacking the poetic touch seemed to be going a little far, but Gelb explained himself. Conservatives, he said, saw Kissinger as Rasputin, anti-Semites saw him as Shylock, and liberals saw him as George III. Rasputin, Shylock, and George would make a formidable and versatile triumvirate, especially if one accepts the recent opinion of historians that George was not insane but only sick and in need of help, but none of them fits Kissinger's self-image, at any rate as publicly revealed.

Because the absence of self-images can be crippling, the task of developing self-acceptable self-images is welcomed by many institutions. The United States Navy's Finance Center, in Cleveland, offers Participative Management Training, a task-oriented training experience directed toward improvement of interpersonal skills. It is craftily devised to bring optimal (best is not enough) results by making attendance completely (not partly) voluntary.

A quick overview of the course, from an article in the *Journal of Navy Civilian Manpower Management:*

"Our adaptation includes the use of several structured consensus tasks, exposure to the Blake and Mouton Managerial Grid, and experience with the Johari Window. We use several instruments to assist participants in appraising their leadership styles and in planning for change. We intersperse through the institute lecturettes on McGregor's Theory X and Theory Y, Maslow's hierarchy of needs, and Herzberg's motivator and hygiene factors. The entire institute is task-oriented."

The paragraph insistently brings to mind the triumphs of other naval task-oriented forces:

Damn the motivator factors! Optimal speed ahead!
Don't give up the lecturettes!

The Animal and Health Inspection Service of the Agriculture Department offers women employees seminars in assertive awareness. The seminars consist of lectures (no lecturettes that insultingly suggest that those listening have a short attention span), discussions, and Danish thumb wrestling. According to R. M. Gurley, the service's training officer, the seminars tone down women on the "super-aggressive, super-hostile side" and help the shy and reticent to deal with their male supervisors. In Danish thumb wrestling, hands are locked in such a way that only the thumbs are free to do battle. Each tries to push the other down. The cost of the seminars to the middle of 1976 was $44,000. The Danes say that thumb wrestling has nothing to do with them.

Institutions have images of themselves, also. "The goal of the U.C.C. is the development of well-rounded persons. It encourages self-directed activity, while giving maximum opportunity for self-realization and for growth in individual self-competency and group effectiveness."*

This last comes, advocates of hemispheric solidarity will be gratified to learn, from Canada. The U.C.C. is the University Community Centre of the University of Western Ontario, London, Canada. Functioning, as it points out, within the framework of the community concept, the U.C.C. has a bookstore which "considers its role to be to create the broadest possible interface of the world of information packages and the whole university community, and to serve as a retail outlet on campus to fulfill other service requirements." This means that the bookstore sells

---

* Self-directed activity sounds as though it would direct itself, which would be humiliating for a well-rounded, self-realized, self-competent, group-effective person.

books. Though a country with a relatively small population, Canada can interface with the best of them.

All right, the second best of them, because Canada cannot interface with Sanford M. Lewis, M.D., of East Orange, New Jersey, who wrote to the *New York Times,* "I too am concerned with the evolution of viable constructs by which complex problems at the medical-legal interface can be effectively resolved for social usefulness." Even against Canada, practiced in ice hockey though it is, Dr. Lewis wins the interface-off.

I have gone to the medical-legal interface only on journalistic assignment, and with hazardous duty pay, but I did go one day on my own time to an interfaith interface. As luck would have it, my ecumenical mood was curdled by the realization that the meeting was troubled by multivariate problems, among them the fact that some of those attending were, like the Japanese, interested only in saving interface, while others were there only in search of interaction that might lead to interpersonal relations, such as going elsewhere and dancing intercheek. I decided to interface up to the fact that I would probably never again attend such a meeting, for I knew that many of the interpersonal relations begun there would end unhappily, possibly even in a category to which a sociologist at the University of Southern California consigned murder and assault—escalated interpersonal altercations. But that was a long way off. I was reminded of the summarizative description of the aims of a research project on romantic love financed by the National Science Foundation:

"The primary aim of this research project is to examine the role of psychological dependency as an antecedent to interpersonal attraction, particularly, though not exclusively, in heterosexual relationships in which the individuals involved label their attraction 'romantic love.' A related, but subsidiary, aim is to assess the potential of the dependency construct to provide the core of a theoretical framework whose predictive domain would encompass not only the milder forms of attraction, such as 'liking' and 'disliking,' but also the stronger forms, such as 'love' and 'hate,' in both like- and opposite-sex relationships. An examination of the relationships between hypothesized dependency variables will be made, as well as an examination of the effect which environmental conditions conducive and nonconducive to fantasy may have upon these variables. Too, the investigation of situational factors which may determine labeling of positive affect in dyadic relationships will be undertaken. Research will involve both laboratory and field investigation."

A bargain at $133,400, though not likely to enrich the language:

"It's no use fighting it, baby. You and I have an interpersonal attraction in an opposite-sex relationship going."

"Take it easy, big boy. You don't understand. In the first place, we're crosscultural. In the second place, the moon is an environmental condition conducive to fantasy. And there are situational factors that may determine positive affect. We are, to put it plainly, the only ones here."

"You're wrong, baby. This is a dyadic relationship if I ever saw one. It's the real thing."

Suddenly she yields. The positive affect is too strong. Her resistance to a dependency construct self-destructs. He works his will on her. They interface.

Interfacing is not always so intense and interpersonal. The Energy Research and Development Administration has published, in the *Federal Register,* a Consumer Representation Plan that "focuses on two functions: Information Input and Information Output." ERDA* announced that it planned to accelerate communication, glean feedback, finalize option papers, make a concentrated and time-constrained effort, and use new public outreach interlocking mechanisms to broaden and sharpen the interface process. The public outreach interlocking mechanisms sound as

---

* The initials were chosen to make up an acronym standing for Erda, the earth goddess, who when not otherwise occupied sings in *Das Rheingold* and *Siegfried* in Wagner's *Ring.* Nobody ever accused Wagner of accelerating communication or making a time-constrained effort.

though they will cancel each other, but that can happen when government agencies go at things in a rush. Time constraint makes waste.

If all government agencies are intent on interfacing, however, there is reason to doubt that there will be enough concerned citizens to go around. Citizens we have in plenty; concerned citizens are so scarce that they have to be shared almost constantly among government departments, wearing a worried look when providing input and evincing relief and enlightenment when receiving output. Some of the citizens were exhausted by overuse and tumbled into the outreach interlocking mechanisms, which had to be interrupted in their broadening and sharpening and brought grinding to a halt. It does appear that a CCC (Concerned Citizens Corps) is needed. However, the demand for a CCC may be reduced by the creation, under a law passed in 1974, of the Office of Federal Procurement Policy. The OFPP's administrator, Hugh E. Witt, has said, "We are the interface* between the executive branch and industry." Witt may be able to procure concerned citizens and distribute them in areas of greatest need.

Outreaching and interfacing in their beginning stages may be seen in a letter written by the environmental review officer of a city in the Middle West. He was asking those with the same job in other cities for help:

"Dear Sir:

"Recently this department became aware of the crucial need to collect sufficient technical information and thereby to implement the methodology of environmental analysis in urban planning. Toward this formidable endeavor, we have researched available information and those organizations displaying excellence in this venue. We therefore wish to present a respectful request for repre-

---

* I was present at a meeting in June 1976 at which a participant said that one of the problems facing us was the lack of a structured interface. I mention this to show that I write about these matters from experience and bear the scars of combat.

sentative examples of environmental and developmental analysis which you have available.

"Our progress to this point in utilizing fundamental environmental requisites is represented by the creation of a manual, but soon to be computerized, environmental data base. Further, we are incorporating existing staff expertise and planning process derived from conventional physical and computer planning capabilities. But, without some superior paradigms which depict attainments made on the 'cutting edge' of technical innovation, we will experience an obvious delay in the 'tool up' phase prior to the urgently needed application.

"If you could perhaps forward several such environmental studies and/or other development feasibility research, or provide referral as to the means and cost of procurement, we would be most appreciative. Any similar assistance which we might provide from our subsequent efforts would certainly be yours promptly upon request. . . .

"Sincerely."

There are briefer ways of putting it—"Brother, can you spare a superior paradigm?"

I cannot believe that anybody well stocked with paradigms could resist the heartfelt yearning evident in the letter. It is, however, as well that only urban planning paradigms were needed because certain other kinds are not readily obtainable. I base this comment on an essay in a book titled *Against the World, For the World*, which looks at the future of American religion. In it the language of the social sciences takes possession of religion, a conversion in keeping with the times.

George Lindbeck, of the Yale Divinity School, who wrote the essay, believes that we are living through a paradigm shift, and that the old paradigms seem increasingly inadequate and the new ones implausible. Lindbeck acknowledges that his conclusion depends "on the adequacy of a paradigm-shift analysis of theological crises," but he does not doubt that a revolution in theological paradigms is going on. Paradigm-shift analysis is not my field—I have no training in it; but paradigms, one gathers with Lindbeck's guidance, do not last forever. The time comes when one says, " 'Twere paradigm enow."*

Christopher Mwoleka is the Roman Catholic Bishop of Rulenge, in Tanzania, and lives in the village of Nyabihinga. Bishop Mwoleka might be thought to be burning with a desire to save souls. Not so. He told a reporter that he wants the villages to be "oriented to God." As social science language goes, that is only a beginning, but Nyabihinga, Tanzania, gets sketchy service from the social sciences. Bishop Mwoleka could hardly expect to equal this statement by Paul Lehmann in *The Transfiguration of Politics: The Presence and Power of Jesus of Nazareth in and over Human Affairs,* published in 1975 by Harper & Row:

"Piety and politics belong intrinsically and inseparably together. Piety is the compound of reverence and thankfulness that forms and transforms the reciprocity between creaturehood and creativity, in privacy and in society, into the possibility and the power of fulfilling human freedom and joy. Politics is the compound of justice, ordination, and order that shapes, sustains, and gives structure to a social matrix for the human practice of privacy and for the practice of humanness in community. In such a matrix, justice is the reciprocity of differences in creaturehood and creativity, experienced as enrichment rather than as a threat; ordination is the insistent priority and pressure of purpose over power in the practice of the reciprocity between creaturehood and creativity; and order is the possibility and the power of so living in one time and place as not to destroy the possibility of other times and places. So piety apart from politics loses its integrity and converts into apostasy; whereas politics without piety subverts both its divine ordination and its ordering of humanness, perverts justice, and converts into idolatry.

"To read and understand the Bible politically and to under-

---

* The pronunciation, I am sorry to say, is paradim, which eliminates "One kiss, one fond caress, They lead the way to happiness, They take me to paradigm." However, it does make possible paradiminuendo, which is a model no longer much followed.

stand and practice politics biblically is to discern in, with, and under the concrete course of human events the presence and power of God at work, giving human shape to human life. The human meaning of politics is to the biblical meaning of politics as the Fall is to the creaturehood and destiny of humanity in a world that has been created and redeemed."

The point, I believe, is that the Biable is viable.

It is possible that neither the man who wants his environmental data base brought up to date nor any of the three theologians just quoted has ever met a payroll, an experience thought in some circles to produce individuals who are matter-of-fact, hard-bitten, and laconic. (The hard biters of the hard-bitten have never been identified.) Nonetheless, people who do meet payrolls speak contemporary American. In a speech to the American Life Insurance Association Convention in San Francisco, in December 1974, Allan D. Schuster, vice president and general manager, Citicorp Realty Consultants, Inc., of New York City, posed this question: "Are we watching a recurring phenomenon or is real estate on the road toward stability shaped by forces of positive change at war with the old ways?" Having cornered himself, Schuster replied that out of the crisis was coming an emerging professionalism. He epitomized this by dropping into his speech ongoing, conceptual, expertise, viability, highly-leveraged, contained multi-purpose communities, societal attitudes, benchmarks, over-leveraged, and macro market research. Research, Schuster let it be known, was indispensable. Holy macro.

Contemporary American is also spoken by trade unionists. Ben Fisher, special assistant to the president of the United Steelworkers of America, was quoted in *New Times* magazine on the question of discrimination against blacks in the steel industry: "It is just not accurate to believe that blacks were confined somehow to the lowest paying jobs; rather, there was some tendency for blacks to be congregated in certain units which had a variety of characteristics including, in some instances, a somewhat lower average pay than some units where there might be a heavy concentration of white employees." Meaning, apparently, that blacks who received lower pay than whites did not have lower paying jobs. Bring back the young-old.

An employment agency in New York, the Craig Computer Centre Agency, sent the personnel managers of companies it dealt with a letter that began with these words: "The purpose of this letter is to historize the philosophical infrastructure Craig Computer Centre abides, regarding applicant referrals." The agency wanted to tell its customers what its policy was. Instead, it historized the philosophical infrastructure Craig Computer Centre abides. I cherish the hope that anybody who historizes philosophical infrastructures will abide not with me, but that they will abide and prosper is certain. They are everywhere. Here is an infrastructure from the August 1975 issue of the *Designer,* published by the American Society of Interior Designers:

"There is a wide gap between multi-disciplinary teams and inter-disciplinary teams. Multi-disciplinary applies when various disciplines provide their views with minimal cooperative interaction. Interdisciplinarity requires coordination among disciplines and synthesis of material through a higher-level organizing concept. . . .

"A good test of interdisciplinarity is whether a team can integrate imaginative ideas originating from different disciplinary perspectives so that the work product reflects an expanded lens of perception of reality."

These views were contributed to the *Designer* by Sherry R. Arnstein, of the Academy for Contemporary Problems. Ms. Arnstein is in the right academy.

Scene in the disciplinary barracks:

"Bad news, Graustark. You're going down to the multis."

"Gee, Sergeant, I thought I was doing so well."

"You were for a while, Graustark. But the inters are too fast for you. Still, look at it this way. Multidisciplinarity is better than unidisciplinarity."

"Unidisciplinarity?"

"Solitary."

"What am I doing wrong, Sergeant? Is it my work product?"

"It's more basic, Graustark. It's your lens of perception of reality. It won't expand."

More modest than the interdisciplinary or multidisciplinary team is the transbinary, which brings together two disciplines (stern and lax), and which has a lens barely open at all. Transbinary is well established in Britain, where transbinary collaboration between universities is encouraged, but it is only at the beginning of its career in the United States. Remember, you heard it here first.

A Fatal Slaying
of the Very Worst Kind

I t is typical of American English that enough is almost never enough. Is there a famine? No, there are famine conditions. Are there kinds of molecules, or ice cream, or postcards, or whatever they may be? No, there are different kinds. Is it the hottest Easter Sunday we've ever had? It is the hottest Easter Sunday we've ever had, regardless of date. When House Speaker Carl Albert announced that he would retire at the end of 1976, was Thomas O'Neill of Massachusetts the heir apparent? Not at all. According to United Press International, he was the apparent heir apparent. Does Jimmy Carter's pollster, Patrick Caddell, give his client, Saudi Arabia, information in confidence? He would rather speak of "the confidentiality of my client situation." Is there an urban crisis? No, said Morris Udall on April 17, 1976, there is an urban crisis situation. Is Italy's economy deteriorating? No, said Edwin Newman of NBC News in a broadcast in May 1976, Italy is in a deteriorating economic situation.

We no longer have rules and prospects and news but ground rules, future prospects, and newsworthy happenings. Airlines tell us to read the instructions in the seat pocket in front of us not for our safety but for our personal safety. Companies do not grow; they enjoy positive growth. The Encinitas Union School District in California announces that it will provide equal employment opportunity not merely through affirmative action but through positive affirmative action. Do new cameras obviate special lighting? They obviate the need for special lighting. Is the horse Rogue's Gambit, subject of a story in the *Washington Post,* one of a kind? No, it is uniquely one of a kind. Does Nelson Rockefeller complain of a misrepresentation by Ronald Reagan? No, he complains of a factual misrepresentation, which cancels itself. Was a woman raped? No, she had a rape experience. Shall we face reality? We can do better. We can face reality as it is. Pillows renovated, a shop proclaims, like new. No trespassing, signs say, without permission.

All this is redundancy, to which Americans have become addicted. We ought to have signs posted that say, "No redundancy without permission." Still, if you have a sunny disposition, there is always comfort to be found somewhere, and I would rather be redundant in the American sense than in the British.

In Britain someone who loses his job is not thereby rendered unemployed or out of work. He is made redundant. A company will not say that it is going to lay people off. It warns that there will be redundancies. The BBC and the newspapers headline Redundancies at Coventry or Cowley or wherever it may be; the British comedian Spike Milligan fifteen years ago invented a character whose occupation was retired redundant.

In the great days of American western movies, the sheriff would often choose some hapless fellow who did not want to become involved, pin a star on him, and say, "I'm namin' yew my deppity." In somewhat the same way the British look at workers and name them redundant, or in the North of England, redoondant. The difference is that the redundants would rather be deputized, and the deppities would rather be redundant.

Given the addiction to jargon among statisticians and among

social scientists generally, it is surprising* that redundant, in the sense of out of work, has not caught on in the United States. The British borrow from us indiscriminately and no questions asked. They—quick learners—are having major confrontations, consulting in depth, satisfying targets, giving the score situation instead of the score, flaunting instead of flouting, making an effort to try, subjecting clothes not to washing but to water process treatment, describing the way people talk as their conversation culture, and—in prestige projects—describing swimming pools and playing fields as leisure complexes. They are also calling for action on a broad front, particularly in areas of cultural disadvantage; making controversial recommendations and advocating controversial teaching methods; holding major official inquiries; lavishing each other with gifts; discussing the country's intervention capability; issuing consultative documents; looking on with approval as disadvantaged children verbalize to their peers; transmuting guest stars into special guest stars; and setting preconditions, which somehow surpass conditions and, when they number more than one, become packages. The BBC has even broadcast a song called, "Life Is the Name of the Game."

In return we should be borrowing from the British, if only on a small scale. It seems the least we could do. However, redundant in the sense of unemployed will never catch on with us. Redundancy in language has preempted the field. Because it has, much American speech and writing is boring, wastes time and effort, and makes reading and conversation a chore. We slog through the laborious and repetitious, and tarry when we should be moving on. Redundancy's cause is triumphant.† A Viking scientist, asked whether the loss of an instrument would mean that the soil-collecting scoop would not function, replied: "No. We have redundancy in that area." By that standard, no car should be without a redundant tire.

Irving S. Shapiro, chairman of the board and chief executive officer of Du Pont, has denied that the company interfered in the

---

* And unexpected. Read on.
† Successfully triumphant. Read on.

editing of two newspapers Du Pont owns in Wilmington, Delaware. "Emphatically not true," he said. Then, the emphatically being not emphatic enough, Shapiro added, "And there are no solid facts which would support a contrary inference."

I once came upon a solid fact that was supporting a contrary inference, and, possibly because the pedestal was Corinthian and the capital Ionic, it was an ill-assorted solid fact and was cracking under the strain. Shapiro did not mention the facts that were once so popular with politicians and editorial writers, the true facts, no doubt because they have been displaced—not in Britain, where the playwright William Douglas-Home has implored the Conservative Party to keep plugging, day in and day out, the true facts about taxation, but in the United States. A press release for Quinn Martin Productions about a television film based on events in Mississippi in the summer of 1964 noted that "the facts hew to actuality." Facts that hew to actuality open up—here I am indebted to Charles Prince of Wales and his splendid English education—new and previously undiscovered vistas. Those who ignore facts that hew to actuality do so at their own risk. In a barbarous world they may suffer the fate that the Prince cheerfully noted befell one of his ancestors. Said ancestor subsequently lost his head at a later date.

I am, of course, discussing what Secretary of State Kissinger called a hypothetical situation that does not now exist. It is only when a hypothetical situation does exist that it warrants our concern. If it is pressing and appears to threaten our security, we may want to get, perhaps from Pentagon spokesman Joseph Laitin, a preliminary final count on which of our allies will stand with us. Preliminary final will have to do because—here again the felicitous phrase was Kissinger's—it will be too early to draw a final conclusion. Those who want to draw conclusions will have to use the nonfinal variety.

When I mention a final conclusion I am speaking in terms of terms. Moderator Bill Monroe on "Meet the Press," November 30, 1974: "I think our time is up in terms of having time for another question." Etcyl H. Blair, director of health and environmental research for Dow Chemical USA: ". . . a series of question-able restrictions have had unfavorable impacts on American workers, in terms of lost job opportunities; on consumers, in terms of higher costs and fewer choices; and on scientists, in terms of lost incentive and lost confidence."

In terms of being necessary, in terms of isn't. Reviewing the PBS series on health, "Feeling Good," in the *New York Times,* John O'Connor remarked that it was "attempting to reach a broader audience in terms of national coverage." He could have said broader national audience and let it go at that. In the same review O'Connor wrote that "Feeling Good" resembles a variant of "The Electric Company," which must be subtly different from resembling "The Electric Company" itself, and that he thought it had been designed for a slightly, but not much, older audience.

Of "Feeling Good" he said in conclusion, "No one may be thoroughly offended, but no one is likely to be adequately satisfied, either." A lack of adequate satisfaction is frustrating, but then, slightly but not much older audiences are known to be slightly if not much harder to please. They seldomly* go in for what O'Con-nor called, in reviewing the CBS situation comedy "One Day at a Time," loud shouting.†

When a forty-five-year-old man from Sanford, Maine, claimed to be the son of Anne and Charles Lindbergh, David Wilentz, the New Jersey prosecutor in the Lindbergh baby kidnaping case, was asked for his reaction. Said Wilentz: "Preposterous and" (there is always an and) "beyond the realm of possibility." Maybe loud shouting, preliminary final, hypothetical situations that do not exist, and preposterous and beyond the realm of possibility are only to be expected. The United States is the most wasteful

---

* Hank Stram, former coach of the Kansas City Chiefs, became a football broadcaster and wondered, during the 1976 Super Bowl, why Dallas threw the ball very seldomly. He seemed unaware that its passes had oftenly been intercepted.

† Loud shouting may be done individually or, as at college athletic contests, in mass unison. The *New York Times* sometimes alternates it with loud yelling.

country in the world, and our use of words is extravagant. The waste has two causes. One is the feeling not seldomly encountered that an idea is more effective if it is repeated and reinforced. This is why Jimmy Carter says that he had a deeply profound religious experience. At any rate, I want to believe that that is why. I would hate to learn that he thought that deep and profound are different. It is certainly why Harper & Row announced early in 1976 that the paperback rights to one of its books had been sold for a "substantial six-figure sum." Even with inflation there is no sizable school of thought that holds six-figure sums to be paltry. I agree that this depends on where you are—life in some urban cities is more expensive than in others, as many a future bride-to-be learns to her sorrow after she is married—and whether you are touched by the revolution of rising expectations. In the late 1940s the former attorney general of California, Robert Kenny, represented a client before a congressional committee in Washington. Kenny's client was distressed about something that had been said about him and had brought a suit for damages. "How much are you suing for, Mr. Kenny?" a reporter asked. Kenny seemed surprised by the question. "The usual million," he said.

The second cause of waste is a failure to understand what words mean. The *New York Times* could not run a headline about an unexpected surprise from Japan if it knew what surprise meant. If it understood what triumph meant, it could not, in reporting an interview with Representative Les Aspin of Wisconsin, describe a spending ceiling on a defense authorization bill as "perhaps his most successful triumph." Aspin probably kept his less successful triumphs to himself, or the *Times* would have trumpeted them as triumphant Pyrrhic victories. *Harper's* magazine, speculating on a replacement for Henry Kissinger as Secretary of State, identified a former diplomat who had successfully convinced much of the foreign affairs community that he was a profound thinker. In view of the new requirement for deep profundity, this may not be enough.

Senator Charles Percy of Illinois, when he had some hope of getting the Republican presidential nomination in 1976, announced that he could be found in the "centrist mainstream" of American politics. It did not help Percy, but, generally speaking, it is a good place for a politician to be. An officer of the Ford election committee recognized this during the Republican primaries. "Ford has got to be pictured in the mainstream," he said, "and Reagan off on the right bank, so to speak." The officer understood that away from the bulrushes and down the centrist mainstream float Presidents and bills that have a good chance of being, in the words of the *New York Times,* successfully passed or, failing that, successfully enacted. Bills from the extremist mainstream do not automatically come under—again in the words of the *New York Times*—a total ban. They may even—*New York Times*—successfully withstand attacks, in spite of earlier impressions that they would unsuccessfully withstand them. Their sponsors may make an effort to try (Senator Birch Bayh) to successfully capture supporters (United Press International) where none had been thought to exist. ("Aha! In my power! Successfully captured at last!") But sooner or later the bill from the right bank or the left will be seen to be coming from one who is only an occasional frequenter (*Gourmet magazine*) of the centrist mainstream, and the bill will be (*New York Times*) successfully stifled.

Time magazine has noted that the National Football League successfully avoided any direct brush with gambling interests from 1963 to 1974, evidently for the benefit of those who thought that the League had unsuccessfully avoided them. *Time* speaks of arguments that were not successfully refuted and of fugitives who successfully eluded their pursuers, and says that the Broadway musical *Candide* was played on an open stage surrounded on all sides by the audience. Encircled on a couple of sides though I was by other assignments, I continued reading *Time* and was rewarded by the news that Rhodesia found itself not merely surrounded by hostile African governments but completely surrounded by them.

I. F. Stone, in the *New York Review of Books,* tells us that it was John Wilkes who established the right of the press to cover parliamentary proceedings when, as Sheriff of London, he successfully prevented the arrest of a printer the House of Commons had charged with publishing its debates. An ounce of successful prevention is worth a pound of successful cure, which explains why Ronald R. Fieve, M.D., chief of psychiatric research at the Lithium Clinic and Metabolic Unit in New York City, hopes to prevent successful suicides among his patients; why another doctor sympathizes with a patient suffering from subjective pain and another reports on tonsils that could not be entirely removed in toto; why countries—Rhodesia is an example—are said to declare unilateral independence, as though there were any other kind; why United Press International speaks of people being rescued safely; why TWA, delivering an unaccompanied child to its parent, guardian, or some other designated person, calls it a positive handoff; why reporters who do what used to be known as reporting are called investigative reporters, and biographers who do what biographers should do are said to write investigative biographies; and why David Sencer, director of the National Center for Disease Control, does not say that an epidemic is passing but that "there is a downslope on the curve of occurrence." Does a downward trend wipe out the previous day's sharp gains by the dollar? It does not. It—United Press International—wipes them out completely.

UPI is often on top of the news:

"Miami (UPI)—A Puerto Rican who said he attempted unsuccessfully to shoot President Ford on Saturday has been charged with threatening the life of the President."

UPI must have been relieved to hear that the attempt was unsuccessful. Otherwise somebody in the Miami bureau might have become redundant.

Dr. John Lundgren, looking after Richard Nixon, said in January 1975, "He still tires and fatigues very easily." When you tire and fatigue, you are really worn out. Lieutenant General James F. Hollingsworth, United States commander in South Korea, said that if the North Koreans attack, "Our firepower will have a tremendous impact on their ground troops, breaking their will in addition to killing them." This dual purpose explains why the United States must have sophisticated weapons.

Hollingsworth's language may have been influenced by his colleague, or as some now have it, his fellow colleague, Major General Henry E. "Gunfighter" Emerson. When President Ford stopped off to visit the Second Division in Korea on his way to the Soviet Union in November 1974, Emerson prepared his men for the President's arrival with these words:

"He's not just our Commander-in-Chief. He's Commander-in-Chief of all the American troops. He's Commander-in-Chief of the whole free world, and he's going to talk to the Russian Communists. He's a hell of a man. He's an All-American football player, and I guess that tells you what kind of a guy he is. He's putting our country back together and he's putting the world back together."

If the language seems more suitable to an inspiring talk by a gutsy coach in a somber locker room at half-time, it should be borne in mind that General Emerson was not getting his men merely ready. In Pentagon parlance, he was getting them operationally ready. Nor were they to join in the country's defense. They were to take their place in the country's defense posture, a responsibility far weightier and more compelling, which is why the Pentagon issues an annual defense posture statement. During the 1976 contest for the Republican presidential nomination, one of the issues between Ford and Reagan was whether the United States military posture was declining. If decline goes far enough, a low profile results.

Jimmy Carter also spoke of the country's military posture. He wanted it reviewed. In addition, he said that the Warsaw Pact forces were "postured for an all-out conflict of short duration and great intensity." In an interview on foreign affairs Carter had this country "in the posture quite often of having to face an accomplished fact of our adjustment of our interests," and endorsed a "rough equivalency" with the Russians as "a very good posture to maintain." Carter must have wanted to leave Plains, Georgia, for Washington and greener postures.

For a man whose political fortunes rested on his not being

associated in the public mind with Washington, Carter took risks. In one speech on foreign affairs he mentioned not only a military and a recent posture but ever increasing unity and understanding, a significant world impact, larger global roles, a new international order, democratic values, political and economic concerns, frequent consultations on many levels, our entire foreign policy apparatus, continuing contacts at all levels, closer and more creative relations, increased coordination among the industrialized democracies, multilateral trade negotiations, basic monetary adjustments, interactions among national economies, a creative partnership, basic global standards of human rights, our own basic ideals, the democratic process, the democratic concert of nations, the strategic umbrella, a pressing need, genuine North-South consultations, sharper confrontations, a more stable and just world order, a major effort, and global economic development. Not exactly a new broom.

Not all postures are military. Henry Kissinger was sometimes said to need a more credible posture in Latin America. This lies somewhere between bending over backward and being standoffish. I was round-shouldered as a boy, which is the opposite of bending over backward, and was often scolded about it. "Straighten up, Edwin," my mother used to say. Questions about my credibility arose in other connections.*

In Washington one day, after President Ford vetoed a bill to which he had given active, rather than inactive or passive, consideration, the Senate overrode the veto by seventy-two to one. The *San Francisco Chronicle* felt obliged to note that seventy-two to one was "well over the two-thirds majority needed." It was 3500

---

* Discussion of somebody's credibility usually means that credibility is something he does not have. Credibility results from a proportion between what you say you will do and what your interests make it reasonable for you to do. It may also arise from being erratic and unpredictable, in which case others will be reluctant to find out whether you mean what you say. The credibility of nuclear deterrents cannot be tested without risking annihilation. There is an old line that covers the situation: Take my word for it.

under the head of interpretive reporting. The veto was of a Railroad Retirement bill that reflected many hopes and aspirations. These now make up one word in Washington—hopesandaspirations—and so technically do not constitute a redundancy. Hopesandaspirations will soon be joined by necessaryandessential, unnecessaryandsuperfluous, fairandequitable, loudandvociferous, goalsandobjectives, helpandassistance, promptandspeedy, procrastinationanddelay, adviceandcounsel, interestandconcern, and reputationfortruthandveracity, which comes from the legal world, where it appears to be thought that a witness can have a well-deserved reputation for telling the truth without having veracity.

Justandlasting and ournation'scapital may appear to belong in the list, but they are not redundancies. They are clichés and they drain words of their meaning. The redundancy also weakens words by implying that they cannot stand alone—advice *and* counsel. In addition, it clutters the language. It impedes the communication that Americans insist they so dearly want by making it necessaryandessential to hack away what is not necessaryandessential to get to the point. I will settle for either goals or objectives and for either equitable or fair, and consider myself well served.

Precision in language can be delightful and devastating. I know this from experience. As a glamorous and commanding figure on the screen, and even more winning and vivacious in person, I am sometimes asked why I do not smile more often while performing. The answer has to do with a program in 1961, on which I appeared with Hugh Gaitskell, then leader of the British Labour Party, and Walter Judd, then a Republican Representative from Minnesota.

My performance was so striking that the mail poured in, in the form of a letter from a clergyman in Connersville, Indiana, who accused me of, without also charging me with, smirking at Representative Judd. The NBC News executive who answered the letter replied that this surely could not have taken place since a smirk was an expression revealing inner malice and that was not part of my disposition. The clergyman replied that in his view and according to a dictionary that lay to hand, a smirk was a smug, silly, self-satisfied smile and that was part of my disposition. We dropped the correspondence.

Since the Judd incident, I have tried to keep a dead pan, and some might say that I have one presently. *Harper's* magazine probably would, if it thought about the matter, because *Harper's* has an unfortunate way of saying that one of its contributors is presently writing a book, or presently completing a novel. Presently is unnecessary in these phrases as well as ill-advised because the primary meaning of presently is soon. Dictionaries ought to insist on that. Giving way and allowing it to mean now—over which, for some people, it has the great advantage of being two syllables longer—creates confusion. It creates almost as much confusion as formerly does. From the *New York Times*:

Ian Smart was formerly a member of the British diplomatic service from 1958 to 1969.

O. Edmund Clubb was former director of the State Department's Office of Chinese Affairs.

Leonard Katz, former reporter with the *New York Post* for more than twenty years, was named director of public relations for Monticello Raceway.*

Leon H. Keyserling was a former government economist.

Just how long, Mr. Keyserling, were you a former government economist?

Keyserling, who speaks English, is unable to reply.

I see. I submit, Mr. Keyserling, that the truth is that you have not at any time ceased to be a former government economist.

Keyserling consults his lawyer, but there is no way out. He agrees that he is still a former government economist and saves himself from a contempt of Congress charge.

It is possible that someone will be described as being presently a former government economist. The closest approach to this came during the 1974 World Series, when Tony Kubek said that Brooks Robinson of the Baltimore Orioles had been voted the "greatest living third baseman of all time." Some insist that, after

---

* Unfortunately for Katz, former reporter is a nonpaying job.

after a pause, Kubek or his partner, Curt Gowdy, added, "Currently." It is established as well as these things can be that during the same broadcast, Gowdy said of Tony Bartirome, trainer of the Pittsburgh Pirates, "He's the only trainer in baseball who used to be a former major leaguer." Presently.

Governor David Boren of Oklahoma is a man noted for what the NBC personnel department calls good oral and verbal communication skills. "My opponent," Boren once said orally and verbally, "already is setting the tone of his campaign to win the runoff. It is the tone of typical old politics—negative mudslinging." In contemporary America mudslinging is not enough. Negative mud must be slung. But then *war* is not enough. Admiral Elmo Zumwalt, retired chief of Naval Operations, has said that he is concerned about the possibility of another operative war in the Middle East. Zumwalt did not think it necessary to add that he preferred an inoperative war, or peace. Operative wars, after all, are full of—United Press International—fatal slayings, which are the worst kind.

Fatal slayings may be said to show human nature at its basest or, as the *San Francisco Sunday Examiner and Chronicle* has it, at its lowest nadir. Anyone in danger of becoming the victim of a fatal slaying faces, as former Secretary of Health, Education and Welfare Caspar Weinberger would put it, a major crisis problem. Particularly vulnerable would be, for the *Dallas Times Herald,* a recluse who likes living alone. Among the impressionable, such a problem may make the mind go, in Timestyle, entirely blank.

The mind that is entirely blank probably would not seem strange to State Senator Roscoe Dean of Georgia, who, when charged with cheating the state of $1424 in travel allowances, said that he was innocent and not guilty. It probably would not seem strange to Ron Nessen, President Ford's press secretary, who argued that published allegations that the CIA was giving money to noncommunist politicians in Italy "make it difficult to work with and continue to have a relationship with friends and allies around the world."

I had a theory—call it an imaginary fantasy—that it was not

the CIA but the CIAO, the dreaded Italian intelligence agency, that had been giving money to Italian noncommunist politicians. I did not pursue it, however, because doing so would have made it difficult for me to work with and have a relationship with Ron Nessen. There are some with whom I work with whom I do not have a relationship, but it tends to make everything take longer.

Others at the White House who worked with Nessen and either did or did not have a relationship with him announced in January of 1976 that President Ford would abide by the new election law totally and completely. That is abiding by the law on a scale scarcely comprehensible, except by the record company that put out a recording of *Così fan Tutte* that was totally complete.

The language in the White House announcement may have been Ford's. He has identified inflation as the universal enemy of 100 per cent of the people, and has described the country as currently facing three serious challenges, all at the same time. In his State of the Union message of January 1976, in which he proposed catastrophic health insurance for everybody covered by Medicare (when my time comes, count me out), he said that we could not realistically afford national health insurance, as though there were some other way to afford it. After losing to Ronald Reagan in the Texas primary, he promised to make a maximum effort in Indiana, and in the Alabama and Georgia primaries even more: a real sincere and very maximum effort.

Had James Schlesinger not been removed as Secretary of Defense, one might have guessed that he had been lending a hand in the press office, since Schlesinger had argued that reducing support costs made it possible to provide more combat capability and effectiveness. This was part of Schlesinger's plan for "turning fat into swords." It might have saved time and trouble to turn it into ploughshares.

Franklin D. Roosevelt, so A. Willis Robertson Professor of Economics at the University of Virginia Herbert Stein has pointed out in an article in the *Wall Street Journal,* holds the record for most times elected President in one lifetime. It is four. Should you want to ask Stein who holds the record for most times elected President in more than one lifetime (or less than one lifetime), you may of course try to reach him by telephone. I thought of it, but instead fancied that he was already engaged in a telephone conversation, talking with Henry R. Luce Professor of Urban Values at New York University Irving Kristol, and that there would be no point in my holding on. With those academic titles, such conversations take a long time:

"Is that Henry R. Luce Professor Kristol? It's A. Willis Robertson Professor Stein here. I'm curious to know, Henry R. Luce Professor Kristol, how you believe urban values are affected . . ." and off they go, the discussion culminating in a proposal by A. Willis Robertson Professor Stein, to which Henry R. Luce Professor Kristol agrees, that they broaden the scope of their inquiry and call Sebastian S. Kresge Professor of Marketing at the Harvard Business School Walter Salmon, Charles Edward Wilson Professor of Business Administration Emeritus at the same institution Robert W. Austin, Ralph Waldo Emerson Professor at the University of Massachusetts Adam Yarmolinsky, Norman Thomas Professor of Economics at the New School for Social Research Robert Heilbroner, Benjamin Franklin Professor of Economics at the Wharton School of the University of Pennsylvania Lawrence Klein, Edward R. Murrow Professor of Journalism at Columbia University Fred W. Friendly, Lawrence Wien Professor of Real Estate Law at the same institution Curtis J. Berger, and Marie Rankin Clarke Professor of Social Sciences at Claremont University Peter Drucker, and ask them what is happening to urban values in a changing world. William Edwards Huntington Professor of History and Social Science at Boston University Sam Bass Warner, Jr., could have told them. They're changing.

This does not get any questions answered about Roosevelt or about Presidents who had more or less than one lifetime, but such a disappointment ought to be taken in calm stride, as the Associated Press said the government of Laos was taking things. If it does make anybody calm but tense, as the *New York Times* found life in Beirut late in 1975, there is room for adjustment through the process the White House recommended for the Middle East, mutual compromise.

Someone in calm stride, so far as I can understand it, is strolling. For a horse, it is a canter. Somebody calm but tense might be trembling nonchalantly. As for mutual compromise, there is no other kind. This is true as well of mutual cooperation, which must be mutual if it is to be co. One-sided cooperation has been tried and found wanting, usually falling short by 50 per cent. An example of mutual cooperation is the Rose Bowl pact between the Big Ten and the Pacific-8 conference, which remains, the Tournament of Roses Association assures us, as firm "as the concrete in Pasadena's historic Rose Bowl stadium." The reasons? Two, says the Tournament of Roses Association—similar athletic philosophies and mutual cooperation.

Mutual cooperation requires a mutual agreement. The British, drawing on their long diplomatic experience, produced such a one with an announcement from Kensington Palace that "Her Royal Highness, the Princess Margaret, Countess of Snowdon, and the Earl of Snowdon have mutually agreed to live apart." Evidently it was a mutual agreement for a mutual separation. The British may want to take a phrase from American reporting of labor disputes: Both sides are far apart. When both sides *are* far apart, a man like President Ford's Secretary of Labor, William J. Usery, Jr., comes in handy. "Usery," an unidentified White House official told the *New York Times,* "is a tremendous guy to make peace on both sides of an issue."

Mutual cooperation must express itself in practical ways.* At the Rose Bowl, evidence of mutual cooperation may be seen in the fact that—a condition spotted by the *New York Times*—

---

* And not only in sports. Manhattan District Attorney Richard Kuh said, while describing a roundup of drug dealers, "All the agencies worked together cooperatively."

both teams are usually closely matched. It wouldn't be much of a game if only one were. It is best when they are coequal.

The concept of coequality is realized on the "Today" show, which has cohosts, though it does not bill coguests. I sometimes acted as cohost when Barbara Walters was the other cohost, but this can no longer happen because Miss Walters, in the summer of 1976, left her cohost copost at NBC to become a coanchor at ABC. It ended gracefully, at a farewell party, with cotoasts.

There were times when a cohost had little to do, partly because of the presence of the other cohost, and occasionally my mind turned to poetry, to Wordsworth and his cohost of golden daffodils. I also found myself thinking of the Atlantic Cohoast and the Pacific Cohoast, as well as the high cohost of living, and (this can become, as was said of the couple whose marriage failed, a bad cohabit), when in a religious mood, of the Lord God of Cohosts. Also of a burglar's associate interrupted in flagrante delicto: "Aha! Cohort in the act!"

The ideal cohost, had he not died before it could come about, would have been George M. Cohan, interviewing the Soviet Prime Minister, Alexei Kosygin, about peaceful coexistence.

In England, as we know, the rot has also set in. A broadcaster on the BBC has spoken of conspirators conspiring together, which suggests that opportunities exist for conspiring separately. It is painful to hear such things on the BBC, which can still, on occasion, speak with economy and directness. One such occasion came in July 1975, when John Stonehouse, a Labour member of Parliament, in prison and awaiting trial, did not eat. The BBC was frank enough to say that it did not know whether he had gone on a hunger strike or had simply lost his appetite.

Remnants of precise British usage survive. A man attempted to attack a notorious criminal with the intention of taking the law into his own hands. The police detained him, then sent him home with what was called appropriate advice. It may have been nothing more than, "I shouldn't do that if I were you, sir." British advice can be highly appropriate, and British ceremonial phrases poetic and succinct. When the House of Commons is to hold a debate in private, the signal is given by a member on the floor, who points to the galleries and says, "Mr. Speaker, I spy strangers." The Speaker then orders the galleries cleared, and the strangers, among them relatives and close friends, troop out.

The British don't always use understatement. At a meeting of shareholders of the British Leyland Motor Corporation, the chairman, Lord Stokes, explaining the disasters that had befallen the company, found his explanation being drowned out by slow clapping. Said Lord Stokes sarcastically, "Well, thank you for your support." Said one of the shareholders, "There is only one support you want because you are a bloody big rupture all the way through." It was a little too long to be ideal, but it undoubtedly enlivened the dialogue situation.

To call somebody a rupture is to speak metaphorically. The British do more of that than we do. The figure of speech is more comfortable for them because of the influence of the English poets and because, in politics, speech in the House of Commons is less declamatory and more spontaneous than speech in the United States Senate and House of Representatives. In Congress the seats face forward. In the House of Commons the government benches and the opposition benches face each other, and anyone who speaks does so with his supporters at his back or stands in their midst, with his adversaries glaring at him. It is an invitation to vivid speech. It is the atmosphere of the duel, the original eyeball-to-eyeball confrontation.

The Prime Minister may be facing the Leader of the Opposition across the floor fifteen or so feet away, with the one listening showing his disdain for what is being said by slumping down and putting his feet up against the table that stands below the Speaker's chair and separates the two front benches. Debate in the House of Commons is often a search for the phrase that stings the other side and delights your own, and the exchanges may be intensely personal. Aneurin Bevan of the Labour Party once pointed across at Winston Churchill and said, "When the Tories are finished with you, they will toss you aside as though you were a soiled glove."

Bevan may have remembered the occasion during the Second World War when Churchill called him "a squalid nuisance." The war years also produced one of Churchill's most scornful phrases, provoked by Mussolini's subservience to Hitler. Mussolini, Churchill said, was "the merest utensil of his master's whim." In any case, Bevan's remark also enlivened the dialogue situation.

Because of their literary tradition, and because so many British politicians have a university debating background, the House of Commons provides an almost universal welcome for a phrase well-turned. One was produced by a Labour member, Sidney Silverman, during a debate over the Middle East in the early 1950s. Ernest Bevin, who was the British Foreign Secretary, had for months been furious about the course events were taking. He felt that British policy was being excessively influenced by supporters of Israel, in both Britain and the United States. Bevin entered the House, spoke briefly and angrily, and left. Silverman rose to comment: "The right honorable gentleman," he said, "blows in, blows up and blows out."

It was a marvelous metaphor. How long Silverman had been nursing it, waiting for the propitious moment, I do not know. From the press gallery of the House of Representatives I heard one that I think could not have been nursed. It was the day that Grace Moore, the opera singer and moving picture actress, was killed in an airplane crash. When word of her death came in, Representative Jere Cooper of her home state of Tennessee asked for permission to address the House. "Mr. Speaker," he began, "a lovely flower has been crushed." Perfect.

The attempt to produce a metaphor sometimes produces a mixed metaphor, which resembles the redundancy. There is too much of it; it is overloaded; and it means that somebody is speaking who does not understand the terms he is using. Figures of speech can be treacherous; not everybody can handle them. And the mixed metaphor is a figure of speech that is out of control.

On the night of the 1976 North Carolina primary a guard at a textile plant in upstate New York heard a news broadcaster—it may have been a media analyst—say, "Reagan could use his victory in North Carolina as a springboard to rekindle his campaign." Throwing springboards on campaign fires was new to the guard, and he kindly wrote to tell me about it.

The most active metaphor mixers are politicians. For some reason—maybe they have to do more to be noticed there—this is especially the case in New York. John Lindsay, when mayor of New York City, presciently said, "It is necessary to lay the foundations for whatever difficult medicine the people will have to swallow." New Yorkers eventually swallowed much difficult medicine, and some of them thought that Lindsay himself was the chief ingredient. His search for other office failed, in keeping with the warning sticker pasted on some medicine bottles: CAUTION: Federal law prohibits transfer of this drug to any person other than the patient for whom it was prescribed. SHAKE WELL.

To Lindsay's successor New York's problems were identified flying objects in City Hall's superstructure. "These are not chickens just now come home to roost," said Mayor Abraham Beame. "They are birds of prey that have been with us for a long time, growing ever more assertive." Given New York's condition and a general disinclination to offend the birds of prey, which when not roosting were hovering unpleasantly in the city's air space, nobody seriously quarreled with Beame's analysis, though one citizen wrote a letter to a newspaper describing the city itself as an albatross bleeding rich and poor alike, which may have been what attracted the birds of prey. Beame's talent as a phrasemaker was overshadowed by the economic crises he had to grapple with. He refused to extend an official welcome to President Sadat of Egypt because, he said, Sadat supported a United Nations resolution that "seeks to revive a new form of racism." To revive something new is no mean trick.*

---

* So is smelling out a mosaic. I wrote in *Strictly Speaking*: "Politicians should be encouraged to stand for what they believe in, not to try to smell out the exact mosaic of attitudes and positions that will appeal to the greatest number." How do you smell a mosaic? G. V. Underwood, Jr., of Hilton Head Island, South Carolina, wanted to know. It takes training.

New York politicians often think about what they, or their constituents, may be called upon to ingest. The Democratic leader in the state assembly, Albert Blumenthal, was enraged by a Republican charge that the Democrats had put the state in a pickle. "We find ourselves in this pickle," he replied, "because you bought that jar and filled it not with pickles but with water, and now you're trying to jam it in the public's face." The Republicans were so stunned by Blumenthal's accusation and a vision of themselves at factory gates as the early shifts arrive, shoving jars of water at workers who recoil and dash off to register as Democrats, that they did not reply, even to say something about a jar of another color. Another Democrat, Stanley Steingut, Speaker of the Assembly, would have known what to do with Blumenthal's jar. The easy thing would have been to carry it on both shoulders, but Steingut, to judge by his public pronouncements, would have put it on the back-room burner, where, from time to time, he likes to simmer legislative matters that he does not consider urgent. This kind of slow cooking goes on elsewhere. A survey on drug use in public schools which had been allowed to simmer in Seattle was said by an administrator, Dr. Robert Collins, to have "got kind of back-burnered because I didn't have time to pursue it in light of the upcoming levy."* Steingut, however, would not have found room for a bill that he thought would derail the ship of state, or which, in the words of Henry Wallace, would have sent the ship of state sailing down untrod paths. Steingut would rather have no legislative activity than that, even though he has recognized the danger of being buried by an avalanche of creeping paralysis.

Remarks of the kind Blumenthal made risk, in the *New York Times*'s flashing phrase, raking up old partisan wounds, which usually lie buried under the fallen leaves of yesteryear. The leaves, when blown away, reveal, etched in the sands of time, the question put by State Senator John R. Dunne of New York: "Who can predict what will remain after those winds of change have run their

---

* Also known as Up-and-Coming Levy, an uncommonly promising young politician of radiant personality.

course?" The winds of change, a relay team, took an early lead on an eight-lap track, with Tartan turf and banked at the curves, and then breezed home.

Old partisan wounds also exist outside New York, for example in Kentucky, where, in the 1975 primaries for governor, a Democrat, Todd Hallenbach, accused his opponent, Governor Julian Carroll, of "going around the state spreading mistruths and innuendoes. Julian Carroll," Hallenbach said, "has washed his hands on the courthouse steps of Kentucky communities like Pontius Pilate." He added, "The political machine has the gun on the people right now but the people pull the trigger and I think they'll pull it in the election booth." A correspondent in Henderson, Kentucky, pointed out to me that there is no Kentucky community named Pontius Pilate and denied that she intended to shoot herself while in the election booth. She thought it unnecessary to go that far to register a protest vote.

Washington produces metaphors that are mixed and mystifying. Senator Howard Baker of Tennessee said, when asked about the possibility of more hearings on Watergate, "The tip of the iceberg is the only thing showing. I'm not sure we can put it together." Representative Wayne Hays of Ohio, when he was chairman of the House Committee on Administration (administration is liable to broad construction on Capitol Hill), was pleased by a compromise on federal election legislation. "I think," said Hays, "this is a package that will fly." Air express.

Representative James Grover of New York put out a press release early in the Nixon Administration in which he announced: "The honeymoon is over between President Nixon and the Democratic-controlled Congress. The gloves are off and it's full speed ahead in attempts by the Democrats to impede the President's program." This means that the gloves must have been on during the honeymoon. It seems excessively formal.

Being around politicians in Washington affects reporters. Helen Thomas, UPI's White House correspondent, wrote this:

"Washington—President Ford said today America's economic

future looks brighter each day. But he accused Congress of drafting a federal spending blueprint that would ignite another inflationary cycle."

Two petitioners to the Federal Communications Commission got into the Washington spirit. They complained that there was not enough controversy on radio and television stations run by schools and colleges. "Educational broadcasters," they said, "should not draw the ivory towers about themselves as some sort of sacred cloak which permits them to choke off efforts for new, diverse, more broadly based groups to have access to radio and television permits." The ivory tower cloak that chokes has been approached only in the Puccini one-act opera *Il Tabarro,* in which choking takes place under both a cloak and cover of darkness. At the opera's climax the choker throws open his cloak and allows the lifeless body of the chokee to fall forward before the horrified eyes of the woman they both loved. This takes place on a barge on the Seine, and although there is no ivory tower, the Eiffel Tower glints metallically in the background.

The sacred cloak that chokes is a versatile weapon and would be more so if it had teeth. This may well be feasible, for there is a source of supply of teeth that legislatures are able to draw on at will. The source was drawn on when, as *Editor and Publisher* reported, sharp teeth were injected into the federal and Illinois fraudulent bidding and antitrust laws as a result of a reporter's brewing a scandal after six years of effort. What made the story news is that teeth go into brews—"Scale of dragon, tooth of wolf, Witch's mummy, maw and gulf Of the ravin'd salt-sea shark, Root of hemlock digg'd i' the dark"—more often than they come out of them.

Teeth are also injected into legislation under the parliamentary system, and the British are a step or two ahead of us here. They are specialists. The *Times* of London wrote: "We already have the machinery for the best sort of state intervention in the Design Council, which ought to be given not just pretty front teeth but molars, too, so it can be the catalyst in this now vital endeavor." A catalyst needs molars so that it can take the ferocious grip for which it is famous. Otherwise, public confidence, which has already taken a nose drop, will die by leaps and bounds.

The greatest metaphor mixer of our time, possibly of all time, is Representative Daniel Flood of Pennsylvania. He did not say, "At issue is a budding military program that six months ago in the first blush of prototype flying looked merely huge but now looms as the fighter plane plum of the century." The looming plum was developed, probably with the help of grafting techniques, by the *New York Times.* Flood did not say, "Angola Cements U.S.-Cuba Rift." The *St. Paul Sunday Pioneer* had the story on that, and aerial reconnaissance showed where the cement was being laid. He did not say, "Against every bone in my body, I'm sitting here twisting both arms." Representative Claude DeBruhl, of the North Carolina legislature, voting for a bill he opposed, tied up his arms that way, but the vote was by voice. Flood did not say that every child has his Achilles heel if only you can find the right niche in which to place him, or "That boy will be all right if we can get him to stop hiding behind his mother's apron strings." Years of research, observation, and practical work led social workers to those conclusions.

Flood did, however, tell a military commander that he was at the Rubicon and that if he did not change his ways he would be a dead duck. On another occasion, Flood questioned a Secretary of the Navy about some missiles. The missiles were, he said, pigeons that Congress had adopted a long time before. "When you get married that closely to something," he said, "you get very unhappy when it does not grow up to be an All-American. This thing is poohing out, and we do not like it." The witness objected only to "poohing out." This may have been out of forbearance, or because the Secretary was embarrassed about Congress's marrying pigeons that came under his jurisdiction and were not chosen as All-Americans.

Charles de Gaulle so angered Flood that Flood asked a Secretary of Defense during a closed hearing: "Do we have any alternative or are all our eggs in one basket if he picks up his marbles and goes home? Are we not in a badly exposed position? Are we not caught with our pants down out there?" The Secretary's reply was deleted from the transcript of the hearing for diplomatic reasons.

Flood's attention was attracted to Latin America by a proposal to build a successor to the Panama Canal. Speaking in the House, he said that a decision had already been made to build it in Panama. Proposals to build in Colombia, Nicaragua, and Mexico, he said, were merely straw projects in a fake horse race for propaganda purposes.

When I first called attention, years ago, to Flood's metaphor mixing, he wrote me that he had not been aware of it. "If I could mix a martini half as well," he added, "it would be a pistol, wouldn't it?" Flood has been a member of the House of Representatives for thirty years. What his life would be like if he left the House after all that time, I do not know. He might find himself, like a recent candidate for sheriff of Allen County, Indiana, sitting naked on the other side of the coin. It is cold on the other side of the coin, especially when the pendulum is swinging in the other direction, and those who find themselves there may want to get up off their hackles and leave, even if they have to cross a mesquite-infested prairie to do so.

The rest of us should help them, and if we really have our pulse on where people's heads are at, we will not be pettyune about it. Otherwise, we may find ourselves split right down to the grassroots.

Myself Will Be Back
After This Message

I t was a day like most others. I had begun it by reading *In My
Own Words,* by the gangster Mickey Cohen as told to John
Peer Nugent. Why Cohen had to tell it to John Peer Nugent if they
were his own words I could not figure out, but the book did live up
to its advertisement, which said that it was bulging with profanity
and malipropisms. Honi soit qui mal i prop.

Over lunch I learned, thanks to the London correspondent of
the *Chicago Tribune,* that United States Ambassador Walter An-
nenberg had delayed retiring from his post for a week so as to attend the royal opening of Parliament, where his seniority admitted
he and his wife to the front row, and with front row seats you could
hardly blame they for waiting. The *Chicago Tribune* often sees
through to the heart of things in that way. A *Tribune* columnist,
Bob Wiedrich, has rebuked a court for failing to say that spanking
a youngster today might save he or she from worse punishment
tomorrow. Right as rain, I thought about lenient courts. Save we

394

from they. Many parents depressed by their children's turning from the path of virtue may find mild corporate punishment to be the answer.

I read on and found the Huntington, New York, Pre-School suggesting to busy parents with a three- to five-year-old, "Why not drop he or she off at the school?" Why not indeed? With the start Huntington can give them, they may grow up to be as clever as Sonny Bono, whose business acumen, the New Haven, Connecticut, *Register* reported, helped land both he and Cher in relatively safe financial strata. This was considerate of Sonny because desperate strata were available at the time. Besides, she had left he.

Some men are confused about who did the leaving. They insert notices in newspapers that say, "Having left my bed and board, I will not be responsible for debts incurred or contracted by my wife." A notice of that kind often ends a relation that began with one more cheerful. Stouffer's Denver Inn posts a sign that greets newly married couples holding wedding parties there. I was lucky enough to see one:

CONGRAD

ULATIONS

BRIAN & LIZ

I wondered whether this was a tradition begun by Congrad Hilton. It makes a good start down the road of life for those who have plighted their trough.

Speaking of weddings, here is a report on the youthful and immature marriage policies of the diocese of Springfield, Massachusetts, offered, with becoming modesty, by the diocese itself. Give the policies time.

I switched on the television set to watch the reflexive reflex, with Brent Musberger of CBS saying, "Phyllis, Irv, and myself will be back at half-time." Brent was followed by a commercial in which a man in a tavern was asked to choose between beers and announced, "I must say that the results were a surprise to myself and the others." Myself switched the set off and turned to a story by United Press International about a professor of psychology in

College Park, Maryland, who concluded that an attractive woman has a greater chance of receiving a light sentence if she has not used her beauty to perpetuate the crime. But would the sentence still be light if the woman's good looks illicited "oohs" and "aahs" in the courtroom? La donna e perpetuum mobile.

The *Telegraph-Herald* of Dubuque, Iowa, which was at hand, reported the King of Nepal coronated in a tradition-rich ritual. There is much we can and do learn from the East. Governor Edmund Brown, Jr., who is, one hears, a devotee of Zen, complained that before the 1976 convention many people had already coronated Jimmy Carter the Democratic candidate. That was done by Democratic party king makers meeting in a smoke-filled room and puffing on Corona Coronas before placing them on Carter's head.

Time magazine does not coronate. It decimates. It wrote, "China took another giant step toward consolidating the governmental and military leadership that was almost completely decimated by the Cultural Revolution and the struggle for power that followed it." To decimate means to reduce by a tenth. I interpret almost completely decimated to mean reduced by an eleventh. *Time* also wrote about an arrangement that "particularly rankles with younger Jesuits." The arrangement was outranked by older Jesuits. Rankle has its privileges.

There are many other wonders in the press, thanks in part to the dangling modifier. The columnists Evans and Novak report travel bills looking for votes—"As the favorite campaigner for conservative Republicans, Reagan's travel bills for himself and his large entourage consistently left his hosts bugeyed." The Associated Press finds annual profits that were somebody's sister and became the chairman of Dunhill's in London—"Since succeeding her brother as chairman in 1961, annual profits have risen from $1,300,000 to $14,000,000." United Press International alters the function of magnets—"President Ford keeps returning to Capitol Hill like a magnet." Or like a flame to the moth. Clive Barnes of the *New York Times* has a conversation with a mind of its own—"During the summer, walking through the ruins of Persepolis in Iran, my conversation with the guide turned to the theatre festival in nearby Shiraz." The *Times* also has a city taking extraordinary precautions—"As the plane nears Riyadh, the six-man security detail gets ready for landing. Unlike Damascus, they do not wear bulletproof vests on this stop." Damascus, jittery, never got off the plane. It couldn't get through the exit with the vest on.

I pressed on. AT&T is sending its shareholders a memorandom on "The Case for Congressional Action." If it catches on with the shareholders, AT&T may want to have it published commercially by Memorandom House. A Columbia Records press release declares Beethoven's late style perfectly congrous in its own terms and the distilation of a lifetime's experience in music.* Columbia offers recordings by the pianist Ruth Laredo of two works by Rachmaninoff, "Lilacs" and "Dasies." Giv me yur anser, do. The *Wall Street Journal* proposes a trial subscription at a savings of $3.50 over the newsstand price; I reject the offer, preferring a number of small saving. The *Judge,* published by the Syracuse University College of Law, reports that Dean Craig Christensen, questioned about the school's financial condition, responded, "While there are not enough funds to do what ought to be done, we're not in too bad of a position in the context of higher education in the seventies." If that is the dean speaking, or the paper, we are in very bad of a position in the context of higher education in the seventies.

Higher education goes on at Annapolis also. The director of candidate guidance, a Navy captain, has advised members of Congress of a meaningful service offered there through the Congressional Pre-Candidate Evaluation program. The captain wrote: "A candidate who receives an excellent or top candidate evaluation and is scholastically qualified, medically qualified and passed their physical aptitude examination will in all probability be offered an

----

* Johann Strauss's music was also perfectly congrous in its own terms. It was the congrous of Vienna.

appointment in the event they received an official nomination."
That seems only fair. If a candidate is passed their examination,
they should be nominated. Anchors ahoy.

The State Department has celebrated the Bicentennial by issuing special passports, with a deep blue cover and the Liberty
Bell printed in red, white, and blue on the pages, and bearing a
request to "all whom it may concern to permit the citizen of the
United States named herein to pass without delay or hinderance."
It is reassuring to see the State Department making that request.
Hindrance used to be hazardous enough. Nowadays hinderance is
the danger and can be disasterous. I have a Bicentennial passport,
and when it has expired I intend to keep it as a rememberance.

The Benton-Franklin Governmental Conference of Richland,
Washington, has announced that it is "accepting resume's in application for the position of secretary" and that "proficiency in typing, filing and standard office procedures are required." Benton
and Franklin want their money's worth. Ours is a mixed economy,
however, and private enterprise is giving government agencies stiff
competition in error making. The Stereo Festival of Great International Artists has advertised Lorin Hollander and the Tokyo String
Quartet playing Brahm's Piano Quintet in F-minor. A local shop
is offering reduced gown's on sale; another is selling groceri'es;
and John has chalked up on a convenient wall that he loves
Glady's. Hall Lebovitz, sports editor of the *Cleveland Plain Dealer,*
has written that the Cleveland Indians took a calculated risk by
hiring as manager Frank Robinson, "who's managing in Puerto
Rico must be regarded as inconsequential." The column was not
libelous, fortunately for Lebovit'z, who's paper might otherwise
have reported, as it sometimes does of others, that he had been
hailed into court.

All hale the *New York Times.* It reported the Greek community in Astoria, Queens, dancing to it's very own drummer. A
Times headline, "Mets Tour of Japan Will Cost About $2-Mil-
lion," worried baseball fans, but the tour was made by the Metropolitan Opera. The *Times* is in a class by it's self. I hate to be

finicky. I would rather, as the *New York Times* has put it, walk spritely on my way. Or read about the tennis-playing Evert sisters, Chris and Jeanne, both of whom, I was glad to see in the *Times*, are still close. How unfortunate if only one were.

So I read on in the *Times*, about the big oil spill that despoiled Portugal's coast, making off with a number of luxury hotels as booty; and about Yugoslavia's charging Croatians in exile with formenting terrorist acts, though surely that is a consequence Yugoslavia would expect in an atmosphere of intellectual fervent; and in the New Jersey *Sunday Record* about the policemen who waited until a suspect who had proceeded them to the door separated from his cainine friends, two Doberman pinchers. The suspect was arrested, but the police, who were not Doberman pinchers, let the dogs go. The *New York Times* tells me about the Italian financial institution known as the Bongo di Roma (its directors sit on the Bongo board), and about the 1000 per cent drop in the value of Chilean currency reported by C. L. Sulzberger. Before that I had thought that a currency could not lose more than 100 per cent of its value, but inflation in Latin America, as Sulzberger suggested, can be fierce. The Associated Press has the Watergate prosecutor attributing a nepharious plot to John Mitchell. There is no mention of the other dephendants. I come upon a story about Thomas D. O'Malley, state treasurer and insurance commissioner in Florida. "I'm not despaired in the least," said O'Malley. "In no way, shape or form do I intend to resign." Or as the *Miami Herald* put it in a headline:

> "I'm Not Despaired,"
> O'Malley Assures,
> Shuns Resignation

It was a great headline. It made me think of the proud boast by the *Birmingham News/Birmingham Post-Herald* on the cover of *Editor and Publisher:* No other media even comes close. A tenable claim. Other medias claiming to come close might fill a stadia, but Birmingham's medias are beyond their reach. So much for medias. As poor, bumbling, passionate, foolish, vengeful, tragic Canio the clown says in *I Pagliacci*, "La commedia e finita" (comedy is finite).

Claims to superiority are common. The restaurants that say that they are best might also fill a stadia, probably the Sugar Bowl, but the wise person has his own favorites. When my mind turns to food—an untoward development, since the legs usually go first, turning, in times of stress, to jelly—I think of smorgasborg, and then omelete assorti. I think next of an 8 per cent fillet mignion served in Amarillo, Texas—8 per cent is as much of that as I want to eat at a sitting; of Lindy's Crab and Seafood Market in Linden, New Jersey, which is open seven days a week and Sundays and holidays; of a restaurant in Buffalo, New York, that specializes in eye rib of beef, lean and succulant, cooked to your indiscriminant taste; and then of a stay at the Hollenden House, in Cleveland, where the restaurant listed appetite provacateurs, among them shrimp scampies, a mischievous but endearing crustacean. I long to go to a restaurant called La Diplemat, in Nashville, Tennessee, and I wonder what is on its menu. Perhaps Kitsch Lorraine, chicken en brochay, and two Irish dishes, O'Grattan potatoes and lemon moran pie.

A mad hunger takes possession of me and I am unindated by memories of the Granada Royale Hometel in Omaha, where a light and airy courtyard lends a sidewalk cafe affect to meals. I remember a roast beefe sandwich I had at the Red Lion Restaurant of the Beverly Hilton Hotel. Ah! Ye roast beefe of Olde England. Alors! Le petit strip sirloin at the Hyatt Regency Hotel at O'Hare Airport in Chicago, served with the Frenchman's favorite wine, Beaujolias. My minds skips to the Chez Bon Dining Lounge near L'Aéroport de Detroit; to the Board Room Restaurant in New York, which serves Les Asparagus de France, though not Les Tomatoes or La Lettuce; and to a plate du jour at a country club in North Carolina, where I saw a woman carrying a L'Tote cosmetics bag by Lancome. Her carriage suggested that her girdle was a Fleur d'Lace.

The French should be gratified that their cuisine is enjoyed across the United States. Stouffer's Denver Inn, where Brian and

Liz were congradulated, serves French Dip, consisting of sliced
Colorado beef on a roll with savory au jus so good it sets you humming. A cup of coffee, a sandwich and au jus. Au jus is turning
up in many places. I was offered a cup of it on an airplane. It appears to be a case of the wandering au jus. At Lake Tahoe, Shrimp
Provenciale is presented as evidence of one restaurant's Continental flare, and the DELInclineTESSEN restaurant features Escargot
Cognac and a galantina sandwich. I thought that anybody who
would drink Escargot Cognac must be galantina indeed, but a
preoccupation with food can lead you astray. When Mario Merola,
the Bronx District Attorney, made some comments about a super-
seder by Governor Hugh Carey, he proved to be talking about the
possibility that Carey would remove one prosecutor from office in
favor of another. I had assumed that the Governor was giving an
unusually large Passover feast for his Jewish friends. This seemed
not out of the question in New York politics.

My mind drifts back to the best, and only, baked lasange I've
ever had, in Hudson Falls, New York. It skips to a motel in Char-
lotte, North Carolina, where it was possible to begin a meal with
anti-pasto, a dish popular with those who dislike Italian cooking
(I am pro-pasto myself), and then, for those unable to make up
their minds about sauces, go on to Veal Parmigiana Milanese. All
roads lead to Rome, or elsewhere.

Mistakes enliven American life. Some, of course, are caused
by pomposity and make those responsible for them appear ludi-
crous. About others there is an innocence that it would be a shame
to lose.* In arguing for a civil tongue, I am arguing for naturalness,

---

* My mistakes in *Strictly Speaking* were caused by innocence. Joe
Ray, a copy editor on the Utica, New York, *Observer-Dispatch,* wrote:
"I was all set to credit you for clever work when I came across a real
blunder on page 139. You had Benjamin Franklin coming out of the
Constitutional Convention of 1776. It was the hot summer of 1787,
not 1776." When I put Campobello in Nova Scotia instead of New
Brunswick, a Canadian commented that geography was not my
province.

Another correspondent thought that religion was not my province even when it leads to mistakes. There is no reason that naturalness cannot be joined to correctness, but even when it isn't, clarity and genuineness can come together. More than this, we Americans don't have as much fun as we could with English. The fun is there to be had, but it requires some knowledge (which need not be formal), some imagination, and a sense of delight in what language can do.

I have been told that my view is cranky and pedantic, that I want to keep the language from growing and to impose a standard and rigid English on Americans. Far from it. Our language should be specific and concrete, personal, so that we don't all sound alike, eloquent when possible (for eloquence is hard to come by), and playful when possible (for wit is given to few). We spend much of our time speaking and writing. Must it be monotonous? One of the most cheerful pastimes is to play on words.

I was looking at an advertisement placed by the realty firm of Cleveland, Duble & Arnold, of Greenwich, Connecticut, for a waterfront estate with deep-water mooring, dock, float, and Har-Tru tennis court. An envious way of life, Cleveland, Duble & Arnold called it, and it seemed just right for me. My envy was insensate and knew no bounds. I had just picked up the phone to put in a bid for the estate when a man burst in.

"You are known to be arboring fugitives," he said in a gutteral voice.

I denied it.

---

either. The Rev. Ralph Kowalski, of the Church of St. Bede in South-field, Michigan, wrote:

" 'Quo Vadis?' was not spoken by St. Peter but to him. It is reported, by usually reliable sources, that Christ, in a vision, confronted Peter when he was retreating from Rome to escape the persecutions. He asked, 'Quo Vadis?' whereupon Peter, in remorse, returned to his see and subsequent martyrdom."

I accepted the Reverend Kowalski's version rather than the rival version in which the question is put by Peter, because it seemed to me to offer a rare opportunity to use the word fraught. "Your book," I said to myself, "is fraught with error."

"Contain your indignance," he said. "There are radicals at large, flaunting the establishment."

I had read in Jack Anderson's column about the flaunting of the law by power-hungry men while they basked in the sunshine of Key Biscayne and San Clemente, and I thought the intruder's time would be better employed in going after them. I had even heard of cases of cavalier flaunting of the law. "Why come after me?" I asked. "Get the cavaliers."

He was not dissuaded. "In this very neighborhood," he said, "a man entered a woman's house with the intent of doing bodily harm to her person. She was in eminent danger. Luckily, the family dog, a laboratory retriever, who can be a holy terrier when aroused, arrived in the niche of time. I'm surprised that you don't know about it. You must be imperious to these things."

I said that I still did not know what he wanted.

"You have been surveilled," the intruder said. "We are well-vexed as to your activities."*

"Where did you get the information that led you to me?"

"It enamated from secret sources."

How would he describe the fugitives he was seeking? He re plied that one of them had gray hair and an unrepossessing face, and was alienated with the government. She was wanted for smuggling and worked with a gang that specialized in falsifying ships' manifolds. She had been in a hospital, inflicted by monogram headaches, and while there had had a tubular litigation, which led to a blood clog in the lungs. They had had to stick a needle in her arm and feed her inconveniently. Nonetheless, she had recovered. An incredulous story.

I was moved to prayer and got out the fur skullcap I had bought in Peru, a llamalke. My visitor told me not to bother, it was all water over the wheel, and the point was that the unrepossessing

---

* A reader in Arlington, Virginia, told me that she does market research. In one study she asked people about their beer-drinking tastes and habits. The study was called "Beer Surveillance—Wave One." I suppose that the surveillers went ashore from the Potomac.

fugitive had been attended by a round-the-clock private nurse, and they could not understand how she got away.

I: A private nurse working round-the-clock may fall asleep.

He: I like a little repertoire as much as the next man, but these wisecracks only add more grist to the fires. Such half-hazard answers do not help to implant the goal of the investigation and risk rendering it mute. Your attitude is getting my dandruff up and becoming a craw in my throat.

I: There is no point in our hurling epitaphs at each other.

He: Can you vouch for the fugitive as a person of integrity and complete moral turpitude?

I: That puts me in a quondam, but in the transitory times we are passing through, I don't see how I can.

He: You are causing irreputable damage to my work, and you will have to bear the blunt of the punishment for it.

Could he not hold his judgment in obeyance? No, he replied; engaging in claudestrian activities was no joke. "I have deep-seeded emotions about this," he said, and he swept out into the bedrizzled streets in a high dungeon.

It occurred to me that the woman he was looking for might be Ma Gauche, a clumsy but well-loved gangster's moll from France. French gangsters rallied behind her shouting, "Dieu et Ma Gauche." I thought the investigator might be malingering outside, and when I opened the door I saw that he was in a large automobile. That clenched it. "Is this car public property?" I shouted.

"It is one of the prerequisites of office," he replied. "What's wrong with you? I crouched my request for information in polite terms, but you were on tenderhooks. You tried to pull a mirage over my eyes."

"That's a spacious argument," I came back. "You gave me a grueling."

He looked at me pityingly. "If you had helped me, you could have been capitulated into instant fame." Flush with victory, he drove off.

I was going out to buy some items at a shop called Sex Fifth Avenue. I turned on the radio to get the weather forecast and heard about a hurricane that was packing winds of up to eighty miles an hour. It was delayed until the packing was done. There was also financial news from India, where the Dhow-Jones industrials had fallen; news about China, for the Orient-oriented; proposals for a dental insurance plan that was opposed on the ground that it would cause wailing and nationalization of teeth; a story about a window dresser arrested while posing a serious threat; and another story about some people who behaved fecklessly and had not a single feck to their names, as a result of which the family fortune was placed in escarole.

Since the hurricane was still some distance away, I was preparing to leave when my visitor came in again.

"What is it this time?" I asked.

"Malocclusion," I thought I heard him say, and I asked whether the condition was giving him much trouble.

"It is not a condition," he said testily, "but an Irish tenor illegally in the country."

"How would anybody recognize him?"

"He cannot shape his vowels."

"But," I said, "that is an affliction so common it is known as the Broadway malady. Besides, he has cut only a narrow swathe in the world of music. Why not leave it to the police?"

"They are laxadaisacal about these things."

"It seems a waste of money to me."

My friend, as I had now begun to think of him, squared his jaw. "You'd better get a new prospective on things. A well-conceived expenditure, thanks to the cascade effect, will return the investment many times."

"Where did you learn that?"

"From the seventeenth-century financier Bernard Baroque."

"Cascade is le mot juste," I said admiringly.

He drew himself up. "Le Moe juste is a Jewish lawyer of French descent known everywhere for his sense of fair play."

I could see that he was becoming upset again, so I changed the subject. "I went to a recital last night by a secretary turned violinist."

"Who was it?"

"Yehudi Amanuensis."

I rubbed my eyes.

"What's the matter?" he asked.

"Conjunctivitis. I begin too many sentences with and."

"Have you heard about the French noblemen who all had the same name?"

"No."

"Pierres of the realm." This time he changed the subject. "What's your favorite restaurant?"

"It's an old-fashioned Russian one. I like to hear the instructions the proprietor gives the waiters."

"What are they?"

"See what the boyars in the backroom will have."

"You must excuse me," he said. "I'm off to dinner, to a small French restaurant I'm fond of. Le Premier Cri. Not pretentious, but it has won a cauldron bleu for its cooking. One dines there al fresno. I am especially fond of their canopies. It will be a sumptuary repast." He turned on his heel, his face betraying, I thought, a soupcan of sadness, and was gone.

"A richly redolent experience," I said to myself. "I must make a commitment of it to paper." And I did, though not before making out a check to the Washington Performing Arts Society so that it could, as it requested, list me as a benefictor. That is how I like to think of myself.

Index